THE WINES AND VINEYARDS OF NEW ZEALAND

THE WINES AND VINEYARDS OF NEW ZEALAND

Michael Cooper

PHOTOGRAPHY BY
ROBIN MORRISON

HODDER AND STOUGHTON
AUCKLAND LONDON SYDNEY TORONTO

Photographic Acknowledgements

Alexander Turnbull Library 16, 17
Auckland Institute and Museum 12, 13, 15 (TOP), 20
Auckland Public Library, from *The New Zealand Farmer*,
    Feb. 1899 21
Corbans Wines 120
Hocken Library 30
Mary McIntosh 11
Morton Estate 182
New Zealand Herald 48, 253
North and South Magazine 47
Quickcut, *Liquor Industry Products*, 1988 50
Dick Scott, from *Winemakers of New Zealand* 14,
    15 (BOTTOM), 18, 23, 24, 27 (TOP), 29, 31, 32, 33,
    35 (BOTTOM), 41; from *Seven Lives on Salt River* 20
Richard Smart 70 (from *100 Jahre Rebsorte
    Müller-Thurgau*), 74
Te Kauwhata Viticultural Research Station 19, 25
Simon Ujdur Jnr 36, 37
Western Vineyards 43
Wine Institute of New Zealand Inc. 44, 45, 53, 253
Wineworths 48
Stephan Yelas 26

Cartography
Maps reproduced by permission of the Department of
    Survey and Land Information.

Copyright © 1984 Michael Cooper
First published 1984
Second edition first published 1986
Reprinted 1987
This edition first published 1988
ISBN 0 340 431377

Book design by Donna Hoyle
Cartography by Sue Gerrard

Typesetting by Glenfield Graphics Ltd, Auckland
Printed and bound in Hong Kong for
Hodder & Stoughton Ltd, 46 View Road,
Glenfield, Auckland, New Zealand.

CONTENTS

FOREWORD

T he world of wine is changing, or rather evolving, more rapidly than ever before, but nowhere has this evolution been so marked as in New Zealand. That the vineyards and cellars of New Zealand today are all but unrecognisable to those who last acquainted themselves with New Zealand wines in the seventies is perhaps not surprising. But in no other wine-producing country known to me is there quite such a contrast between 1988 and, say, 1983.

All the more need then for a guide as well informed as Michael Cooper to this exploding source of good to fine wine – and all the more difficult is his task of keeping his readers up to date.

The third edition of THE WINES AND VINEYARDS OF NEW ZEALAND has been comprehensively rewritten and updated to include such promising new wine regions as Central Otago, the world's most southerly, and the most exciting of those new winemakers whose produce New Zealand has been launching on to an ever more enthusiastic marketplace.

This book not only, and unusually, fills a legitimate gap on the international wine bookshelf; it is scholarly, wide-ranging and delightfully easy on the eye.

JANCIS ROBINSON
London 1988

PREFACE

The world of New Zealand wine is constantly shifting. No sooner has one's ink dried on the page than another label has debuted or been dropped, another winemaker switched employers, another company changed hands, another winery been founded.

This impermanence poses a real challenge for those who chronicle the New Zealand wine industry as it emerges at breakneck speed from its recent backwater status into the spotlight of international recognition. At best, a chronicler can only hope to capture the essence of the industry as it exists at the time of writing – in this case the winter of 1988.

Every night I open one or two bottles of New Zealand wine. My tasting notes are the foundation on which the opinions expressed in this book about the quality of each vintner's wines rest.

A deep understanding of the wine industry, however, requires more than an acquaintance with its end products – behind the labels are the people, a highly individualistic, indefatigable community of viticulturists, oenologists, administrators and marketers. After a month-long national vineyard tour, my most lasting impression was of the burgeoning array of modern-day pioneers who, frequently in relatively unproven regions, are now staking their livelihoods on the future success of New Zealand wine. For their uniformly warm reception and willing co-operation, my thanks are due.

Other pens than mine have already written of this unique, fascinating industry: there has been Dick Scott's elegant treatise, *Winemakers of New Zealand*, for instance, published in 1964, which examines winemaking here up to the early 1960s – in acknowledging his contribution I would like to feel the historical section of this book helps to complete the picture up to the present day. Another heavyweight which pulls no punches is Frank Thorpy's *Wine in New Zealand*, first published in 1971 and revised in 1983.

Many individuals have made important contributions to this third edition of *The Wines and Vineyards of New Zealand*. Simon Ujdur gave patiently of his time and was an indispensable source on the history of Birdwood Vineyards. Dr Richard Smart and Doris Zuur read chapter two in manuscript form and Joe Babich read chapter three; I am indebted to these individuals for their invaluable observations and suggestions.

Renewing the partnership formed with Robin Morrison in the first edition was an immense pleasure: the unique style of his photography brings the contemporary industry to life to a degree no writer of prose could ever hope to rival.

Special thanks are due to my long-time employers, Peter and Joe Babich, who freed me from my normal duties long enough to research and write this new edition. Thanks, too, to Noeline Sadgrove, who typed the manuscript with her customary efficiency. For permission to use material first published in my monthly column in *North and South*, I am indebted to that magazine's publisher. Philip Gregan, deputy executive officer of the Wine Institute, handled my numerous requests for material with unflagging cheerfulness and promptness.

To Linda, my wife, for her unfailing help in a multitude of ways, my deepest thanks.

MICHAEL COOPER

INTRODUCTION

The pleasures of wine have been known to man for over seven thousand years, ever since the people of Asia Minor first converted grapejuice, by inadvertence or a happy miracle, into the true monarch of beverages. Cultivated in ancient times throughout the Mediterranean Basin, wine came to fulfil a multitude of purposes – restorative, medicinal, religious and domestic – and became inseparable both from the humble pleasures of daily life and the exhilarating pomp of great occasions. Hundreds of years before the birth of Christ, grapes were being grown in France, to spread throughout Europe into what are now known as some of the great wine-producing regions of the world. Names like Bordeaux, Burgundy and the Rhine have a special redolence for the wine lover, evoking visions of luscious purple grapes ripening under clear skies, soft green vines spilling down steep hillsides, or pale grape flowers blooming over the dark red soil of the Rheinhessen.

Explorers, pioneers, missionaries and colonists spreading into new worlds over the centuries, brought with them the techniques of winemaking, and above all the desire to perpetuate in their new lifestyle a most enjoyable element of the old – the benefits and joys of consuming wine.

Different soils and climates, viticultural histories marked by constant trial and error, have led to the successful establishment of many New World wine industries, the most familiar to New Zealanders being those of California, South Africa, and Australia.

This book begins with the history of our own winegrowing. It is the tale of small isolated efforts, early failures, and tiny but significant successes, which eventually contributed to the growth of one of New Zealand's most promising industries. It not only traces the introduction of grape varieties to early New Zealand, and the vagaries of their cultivation, but looks at perhaps the most important side of New Zealand viticulture, the people who pioneered winegrowing in the nineteenth century, those who learned the value of research in the early twentieth century, those who lent their talents to the burgeoning of the industry in the 1960s, and finally the ones who remain the inspiration for wine production in New Zealand today.

The second and third chapters deal with the realities which New Zealand winemakers are involved with all year round – those of the vineyard and those of the winery.

Chapter two takes a close look at our climate and soils in relation to vine cultivation, and then at all the major grape varieties. Then follow sections on vineyard practice and the national development of wine research, both essential to an understanding of wine production in New Zealand.

Chapter three explores in detail the transformation of the black and green grape varieties into the different wines: white, red, rosé, sparkling, sherry and port.

The heart of the book follows: the fourth chapter is a region-by-region commentary on every wine company of importance. I have visited almost all at least once, and returned to some, of course, many times; there is nothing to compare with the satisfaction not only of knowing the soils, terrain and vines of different regions and vineyards, but of understanding the goals and dreams of the winemakers themselves. This chapter explores the perfumes, tastes and myriad delights which New Zealand wines offer, linking them to their origins, and presenting what I hope is a fair, intelligible and nonetheless personal account of their character. Photographs, maps and labels fill out the picture of what is, in my opinion, one of New Zealand's most complex and endlessly fascinating industries.

The final chapter is concerned with two things of great importance to all wine lovers – the pocket and the palate. A section on the buying of New Zealand wine maps out the tempting range of choices offered to the consumer, and touches on both the last decade's vintages and the wine competitions, in the belief that if such knowledge is within the reach of everyone, it can only serve to enhance the appreciation of wine drinking. For those who want to take advantage of the excellent aging qualities of many New Zealand wines, there are notes on cellaring.

Finally, there is the section on tasting and drinking wine. This offers simple guidelines only, as there are no special mysteries here – the real miracles have occurred already, with the tender cultivation of the grapevine, the careful fermentation of the juice, and the subtle ministrations of the winemaker as he or she has coaxed a wine into clarity, balance and fragrance.

Hugh Johnson, a perceptive author of formidable knowledge and impeccable accuracy, wrote in *Hugh Johnson's Wine Companion*, first published in London in 1983: 'New Zealand's natural gift is what the winemakers of Australia and California are constantly striving for: the growing conditions that give slowly ripened, highly aromatic rather than super-ripe grapes. It is too soon to judge yet how good her eventual best wines will be, but the signs so far suggest that they will have the strength, structure and delicacy of wines from (for example) the Loire, possibly the Médoc, possibly Champagne.'

Johnson is the world's most authoritative and widely read writer about wine. Thus the winemakers of New Zealand, with all their natural advantages and with superb wines already in the bottle, begin to stir up excitement in the leading wine centres of the world.

CHAPTER ONE

The History of New Zealand Wine

THE NINETEENTH CENTURY

FROM THE REVEREND SAMUEL MARSDEN'S CONVICTION THAT THE MAORI SHOULD BE TAUGHT AGRICULTURE AND HANDICRAFTS AS A PRELUDE TO CONVERSION TO CHRISTIANITY, STEMMED IN 1819 THE FIRST RECORDED PLANTING OF GRAPEVINES IN NEW ZEALAND.

JAMES BUSBY WAS BORN IN EDINBURGH IN 1801. WHILE BRITISH RESIDENT AT THE BAY OF ISLANDS BETWEEN 1833 AND 1840, HE MADE THE EARLIEST RECORDED NEW ZEALAND WINE.

Vitis vinifera, the great species of vine for winemaking, originated in the northern hemisphere and stayed there, until carried south in the ships of the early colonists. Thus the grapevine sank its roots into New Zealand soil during the first years of European settlement. Such eminent enthusiasts as Samuel Marsden, who made the first known planting of grapevines in New Zealand and James Busby, our first recorded winemaker, ensured that grapes were among the early pioneering fruits.

In traditional Maori society there were no alcoholic beverages. Without the benefit of the grapevine as a native plant, the pre-European Maori sometimes made a non-intoxicating drink from the juice of poisonous tutu berries. The colonists attempted to make 'wine' from the same plant – with startling results. Exploring the area north of Wakatipu in March 1864, A.J. Barrington noted in his 'Diary of a West Coast Prospecting Party' that: 'Simonin [a Frenchman in the group] gathered a handkerchief full of tutu berries, beat them up, squeezed them, and got a pint of wine, which was a first-rate drink. The refuse, or seed, he threw on the beach, which the dog ate. In an hour afterwards he showed every symptom of being poisoned, foamed at the mouth, and lay down in fits; I believe he would have died but for a good supply of salt and water we managed to pour down his throat'.[1]

Fortunately the fruit of the tutu plant never won favour as the basis for a potentially unique antipodean wine industry.

When Charles Darwin called at the Bay of Islands in 1835 during the global voyage of the *Beagle*, he saw well-established grapevines. Samuel Marsden, on his second trip to New Zealand as Anglican missionary and chief Chaplain to the Government of New South Wales, had decided to make a settlement at Kerikeri. In his journal for Saturday 25 September 1819 he wrote: 'We had a small spot of land cleared and broken up in which I planted about a hundred grape-vines of different kinds brought from Port Jackson. New Zealand promises to be very favourable to the vine as far as I can judge at present of the nature of the soil and climate'.[2]

Other early colonists followed Marsden's example and planted vines in the North. Lieutenant Thomas McDonnell R.N., who had settled at Hokianga ('I think in the year 1830') and later at Kaipara, told a House of Commons Select Committee on New Zealand in a report printed in July 1844 that he had 'cultivated the vine to a great extent at Hokianga: I have nearly four hundred varieties of the grape-vine'.[3] Further north at Whangaroa Harbour, William Powditch was also growing grapes and he gave vine cuttings and viticultural advice to his neighbours.

These early vinegrowers are not known to have attempted winemaking. The honour of being the first to produce wine in New Zealand therefore belongs to James Busby. A Scot, Busby emigrated to Australia in 1824, published a series of pamphlets fervently advocating the pursuit of winemaking in Australia and New Zealand, and established a forty-acre (16.2ha) vineyard in the Hunter River Valley of New South Wales. He is widely regarded as the father of Australian viticulture.

After Busby was appointed in 1832 to the position of first British Resident in New Zealand, a small vineyard appeared between the house and the flagstaff at Waitangi. Writing to his brother in 1836 Busby told how 'the vines were planted out under the most favourable circumstances, just after a soaking rain. I think the majority of them are likely to survive'.[4]

The vines flourished, and the wine Busby made and sold to Imperial troops also found favour in 1840 with the French explorer Dumont d'Urville. Touring Busby's estate, d'Urville saw 'a trellis on which several flourishing vines were growing . . . with great pleasure I agreed to taste the product of the vineyard that I had just seen. I was given a light white wine, very sparkling, and delicious to taste, which I enjoyed very much'.[5]

Within a decade of their establishment Busby wrote that his vines were under attack, prey 'to the ravages of horses, sheep, cattle and pigs. The leaves are ripped off as soon as they come out'.[6] The vineyard was completely destroyed in 1845 by British soldiers camped at Waitangi during the clashes with Hone Heke. Although Busby thereafter channelled into land speculation the energies he once devoted to viticulture, he deserves to be remembered as the pioneer whose enthusiasm for the spread of vinegrowing yielded the first New Zealand wine.

Other early outposts of viticulture included Port Nicholson and Auckland. A propagandist for the New Zealand Company, the Honourable Henry William Petrie, spent a year with the first settlers at Port Nicholson before returning to England in 1841. Petrie later wrote that: 'When I quitted the Colony, several vines had been planted, but had not then produced grapes. I myself took about one hundred cuttings of different sorts from Sydney, many of which were flourishing . . .'[7]

At Auckland, vines were planted from the very beginning of European settlement. The first colonists arrived in September 1840; in 1843 the Agricultural and Horticultural Society of Auckland reported that 'the vine plants brought from Sydney in October 1840, have already produced grapes, and others procured from different sources, and planted subsequently in gardens, have thriven surprisingly . . . the experiments carried on in the gardens will show what success may be reasonably anticipated, and ultimately lead to the formation of extensive vineyards'.[8]

At the Agricultural and Horticultural Society's exhibition held in March 1849, the wine on display was from Northland, rather than Auckland. *The New Zealander* reported that 'the attendance was both numerous and select, His Excellency the Governor and Lady Grey, and almost all the elite of Auckland being present . . . There were half a dozen bottles of a claret from Wangaroa [sic] manufactured without any of the necessary means of wine making. It was much too new to form even an idea of its quality, but its colour was clear and good'.[9]

The 'claret' was probably made by French Marist missionaries. The first Catholic Bishop of the South Pacific, Bishop Pompallier of Lyons, had arrived at Hokianga in 1838 with French vine cuttings on board. To supply the missionaries' need for table grapes and for sacramental and table wines, vines were planted wherever mission outposts were established. An ancient vine, believed to be descended from one of Pompallier's plantings, was still growing wild at his ship's Kohukohu landing place in Hokianga Harbour as recently as 1984, when it fell victim to a local weed-spraying project.

Brother Elie-Regis at Whangaroa wrote to Lyons in May 1842: 'We cultivate the vines, they do very well here, the first which we planted three years ago already commence to bear fruit'.[10] In 1851 Catholic priests established the first vineyard in Hawke's Bay and the oldest winemaking enterprise in New Zealand, the Mission Vineyards, is descended from these early ventures.

Failure was common. Petrie had observed in the 1840s that a major drawback to the spread of the grapevine was that the English knew little about viticulture. 'To cultivate them [vines] to any extent, we shall require French and German cultivators, to whom the most liberal encouragement should be given.'[11] French peasants did plant vines at Akaroa in 1840 and three years later German winemakers arrived at Nelson, but by the late nineteenth century little trace remained of either venture. Two shiploads of German vintners who had been promised perfect opportunities

DUMONT d'URVILLE, REGARDED AS ONE OF CAPTAIN COOK'S MOST TALENTED SUCCESSORS AS A PACIFIC EXPLORER, PENNED THE OLDEST SURVIVING TASTING-NOTE ON A NEW ZEALAND WINE.

BISHOP POMPALLIER'S RELIGION AND NATIONALITY WERE SEVERELY FROWNED UPON BY HIS RIVAL MISSIONARIES, BUT HIS PLANTING OF VINES, FROM AROUND 1838, SOON TRIGGERED A MORE WIDESPREAD SCATTERING OF THE GRAPEVINE AROUND NEW ZEALAND.

for viticulture by the New Zealand Company, arrived on our shores, contemplated the steep bush-clad hills surrounding Nelson, and left for South Australia.

At Akaroa grapevines sprouted in clearings around the small clay cottages and wine was made, but heavy forest cover and the spread of British influence on Banks Peninsula combined to defeat hopes for a flourishing winegrowing industry. A Government report near the end of the century pointed to the temporary nature of most early attempts to make wine in New Zealand: 'The wine industry [at Akaroa] prospered so long as those by whom it was started remained at the helm, but immediately they began to die off, the vineyards became neglected, and in consequence the vines died out'.[12]

An Englishman was the first to prove the commercial possibilities for winegrowing in the colony. Charles Levet, a Cambridge coppersmith, and his son planted seven acres (2.8ha) of mainly Isabella grapes on an arm of the Kaipara Harbour and from 1863 to 1907 earned a living from making and selling wine. The Levets regularly shipped wine to Auckland customers including, in the 1890s, the Earl of Glasgow in Government House. After more than forty years of winemaking, father and son died within two years of each other and the trickle of wine from the Kaipara ran dry.

The most successful non-British winemaker was a Spaniard, Joseph Soler, who made his first wine at Wanganui in 1869 and until his death in 1906 sold wine all over New Zealand. From grapes grown on his two and a half acre (1ha) property in Wanganui and other grapes purchased by the canoe-load from Wanganui River Maori, each year Soler produced around 20,000 bottles of wine.

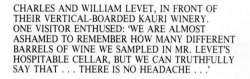

CHARLES AND WILLIAM LEVET, IN FRONT OF THEIR VERTICAL-BOARDED KAURI WINERY. ONE VISITOR ENTHUSED: 'WE ARE ALMOST ASHAMED TO REMEMBER HOW MANY DIFFERENT BARRELS OF WINE WE SAMPLED IN MR. LEVET'S HOSPITABLE CELLAR, BUT WE CAN TRUTHFULLY SAY THAT . . . THERE IS NO HEADACHE . . .'

Soler's entries at first won three of five gold medals awarded at the Christchurch International Exhibition in 1906. Then Cabinet intervened at the urging of rival Australian entrants and ordered a retasting. This time, Soler emerged totally triumphant by capturing all five golds.

Later that year, however, Soler died and his sons abandoned the effort to grow grapes in a region climatically ill-suited to viticulture. They went sheep-farming.

There were numerous other small vineyards scattered around the country in the second half of the nineteenth century. Five settlers with eight acres (3.2ha) of grapes between them were 'principally engaged in vine-growing' on the Mangawhai River south of Whangarei. The largest vineyard, according to *The Daily Southern Cross* in March 1875, was the 'well-known and old-established one of Mr Wendolin Albertz, who has three acres in a high state of cultivation . . . There are about 1,000 gallons of wine on hand in the cellars . . . Mr and Mrs Albertz were most hospitable, and produced a wine at once pleasant, wholesome and invigorating; a wine entirely free from adulteration, of a good bright colour, light in strength and having a fine bouquet'. The newspaper's 'rambling reporter' enthused: 'The wine made throughout the district is of fine colour and flavour, and only wants to age to make it equal to foreign wines usually imported, and better than some Australian'.[13]

The prospect of winemaking on a much grander scale emerged briefly when Sir George Grey, long an advocate of viticulture, became Prime Minister from 1877 to 1879. At his Government's request the Waste Lands Board reserved a block of 26,000 acres (10,500ha) in the Hokianga district, 'it being the object of Sir George Grey to establish there a settlement of skilled winegrowers', the *New Zealand Herald* reported.[14] A year later a Scottish promoter planned to settle vignerons from the south of France on the land, but in the end Grey's scheme failed to get off the ground.

By 1884 a German settler, Heinrich Breidecker, had a small two-acre (0.8ha) plot of Isabella vines trained along low manuka poles at Kohukohu in the Hokianga. With additional grapes bought from local Maori, Breidecker in most seasons to the end of the century produced and sold 1200 gallons (5400L) of wine at 10/– a gallon.

SIR GEORGE GREY DEMONSTRATED AN EARLY INTEREST IN WINEMAKING WHEN, AS A YOUTHFUL GOVERNOR OF SOUTH AUSTRALIA, HE DESPATCHED IN 1841 THE FIRST CASE OF WINE MADE IN THAT STATE TO QUEEN VICTORIA.

HEINRICH BREIDECKER AND HIS SON JOHANN STAND READY TO WELCOME THE GOVERNOR, LORD RANFURLY, WHO VISITED IN 1899. ACCORDING TO THE DEPARTMENT OF AGRICULTURE, THEY PRODUCED 'A GOOD UNADULTERATED WINE'.

Generally, however, there was little wine being made in New Zealand in the latter part of the century. Partly to blame was the onslaught of a powdery mildew (oidium) from America which had invaded European vineyards at mid-century. Oidium first appeared as small whitish patches on young leaves and shoots, and eventually attacked all the green parts of the vine. The grapes became covered with a felt-like mould and split open, exposed to the ravages of fungi and insects.

When in 1876 oidium invaded the vineyards of Wendolin Albertz and those of his fellow winegrowers on the Mangawhai River, the *Southern Cross*'s 'rambling reporter' observed on 27 March that 'nothing but leaves and wood are to be seen where last year tons of grapes were gathered'. The devastation was widespread. Evidence submitted to a Government committee in 1890 told how 'the chief difficulties with vine cultivation in New Zealand now arise from the presence of minute fungi, which in some seasons reduce the plants to such a condition that no fruit can be perfected'.[15]

Also inhibiting the development of a substantial local wine industry was the pattern, prevalent in northern European countries, of wine consumption by the educated elite rather than by the working class, whose members much preferred beer and spirits. Working men occasionally enjoyed wine as part of a 'fence' – a blend of spirits and port or sherry – but it was the well-to-do who consumed most of the wine in nineteenth-century New Zealand. Traditional perceptions of wine as a 'class' drink lingered.

Portuguese ports and Spanish sherries were most in demand. Australian wines, despite favourable customs duties, were not popular, being regarded as 'an inferior sort of wine', drunk only by those possessing 'a very poor palate indeed'.[16]

THE ONE-ROOMED SHANTY 'DEW DROP INN', ERECTED IN 1903, WAS SITED ON THE DOUGLAS SADDLE IN BACK-COUNTRY TARANAKI. BY THE END OF THE CENTURY MOST OF THESE HUMBLE, ILL-SUPERVISED GROG SHOPS HAD DISAPPEARED.

The prosperous were equally uninterested in New Zealand wines. Fruit winemaker E.C. Mouldey, of Christchurch, observed that his wine was 'usually bought by the working people'.[17] Israel Wendel, a native of Alsace-Lorraine, who from the early 1870s sold wine made in the basement cellar of his Symonds Street, Auckland, house, described his customers as 'the poorer classes'.[18]

The fledgling wine industry was soon further undermined. The rigours of pioneering life made for hard drinking and public drunkenness was common, much more so than today. Cabin passengers sailing to New Plymouth in 1841 had each been allocated a bottle of beer every second day, a bottle of wine every third day and a pint of spirits every fourth day. The grog shops of the early settlements had set a pattern of squalid drinking conditions that prevailed through the century. Perhaps inevitably, there was a strong reaction.

The 1860s witnessed the foundation of a large number of temperance societies which increasingly called for the total prohibition of liquor. The Licensing Act of 1881, which severely restricted the conditions under which new liquor licences could be granted, was the prohibition movement's first major success, and from 1881 to 1918 there were more and more restrictions.

These laws severely inhibited the development of the wine industry. Representing the New Zealand Viticultural Association before the Industries Committee in 1919, Dawson Smith told how the viticultural pioneers 'had a very uphill fight . . . owing undoubtedly to the prejudice which you would naturally expect in respect of an article of that description made in the Colony'.[19] The annual consumption of local and imported wines dropped from two bottles per capita in 1882 to less than one bottle by 1894. Later *The New Zealand Graphic* disapprovingly noted the 'difficulty in the way of obtaining wine licences for the retail sale of our native wines'.[20]

Winegrowers succeeded in extracting a few concessions from Government before the power of the prohibition movement peaked in the early twentieth century. These reforms were sparked by the Colonial Industries Commission, which reported in 1880 that 'wine of good quality is produced in various parts of the colony, and that, but for the restrictions placed upon it by the existing licensing laws, this industry is likely to grow to considerable proportions. They find, however, that no provision being made by the law for retailing colonial wine, except by obtaining a public-house licence, the trade is practically suppressed.

'They are of opinion that it ought to be encouraged, both on the ground of its affording remunerative occupation in a new branch of agriculture, and on that of its supplying the public with a cheap and wholesome beverage. They therefore have the honor to recommend that special facilities should be provided in the Licensing Bill now before Parliament for the sale of New Zealand wines by retail or for consumption on the premises.'[21]

In 1881 special licences were introduced to govern the sale of New Zealand wine. Previously vineyard sales had been banned and hotels had been the sole legal outlet. Vineyard sales were now authorised but restricted to a minimum quantity of two gallons (9.1L) for consumption off the premises.

A new wineshop licence was also created which allowed consumption on or off the premises – mercifully without the two-gallon (9.1L) requirement. Only four of these licences were ever issued. Then in 1891 Parliament awarded winemakers the right to operate their own stills to produce spirits for wine fortification, thereby releasing them from the financial burden of having to purchase heavily taxed imported spirits.

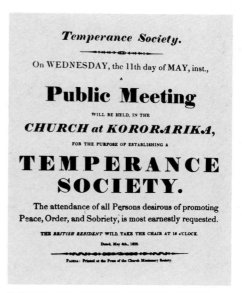

Temperance Society.

On WEDNESDAY, the 11th day of MAY, inst.,

A

Public Meeting

WILL BE HELD, IN THE

CHURCH at KORORARIKA,

FOR THE PURPOSE OF ESTABLISHING A

TEMPERANCE SOCIETY.

The attendance of all Persons desirous of promoting Peace, Order, and Sobriety, is most earnestly requested.

THE *BRITISH RESIDENT* WILL TAKE THE CHAIR AT 1? o'CLOCK.

Dated, May 6th, 1836.

PAIHIA: Printed at the Press of the Church Missionary Society.

THE EARLY TEMPERANCE SOCIETIES CALLED FOR A HALT TO DRUNKENNESS AND ABSTENTION FROM SPIRITS – BUT NOT WINE. JAMES BUSBY, NEW ZEALAND'S FIRST RECORDED WINEMAKER, CHAIRED THE MEETING IN KORORAREKA IN 1836 – ADVERTISED ABOVE – WHICH FOUNDED THE NEW ZEALAND TEMPERANCE SOCIETY.

At the end of the century, the future of the wine industry hung in the balance. On the one hand, pressure mounted for the prohibition of alcohol; on the other, there were many attempts to find new industries that could boost the country's economy. Increasingly through the 1890s the wine industry came to be viewed as a new and potentially major avenue for economic development. According to Wairarapa winemaker William Beetham the feeling of the times was that 'anything that adds to the value of land, and to the prosperity of the country and the people, might well be taken in hand by the Government'.[22] In this context, development of the wine industry 'would add value to a large area of land in New Zealand that is not of very great value at the present time'.[23] A Government viticultural expert received in 1895 'letters from several agriculturalists, asking for information regarding the viticultural industry' who 'one and all express their willingness to plant vines on a large scale . . .'[24]

New vineyards appeared as several Hawke's Bay landowning families explored the economics of winemaking. Their interest was aroused by Beetham, who as a young man had spent several years in France and returned, as he later put it, 'sure that a very large area of New Zealand could be profitably planted with the vine, and that excellent wine could be made'.[25] Beetham planted his first vines in 1883 and by 1897 he was producing about 1850 gallons (8410L) of wine from Pinot and Hermitage grapes.

PICKERS HARVESTING WILLIAM BEETHAM'S LANSDOWNE VINEYARD AT MASTERTON IN 1897 WERE REWARDED WITH PAYMENT OF TWO SHILLINGS EACH PER DAY.

During the 1890s New Zealand wines enjoyed a decade of unprecedented popularity, when they accounted for almost a quarter of all commercial wines sold in the country. Beetham's brother-in-law, J.N. Williams, planted an acre of Pinot grapes at Hastings in 1893 and later expanded the vineyard to seven acres (2.8ha) producing 4000 gallons (18,184L) of claret and hock per year. At the Te Mata Station, Bernard Chambers planted his first vines in 1892, and by 1909 he was making 12,000 gallons (54,552L) of claret, hock and Madeira.

In 1894 a *New Zealand Farmer* reporter in Hawke's Bay wrote: 'The fame of the Marist fathers being quoted on all sides as successful labourers in the vineyard . . . inclined my footsteps to Meeanee . . . High fences that shut out the world and worldly fancies were pierced by white gates that led the visitor into a garden full of fruitful trees, graceful shrubbery and beds of flowers. Right and left were vineyards'.[26]

The vineyards attached to the Mission house were often severely flooded, although newer plantings on higher ground were less vulnerable. Over three acres were established in Pinot Noir, Meunier, Black Hamburgh, Chasselas and Sweetwater vines.

In producing wine and selling their surplus on the local market, the Mission fathers made no concessions to popular taste preferences. 'Two principal wines are made, a white and a red, both of a stomachic and tonic character, and neither of them given a name. Wine to please an Anglo-Saxon and a public-house palate he does not make. The gilt foil about the cork, the gay label, the mixture entitled wine by a stretch of courtesy in which sugar and spirit play principal parts, are not in favour . . .'[27]

The expansion of winemaking activities had earlier come under renewed threat when in 1893 it seemed for the first time that a total prohibition of liquor might be imposed in New Zealand. The prohibitionists succeeded, by Act of Parliament, in having the issues of 'continuance', 'reduction' and 'no-licence' put to a three-yearly popular vote. When the Clutha electorate voted no-licence in 1895 and was soon followed by others, the wine industry, regardless of its recent growth, faced a real threat of extermination. It took an outsider to resolve the dilemma.

Romeo Bragato, a Dalmatian-born graduate of the Royal School of Viticulture and Oenology in Italy, came to New Zealand in 1895 on loan from the Victorian Government to investigate the possibilities for viticulture and winemaking in the Colony. Bragato travelled widely through the country and furnished Prime Minister Richard Seddon with a very favourable report. Seddon was thereafter to become a powerful political supporter of winegrowers, on the dual grounds that 'this colony had great capabilities in the matter of viticulture' and that 'he did believe that if [settlers] had light wines available . . . it would probably keep people from drinking something stronger'.[40]

Bragato wrote that 'there are few of the places visited by me which are unsuitable to the cultivation of the vine'. Hawke's Bay and Wairarapa were 'pre-eminently suited' to viticulture. The potential for winemaking was enormous. 'The land in your Colony, if properly worked, should yield a very large quantity of grapes per acre from which wine of the finest quality, both red and white and champagne could be produced . . . I look hopefully forward to the development in the near future of an industry that will by far eclipse any other that has hitherto been prosecuted here.'[41] Bragato's enthusiasm tipped the balance in favour of the industry's expansion, vinegrowers' associations sprang up in North Auckland and Central Otago, and a general surge in vineyard plantings followed.

Bragato's other major contribution to New Zealand winemakers in 1895 was the identification of phylloxera, a parasitic disease of the vine that rampaged like a prohibitionist zealot through French vineyards in the 1870s. In New Zealand it had wiped out entire vineyards; Government Viticulturist S.F. Anderson recalled in 1914 that 'from the invasion of many of the vineyards by the phylloxera many promising starts fell through'.[42]

The Government was thus early in receipt of sound advice, but it failed to act decisively. Following Bragato's positive identification of phylloxera, infected vines were destroyed, prompting the *Auckland Star* to declare in December 1898 that 'phylloxera is gone'.[43] The *Star* was wrong. The Department of Agriculture chose to ignore Bragato's advice to distribute phylloxera-resistant vines grafted on American rootstocks. The replacement vines supplied by the department proved equally susceptible to phylloxera, which recurred massively in 1901.

ROMEO BRAGATO, A GRADUATE OF THE ROYAL SCHOOL OF VITICULTURE AND OENOLOGY AT CORREGLIANO, ITALY, WAS NEW ZEALAND'S FIRST GOVERNMENT VITICULTURIST. HE WAS BORN IN THE VILLAGE OF MALI LOSINJ IN DALMATIA. IN NEW ZEALAND, CONSCIOUS OF ANTI-'AUSTRIAN' FEELING, HE APPEARS TO HAVE PREFERRED AN ITALIAN IDENTITY.

THE PHYLLOXERA APHID ATTACKS THE VINE BY SWARMING OVER ITS ROOTS AND SUCKING ON THE VINE'S SAP. TUMOURS DEVELOP ON THE DAMAGED ROOTS, CAUSING THE VINE TO WEAKEN AND EVENTUALLY DIE.

THE PREMIER VINEYARD
OF NEW ZEALAND

Tom McDonald of McWilliam's, the Vidal brothers, Robert Bird of Glenvale, John Buck of Te Mata: all rank among the leading names of twentieth-century winemaking in Hawke's Bay. The reputation of Henry Stokes Tiffen, founder of the now vanished Greenmeadows Vineyard, was built in an earlier age. Yet a Conference of Australasian Fruitgrowers held in Wellington in 1896, heard that 'more pioneer work in viticulture has been done at the Greenmeadows Vineyard, Taradale, than elsewhere. Here we find the premier vineyard of New Zealand'.[28]

HENRY STOKES TIFFEN 1819–1896.

Tiffen's interest in winemaking was only fully aroused after almost fifty years' residence in New Zealand. Born in Kent in 1819, a printer's son, he arrived in the country in 1842 as a surveyor for the New Zealand Company. In 1857 he and two partners purchased from the Government several thousand acres of hills and flats in the districts west of Napier; the property was later divided by agreement, Tiffen naming his share Greenmeadows, and subsequent astute land speculation soon made him a wealthy man. He was the first Hawke's Bay County Chairman and by 1890, when, in his seventies, he plunged into commercial winemaking, Tiffen was a leading provincial figure.

Although grapes were first planted at Greenmeadows at an early date (probably soon after 1857) and Tiffen even advertised his willingness to distribute free vine cuttings, his entry into wine production came much later, following an 1890 visit to Wairarapa landowner William Beetham. Tiffen inspected Beetham's tiny vineyard, planted in Hermitage and Pinot varieties, and was deeply impressed with his wine. In Beetham's words: 'He paid us a visit and saw my vineyard; he lunched with us and tasted our wine. He said, "This is enough for me", went back to Napier and planted a vineyard'.[29]

By 1894 Tiffen had despatched his manager, S.F. Anderson, to Australia to study the wine industry and had himself been visited, in March 1894, by a *New Zealand Farmer* reporter, who later wrote: 'I betook myself to Taradale in order to see Mr Tiffen's young vineyard at Greenmeadows. Here, in an area of 36 acres, nearly two-thirds of it planted to vines, was a good beginning made . . .'[30]

Pinot Noir and Meunier, both classic red varieties, were the dual mainstays of Greenmeadows' wine production. In 1896 the *Farmer* observed that 'the vines, all young, some younger than others, were in fine and healthy condition, of vigorous growth, and fairly laden with fruit . . . All the Pineaus – P. Noir, P. Meunier, P. Blanc and P. Chardonnay – have coloured well and developed a high degree of saccharine and richness'.[31] Romeo Bragato, the touring Victorian Government wine expert, had visited Greenmeadows in 1895, and strongly urged Anderson to cultivate the Cabernet Sauvignon variety. However, when the *Farmer* returned in 1897, 'Pinot noir and P. meunier were still the chief reliance as yet, though Shiraz would be in bearing for winemaking in a year or two . . . Outdoor grown table grapes, Black Hamburgh and Chasselas, were doing well and marketing right well'.[32]

The 1896 vintage yielded 2400 gallons (10,910L) of table wine, all red – a production level which climbed, by 1913, to 6000 gallons (27,276L) of both white and red wine, and if one accepts Bragato's estimate that a vineyard should yield between 350 and 400 gallons (1591–1818L) per acre, it is clear that much of the Greenmeadows grape crop was never converted into wine. Greenmeadows also boasted an orchard, producing apples, plums, peaches and apricots, and naturally grapes were also grown for the domestic table. Even the Pinot wine varieties, sold to fruit shops at fourpence per pound, found much favour with the local public for eating.

A regiment of children was hired at each vintage to bring in the harvest. S.F. Anderson kept a diary which portrays vividly the 1898 vintage: 'Commenced gathering the grapes on the 21st March 1898. Weather very fine, cool and bright. Therm. from 60 to 75 maximum – going down to 45 at night.

'Commenced picking with 50 pickers. 15 girls and 35 boys with 3 men to look after them. 8 men in press house. Picked 5 days with 50 . . . The fermentation was good, the colour also good. No acetic smells, mould, sinking of the skins and no flies like last year. This is possibly owing to the higher sugar percent. The P.N. [Pinot Noir] going 22 by the H.R.S. [Hunter River Saccharometer] and the P.M. [Pinot Meunier] going 21.

'Amount gathered for wine off the 30 acres nearly 25 tons 15 cwt 13 lb = 57,593 lb ÷ 16 = 3,600 gallons nearly.'[33]

GREENMEADOWS VINEYARD. TARADALE, HAWKE'S BAY.

The Following Wines can now be obtained from the

Napier Wine and Spirit Merchants.
OR FROM THE ABOVE VINEYARD.

Hock (Pedro Ximenes in pints only..	Vintage 1895.	Per doz.—13s.
Burgundy (Pinots Noir or Meunier)	Vintage 1895.	Per gall.—10s.
Burgundy (Pinots Noir or Meunier)..	Vintage 1896.	Per gall.— 9s.
White Burgundy (Pinots)..	Vintage 1897.	Per gall.— 8s.

All these Wines are thoroughly matured, and are guaranteed not to ferment and lose quality. They are natural, pure grape wines, unfortified.

AN ADVERTISEMENT FOR GREENMEADOWS VINEYARD'S WINES, AS IT APPEARED IN THE *NEW ZEALAND FARMER* IN FEBRUARY 1899. FOUR-YEAR-OLD, 'THOROUGHLY MATURED' WHITE WINE IS A RARE SIGHT TODAY.

In a compact, modern winery, the grapes were carried aloft by elevator, where they descended into a de-stemming and crushing device, then into a mobile wine press mounted on rails, and finally into a row of 1100-gallon totara fermenting vats. Following the fermentation the new wine was drawn off into casks. 'It is all plain sailing and matter of fact', noted the *Farmer* approvingly. 'The wine-house is now fully furnished with tuns and barrels and vats.'[34] Freshly arrived in 1897 were a dozen great oval casks dubbed ' "the Twelve Apostles", from Cassel (made in Germany) of good solid oak . . . the sight of these tiers of casks would make a staunch Prohibitionist grieve'.[35]

And what of the wine? William Beetham, whose Masterton-grown wine had so enthused Tiffen in 1890,

himself paid a visit to Greenmeadows in 1895, 'in company with Mr. Bragato . . . we tasted some of the wine, which was excellent'.[36]

Anderson's diary for the 1899 vintage records the claret was 'made of 1848 lbs. Shiraz 674 lbs. Cabenet [sic] and 240 lbs. Malbec'.[37] Advertised as 'natural, pure grape wines, unfortified', most of the Greenmeadows range was believed unready for sale until the wines had been matured for three years in casks. According to contemporary opinion, the final product was indeed worthy of the long wait. In company with others, a *Farmer* reporter tasted the 1895 vintage at one year old: 'The colour, the clearness, and the bouquet are there already . . . As far as pronounced upon by one who should know, the character of the wine is high'.[38]

A reporter in a later edition of the journal warmly praised the Burgundy, based on Pinot Noir and Meunier: 'I came across a bottle of Burgundy in private life, and it bore on the bottle the Greenmeadows label. The excellence of the wine had drawn my curious attention to the label, and I was both surprised and pleased to find wine so matured and of such high-class quality produced, so to speak, at one's elbow. For good, sound, light wine we have really no occasion to go outside the colony'.[39]

Henry Tiffen died in February 1896. 'Even to the last he was actively engaged in trying to show by practical example how the rich lands of the Ahuriri Plains could be profitably worked as fruit farms and vineyards', read his obituary in the *Hawke's Bay Herald*. Greenmeadows was then cut into large blocks and sold.

Mrs Amelia Randall, Tiffen's daughter, who inherited ninety-five acres (38.46ha), at first carried on winemaking, even expanding the vineyard to thirty-five acres (14.16ha) by 1905. But in 1903 Anderson was appointed manager of a new Government experimental station at Arataki, and later succeeded Bragato as Government viticulturist based at Te Kauwhata. A prohibitionist, William Jarvis, was eventually appointed manager at Greenmeadows, and he helped persuade Mrs Randall to cease wine production. The decision was hastened by the deteriorating economics of the venture, caused in part by her own reluctance to use sugar to ensure stable alcohol levels in the wine.

By 1914 the vineyard had contracted to five acres (2ha). The final act came in 1921, when Wadier Corban journeyed south to Taradale, purchasing sufficient barrels, crushers, bottling machines and other equipment to fill a train for the return trip to Henderson. The Randall property, once the site of 'the premier vineyard of New Zealand', was henceforth known solely as an orchard.

W. HEATHCOTE JACKMAN (RIGHT) AND A NEIGHBOUR. ROMEO BRAGATO WROTE THAT JACKMAN'S 'EXCELLENT WINES, BOTH WHITE AND RED . . . WERE A POSITIVE PROOF OF THE SUITABILITY OF BOTH SOIL AND CLIMATE FOR THE MAKING OF CHOICE LIGHT WINES OF DRY QUALITY'.

'The largest and most successful vine-grower up North' at the turn of the century was W. Heathcote Jackman, observed the *Graphic*.[44] Jackman, who had arrived in New Zealand in 1866, later established a thriving general store and gum-trading post at Whakapirau, on a north-east arm of the Kaipara Harbour. A few hundred metres along the shore, behind his house, 'Heathcote' − which still stands − he planted a model vineyard in the 1890s.

When phylloxera inspectors arrived at Whakapirau in the summer of 1898−99, they discovered in Jackman's vineyard 'a large quantity of vines cultivated . . . 4½ acres of trained vines, about six thousand . . .'[45] The vineyard had been established in classic varieties: Cabernet Sauvignon, Pinots, Chasselas, Riesling and Shiraz.

Jackman's wines were dry − he avoided adding sugar except in poor years − and when his customers baulked at their lack of sweetness they were 'educated up to them'. Bragato was much impressed, telling an audience of fruitgrowers that he 'had tasted wine, that of Mr Jackman in the Kaipara, equal, and very likely superior, to any wine imported into the country. (Applause)'.[46]

Then phylloxera ravaged Jackman's vineyard, eventually forcing him to replant with grafted vines. In a desperate bid to restore his vineyard's productivity, he broke into a Ngati Whatua mausoleum at Whakapirau, housing bones from the Ngapuhi massacre of 1825, and ground them into vineyard fertiliser.

After Jackman fell ill in 1913, his vineyard slid into neglect and eventually his barrels, press and corking machine were sold to the nearby Silich family. Dick Scott, who has recently shed new light on Jackman's winemaking contribution, found on revisiting 'Heathcote' that the 'cellar building, still leaning drunkenly in 1976, a few vat hoops rusting on the earth floor, has since collapsed and disappeared. And the last remaining vine, then a thick trunk straggling up a tree, has died'.[47]

Perhaps the most important of all nineteenth-century developments in the wine industry was also one of the very last. In the 1890s, Dalmatians in the kauri gumfields of the Far North began to make wine.

The promise of quickly acquired wealth attracted the first wave of Dalmatians to New Zealand. Gumdigging required little investment other than hard work and offered a solid financial return. There were over five hundred Dalmatians on the northern gumfields by the 1890s and their presence quickly attracted widespread criticism. The Dalmatians were seen as transitory, and indeed before 1920 most had no intention of settling here. This was directly at odds with the official view of 'settling the North', which held that gumdiggers should be prepared to invest the fruits of their toil in the development of self-sufficient northern farms. New Zealanders at the time tended to mistrust persons of non-British origin, so racial prejudice was also brought to bear on the Dalmatians.

The wine produced and sold in the North further aroused hostility against the Dalmatians. It was alleged before the Commission on the Kauri Gum Industry in 1914 that the wineshops in the gumfields 'should not be allowed to continue in any shape or form, and that they were conducive to great immorality'.[49]

It was widely believed that Dalmatians were trafficking in wines to the injury of the Maori. 'A great deal of feeling against these men in the Far North is due to many of them being wine growers, and the belief that Maori women are able to get, through them, intoxicating liquors . . .' The Aliens Commission in 1916 thundered, 'Where young and vigorous men, attractive young women, free from conventional social restraints and abundance of intoxicating liquors are found together, debauchery will certainly result . . .'[50]

Gumfields poet Ante Kosovich conveys a bitter impression of gumfields life in this excerpt from his 1908 poem 'Longing for Home'[48] (translation by Amelia Batistich):

Ah! Dalmatia, if I could but give
*   you news of your dear sons,*
how this wild, hard country beat
*   them down,*
in what plight they find themselves
in the lonely hell of gumfields.

Anti-Dalmatian sentiment intensified during the First World War and in 1918 many Dalmatians were put in prison camps, or pressed into state service building roads and railways, and scrub-cutting. After the war the financial return from gumdigging was on the decline. The decision of many to settle permanently and take up other occupations was a development of much significance in this generally unhappy period for Dalmatians in New Zealand.

Although Dalmatians are known to have grown vines at Pahi in north Kaipara as early as 1896, the most successful attempt at settlement in the North was at Herekino, south of Kaitaia, where vines were first planted in 1901. By 1907, fourteen tiny vineyards were producing about 2000 gallons (9092L) of wine per year. 'It is a curious fact,' observed *The Auckland Weekly News* in May 1906, 'that although men of British blood were the first to prove that the vine would flourish in New Zealand, and even now have the largest and most up-to-date vineyards, the expansion of vine-growing is due at the present time largely to the efforts of foreigners.'[51]

Pride of place among Yugoslav winemakers in this period belongs to the Frankovich brothers, established on the Whangaparaoa Peninsula north of Auckland in 1899. They had eleven acres (4.5ha) of vines planted by 1913 and each year produced about 4000 gallons (18,184L) of wine. As more Dalmatians chose to settle after the war, and small vineyards spread across Northland and Auckland, the immediate future of the wine industry in New Zealand became, largely, whatever the Dalmatians would be able to make of it.

DALMATIAN DIGGERS ENJOY A SHORT RESPITE FROM GUMFIELDS TOIL. FROM PROBING NORTHERN SOILS WITH SPEARS IN THE QUEST FOR KAURI GUM, MANY LATER TURNED TO WINE PRODUCTION.

JOSIP BALICH, BESIDE THE MODEL-T VAN FROM WHICH HE CANVASSED DOOR-TO-DOOR OFFERING GOLDEN SUNSET WINES – WARMLY RECOMMENDED FOR MEDICINAL PURPOSES.

JOSEPH SOLER, OF WHOSE WINE A MASTERTON MAGISTRATE WROTE IN THE 1880s: 'I HAVE JUST HAD A CASE OF SOLER'S WANGANUI WINE SENT TO ME; IT IS QUITE EQUAL TO THE BEST AUSTRALIAN AND IS A CREDIT TO THE COLONY – THE CONSTANTIA IS SPECIALLY EXCELLENT'.

Looking back, what style of wine had been made in New Zealand in the colonial era? What, if any, were its virtues?

The best of the wine was vastly superior to many of the overseas wines available in New Zealand. *The Daily Southern Cross* saw fit in December 1875 to call upon settlers 'to enter largely into the culture of the grapevine . . . as a means of placing in the market a description of wholesome beverage free from any of the deleterious adulterations so freely used in some of the imported wines'.[52]

Public preference, however, provided no incentive to winegrowers to produce high-quality table wines. At the close of the century the *New Zealand Farmer* observed that 'natural uneducated British taste, when it calls for wine, craves something that is red and sweet and strong. Good wine of a lighter kind might be better for the average drinker, but the ascent to that better state of affairs seems long and slow'.[53]

Some early wines must have been of low quality. Many growers, including Levet, used the Isabella grape to make wine. Although growers of the era were much divided on the merits of *labrusca* varieties, Bragato's opinion was quite firm. Isabella was 'a very inferior grape from whatever point of view it may be regarded . . . for winemaking its "foxy" flavour, lack of sugar and excess of acidity make it most unsuitable'.[54]

Vineyards had successfully been established on a small scale in the North so far as growing grapes was concerned, declared the *New Zealand Mail* in October 1882, 'but the wine, though considered good by some persons, has in no case acquired a character such as to render it an article in steady demand'.[55] Charles Levet, successfully growing wine on the Kaipara, undoubtedly would have disagreed. Nevertheless, in 1896 William Beetham opposed suggestions that New Zealand should provide samples of wine for analysis by a leading London authority. 'Where are the vineyards? Where is the natural wine? A concoction of a little grape-juice and sugar that is called by some people wine, is not a wine of the country.'[56]

Beetham himself had cultivated mainly Pinot and Hermitage vines and produced a wine praised by Bragato in 1895 as 'Hermitage wine six years old, and certainly of prime quality'.[57] Soler's Wanganui wines were principally derived from classic French and Spanish grapes, and, long before the memorable success in Christchurch, won awards at the Melbourne International Exhibition in 1880.

In a paper entitled 'On Vine-growing in Hawkes Bay' read before the Hawke's Bay Philosophical Institute in August 1890, the Reverend Father Yardin of the Meeanee Mission related how: 'When leaving New Zealand, Comte d'Abbans, the French Vice-Consul at Wellington, took with him some twenty bottles of 1885 to 1888 wine of different qualities, made at Meeanee . . . the Comte subsequently obtained the opinion of some of the best wine merchants in Paris, who have unanimously pronounced it unmistakably superior to anything produced in Australia'.[58] Bragato found the Mission wines 'most exquisite', recalling 'the liqueur wine produced on the Greek Archipelago. islands'.[59]

The Hawke's Bay vineyards were widely planted in quality vines. In 1915 the Mission had all classical varieties: Cabernet Sauvignon, Pinot Noir, Meunier, Pinot Gris, Palomino, Pedro Ximenes and La Folle Blanche. At Greenmeadows Vineyard, the 1899 Claret was produced from Shiraz, Cabernet Sauvignon and Malbec grapes – a blend favoured these days by at least one leading Australian winemaker.

At the Franco-British Exhibition held in London in 1908, the experimental viticultural station at Te Kauwhata won a gold medal for a wine 'approaching the Bordeaux clarets in lightness and delicacy'[60] – final proof that high-quality wine, albeit in small quantities, was indeed made during this obscure era of New Zealand winegrowing.

WINEGROWING FROM 1900 TO 1960

Those who had endured the struggle to make wine in the generally adverse social climate of nineteenth-century New Zealand enjoyed in the early 1900s a notable rise in fortune.

In 1901 the Government recalled Romeo Bragato to recommend how New Zealand should attack the phylloxera problem. Bragato declared that winegrowers had been wrongly advised by the Department of Agriculture – and repeated his earlier view that phylloxera could be controlled only by a complete replanting of vineyards on phylloxera-resistant rootstocks. In 1902 Bragato accepted the newly created post of Government Viticulturist and took personal charge of the war on phylloxera.

The Government station at Te Kauwhata was promptly upgraded. Originally a wattle plantation where vines had first been planted in 1897, by 1905 the station possessed an eight-hectare vineyard and a small new winery. The original vines were ripped out and replaced with vines grafted on phylloxera-resistant American rootstocks. Vines from all over Europe were imported and tested for their suitability for grafting and adjustment to New Zealand growing conditions. Many vineyards were replanted in this period with vines supplied from Te Kauwhata, and the second Government vineyard established in 1903 at Arataki in Hawke's Bay.

At Te Kauwhata, Bragato also embarked upon a programme of experimental winemaking. The *New Zealand Herald* in December 1902 recorded that thirty fruitgrowers had visited Te Kauwhata, where they 'inspected the cellar and tasted the wines made by Mr Bragato from last year's vintage. A red Hermitage wine was the first submitted, and this was pronounced excellent . . . Wines from the Pineaus and from the Carbenet [sic] were also tried, being of undoubted high quality. Mr Bragato . . . expressed the opinion, that in Auckland not only would the vine flourish magnificently and produce heavy crops of grapes, but that there could be produced from these grapes wines equal in quality to the best in the world'.[61]

TE KAUWHATA VITICULTURAL RESEARCH STATION, PHOTOGRAPHED SOON AFTER THE TURN OF THE CENTURY. THE ORIGINAL WINERY (RIGHT) STILL STANDS, BUT OF THE HOUSE ONCE OCCUPIED BY ROMEO BRAGATO, NO TRACE SURVIVES.

Bragato's vineyard foreman at Te Kauwhata, T.E. Rodda, later described his boss as a man alienated from most of his staff by an impulsive and abrasive personality. Nevertheless, sometimes late at night during vintage 'Bragato would come to light with a supper of dry water cracker biscuits, sardines, pickled olives, and claret. I could eat the biscuits and sardines, but could never acquire a taste for the olives. Sometimes when Bragato was in a good humour he would give us a lot of information in respect of winegrowing in Dalmatia'.[62]

Under Bragato's tutelage – his handbook *Viticulture in New Zealand* sold 5000 copies – and with the aid of the Government research stations, the wine industry looked set to prosper. New people were drawn to the industry, especially the Dalmatians who planted vines and began to produce wine at Henderson.

The Dalmatians came to Henderson as gumdiggers, buying land at easy prices with money accumulated on the northern gumfields. When the gum ran out, many turned to agriculture, establishing small mixed holdings of fruit trees, grapevines and vegetables. Small-scale winemaking was often an integral part of these essentially peasant enterprises.

In 1902, the same year that the Lebanese A.A. Corban established four acres (1.6ha) in vines at Henderson, Stipan Jelich at Pleasant Valley made the first wine at what has now become the oldest surviving Dalmatian vineyard in New Zealand. 'In this way', Bragato observed, 'many of these men, who were formerly looked at askance and regarded by some as undesirable immigrants, may now be counted as sober, industrious and thrifty settlers . . .'[63] By May 1910 *The Weekly News* enthused that 'the vineyards in the Henderson and Oratia districts . . . stand out as [a] striking example of what may be accomplished in the way of converting the once despised gumlands into highly profitable country'.[64]

THE SMALL TIN SHED WITH LEAN-TO IN THIS RARE 1902 PHOTOGRAPH WAS THE ORIGINAL PLEASANT VALLEY WINERY.

ASSID ABRAHAM CORBAN – PHOTOGRAPHED BY THE ELDEST OF HIS TEN CHILDREN, KHALEEL, AN AMATEUR PHOTOGRAPHER OF TALENT – STANDS GUARD OVER YOUNG VINES TO PROTECT THEM AGAINST BIRDS.

WADIER CORBAN, SON OF THE GREAT PIONEER A.A. CORBAN, AT THE AGE OF 90, IN FRONT OF THE HISTORIC DEPOT USED TO SELL CORBANS WINE DURING THE PEAK ERA OF PROHIBITION INFLUENCE.

A handwritten register (below) kept by S.F. Anderson, Government Viticulturist after Bragato, gives details of almost every vineyard producing wine in 1913. Seventy winemakers were producing a total of 81,450 gallons (366,525L) of wine a year.

The wine yields per acre vary partly because many growers marketed a portion of their crops as table grapes. Deep Creek, the address given for several vineyards, is today the North Shore suburb of Torbay.

The list is an invaluable roll-call of pioneer winemakers on the eve of World War One.

RECORD OF PERSONS GROWING OUTDOOR VINES FOR WINEMAKING AS AT MARCH 1913

Name	Where Situated	Acreage	Gallons of Wine Made	Name	Where Situated	Acreage	Gallons of Wine Made
Asser, Percy	Tauranga	¼	400	Kunicich, Teda	Puhata, Herekino	4½	1500
Borich, Ante	Kumeu	8	2000	Knudson, Thomas	Kawakawa	½	200
Bedlington, S.W.	Waiou Valley, Whangarei	¼	100	Lemon, Alen	Taumarere, Bay of Islands	½	300
Bedlington, Percy	Waiou Valley, Whangarei	1¼	400	Lightfoot, Theo	Kerikeri, Bay of Islands	1	400
Beer, Henry	Birkdale, Auckland	10	5000	Long, Arthur	Deep Creek, Auckland	1½	400
Bridson, T.A.	The Wade, Auckland	¼	100	Lunjevich, Peter	Puhata, Herekino	4	800
Battersby, George	Albany	¾	300	May, Norman	Hupara, Kawakawa	2½	1000
Bacich, John	Uwhiroa, Herekino	2	700	Marinovich Bros.	Oratia, Auckland	8	2000
Breidecker, J.B.	Kohukohu, Hokianga	2	800	Milicich, Peter	Main Road, Henderson	6	1800
Batty, Alfred	Whau Valley, Whangarei	½	100	Mission Vineyards	Greenmeadows	8	2700
Borich Bros.	Manukau Road, Avondale	6	2000	Mariner, H.	Redvale, Auckland	4½	2000
Bilich, Martin	Lincoln Road, Henderson	2	800	Orsulich, John	Red Hill, Te Kopuru	2	100
Buchanan, W.	Paeroa, Thames	¼	200	Paynter, J.W.	Blenheim	¼	150
Barbalich, Nicholas	Shortland, Thames	2	200	Pye, W.A. & Sons	Red Vale, Auckland	4	300
Bray, Frank	Swanson	5	750	Pechar Bros.	Tokatoka, Northern Wairoa	6	—
Chambers, Bernard	Te Mata, Hawke's Bay	35	10,000	Potter, A.F.	Whangarei	¼	100
Corban, A.A.	Henderson, Auckland	8	2000	Randall, Mrs A.M.	Greenmeadows, Hawke's Bay	5	6000
Crapp, Algernon	Omokaroa, Tauranga	7½	650	Radaly, Joseph	Henderson	5	500
Clemow Bros.	Deep Creek, Auckland	7	1000	Steinmetz, B.	Greenmeadows, Hawke's Bay.	4	2300
Cox, H.B.	Redvale, Te Kopuru	2	400				
Chaytor, W.	Albany	7	2000	Sunde Bros.	Oratia, Auckland	2	—
Cottle, Capt.	Greenhithe	1	400	Sowerby, Mrs	Deep Creek, Auckland	¼	100
Donald, Thomas	Te Mata, Hawke's Bay	2	600	Smith, Alfred	Deep Creek, Auckland	½	200
Dragicevich, Tony	Te Kopuru	1	100	Smith, Cholmondely	Deep Creek, Auckland	2	1000
Devcich Bros.	Puriri, Thames	½	—	Schrieder, Carl	Moturata, Kohukohu	1½	200
Franicevich, Mate	The Wade, Auckland	3	400	Trafford, E.	Kohukohu	1½	500
Frankovich Bros.	Whangaparaoa	11	4000	Te Kauwhata	Te Kauwhata	20	9500
Freeth, G.	Mt Pleasant, Picton	8	2000	Urlich, Stephen	Uwhiroa, Herekino	3	900
Glamuzina, M.	Red Hill, Auckland	1	200	Vella, John	Oratia, Auckland	6	2000
Gray, Margaret	Omakra, Kohukohu	½	200	Vella, Peter	Kumeu	5	1500
Glucina, Ivan	Oratia, Auckland	2½	500	Veza, George	Uwhiroa, Herekino	1	300
Grischka, Peter	Te Ari, Gisborne	3	300	Vidal, Anthony	Te Awanga, Clive Grange	7	—
Harris, Claude	Ruatangita, Whangarei	2¾	600	Watt, W. Ross	Kiwitahi, Morrinsville	¼	300
Hannah, J.	Bay of Islands	¾	200	Yelas, Stephen	Henderson	4	1300
Hows, Ivan	Whangaroa	1	200				
Jackman, W.H.	Whakapirau, Kaipara	5	1500				
Kokich, Stephen	Swanson	1½	—				

The influence of the prohibition movement, however, peaked in the second decade of the century – with disastrous consequences for the winegrowers. Prohibitionists achieved their first victories in wine districts in 1908 when Masterton and Eden – an Auckland electorate including part of Henderson – voted 'no-licence'. Denied the right to sell, although not to make, wine within a no-licence area, many winemakers were forced out of business.

A change emerged in the Government's attitude towards the wine industry. The minimum area in vines required before a winemaker could operate a still was raised in 1908 from two to five acres (0.8 to 2ha). Then cheap South African wines were imported on low preferential tariffs and made rapid inroads in the local market.

Bragato sought to counter the prohibition threat by arguing that wine contributed to the sobriety rather than to the drunkenness of a nation. 'As an agency in the cause of temperance the viticultural industry operates powerfully . . . It is a fact beyond contention, except by the bigot, that in wine-drinking countries the people are amongst the most sober, contented, and industrious on the face of the earth.'[65]

CORBANS COUNTER-ATTACK THE PROHIBITIONISTS AT THE AUCKLAND SPRING SHOW BEFORE THE KEY 1919 LIQUOR POLL.

Bragato's vision of a thriving wine industry, which underlay his proposals for the training of viticultural cadets at Te Kauwhata and the publication of periodic technical bulletins, now encountered resistance even within the Department of Agriculture. A letter published in the *Evening Post* in December 1907 referred to 'a curious difference of opinion between Signor Bragato, Government Viticulturist, and his chief, Mr J.D. Ritchie, who "doubted whether the wine grape will receive much attention in the near future" '.[66] The vineyard areas at Te Kauwhata and Arataki were restricted and in 1908 Bragato lost control of both stations. Frustrated, and severely disillusioned, he resigned his post in 1909 and left the country for Canada. Eventually he was to commit suicide there, following a domestic crisis.

The Viticultural Division of the Department of Agriculture was disbanded and research at Te Kauwhata shifted to horticulture. Public interest in winemaking waned; by 1909 Te Kauwhata had available a large amount of grafted vines, for which there were few buyers.

A *New Zealand Truth* reporter, journeying by train from Wellington to Hawke's Bay in 1911, sat next to 'a good-natured winemaker with tasty samples of his industry in a handy kit-bag'. It was J.O. Craike, manager of Te Mata Vineyard, returning from Wellington with orders for his hock, claret and Madeira. *Truth* asked him how winemakers would fare if prohibition were carried on a national basis?

' "Ruined − our industry will be absolutely ruined," Craike emphatically replied . . . "The worst feature of this prohibition craze," the winemaker complained, "is the fact of the Government some years ago having encouraged people to grow grapes and make wine. Much public money had been spent in fostering the industry . . . Now . . . when there was the prospect of a fair return for labour and capital expended . . . came the possibility of ruination by National Prohibition, which the Government in turn was now fostering. If this industry is wiped out . . . it will be a downright injustice to a section of the community worthy of better treatment." '67

Late in 1911 a new organisation surfaced to defend the winegrowers against the prohibitionists. The New Zealand Viticultural Association promptly petitioned the Government for help 'to save this fast decaying industry by initiating such legislation as will restore confidence among those who after long years of waiting have almost lost confidence in the justice of the Government. Through harsh laws and withdrawal of Government support and encouragement a great industry has been practically ruined'.68

Bragato had noted in 1903 that the sale of cheap fake wines was damaging the reputation of all New Zealand wines. Stories such as that appearing in the *New Zealand Times*, describing an incident at Don Buck's camp near Henderson, were not unusual. In November 1912 the camp was 'the scene of a drunken orgy, culminating in the death of a man called Harry Whiteside . . . A woman volunteered the statement that there had been considerable carousing, and yesterday a two-gallon keg of wine was brought to the camp . . . Some time before it had been reported that a wine highly fortified with some cheap spirit was being sold to gumdiggers, mill hands, and others. Austrian winegrowers received the blame'.69

The Viticultural Association publicly condemned the widespread practice of wine adulteration and called for the licensing of winemakers and regular checks on winemaking standards. Soon after, the whole issue of wine adulteration came to a head.

During debate on the Licensing Amendment Act of 1914, Prime Minister W.F. Massey launched a sweeping attack on 'the manufacture and sale of what is called Austrian wine. I do not know whether the name is a misnomer or not [Dalmatia was then a reluctant part of the Austro-Hungarian Empire] but it is a liquor that is sold in the district north of Auckland. I have never seen the stuff, but I believe it to be one of the vilest concoctions which can possibly be imagined. I do not know what its ingredients are, but I have come across people who have seen the effects of the use of Austrian wine as a beverage, and from what I have learned it is a degrading, demoralising and sometimes maddening drink . . .'70 Massey's sentiments towards wine in general are only too clear in this statement. An amendment subsequently introduced by Massey tightened Government control of the industry through the creation of a new system of winemakers' licences and a string of accompanying restrictions.

The close of war brought no respite for the harassed vintners. The Licensing Amendment Act of 1918 determined that, if national prohibition were carried, the liquor trade should receive no financial compensation for its losses. The wine industry would simply be forced to close down.

When Eden electoral boundaries were altered, all of Henderson became

THE OPPONENTS OF PROHIBITION ARGUED − AS IN THIS 1905 CARTOON BY E.F. HISCOCKS − THAT ABOLITION OF THE LEGAL TRADE IN LIQUOR WOULD IN FACT INTENSIFY THE SOCIAL PROBLEMS THE PROHIBITIONISTS SOUGHT TO CURE.

a no-licence area, forcing winegrowers to erect depots away from their vineyards, in 'wet' areas, from which to sell their wine.

Then in 1919 New Zealand voted in favour of national prohibition. Only the crucial, primarily anti-prohibition votes of returning servicemen tipped the balance and rescued the winegrowers from economic oblivion.

The 1920s and 1930s witnessed a slow, but definite, expansion in the wine industry. Support for prohibition at the polls gradually slumped. The failure of prohibition in the United States turned opinion against the movement in New Zealand, and the prohibitionists' refusal to accept the efficacy of reforms that fell short of complete prohibition hastened their decline. The prohibition tide had been stemmed; there then came a long period of stalemate between 1918 and 1939 during which there was no significant legislation on liquor. The New Zealand Viticultural Association wound down its activities and slipped into recess.

With winemaking once more a feasible proposition, new vineyards were planted and wine production increased. This was the period of the main settlement of Yugoslavs in West Auckland, bringing to the area, according to the *New Zealand Herald* in July 1935 'something of the charm of a home industry with simple apparatus and unpretentious sheds'.[71] The influx was reflected in the rapidly rising numbers of licensed winemakers. There were forty in 1925 (barely more than half the seventy winemakers listed by S.F. Anderson in 1913); by 1932 there were a hundred.

Hawke's Bay lacked cheap land and close markets of the size that made Auckland attractive to European immigrants. The trend there was to fewer and larger vineyards, and specialisation in winemaking was more advanced. Friedrich Wohnsiedler established a vineyard at Waihirere near Gisborne in 1921; Tom McDonald bought his first land in 1927; and in 1933 Robert Bird founded Glenvale Vineyards at Bay View.

The Government continued to treat the industry in an apathetic and frequently hostile manner. Legislation passed in 1920 prevented any further issue of wine-bar licences. Since the hotels and merchants selling imported wine regarded the local industry as a competitor to be obstructed in every way possible, growers were forced to rely heavily on door sales, hunting prospective buyers on foot through the 'wet' areas of Auckland.

The laws regulating the industry were harsh and in a mess. The Customs Department supplied winemakers with brandy to fortify their wines; the Health Department prosecuted its use. Some of the first regulations drawn up for the control of winemaking in 1924 would have forced many growers out of business had they been rigidly enforced. The addition of water (commonly used to reduce acidity) was prohibited; wine could be made

AFTER WEST AUCKLAND VOTED 'DRY' IN 1908, A.A. CORBAN WAS UNABLE TO SELL WINE FROM HIS CELLAR (LEFT). THE SMALL WHITE BUILDING (RIGHT), WHICH STILL SURVIVES, WAS POSITIONED ACROSS THE RAILWAY LINE IN A 'WET' ELECTORATE AND FOR SEVERAL YEARS SERVED AS THE CORBANS SALES DEPOT.

FRIEDRICH WOHNSIEDLER, BORN NEAR WÜRTTEMBURG IN GERMANY, WHOSE WAIHIRERE WINES, NEAR GISBORNE, FLOURISHED FROM 1921 UNTIL HIS DEATH IN 1956. HIS NAME LIVES ON, HOWEVER, ON THE LABEL OF NEW ZEALAND'S FASTEST-SELLING VARIETAL MÜLLER-THURGAU, MONTANA WOHNSIEDLER.

ROBERT BIRD, THE ENGLISHMAN WHO FOUNDED GLENVALE WINES AT BAY VIEW, NEAR NAPIER, WAS ALREADY FIFTY-ONE WHEN HE FIRST PLUNGED INTO COMMERCIAL WINEMAKING.

CHARLES WOODFIN, AN ENGLISHMAN WHO LEARNED WINEMAKING IN BORDEAUX, WAS APPOINTED GOVERNMENT VITICULTURIST IN THE 1920S. TALES STILL ABOUND OF HIS HELPFULNESS TOWARDS THE STRUGGLING WINEMAKERS OF THAT PERIOD.

only from grapes, thus making fruit wines illegal. Despite the existing restrictions on its production and purchase, only wine spirit could be used for fortifying. Government insensitivity was further demonstrated when a fresh wave of cheap imported wines was allowed in to threaten the local market.

The outcome was the emergence of a new organisation destined to shape the course of New Zealand wine history. Formation of the Viticultural Association of New Zealand – not to be confused with the earlier New Zealand Viticultural Association – was a response by winegrowers to the several adversities facing the industry. The major problems appear in the minutes of a meeting of winemakers held in Henderson in July 1926: 'The industry is likely to be ruined by importation of wines from abroad which are at present practically coming in duty free, and also by the sale of non-genuine grape wines which are being sold, thus prejudicing the public against the genuine grape wines'.[72]

Wine adulteration remained a common practice. A customs officer who called on John Vella at Oratia in 1926, inspected his vineyard and found only 'four rows of a little over a chain each in length. He admitted frankly that he had used raisins in making wine, using the wine so made for blending with wine made from grapes . . . He labels his wine as being made from the best of grapes'.[73] In the same year, Fred Sherwood at Henderson was prosecuted by the Health Department and convicted for selling wine made from apple juice and coloured with aniline dye.

One of the biggest problems for the wine industry lay in its own vineyards. Most *vinifera* vines were in a very low state of health. Blight and viruses had left the vines so weakened that it was widely believed that the *vinifera* varieties could not successfully be grown in New Zealand.

Oidium, according to Government Viticulturist Charles Woodfin in 1928, was still 'well-known through the viticultural areas of New Zealand, where it causes losses in both vineyards and vineries [glasshouses]. Few of the European vines are proof against the attacks'.[74] Grafting onto phylloxera-resistant roots had also hastened the deterioration of classical varieties. The imported rootstocks were infected with virus. Grafting enabled the virus to infiltrate the scion wood and sap the energy of the vines.

Bragato's decision to import native American rootstocks also backfired when many growers chose not to graft onto *vinifera* vines and simply planted the American varieties. These, according to Bragato's successor S.F. Anderson in 1917, were very inferior for winemaking, 'owing to a peculiar black-currant or . . . "foxy" flavour . . . The American class of vine is, moreover, deficient in the natural saccharine for winemaking. Owing, however, to their hardiness in resisting fungoid diseases they are grown very largely in the north of New Zealand'.[75]

At the turn of the century, fear of prohibition had encouraged many growers to search for a dual-purpose grape that if necessary could be sold as a table variety. When one of the American Isabella vines on George Pannill's property at Albany near Auckland produced exceptionally bountiful fruit, growers flocked to procure cuttings. Although the 'Albany Surprise' proved to be exceedingly productive and disease-resistant, its wine proved to have less admirable qualities.

In the 1930s F.E. Hewlett of the Maungatapu Vineyard near Tauranga planted out two acres (0.8ha) of vines 'recommended by Te Kauwhata as being a variety from which nearly all New Zealand wines were made. From the time of planting the cuttings, it takes three years to get any grapes at all; and four years for the yield of even a small crop. Thus it took four years for us to find out that the Albany Surprise grape produced excellent crops of pleasant tasting grapes which, when fermented, produced a very poor quality wine'.[76] In 1960 Albany Surprise was still the most widely planted grape variety in New Zealand.

Another contribution to the declining standards of the national vineyard came in 1928, when Franco-American hybrid vines were imported and distributed from Te Kauwhata. The hybrid vines had been developed during the fight against phylloxera. By crossing European with American varieties, French scientists had endeavoured to produce vines coupling the disease-resistant qualities of the American varieties with the superior winemaking characteristics of *vinifera* grapes. Unfortunately, the coarse *labrusca* flavours emerge strongly in most hybrid wines, and eventually the hybrid vines were banned from all of the best French winegrowing regions.

Government Viticulturist Charles Woodfin was well aware of the inferior winemaking characteristics of the hybrids, but considered that they 'should prove valuable for cultivation in the districts where humid climatic conditions are favourable to the development of fungous diseases'.[77] The hybrids proved popular, and by 1945 the Department of Agriculture was strongly urging the cultivation of Seibel and Baco hybrid varieties in Henderson and the Waikato. Gone was the attention devoted in Bragato's time to the low-yielding *vinifera* varieties. Government policy now encouraged the production of cheap ordinary wine from the high-yielding hybrid vines, a switch that suited the struggling winemakers of the 1930s by presenting winemaking as a more attractive commercial proposition, but left growers stranded when the call went out for higher-quality table wine in the 1960s.

The Depression failed to arrest the slow progress of the wine industry during the inter-War period, but certainly no one had very high hopes of it, and on the eve of Labour's ascension to power in 1935 there was little hint of future prosperity for the impoverished growers. As Tom McDonald, the legendary winemaker, later put it, they were forced 'to sell the grapes to get the money to buy the sugar to make the wine'.[78]

In fact, Labour's long tenure in office was to prove of great benefit to the winegrowers. Rex Mason, MP for Auckland Suburbs and then Waitakere, was appointed Minister of Justice in the new Government, and was thus ideally positioned to advance the interests of his winegrower constituents. Labour's determination to aid the wine industry became clear from 1938. Te Kauwhata received an injection of additional funds to upgrade facilities and expand its research activities, and a new viticultural inspector, B.W. Lindeman, was appointed.

Then – at the request of the winemakers – the Government raised the duty on Australian and South African wines, enabling New Zealand wines to compete on a price basis with imported wines, which previously had dominated the market. From 1938 the quantities of wines and spirits that could be brought in were slashed, and for several years import licences were held at fifty percent of their former value.

Sales of local wines soared. Not even sharp increases in the rate of sales tax on wine – from the five percent first introduced in 1932 to ten percent in 1940 and then forty percent in 1942 – inhibited demand. Merchants, required by the Department of Industries and Commerce to buy two gallons of New Zealand wine for every gallon they imported, suddenly found themselves forced to clamour for local brands that they had long held in disdain.

An influx of American servicemen in 1942 on leave and in search of liquor – any liquor – further excited the demand for New Zealand wine. As one grower put it: 'I sold some wine to an American serviceman for ten shillings a gallon – he was very happy. Then a fortnight later I heard that wine was being sold for thirty shillings a gallon. So I bought a

TOM McDONALD – REVERED BY MANY WINE LOVERS FOR HIS TRAIL-BLAZING CABERNET SAUVIGNON OF THE 1960s – IS PICTURED HERE IN HIS EARLY TWENTIES SLEDGING OUT THE 1929 HARVEST FROM HIS HAWKE'S BAY VINEYARD.

distillery, put in a cellar, and planted five or six acres in grapes. In 1943 in went another five acres . . .'[79]

With wine selling easily and at top prices, the financial position of winegrowers rapidly improved. Brick wineries supplanted tin sheds, concrete vats replaced wooden, and many sideline winemaking operations emerged as profitable small businesses. Wartime conditions created a spring climate for winegrowers, and they sank deep roots.

EASTERN VINEYARDS, NOW VANISHED, WAS ESTABLISHED BY GEORGE ANTUNOVICH IN STURGES ROAD, HENDERSON, IN THE FOOTHILLS OF THE WAITAKERE RANGES, AUCKLAND, IN 1939.

Unfortunately, quality took a back seat in the wartime rush for easy profits. With demand for wine exceeding the supply, growers made up the difference less from grapes than from sugar and water. There is ample contemporary evidence to show that huge amounts of 'plonk' were made and sold in the name of wine during the War. In 1946 the Royal Commission on Licensing was scathing in its criticism of New Zealand wine. 'Most of this New Zealand wine . . . has been far inferior to that which could be imported. The Department of Agriculture states that more than 60 percent of the wine made by the smaller winemakers is infected with bacterial disorders . . . [and] a considerable quantity of wine made in New Zealand would be classified as unfit for human consumption in other wine-producing countries.'[80] In the same year Mr F. Langstone, MP for Mt Roskill, told Parliament that 'most of the wine in New Zealand today is a concoction; it is not wine. There are no more grapes and grape-juice in a lot of it than there are in my boot'.[81]

Records deposited in National Archives show that although the Food and Drug Act prohibited the use of water in winemaking, and limited the addition of sugar to grapejuice to a maximum of two pounds per gallon (1kg per 4.5L), most New Zealand wines of this period – when they were made from grapes – were vinted from the Albany Surprise variety, contained at least twenty-five percent added water and three and a half to four pounds of added sugar per gallon (1.75 to 2kg per 4.5L).

The law itself was partly responsible for the low overall standard of winemaking. Growers with less than two hectares of vines, prevented from operating their own stills, were unable to properly fortify their wines. New Zealand sherries and ports contained only fifteen to sixteen percent alcohol by volume, compared with nineteen percent for their imported equivalents. According to Lindeman, 'the fact of the wines not being fortified to a sufficient strength leaves them open to infection from various wine diseases which produce in the wine, through bacteria, acetic or lactic acid and various other elements which when absorbed by the system have a very deleterious effect'.[82]

The Department of Agriculture moved to tighten its control over winemaking practices, by drawing up a set of proposed regulations that caused much resentment amongst small-scale winemakers. The small growers argued that the regulations would force them to make major structural alterations to their wineries and, in the words of the Royal Commission on Licensing, 'prevent them from using water and certain colouring, flavouring, and sweetening substances which they had always used . . . and . . . from using a still unless they had 25 acres (10.1ha) of fully bearing grapes'.[83]

The smaller winemakers were convinced that the Department of Agriculture was in league with the larger wine companies. The proposed new regulations – which were never implemented – and the actions of the Government instructor, Lindeman, were correctly perceived by the smaller growers as favouring the large companies at their expense.

In July 1943, at a meeting of the Viticultural Association held at Henderson, the swelling ill-feeling between large and small-scale growers came to a head. Several non-Dalmatian members, notably the Corbans, broke away to form the New Zealand Wine Council and (for geographic reasons) the Hawke's Bay Grape Winegrowers' Association. From then until the formation of the Wine Institute in 1975, the internal politics of the wine industry were dominated by an extreme divisiveness rooted in the contrasting economic fortunes of large and small-scale growers. When the Viticultural Association on the one hand – composed mainly of small-scale growers of Dalmatian origin – and the Wine Council and Hawke's Bay Grape Winegrowers' Association on the other – representing primarily large-scale non-Dalmatian companies – were not pursuing individual paths on matters affecting the wine industry, they spent rather less time in co-operation than at each others' throats.

A separate splinter group was led by a Slovenian of independent vision, Paul Groshek. During the Depression Groshek established two acres (0.8ha) of Albany Surprise and Isabella vines at Muaga Vineyards in Henderson, and those who came to inspect the maze of cellars he had tunnelled into the hillside, and stayed to support his pleas for greater consumption of table wine, swore that he gave away more than he ever sold.

Groshek's reputation has lingered as an unorthodox industry spokesman. He used to write poetry in praise of wine, and was in the habit of flourishing before-and-after photographs of sickly animals miraculously restored to health by the healing qualities of Muaga wine. Until his death in 1964 Paul Groshek made a unique contribution to the wine industry's long fight against public indifference and Government restriction.

The sale of wine in restaurants, and tax adjustments to encourage the production of light table wines were among far-sighted recommendations made to improve New Zealand wine standards by the Royal Commission on Licensing in 1946. However, the main part of the Commission's Report recommended nationalisation of the breweries, a course that failed to commend itself to a Labour Government in decline at the polls, and the Report, including the potentially valuable section on the wine industry, was shelved.

A first step towards making New Zealand wine more freely available to the public was taken in 1948, when the wine-reseller's licence was created, and tailored to meet the retail marketing needs of the winemakers. The licence opened up a whole new avenue of sale, by allowing growers and others to establish retail outlets for New Zealand wine throughout the country.

A COLLECTION OF OLD NEW ZEALAND WINE BOTTLES UNEARTHED A DECADE AGO AT EASTERN VINEYARDS, HENDERSON. ONLY THE BABICH COMPANY NAME SURVIVES TODAY. NOTE PAUL GROSHEK'S MUAGA BOTTLE, CARRYING FOR ALL TO READ THE DECLARATION: 'NEW ZEALAND CAN DO IT'.

HENDERSON WINEMAKER PAUL GROSHEK, PHOTOGRAPHED AT THE ENTRANCE TO HIS UNDERGROUND CELLARS NOT LONG BEFORE HIS DEATH, WROTE THAT 'WINE IS LIKE A GARDEN OF FLOWERS, THE SOUND OF MUSIC, A BEAUTIFUL SONG, OR THE SIGHT OF A GREAT PAINTING'.

BIRDWOOD VINEYARDS

One winery which languished during the latter years of the Second World War, but in a surviving May 1939 price list claims to have been 'one of the largest vineyards in the Dominion', was Birdwood Vineyards. For a winery once popular, Birdwood has been too swiftly forgotten.

The founder of Birdwood Vineyards and its driving force through the successful decades of the 1920s and 1930s was Simun Mijo (Simon Mitchell) Ujdur. Born in Gradac, Dalmatia, in 1882, Ujdur was barely a teenager when he arrived in New Zealand in 1895. After five years' gumdigging, he returned to Europe and three years' service in the Austrian Navy before finally settling permanently in New Zealand.

SIMON UJDUR (LEFT, WEARING SUIT), THE ORIGINAL WINERY (CENTRE), AND THE FIRST HOMESTEAD (RIGHT) ALL FEATURE IN THIS HARVEST PHOTOGRAPH OF BIRDWOOD VINEYARDS, DATING FROM AROUND 1918.

SIMUN MIJO UJDUR, 1882-1953.

Initially Ujdur set up a photography studio in Auckland, capturing on film a parade of weddings, schoolchildren, funerals, arrivals and departures. By 1911 he was ready to buy land, choosing a property where Birdwood and Glen roads link, near the base of Don Buck's Hill, Massey. (As an 'Austrian' alien, Ujdur registered the land in the name of a New Lynn resident, Mr Hunter, and only transferred the title to his own name in 1921.)

The year 1915 brought the first vintage at Birdwood Vineyards, in a makeshift winery built out of motorcar packing crates. Business grew steadily through the 1920s,

surviving the Depression. By 1939 Simon Ujdur stated – in the same price list – that he had, 'not by bluff but by actual survey', twenty acres (8ha) in grapes. The principal grape varieties were Albany Surprise and Black Hamburgh, along with some Pinots and Malbec.

Under the Birdwood Vineyards label – featuring a phoenix, the mystical bird that rose from the ashes with renewed youth – Ujdur offered for sale a range of five ports, three sherries, a Frontignac, Madeira, cider and vinegar. For 'those who cannot digest sweet wines', a claret was produced at fifty shillings per dozen. Prospective customers were assured that 'experience will prove we equal the best in quality and beat anything and anyone for value'.

Chairman of the Viticultural Association of New Zealand from its formation in 1926 until 1946, Ujdur was an influential spokesman for the primarily Dalmatian winegrower interests he represented. He was also the owner of a crowded personal library running to many thousands of volumes.

Ironically, during the war era of booming wine sales, Birdwood Vineyard's own fortunes entered a long period of decline. In 1944 the Customs Department, convinced that Ujdur was illegally selling spirit (as 'brandy', rather than using it for fortifying wine), slapped a two-year ban on Birdwood's production and sales. Appeals by Simon Ujdur to Walter Nash eventually brought permission for his accumulated wine stocks to be released – but only on the harsh condition that it was all to be distilled into fortifying spirit. To ensure no stocks were sold as wine, Government officials now poured green colouring powder into all Birdwood white wines and black powder into the reds. Distillation took three years; five years of normal trading was lost. According to his nephew, Simon Ujdur junior, 'those unnecessary and unpalatable terms shortened S.M. Ujdur's life by at least 10 to 15 years'.[84]

A NEW FERMENTATION VAT – MADE BY HENDERSON COOPER PETER BAKARICH – ARRIVES AT BIRDWOOD VINEYARDS, AROUND 1930.

At the end of the war an aging Simon Ujdur wrote to his brother George – then in an Egyptian refugee camp, fleeing the Germans – urging him to bring his family to New Zealand to help run the winery. George and his son, Simon, arrived in Wellington in 1946 and walked straight into the trading fiasco.

Simon Ujdur died on Christmas Day 1953. His nephew remembers him as someone who 'took to me and loved me as though I was his real son. He was a humanitarian in every sense of the word, an achiever, a survivor, artistically creative and a tireless fighter for just causes'.[85]

Sadly, at a time when New Zealand wine sales were falling after wartime import restrictions were lifted, Simon Ujdur's estate was bitterly contested in court. Under the combined burden of death duties and litigation expenses, the winery slid into debt.

Relief came at the end of the 1950s when the sales of local wine began to climb again. In 1959 Simon Ujdur junior started renovating the cellar and built a new wine bar. He and his father employed outside labour and new labels were designed, reading for the first time 'G Ujdur and Sons'.

But the phoenix faltered. Heated disputes between Simon Ujdur's two nephews, Simon junior and Anthony, were paralysing their working relationship. Josip Babich was consulted in an endeavour to sort out the matter. His verdict: 'At Birdwood there's enough potential for all of you if you will only work and co-operate.' Moscow Yelas was the next to be approached. His conclusion: 'All the other vineyards are getting bigger and stronger – if you split, your ship will be stranded.' Finally, Dudley Russell, of Western Vineyards, pointed the way: 'One brother should buy the other out.'

The brothers accepted Russell's advice. An independent valuer put a figure on the land, buildings and chattels of £20,000. A ballot was held in 1963 and won by Anthony. He, as agreed, bought out his brother. Simon Ujdur junior was henceforth banned from the premises.

The year 1970 marked the final vintage at Birdwood Vineyards. The five hundred buyers and onlookers who flocked to a huge auction held in 1977 saw a 1936 caterpillar tractor sold for $350 and an old crusher, press, filter, pumps, corkers, vats and hundreds of forty-four gallon (198L) barrels all pass under the hammer.

Part of the Birdwood estate now forms the Waitemata City Council's Birdwood Depot and the rest is incorporated into Te Rangi Hiroa Reserve. The winery and the old homestead are still standing – remnants of the golden era at Birdwood.

THE ENTRANCE TO BIRDWOOD VINEYARDS, PHOTOGRAPHED AROUND 1926.

SIMON UJDUR JNR.

The wartime wine boom collapsed in the late 1940s after the easing of import restrictions when another wave of Australian wine entered the local market. The nation's political leaders certainly appear to have preferred overseas wines; when Walter Nash asked someone to 'go to Bellamy's and bring up a bottle of New Zealand wine the person sent returned with one half-pint bottle, which represented all the New Zealand wine that Bellamy's cellars could produce'.[86]

The market for local wines tightened and by 1949 prices had fallen appreciably below wartime levels. Then industry fears of competition from overseas wine companies venturing into the New Zealand market were aroused when between 1947 and 1950 McWilliam's Wines of Australia established vineyards and a winery in Hawke's Bay. Winegrowers viewed the intrusion of foreign wine interests with such concern that the three principal growers' organisations came together in a shaky alliance to form the Wine Manufacturers' Federation, a body that lasted five years until it was torn apart by its own internal feuds.

At mid-century the industry was still failing to capitalise on New Zealand's potential for the production of world-class table wine.

A new impulse was felt when George Mazuran was elected president of the Viticultural Association in 1950. Convinced early that the future prosperity of the wine industry hinged on relaxation of the country's restrictive licensing laws, Mazuran subsequently carved out a long career for himself as one of the most successful political lobbyists that New Zealand has known. The efforts of Mazuran and the Viticultural Association yielded an impressive string of legislative concessions from successive Governments that laid the foundation for the industry's phenomenal growth rates of recent decades.

WALTER NASH, PRIME MINISTER DURING THE LABOUR ADMINISTRATION, 1957–60, ADDRESSES AN EARLY VITICULTURAL ASSOCIATION FIELD-DAY. ON HIS LEFT SITS THE HON. H.G.R. MASON. BEHIND, STANDING, ARE PETER FREDATOVICH SNR, OF LINCOLN VINEYARDS, MATE SELAK, AND MATE BRAJKOVICH, OF SAN MARINO VINEYARDS.

The early 1950s under a new National Government brought a series of measures designed to boost the ailing wine industry. The wartime forty percent sales tax was halved. Then in 1953 separate licences were created for the manufacture of grape and fruit wines – and no person or company was allowed to hold both. The idea was to prevent the sale of fruit wines masquerading as genuine grape wine.

The winegrowers' annual dinner and field-day for Parliamentarians and Government officials was launched in 1952 and subsequently brought the wine industry to the favourable attention of a host of politicians. The field-day transformed the traditional European harvest celebrations into a superbly effective public relations exercise. MPs gained the background knowledge, and industry leaders the social contacts that together assured the wine industry of an accessible and responsive legislature.

Mazuran's assiduous lobbying soon paid off. A crucial breakthrough came in 1955 when Parliament reduced the minimum quantities of wine that could be sold by winemakers and wine resellers, from two gallons (9L) to a quart (1.14L) for table wines and – temporarily – to a half-gallon for fortified wines.

GEORGE MAZURAN, REGARDED WITH AMUSEMENT BY SOME MPS FOR HIS 'QUAINT' WAYS, NEVERTHELESS CARVED OUT A CAREER FOR HIMSELF AS ONE OF THE MOST SUCCESSFUL LOBBYISTS NEW ZEALAND POLITICS HAS KNOWN.

An even more important contribution to the resurgence of interest in the wine industry was made by the Winemaking Industry Committee, set up in 1956 to investigate all aspects of the manufacture and sale of New Zealand wine. For several years the breweries had succeeded in preventing the spread of wine-resellers' licences, on the grounds that such outlets were unnecessary where New Zealand wine could already be bought from hotels. In a decision of cardinal significance, the Committee recommended that the existence of other forms of licence should not affect the spread of wineshops and that wine-resellers' licences should be more freely granted. The outcome was the doubling in number of New Zealand wineshops by 1965.

Encouraging the spread of wineshops across the nation was the 1957 Committee's essential achievement. There were other useful proposals. The Committee suggested the formation of a Viticultural Advisory Committee consisting of winegrowers and departmental officials; that restaurants should be licensed to serve New Zealand (and no other) wine; and that the provision allowing the sale of dessert wine in half-gallon quantities should be made permanent. Together, the recommendations received widespread legislative support.

The incoming Second Labour Government rendered further assistance to the winegrowers. Imports of wines and spirits dropped in 1958 and 1959 to half their former volume. Another shot in the arm came with the high taxes slapped on beer and spirits in the 'Black Budget' of 1958. *The Weekly News* in September 1958 declared that the beer drinker 'was rocked on his heels by the sharp bump upwards in beer tax that came with the Nordmeyer Budget. Today, New Zealanders who wend their way homeward after 6 p.m. with brown parcels under arm will often have a bottle of wine as well as the traditional nut-brown brew'.[87]

The effects of Labour's moves are well described in the 1959 Annual Report of the Department of Agriculture. The tax and licensing adjustments had 'created an immediate and unprecedented demand for New Zealand wines. The market position for New Zealand wines changed from one of difficult and competitive trading to a buoyant market capable of absorbing all the wine that producers could supply'.[88] Shortly after, the law was eased to remove restrictions on wine sales in no-licence districts and to allow single bottle sales of fortified wine.

WINEGROWING FROM 1960 TO 1988

Our southern outpost of the earth's millions of hectares of vines presently covers an area estimated by the Wine Institute after feverish planting in 1987 and 1988 to be 6000 hectares – over fifteen times larger than that surveyed in 1960, when there were 387 hectares planted. This rapid growth rate has involved the New Zealand wine industry in a number of drastic changes.

One outstanding feature, especially of the 1960s, was the heavy investment by overseas companies in New Zealand wine. Foreign interests often staked their claims through investment in previously family-controlled wineries. McWilliam's led the way, establishing vineyards and a winery in Hawke's Bay between 1947 and 1950. In 1961 McWilliam's joined forces with McDonald's at Taradale to form what then became the largest winemaking group in the country.

Takeovers soon became commonplace. Like McWilliam's, Penfolds of Australia decided that the establishment of vineyards in New Zealand would best serve their interests in the local market. In a new company, Penfolds Wines (NZ) Ltd, founded in 1963, the parent company in Australia owned sixty-two percent of the capital and local brewers and merchants held the rest. Later Gilbey's moved into Nobilo at Huapai and Seppelt's of Australia became involved with Vidal at Hastings.

All three companies reverted to New Zealand ownership in the 1970s as foreign investors pared their overseas operations. Control of Nobilo passed to a triumvirate of the Public Service Investment Society, Reid Nathan Ltd and the Development Finance Corporation; George Fistonich of Villa Maria acquired Vidal; and Penfolds was bought by Frank Yukich, formerly head of Montana. Meanwhile, Rothmans entered the wine industry through the purchase of a controlling share in Corbans.

The greatest impact by foreign capital on New Zealand wine was made through Montana. Montana was established during the Second World War by a Dalmatian immigrant, Ivan Yukich, as a one-fifth hectare vineyard high in the Waitakere Ranges west of Auckland. A subsequent crash expansion programme culminated in 1973 when Seagrams of New York acquired a forty percent share in Montana. American finance and expertise subsequently enabled the company to emerge as the dominant force in the New Zealand wine industry.

Having failed to prevent the emergence of an indigenous wine industry, local wine merchants and brewers began to display a more positive attitude towards New Zealand wine. Hotel bottlestores throughout the country now stocked and promoted the products of the vineyards in which the breweries had a financial stake. Their involvement in wine could be incestuous; in 1980, for example, two-thirds of McWilliam's shares were held by New Zealand Breweries, Ballins and Dominion Breweries between them.

With a view to the establishment of a brandy industry in New Zealand, in 1964 Government gave permission for winegrowers to carry out experimental brandy distillations. Despite the production of several sound brandies and the discovery of suitable grape varieties – notably Baco 22A – nothing eventuated. The Government, not convinced that a brandy industry would be economically viable, hedged on the allocation of licences. Also the short supply of grapes for processing into wine left none to spare for brandy.

The wine industry derived greater benefit from a proliferation of new forms of liquor licences. From the 1960s the trend towards liberalisation of the licensing laws, evident since 1948, grew much more decisive. Restaurants were licensed in 1960 and taverns in 1961. Theatres, airports and cabarets became licensed between 1969 and 1971, offering new avenues for wine sales. The creation of a permit system in 1976 gave belated legislative recognition to the BYO wine phenomenon by allowing the consumption of wine in unlicensed restaurants. Another amendment that year introduced vineyard bar licences, to enable the sale of wine by the glass or bottle at vineyards for consumption on the premises.

The emergence, relatively recently, of contract grapegrowing has reshaped the structure of the viticultural industry in New Zealand. Traditionally, wineries had grown all their own grape requirements. Viticulture and winemaking formed integral parts of each winery's activities. This pattern altered in the late 1960s when several companies, seeking to avoid the heavy capital expenditure required to establish new vineyards, persuaded farmers to plant their surplus acres in grapevines. The wine companies provided vines, viticultural advice and assistance with financial arrangements in return for guaranteed access to the fruit of the new vineyards.

Vineyard acreages tripled between 1965 and 1970 as contract grapegrowing swept the Gisborne plains. An average winery bought in four percent of its grape requirements in 1960. Today contract grapegrowers produce and sell in excess of three-quarters of the country's grape crop.

Since 1970 Auckland has lost its former pre-eminence as New Zealand's major grapegrowing region. Auckland's share of the national vineyard area dropped between 1970 and 1986 from nearly fifty percent to 5.6 percent. Shifts occurred within the province in this period as many Henderson wineries developed new vineyards further north, in the more rural Huapai-Kumeu area.

ANDRÉ SIMON, THE LEGENDARY WINE WRITER, WITH GEORGE MAZURAN. MOST OF THE DESSERT WINES SIMON TASTED DURING HIS 1964 TOUR OF NEW ZEALAND VINEYARDS, HE LATER WROTE, LACKED 'ANY TRACE OF BOUQUET OR BREED'.

Although vineyard expansion was slow in Auckland and the Waikato, further south in Marlborough, Hawke's Bay and Poverty Bay the pace has been hot. Corbans' plantings, for example, spread from Henderson to Kumeu and Taupaki, and then to the East Coast and finally Marlborough. Cooks in the late 1960s established vineyards and a winery at Te Kauwhata, later contracted growers in Poverty Bay and then acquired vineyards at Riverhead (Auckland) and in Hawke's Bay. Montana planted at Mangatangi south of Auckland before contracting large acreages in Poverty Bay and pioneering the spread of viticulture to Marlborough.

According to the then Viticultural Association chairman, George Mazuran, quoted in *The Weekly News* in April 1971, the wine boom of the 1960s 'was achieved at the expense of quality'. During the 'Cold Duck' era twenty years ago an undiscriminating and unsuspecting public snapped up large quantities of cheap adulterated sherries and table wines. Charged Mazuran: 'Some growers have been getting away with blue murder'.[89]

The 1970s brought an overall improvement in wine quality and heavy emphasis on the production of table wines. Wine production rose between 1960 and 1983 from 4.1 million litres to 57.7 million litres. This, said Alex Corban, means that New Zealand had 'probably the fastest growing wine industry in the world'.[90] The growth area was table wines, which captured twelve percent of the market in 1962. Today that figure stands at over eighty-three percent and slightly sweet, fruity white table wines dominate the market.

The predominance of these wines reflects the sweeping changes in the composition of New Zealand vineyards. Twenty-five years ago less than one-third of the vines planted in New Zealand were of classical European varieties – the most common varieties were the heavy cropping but poor wine-producing Baco 22A and Albany Surprise. As a Cooks publication has noted: 'The first is prohibited in most European winemaking districts. The second would be if anyone proposed to plant it'.[91]

By 1986 the classical Müller-Thurgau variety was three times as heavily planted in New Zealand as any other variety. Cabernet Sauvignon is now the major variety for red wine. Classic varieties now constitute over ninety-eight percent of all vines in New Zealand.

Twenty-five years ago New Zealanders each drank an average of two bottles of wine annually – today the average is eighteen bottles. This increase in wine consumption reflects the much greater awareness of wine in the community.

Lindeman had observed back in 1939 that New Zealanders showed 'not only a lamentable ignorance of wine, but also a very conservative attitude toward it'.[92] Soon after, thousands of New Zealanders stationed in European wine districts during the Second World War had their first fumbling encounters with wine. An anonymous 'Kiwi Husband' writing in the magazine *Here and Now* in January 1952 recalled that most New Zealand soldiers made their first acquaintance with wine only when the supply of beer ran dry. 'It was a rough and ready meeting, and many of us dealt with wine in the manner to which we had become accustomed. We drank it from the bottle, and by the bottleful, often with sad results to ourselves and a total absence of respect for the vintage . . . It was consumed in quantities that horrified the inhabitants and tortured our stomachs. We drained the countryside of mature stocks and caught up with the harvest. We collected our wine in water carts that held some hundreds of gallons and imparted a taint of chlorine and foul lime sediments; we dispensed it in jerrycans designed for petrol and drank it from the mugs we used for hot tea. And we abandoned it for beer whenever we had the chance . . .'[93]

Some, like 'Kiwi Husband', later developed a more appreciative understanding of wine. The migration of thousands of continental Europeans to New Zealand introduced large groups of Italian, Yugoslav and Greek wine drinkers into our midst. Countless New Zealanders passing through Europe during the post-war boom in overseas travel were exposed to the traditional European enthusiasm for wine.

Rising affluence at home encouraged many New Zealanders to seek new experiences in food and drink. The mushrooming restaurant trade very profitably promoted wine as an essential aspect of 'the good life'. No longer, as in Groshek's day, was wine viewed as 'plonk', to be consumed in shame 'behind hedges and bullrushes'. Wine has become fashionable. The industry's own marketing efforts, the improved availability of quality wine and the emergence of wine columnists, wine competitions and wine clubs have combined to raise the level of public wine awareness in New Zealand to new heights.

Yet the turmoil in the wine industry in the 1970s produced a number of casualties. To switch from the manufacture of fortified wine to the production of classical table wines required heavy expenditure. While some companies acquired the necessary technical and marketing abilities, others fell behind in the race to expand and improve.

The failure of Western Vineyards, Spence's and Eastern Vineyards to lift their winemaking standards beyond those prevailing in the 1960s contributed to their demise in the late 1970s.

Western Vineyards – founded by nineteen-year-old Dudley Russell in the Waitakere Ranges in 1932 – had helped pioneer the modern era of classical table wines and enjoyed formidable competition success in the sixties. At its height of production, the winery put out 35–40,000 gallons (157,500–180,000L) of wine a year, with its Cabernet Sauvignon, 'Gamay de Beaujolais', Pinot Chardonnay and private bin Flor Sherry all enthusiastically received.

The stunning forty-acre (15ha) terraced vineyard in 1964 excited André Simon to jot in the visitors' book: 'I have never seen a more picturesque vineyard anywhere but in Tuscany'. For many years thereafter, Western

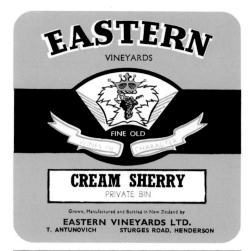

SO STUNNINGLY BEAUTIFUL WAS DUDLEY RUSSELL'S WESTERN VINEYARDS, ITS TERRACED VINES WERE SEVERAL TIMES FEATURED ON THE COVERS OF POPULAR MAGAZINES.

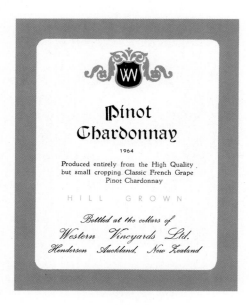

Pinot Chardonnay
1964

Produced entirely from the High Quality but small cropping Classic French Grape Pinot Chardonnay

HILL GROWN

Bottled at the cellars of
Western Vineyards Ltd.
Henderson Auckland New Zealand

THE HISTORIC FIRST MEETING OF THE PROVISIONAL EXECUTIVE COMMITTEE OF THE WINE INSTITUTE, HELD ON 1 OCTOBER 1975. (FROM LEFT) TERRY DUNLEAVY (ACTING EXECUTIVE OFFICER), MONTANA; PETER FREDATOVICH, LINCOLN; RUSSELL GIBBONS, MONTANA; GEORGE MAZURAN (DEPUTY CHAIRMAN); ALEX CORBAN (CHAIRMAN); MATE SELAK; TOM McDONALD, McWILLIAM'S; STAN CHAN, TOTARA SYC; MATE BRAJKOVICH, SAN MARINO; PETER BABICH.

Vineyards' advertisements brandished this memorable Simon quote – minus the last three words.

But in his later years, Dudley Russell began to lose interest in winemaking; beef farming increasingly absorbed his energies and investments. After his eldest son chose not to enter the family wine business, Russell announced in 1979 that the 1978 vintage had been his last; the vineyard would be uprooted and all wine stocks auctioned off. He died less than a year later, aged sixty-seven.

Other old-established wineries in the Henderson Valley have suffered drastic declines in production. Vineyards seeking a permanent place had to acquire the sophistication necessary in an increasingly competitive market or face an uncertain future.

A labyrinth of many years' negotiations finally achieved in 1975 the formation of a single, united wine organisation to represent all New Zealand winemakers. It was agreed that the industry had grown too large, its problems and aspirations too complex, to allow the pursuit of sectional interests to jeopardise development.

Management of the new Wine Institute was vested in a seven-member executive consisting of the elected representatives of three categories of winemakers grouped according to annual levels of production. The formula agreed upon – two representatives each of the small and medium-sized growers and three representatives of the big companies – ensured that, at least initially, a majority of executive members would belong to the Viticultural Association. The large companies were relying upon their belief that the wine industry fell 'into three different categories rather than two, and that the kind of representatives who would emerge from the middle group would tend towards the view of the larger companies rather than the smaller growers'.[94]

The Wine Institute's existence is recognised by statute in the Wine Makers Levy Act 1976, which requires all licensed grape winemakers to fund the Institute's activities via a compulsory annual levy based on sales, and also the Wine Makers Act 1981, which governs the grant and renewal of licences. In 1988 the Wine Institute had 117 members.

Fundamentally a pressure group, the Wine Institute has recently summarised its functions as 'representational, regulatory and promotional, in approximately that order of importance'.[95] Apart from lobbying, a multitude of tasks are accomplished, from behind-the-scenes subcommittee work on such areas of special concern as viticulture, winemaking regulations and tariffs, to more visible promotional activities, including the co-ordination of export campaigns and administration of the country's leading wine competition, the Air New Zealand Wine Awards.

Responsible for the day-to-day conduct of the Institute since its inception has been its indefatigable executive officer Terry Dunleavy. Dunleavy, who stood unsuccessfully as the National Party candidate for the Napier electorate in 1969 before entering the wine industry in 1971 as sales manager for Montana, has recently been memorably described by Robert Joseph of *Wine* magazine, as looking 'like a cross between an old Fleet Street newshound and a hard-bitten union negotiator'.[96] With his political bent and powerful administrative and journalistic abilities, Dunleavy has had a marked personal impact on the wine industry.

The wine industry encountered sustained criticism in 1979 when it became widely known that the illegal practice of wine-watering was common in New Zealand. Many wineries had taken advantage of the continuing shortage of wine in the market place to 'stretch' their products. Several scientific studies yielded evidence suggesting that consumers annually had been paying for up to fifteen million litres of tap water masquerading as wine.

Amendments to the Food and Drug Regulations in 1980 dropped the previous prohibition of water addition and set a scale of minimum grapejuice levels: ninety-five percent for premium or varietal wines, eighty percent for non-premium table wines and sixty percent for dessert wines. A pledge by the Health Department to tighten its surveillance of the regulations led to a marked lift in the quality of 1980 vintage wines.

Yet the whole issue flared again in 1981 when several firms released large volumes of 'flavoured wine', especially in casks. 'Flavoured wine' by law was able to contain as low as forty percent grapejuice. Confronted by a heavy barrage of adverse publicity – and an impending grape glut – the winegrowers finally agreed in 1982 to support moves to prevent watering. Amendment No. 7 to the Food and Drug Regulations dropped altogether the 'flavoured wine' category. From 1983 table wines were permitted to contain only fifty millilitres of water per litre of wine, where the water had been used as a processing aid for legal additives. In effect, table wines of any description must now be produced almost wholly from grapejuice, although the sixty percent minimum juice level for dessert wines remains.

In 1979 the wine industry had been referred for study to the Industries Development Commission as part of the Government's policy on economic 'restructuring'. In its 'Wine Industry Development Plan to 1986', published in December 1980, the Commission sought to 'assess the potential of the wine-producing industry to contribute to the future growth of the economy, taking into account the interests of the wine-producing industry, consumers, and the distributive trades, and recommend a strategy for future development'.[97]

The Commission's essential conclusion was that the wine industry deserved special encouragement. The industry employed 3000 people and turned out a product with eighty-five percent domestic content. Nevertheless, the IDC strongly criticised the price of most New Zealand wine as being too high for the future welfare of the industry. Soaring costs were threatening to push the price of a bottle of wine beyond most New Zealanders' reach.

The IDC produced a series of valuable recommendations designed to contain escalating costs through the encouragement of stiffer competition

TERRY DUNLEAVY, EXECUTIVE OFFICER OF THE WINE INSTITUTE, BRINGS TO HIS ROLE EXTRAORDINARY ENERGY AND A PASSION FOR THE CUT-AND-THRUST OF POLITICS.

in the market. In the Commission's view, over-protection of the local industry from imported wine had placed a burden on the consumer unjustified by the wine industry's 'poor' export performance. Distortion of competition in the wine market also derived from the commercial dominance of a select cluster of wineries, merchants and resellers described by the IDC as 'a highly cartelised group characterised by their oligopolistic influence in the market'. The lack of real competition had encouraged an unhealthy 'cost-plus attitude to escalating costs . . . to a point where consumer resistance to price shows incipient signs of developing into a major constraint upon consumption . . .'[98]

Several, although not all, of the IDC's recommendations won Government acceptance. Foreign wines were freed from import licensing in 1981, although not from tariff restrictions. In an effort to stimulate greater competition in the wholesale distribution of wine, a new class of wine distributor licence was created. And sales tax on wine was altered from a value basis to a volume rate, producing a drop in the retail price for the better class wines.

Yet as early as 1982 serious doubts arose about the successful achievement of the aims of the Wine Industry Development Plan. The plan had projected an annual per capita consumption of New Zealand wine of fifteen litres by 1986, but consumption eased from 12.5 litres in 1981 to 12.1 litres in 1982, then to 12.0 litres in 1983. The drop in sales, largely linked to heavier imports and consumer price resistance, proved a serious setback to an industry geared to rapid growth.

Heavy overplanting of new vineyards in the early 1980s helped raise the spectre of a wine glut. With a gradual phasing-out of tariffs on Australian wines due to commence in 1986, the coming surplus brought consternation to some contract growers and wine companies.

1983 involved much speculation about mergers and takeovers. Brierley Investments' proposal to merge three major companies – Cooks, McWilliam's and Penfolds – was judged by the Examiner of Commercial Practices to be likely to be contrary to the public interest. Later, discussion centred on a possible Penfolds-McWilliam's merger. Cooks announced plans late in 1983 to severely *reduce* its production.

The history of wine in New Zealand can be portrayed as an industry embarked on a century-old rollercoaster ride, soaring and plunging through successive periods of growth and optimism, decline and disillusionment. Between mid-1985 and early 1986, following the sustained prosperity of the 1960s and 1970s, the rollercoaster once again turned groundwards, carrying three privately owned wineries – the Villa Maria/Vidal stable and Delegat's – into receivership and, by their own admission, Nobilo and Glenvale to the brink of it.

The industry's recent crisis was partly rooted in the over-zealous planting of grapevines referred to earlier. For over two decades, from the early hints of the wine boom in the late fifties until about five years ago, wine grapes were in short supply. Winemakers understandably eager to cater for the burgeoning demand for New Zealand wine, and determined in some instances to expand their share of the market, reacted by committing themselves to a multitude of long-term contracts with grapegrowers. The industry needed 55,000 tonnes of fruit from the bumper 1985 vintage to satisfy the current thirst for wine – but crushed 78,000 tonnes. Production climbed by forty-three percent on 1984, sales rose only two percent, and a surplus resulted of record proportions.

Two committees of Government officials which studied independently and in depth the issue of the wine industry grape surplus reached identical conclusions on its principal cause. In the view of the 1983 'Hartevelt'

Committee, 'both growers and companies appear to have ignored the mounting evidence that trends since 1980 have been unsustainable . . . the surplus is seen as an inevitable result of a production system which lost touch with the market for the final product'.[103]

Two years later, the interdepartmental overview committee which conducted a 'mid-term' review of the Wine Industry Development Plan was concerned that 'despite all the recent debate on the subject, significant overproduction of wine in any given year is still possible . . . The problem arises from the industry's ability to divorce itself from market realities . . .'[104]

Discontent within the wine industry focussed most angrily on the Labour Government's November 1984 Budget, which lifted the sales tax on

ROBBIE (LEFT) AND DON BIRD, FORMERLY OWNERS OF NAPIER'S GLENVALE WINERY, WHO SOLD OUT TO VILLA MARIA ESTATE IN THE AFTERMATH OF THE 1985–1986 DISCOUNT WAR.

fortified sherries and ports by fifty-four percent, from $1.05 to $1.62 per bottle, and on table wines from fifty-four cents to ninety-nine cents per bottle – a searing hike of eighty-three percent. According to the Wine Institute, these abrupt tax changes conflicted with its own Industry Study and Development Plan – which in 1981 met with the approval of the Industries Development Commission – whereby vintners had received 'a promise of five years of a taxation regime which was stable [and] . . . varied only by subsequent annual movements in the Consumer Price Index'. But from the viewpoint of Finance Minister Roger Douglas and Trade and Industry Minister David Caygill, they were remedying a position whereby the industry had 'received very favoured treatment with regard to alcohol tax'. In concert with the over-enthusiastic expansion of vine plantings and the slowdown in consumption growth, this brutal tax hike brought the wine industry to its knees.

The decision by the giant Cooks/McWilliam's company – formed by a merger in September 1984 – to unload its surplus stocks by cutting prices then set alight the ferocious price war of 1985–86. Cooks was founded to specialise in fine table wines, and has made a cluster of memorable Chardonnays and Cabernet Sauvignons, but in its vigorous pursuit of the cheap quaffing wine market it arranged purchase contracts with grapegrowers beyond its needs.

With the demand for wine slackening, Cooks/McWilliam's and

WINE BARGAINS SUCH AS THOSE ADVERTISED IN LATE 1985 BY WINEWORTHS, AN AUCKLAND WINE-RETAIL GROUP, CREATED A BONANZA FOR WINE LOVERS BUT BROUGHT SEVERE FINANCIAL ANGUISH TO THE PRODUCERS.

subsequently Villa Maria/Vidal, Penfolds, Montana, Delegat's, Corbans and Glenvale chopped their ex-winery trade prices to as low as one-half the production cost. Wine lovers snapped up leading brands selling at unprecedentedly low prices: McWilliam's Marque Vue sparkling at $2.45, Cooks Chasseur casks at $7.95 or Montana's Marlborough range of varietals at $4.95. The cut-throat discounting brought an explosion in the sale of cheap sparkling wines and casks, sliding demand for the wineries which stayed aloof from the price slashing, and a battle for life for the family vineyards lacking corporate financial backing.

In February 1986 the Government intervened. According to Douglas Myers, chief executive of Lion Corporation, which then owned Penfolds, 'We came together with Mr Douglas, the major companies in the wine industry – Brierley, Rothmans, Montana and ourselves – and the Government asked us what the problems were and what do you want us to do? Within a fortnight a package was announced'.[105]

The Government's decision to provide adjustment assistance partly stemmed from its belief that, without some form of direct intervention, the prospects for an efficient and lasting solution to the oversupply problem were dim. It also accepted that, in hindsight, the Wine Industry Development Plan had encouraged the industry to expand to an unrealistic extent, and that the sales tax increases of 1984 had had a strong negative impact on wine consumption.

The Government was also fully aware that 'the consequence and incidence of costs resulting from the expansion and subsequent overproduction of grapes would not necessarily fall where they belonged . . . The small and medium-sized wine companies, without the same backing as the large wine companies and therefore unable to sustain such losses over a long period, were more likely to be victims of the actions of the larger wine companies through no fault of their own. Furthermore, some grapegrowers faced the possibility of bankruptcy'.[106] Cynical observers also noted that several marginal Labour-held electorates – Wairarapa, Tasman, Gisborne and Hawke's Bay – included important grapegrowing areas. The looming prospect of another bumper harvest in 1986 added urgency to the issue.

The Government's offer, up to ten million dollars to fund a vine-uprooting programme, surprised the wine lobby, which had campaigned for reform of the sales tax. The 'Hartevelt' Committee had in late 1983 specifically advised the National Government against offering viticulturists any financial incentives to diversify out of grapegrowing – on the grounds this would create an awkward precedent. Following the Government's decision to pay grapegrowers $6,175.00 per hectare to eradicate up to twenty-five percent of the national vineyard, 1517 hectares of vines were torn from the soil.

The heaviest vine pulls were on the East Coast: Hawke's Bay lost 534 hectares of vineyards and Poverty Bay/East Cape 586 hectares. In the South Island, 210 hectares were removed; in Auckland, 161 hectares. Müller-Thurgau, the grape variety upon which most bulk white wines are based, suffered the severest losses: 507 hectares, notably in Hawke's Bay and Gisborne. Other major losses were 137 hectares of Palomino, in Hawke's Bay, Auckland and Gisborne; 109 hectares of Gewürztraminer, particularly in Gisborne and the South Island; plus fifty to 100 hectares each of Chenin Blanc, Riesling, Chardonnay, Chasselas, Muscats, Cabernet Sauvignon and hybrids. According to George Fistonich of Villa Maria/Vidal, over sixty grapegrowers quit the industry.

Although some small winemakers viewed the whole exercise as a means of letting the major wineries – those with the worst grape surpluses – off a hook of their own fashioning, almost forty percent of the

Government's vine-removal grants were paid to smaller wineries that removed their own vines or to growers who usually supplied them. Tremendous relief was felt in most quarters of the wine industry as its production base was reduced to a size more suited to market requirements.

The industry's travails also resulted in a severe loss of investor confidence

A SYMBOL OF THE MUCH-DISCUSSED GRAPEVINE EXTRACTION SCHEME – A MOUND OF UPROOTED VINES IN AN AUCKLAND VINEYARD.

and sweeping ownership changes at Montana, Penfolds, Villa Maria/Vidal, Cooks/McWilliam's and Delegat's. Peter Masfen, son-in-law of the late Rolf Porter – an early Montana financier – who, as Montana's deputy chairman and longest-serving director is no newcomer to wine, has gained control of Montana through Corporate Investments, in which he has a majority stake. Seagram's decision to divest itself of its forty-three percent shareholding in Montana is not difficult to understand – in the half-year to 31 December 1985 the company chalked up a net loss of $4,621,000.

In August 1986 Montana succeeded in a takeover of Penfolds Wines (NZ), thereby creating the country's biggest wine company, commanding over forty percent of the market for New Zealand wines.

The Villa Maria/Vidal stable – formerly controlled by George Fistonich and a silent partner, John Spencer of Caxton Mills – had for years lived dangerously by aggressively pursuing and capturing a hefty slice of the extremely price-sensitive bottom end of the market, without the protection of the distribution and retail ties enjoyed by most of its principal rivals, or their huge capital reserves.

A new company, Villa Maria Estate Limited, has been assembled which swiftly cleared the $4 million debts owed by the old Villa Maria Wines – and then stunned the wine industry in early 1987, by buying the troubled, family-owned Glenvale winery in Hawke's Bay. The majority shareholders in the new company are the families of George Fistonich (managing director of Villa Maria Wines) and Grant Adams, deputy chairman of the investment company Equiticorp. Adams, who is an avowed wine buff, was a Cooks director between 1976 and 1983, until the Brierley takeover forced his resignation, and admits his involvement is 'a bit of a crusade'. Villa Maria's current strategy is to shrink its production and concentrate

NEW ZEALAND WINE PRODUCTION AND SALES
(incl. exports)
1980-1987 (Millions of litres)

	Production	Sales
1980	46.6	37.0
1981	44.0	38.8
1982	47.0	38.7
1983	57.7	38.8
1984	41.7	42.6
1985	59.6	43.4
1986	42.4	51.8
1987	37.7	47.6

SOURCE: Wine Institute of N.Z.
Annual Report 1988

REFRESHING, FRUITY BUT BLAND, COOLERS
APPEAL MORE TO YOUNGER CONSUMERS
LOOKING FOR A LOW-ALCOHOL THIRST-
QUENCHER THAN TO AVOWED WINE BUFFS.

more on bottled varietal wines.

Corbans bought the vineyard and winery assets of Cooks/McWilliam's in early 1987 for $20 million. This move surprised few observers: Corbans is a subsidiary of Magnum Corporation, itself a subsidiary of Brierley Investments – as was Cooks/McWilliam's. The enlarged Corbans has now clearly emerged as the second largest wine company in the country, holding around thirty percent of the market.

Delegat's, too, has been restructured, with Wilson Neill, one of New Zealand's most powerful liquor retailers, having gained a substantial interest in 1987.

Aside from the industry's upheaval, a more heartening recent development, has been the emergence of Canterbury and latterly Martinborough as successful new wine regions. Canterbury's cool, dry climate has attracted a cluster of new wineries – Giesen, Amberley, Larcomb, Glenmark and Torlesse – to join the proven Pinot Noir specialist, St Helena. Martinborough's warm summers, dry autumns and gravelly soils have also encouraged a flush of viticultural enthusiasm, with Martinborough Vineyards, Dry River and Ata Rangi prominent arrivals in the district.

Poverty Bay has clearly emerged as the most heavily planted region in New Zealand, with 1425 hectares under vines (according to the 1986 vineyard survey, which covered only about ninety-one percent of total plantings. These area figures are thus conservative). Hawke's Bay, with 1032 hectares, is a shade ahead of Marlborough's 934 hectares, with Auckland (221 hectares) and the Waikato (206 hectares) still of real, although declining, importance. Given the fertility of Gisborne and Hawke's Bay, these two regions now produce over seventy-five percent of the nation's grape crop. New Zealand wine, therefore, is primarily of Hawke's Bay and Poverty Bay origin.

Hard on the heels of the chronic oversupply problem of 1985–86, 1987 and 1988 brought what was inconceivable a year or two earlier – a wine shortage. The 1986 – following the vine-pull scheme – and low-cropping 1987 and 1988 vintages each yielded up to twenty percent (or ten million litres) less wine than the current level of sales.

Company profitability returned as wine prices rose in response to the shortage. Demand, however, declined: economists have demonstrated convincingly that wine in New Zealand has a 'price elasticity of demand of minus one'; that is, for every one percent variation in price there is a corresponding opposite variation in demand.

The emergence in 1986 of wine coolers – blended from a minimum of forty percent wine and assorted fruit juices, syrups and mineral waters – has also contributed to the draining of surplus wine stocks. New Zealanders in the summer of 1986–87 snapped up five million bottles of lightly carbonated wine coolers.

By mid-1988, so acute had become the shortage of New Zealand wine that the two industry giants, Montana and Corbans, turned to the production of cask wines based on kiwifruit. Although clearly packaged as fruit wines, these bulk casks were marketed as an alternative to grape wines, in a bid to prevent loss of market share to Australian wine imports, until the fruit from extensive new vineyards planted in 1987 and 1988 comes on stream.

Looking ahead, much industry concern centres on the impending impact of Closer Economic Relations with Australia. The Government, although funding the vine-uprooting scheme, has also moved to speed up the removal of barriers against overseas wines.

A radically liberalised tariff structure was unveiled in late 1985. Part of the Labour Government's Wine Industry Assistance Package – which also featured the Grapevine Extraction Scheme – this new regime is centred on a series of annual tariff reductions and quota increases.

By the middle of 1990 there will be no quantitative restraints on the volume of overseas wine which can be brought into New Zealand. The heavy duties with which cheap imported wines, valued at less than $2 per litre FOB (free on board), are at present saddled will be slashed in 1990.

The first of a series of five tariff reductions which by mid-1990 will effectively free Australian wine from import duties in New Zealand, came into force in July 1986. Wine imports from other countries will from mid-1990 carry a twenty-five percent tariff. As one industry figure put it: 'The Government patted the wine industry on the head with one hand and gave it a kick in the pants with both feet.'

Much debate has swirled around the issue of the rate of sales tax (now called excise) on New Zealand wines. For much of the period between 1978 and 1988 budgets argued the case for increased liquor taxes on the grounds of the need to recoup from drinkers the social costs of alcohol abuse. Influenced by Treasury advocates, governments more and more adopted a policy that their net alcohol content should be the basis for fixing rates of tax on alcoholic beverages: the stronger the drink, the higher the tax.

The alcohol in table and fortified wines in mid-1988 was taxed at $12 per litre; by comparison standard bottled beer carried $15.50 per litre of alcohol and spirits $28.00 and above. Thus in mid-1988 wine appeared to some observers to be still favourably treated with regard to excise.

The Wine Institute, however, strongly disputed the validity of the Government's 'alcohol equivalence' policy. New Zealand, it argued, saddled its highly promising wine industry with a more severe sales tax than almost any other wine-producing nation in the world. It also contended that wine makes only a very minor contribution to the social costs of alcohol abuse. Further – and this argument is particularly cogent – the inability of successive governments to 'announce and follow a clear, fully defined, long-term policy objective and an agreed method for adjusting tax rates through time has not provided the wine industry with the stability it needs to adequately plan ahead . . . The wine industry is essentially an agri-culturally based industry with relatively long production lead times . . .'[107]

In what must be viewed as a triumph for the wine lobby, in June 1988 the Excise Review Committee concluded that for excise purposes table wine should be treated as a separate product and not categorised with other alcoholic beverages. Noting that wine consumption is not a major contributor to such social costs as those incurred by traffic accidents, the committee recommended that the tax on table wine should be pared from $12 to $10 per litre of alcohol, a recommendation, however, that arrived too late for possible inclusion in the 1988 Budget.

Samuel Marsden observed nearly 170 years ago that 'New Zealand promises to be very favourable to the vine'.[108] That distant prediction has lately been brilliantly fulfilled – leading one overseas enthusiast to even suggest that New Zealand should be planted in a sea of Sauvignon Blanc vines stretching from North Cape to Stewart Island.

With overseas wines now starting to command a greater share of the New Zealand market, however, the wine industry's most urgent tasks are to repel the worst of the forthcoming Australian onslaught, while ensuring that export sales strongly surge ahead on the rising tide of international applause for New Zealand wines.

WINE EXPORTS —
Breaking Through the Confidence Barrier

'There is a rumour Sir Edmund Hillary left a case of this red wine on top of Mt Everest,' said actor Tony Britton during a 1977 episode of the British television comedy, *Robin's Nest*. Richard O'Sullivan, sipping with trepidation on a glass of Château Kiwi, responded: 'If it tastes anything like the white wine, I don't blame him.'

Eight years later David Lucas, the founder of Cooks, entered a London wine bar. Stunned to see bottles of Cooks New Zealand Medium White (sold in New Zealand as Chasseur) on several tables, Lucas, as he later told the story, purchased his own bottle, then, having retreated into a corner, slowly broke down.

For over a century enthusiasts have predicted a buoyant overseas trade in New Zealand wine. Walter Brodie, for instance, ignoring the almost total absence of wines in the colony, declared in 1845 that 'New Zealand, in a few years, will export much wine'.[99] Brodie was wrong. Andrew Tod, a Scotsman who made wine in Wanganui as early as 1873, later shipped a batch home, and in December 1874 the *Dundee Advertiser* reported: 'We have seen some samples of the New Zealand wine . . . it appears to be of excellent quality, and has improved rather than deteriorated in bouquet by the long voyage'.[100]

This, the first recorded export of New Zealand wine, came to nought. In 1934 the British newspaper the *Daily Mail* enquired whether there were any 'New Zealand or West Indian wines that could be offered in this country?' Observed the paper generously: 'We Englishmen are prepared to try anything once'.[101]

A small, steady overseas trade in New Zealand wine has been maintained since 1963. From an insignificant $43,000 in the year to June 1972, sales reached $1,243,000 in the year to June 1983, and recently soared to $11.6 million in the year to 30 June 1988.

There is no doubt that New Zealand's top wines possess the quality to compete on world markets. The country's cool-climate growing conditions – an advantage enjoyed by few other viticultural regions – yield fragrant, naturally crisp, deep-flavoured wines that rival the premium wines of France and Germany. Jancis Robinson, of British television's *Wine* programme, has commented that 'New Zealand has led the world in showing how good Müller-Thurgau can be' and Huon Hooke, in the *Australian Financial Review* has observed that 'Te Mata Coleraine Cabernet/Merlot 1982 is a red . . . with a tightness of structure and firmness of backbone that has been achieved by very few, if any, Australian winemakers'. Such comments have encouraged the growing international respect for New Zealand wines.

The difficulty until recently lay in converting this critical applause into concrete sales. An interdepartmental committee in 1985 described the winemakers' export performance as 'lacklustre'[102] and the industry narrowly failed to achieve its own goal, set in 1978, of over $5 million per year in export earnings by the mid-1980s.

New Zealand wine exporters operate in a tough, competitive environment. There is a drastic worldwide wine surplus: the EEC's wine lake, for example, holds the equivalent of fifty billion bottles. European wine industries enjoy the benefits of heavy state subsidies, enabling them to undercut their opposition.

It is clear that New Zealand, by world standards a very small wine producer, saddled with higher freight and production costs than those of the traditional wine countries, must avoid cheaper volume markets and build its future around supplying the world with top-flight Sauvignon Blancs, Chardonnays and Cabernet Sauvignons capable of commanding premium prices.

With the domestic market now being rapidly opened up to increased competition from abroad, especially from Australian wines under CER, a powerful commitment to export is evident in many wineries. But only recently have the vintners possessed sufficient volumes of premium table wine to think seriously of exporting. Corbans until the early 1980s dominated activity with their sales of Select Medium Sherry to the western provinces of Canada.

Further south, Corbans also has its own importing company in California, and by 1981 its labels were on the shelves of 400 retail outlets. Californians have also been able to order Penfolds wines – under the label Château St Philippe – by mail or telephone, and even have them delivered to the door carrying personalised labels. This is an affluent market, conscious of Pacific developments, and open to new wines.

Other promising footholds have been established in Japan, Sweden and the Pacific Islands.

The fastest growing markets for New Zealand wines, however, are the United Kingdom and Australia. In the year to June 1988, the United Kingdom absorbed 117,333 cases and Australia 91,170 cases.

The United Kingdom is the toughest wine market in the world to crack, with thousands of brands available. Nevertheless, acceptance by the British wine trade, and its internationally influential wine press, is crucial to the worldwide acceptance of New Zealand wines. The annual tasting at New Zealand House in London has generated enormous favourable publicity and now stands as one of the most popular events on the crowded London wine calendar.

But sales have only lately surged ahead on the tide of critical acclaim. Cooks, despite sales of up to 15,000 cases per annum, lost money with its own sales and administration office. Their new agent, Dent and Reuss, the wine and spirit subsidiary of cider giant Bulmer's, aims to exploit New Zealand's positive food image to position the Cooks range at the top end of the market. Seagrams are also promoting Montana to the British trade.

To add depth to the New Zealand range, expatriate New Zealander Margaret Harvey runs a fledgling business distributing the wines of smaller vineyards, notably Delegat's and Matua Valley. Selaks and Morton Estate have appointed distributors and recently the long-established London wine merchants Deinhard and Company have added Babich to their agency portfolio.

The successes of another small winery, Hunter's, have added another feather to New Zealand's cap. At the 1986 London *Sunday Times* Wine Club festival, the winery topped the popular vote with its Fumé Blanc 1985 – awarded a bronze medal at the 1985 National Wine Competition, then a silver at the 1986 New Zealand Easter Show – and repeated the performance in 1987 with its 1986 Chardonnay – awarded a silver medal at the 1987 Easter Show – and in 1988 with its 1987 Fumé Blanc – awarded a gold medal at the 1988 Easter Show.

New Zealand's other most valuable market for wine lies across the Tasman. Critics in both countries agree that New Zealand's Sauvignon Blanc is superior to Australian versions, its Gewürztraminers more intensely spicy, its Chardonnays of equally high interest. The market is close, transport costs are reasonable, tariff barriers are virtually non-existent and the locals are relatively sophisticated about wine. According to Corbans general manager, Paul Treacher, however, 'the difficulty is persuading Australians that New Zealand wine is fit to drink'.

Montana established an important bridgehead in Australia in 1984 with a carefully researched launch on the Queensland market. Wohnsiedler Müller-Thurgau soon emerged as its most popular wine, followed by the bottle-fermented sparkling Lindauer and Marlborough Sauvignon Blanc. Chablisse, a blended dry white pitted in direct competition with hundreds of Australian equivalents, was soon dropped from the range. The company has since pushed into Sydney and Melbourne.

Other vineyards – Corbans, Coopers Creek, Te Mata, Matawhero, Matua Valley and Selaks – have also established an enduring presence on Australian wineshop shelves. As Terry Dunleavy, executive officer of the Wine Institute, put it: 'Our winemakers have now broken through their own confidence barrier.'

NEW ZEALAND'S STATUS AS THE FEATURED NATION AT THE 1988 LONDON WINE TRADE FAIR CONFIRMED THE COUNTRY'S ARRIVAL AS A MUCH-TALKED-ABOUT FORCE IN THE INFLUENTIAL UK WINE MARKET. IN THE ROOF GARDEN OF THE KENSINGTON EXHIBITION CENTRE, INVITED MEMBERS OF THE WINE TRADE, WINEMAKERS AND THE WINE PRESS MINGLE AND SIP NEW ZEALAND-GROWN SAUVIGNON BLANCS.

NOTES FOR CHAPTER ONE

1. Barrington, A.J., 'Diary of a West Coast Prospecting Party' in Taylor, N.M. (ed.) *Early Travellers in New Zealand*, Oxford 1959, p. 402.
2. Rawson-Elder, J., *Letters and Journals of Samuel Marsden*, Otago University Council, 1932.
3. *Report from the Select Committee on New Zealand*, House of Commons, London, July 1844, p. 6.
4. Quoted in Scott, D., *Winemakers of New Zealand*, Southern Cross Books, Auckland, 1964, p. 16.
5. Wright, Olive, *Voyage of the Astrolabe 1840*, Wellington, 1955. See Thorpy, F., *Wine in New Zealand*, Collins, Auckland, 1st edn 1971, p. 20.
6. See Scott, D., *op. cit.*, p. 16.
7. Petrie, H.W., *An Account of the Settlements of the New Zealand Company*, London, 5th edn 1842, p. 59.
8. The Annual Report of the Agricultural and Horticultural Society of Auckland, quoted in *The Southern Cross* newspaper, 25 November 1843, p. 4.
9. *The New Zealander*, 7 March 1849, p. 3.
10. Quoted in Thorpy, F. *op. cit.*, p. 26
11. Petrie, H.W., *op. cit.*, p. 60.
12. Bragato, R., *Report on the Prospects of Viticulture in New Zealand*, Department of Agriculture, 1895, p. 6.
13. *The Daily Southern Cross*, 31 March 1875, p. 3, and 27 March 1876, p. 3.
14. Scott, D., *op. cit.*, p. 38.
15. The Flax and Other Industries Committee, Report on the Wine and Fruit Industry, Appendix to the Journals of the House of Representatives, 1890, (I-68), p. 9.
16. Eldred Grigg, S., *Pleasures of the Flesh*, A.H. & A.W. Reed, Wellington, 1984, p. 77.
17. *Ibid.*, p. 80.
18. *Ibid.*, p. 80.
19. Report of the Industries Committee, AJHR (I-12), p. 233.
20. *The New Zealand Graphic*, 8 July 1899, p. 45.
21. Report of the Colonial Industries Commission, AJHR (H-22), 1880, p. 3.
22. Beetham, W., The Flax and Other Industries Committee, *op. cit.*, p. 18.
23. *Ibid.*
24. Bragato, R., *op. cit.*, p. 3.
25. Beetham, W., in *Conference of New Zealand Fruit Growers and Horticulturists*, Dunedin, June 1901, p. 75.
26. *New Zealand Farmer*, April 1894, p. 128.
27. *Ibid.*
28. Hanlon, L., in *Proceedings of The Conference of Australasian Fruitgrowers*, Wellington, May 1896, p. 90.
29. Beetham, W., *ibid.*, p. 101.
30. *The New Zealand Farmer*, April 1894, p. 128.
31. *Ibid.*, April 1896, p. 126.
32. *Ibid.*, April 1897, p. 115.
33. Anderson, S.F., diary, unpublished.
34. *The New Zealand Farmer*, April 1896, p. 126.
35. *Ibid.*, April 1897, p. 115.
36. Beetham, W., *op. cit.*, p. 101.
37. Anderson, S.F., *op. cit.*
38. *The New Zealand Farmer*, April 1896, p. 126.
39. *Ibid.*, April 1897, p. 115.
40. New Zealand Parliamentary Debates, Vol. 127, 1903, p. 439.
41. Bragato, R., *op. cit.*, pp. 8–10.
42. Anderson, S.F., 'Grape Culture', *New Zealand Journal of Agriculture*, 20 May 1914, p. 507.
43. *Auckland Star*, 1 December 1898, p. 32.
44. Scott, D., *Seven Lives on Salt River*, Southern Cross Books/Hodder & Stoughton, Auckland, 1987, p. 65.
45. *Ibid.*, p. 65.
46. *Ibid.*, p. 65.
47. *Ibid.*, p. 73.
48. Kosovich, A., 'Uzdisaj Za Danovini' ('Longing for Home') 1908. Translation by A. Batistich, made available by S. Jelicich.
49. Report of The New Zealand Commision to Inspect and Classify the Kauri Gum Reserves in the Auckland Land District, 1914, AJHR (C-12), p. 20.
50. Quoted in the *Auckland Star*, 19 September 1916, p. 8.
51. *The Auckland Weekly News*, 31 May 1906, p. 47.
52. *The Daily Southern Cross*, 14 December 1875, p. 3.
53. Quoted in Scott, D., *Winemakers of New Zealand*, Southern Cross Books, Auckland, 1964, p. 32.
54. Quoted in Thorpy, F., *op. cit.*, pp. 52–3.
55. *New Zealand Mail*, 21 October 1882, p. 17.
56. Letter, William Beetham to J.D. Ritchie, Secretary of Agriculture, 30 September 1896, National Archives, Wellington.
57. Bragato, R., *op. cit.*, p. 7.
58. Yardin, Reverend Father, 'On Vine-growing in Hawke's Bay' in Transactions and Proceedings of the New Zealand Institute, Vol. 23, 1890, p. 530.
59. Quoted in Scott, D., *Winemakers of New Zealand*, Southern Cross Books, Auckland 1964, p. 25.
60. Thorpy, F., *op. cit.*, p. 36.
61. *New Zealand Herald*, 12 December 1902, p. 7.
62. Rodda, T.E., 'Recollections of an Early Pioneer of the Department of Agriculture, New Zealand', Auckland Historical Society Miscellaneous Manuscripts, Auckland Institute and Museum, M.S. 808 76/28–31.
63. Quoted in Scott, D., *op. cit.*, p. 57.

64. *The Auckland Weekly News*, 5 May 1910, p. 26.
65. Bragato, R., *op. cit.*, p. 12.
66. *Evening Post*, 13 December 1907.
67. *New Zealand Truth*, 4 February 1911, p. 8.
68. Quoted in Thorpy, F., *op. cit.*, p. 38.
69. *New Zealand Times*, 19 November 1912.
70. New Zealand Parliamentary Debates, 1914, Vol. 168, pp. 829–30.
71. *New Zealand Herald*, 12 July 1935.
72. Quoted in *Wine Review*, Winter 1966, Vol. 3, No. 2, p. 21.
73. Thomas, W.C., Memorandum, 20 December 1926, National Archives.
74. Woodfin, J.C., 'Control of Vine Diseases and Pests Occurring in New Zealand', New Zealand Department of Agriculture, Bulletin No. 134, 1928.
75. Anderson, S.F., 'Outdoor Culture of the Grape Vine in New Zealand', *New Zealand Journal of Agriculture*, February 1917, p. 101.
76. Hewlett, F.E., 'Historical Background to the Establishment of the Maungatapu Vineyard', Journal of the Tauranga Historical Society, No. 8 October 1957, p. 11.
77. Woodfin, J.C., 'Grape Vines for New Zealand Conditions', *New Zealand Journal of Agriculture*, 20 February 1928, p. 106.
78. McDonald, T.B., quoted in *Wine Review*, Vol. 8, No. 1, Autumn 1971.
79. *Wine Review*, Vol. 12, No. 4, Summer 1975.
80. The Report of the Royal Commission on Licensing, 1946, p. 255.
81. New Zealand Parliamentary Debates, 8 October 1946, Vol. 275, p. 712.
82. Lindeman, B.W., letter to the Government Analyst, 15 March 1943, National Archives.
83. The Report of the Royal Commission on Licensing, 1946, p. 262.
84. Personal communication.
85. *Ibid.*
86. New Zealand Parliamentary Debates, 1955, p. 3461.
87. Bolster, T.N., 'Lucky Break for New Zealand Winemakers', *The Weekly News*, 24 September 1958.

88. Annual Report, Department of Agriculture and Fisheries, 1959.
89. *The Weekly News*, 5 April 1971, p. 4.
90. Corban, A., address to an International Wine Symposium, Auckland 1978.
91. Company Brochure, 1979.
92. Lindeman, B.W., Report on the Possibilities of Expansion in the Wine Industry of New Zealand, 3 March 1939. Unpublished. National Archives.
93. 'Observations at the Shrine of Bacchus', *Here and Now*, 2, No. 4, January 1952, p. 2.
94. Minutes of a Meeting of the New Zealand Wine Council, 16 July 1974. See Cooper, M. 'The Wine Lobby: Pressure Group Politics and the New Zealand Wine Industry'. University of Auckland M.A. Thesis, 1977, p. 150.
95. Wine Institute submission to the Working Party on Liquor, 1986, p. 2.
96. *Wine*, August 1986, p. 37.
97. Report of the Industries Development Commission: The Wine Industry Development Plan to 1986, 1980.
98. *Ibid.*
99. Quoted in Scott, D., *Winemakers of New Zealand*, Southern Cross Books, Auckland 1964, p. 14.
100. *Listener*, 8 February 1971, p. 49.
101. *New Zealand Herald*, 12 July 1935.
102. The Inter-Departmental Overview Committee Mid Term Review of the Wine Industry Development Plan to 1986, 1985, p. 94.
103. Report To Prime Minister On Investigation of Grape Surplus by Officials Committee, 1983.
104. The Inter-Departmental Overview Committee, *op. cit.*, p. 34.
105. Quoted in *Southern Horticulture*, February 1986, p. 10.
106. Garrett, R. and Smith, S., Wine Industry Assistance Package, Ministry of Agriculture and Fisheries, 1987, p. 9.
107. Ayto, J., A Review of the Policy and Economics of Selective Taxation on Wine, 1986, p. 11.
108. Rawson-Elder, J., *op. cit.*

CHAPTER TWO

Viticulture

CLIMATE AND SOILS

*S*everal basic factors influence the emergence of all wine styles — climate, the soil, grape varieties and the winemaker.

Grapes are more responsive to climate than most other fruits, and during the growing season the amount of rainfall, hours of sunshine and degrees of heat all have an eventual effect on the quality of the crop. Variations in soil types also influence the character and quality of wine: although vines grow in a wide variety of soils, heavy clays and poorly drained soils are less suitable than gravelly or sandy soils.

The careful selection of soils and climatic zones, however, must be matched by the planting of suitable grape varieties. In New World wine countries, the selection of grape types involves a very considered judgement about grape quality, hardiness and yield. And, although wines are often said to be produced in the vineyard rather in the winery, the winemaker's equipment is important too, as well as his or her mastery of the skills of harvesting, crushing, pressing, fermentation, clarification and maturation.

CLIMATE

Over the years some curious notions have flourished about the suitability of New Zealand's climate for viticulture. Last century, despite the labours of many winegrowers, it was widely believed that vines would not perform well outdoors. Bragato encountered – and rejected – the popular assumption that grapes could be cultivated only in 'vineries' (glasshouses).

The early colonists worried, not without reason, about vine diseases and the difficulty of ripening grapes fully in our temperate climate. Certainly, no one appears to have argued that New Zealand is too hot for winemaking. S.F. Anderson, Government Viticulturist, in February 1917 stated in the *New Zealand Journal of Agriculture* that a natural sweet wine cannot be made in our temperate climate: 'The long dry autumn where the grapes can hang without injury until partially desiccated is not met within our climate'.

In the viticultural sense New Zealand has a cool climate ideal for the production of light table wines. If New Zealand is compared with the European wine areas, the climate most closely resembles grapegrowing conditions in the north of Europe: Bordeaux, Burgundy, Alsace, the Rheingau and the Mosel. Germany lies further north of the Equator than any other quality wine producer: New Zealand lies the furthest south. Both are cool-climate grapegrowing regions noted for their elegant white wines.

Latitude

Precise parallels cannot be drawn between the latitudes north and south of the Equator that offer the best prospects for making wine. The moderating influence of the Gulf Stream in Europe allows vines to be grown closer to the polar regions than in the southern hemisphere. Alone in vast seas, New Zealand encounters cooler temperatures than regions at comparable latitudes in the northern hemisphere. Hawke's Bay has a climate similar to that of Bordeaux, yet Bordeaux lies in latitudes parallel to Timaru, in the south of New Zealand.

Temperature

Temperature, sunshine and rain are the three essential climatic influences on grapevines. To fully ripen, grapes must receive a certain amount of heat during the growing season. Research in the United States has demonstrated that the single most important aspect of climate for viticulture is temperature.

Heat summation, an empirical tool designed to evaluate the potential for viticulture of various parts of California, measures the amount of heat received during the growing season, above the minimum required for active growth. 'Region One' climates accumulate up to about 1370 'degree days', which is the sum of the growing season's mean daily temperatures above 10°C (50°F), the temperature at which the sap rises in the vine. Region One climates are characterised by moderately cool weather under which ripening proceeds slowly.

Such areas, including Bordeaux (1250–1400°C) and Burgundy (1120–1180°C), the Rhine (1050–1250°C) and the Mosel (950–1150°C), produce the world's finest table wines. Sugars can be a problem and acidities tend to be high. The cool weather brings to the fruit optimum development of its aroma and flavour constituents.

The major wine regions of New Zealand all possess Region one climates for grapegrowing. In his Report on the Prospects of Viticulture in New Zealand (1895), Bragato recognised that 'so far as the temperature and the brightness of the sun's rays are concerned, no fear need be entertained but that the greater part of New Zealand will adequately satisfy the demands of the vine'. He was right.

The heat summation method of analysis proven successful for California may not, however, apply equally well to all other viticultural regions of the world. In the Hunter Valley of New South Wales, for instance, fine red and white wines are produced in a consistently warm climate, defying assumptions to be derived from the heat summation method about the suitability of that area for making wine.

Dr Richard Smart, New Zealand's world-ranked viticultural scientist, has challenged the Californian method on several grounds, including that it is an unnecessarily complicated way to calculate how hot a region is, the mean temperature of the warmest month being equally useful. Smart has also argued that, since the length of the vine's growing season varies with temperature (being shorter in hotter regions), the use in heat summation calculations of a fixed ripening period (October–April in the southern hemisphere) cannot be recommended.

Smart also argues that differences between summer and winter temperatures are important. Bordeaux and the Loire are among the few European wine regions having maritime climates; most are continental, with warm summers followed by very cold winters. By contrast, most New Zealand regions are maritime, with a relatively small summer-winter temperature difference.

New Zealand has thus started to develop its own climatic recipes for successful viticulture. Dr David Jackson, of Lincoln College, a crucial figure in the emergence of Canterbury viticulture, has recently formulated a new Latitude Temperature Index for calculating an area's grape-ripening potential.

Jackson argues that the conventional heat summation method puts too much emphasis on summer temperatures, and that New Zealand's position in low latitudes, relative to northern-hemisphere wine districts, gives it a longer growing season which compensates for its cooler summer temperatures. His system therefore is based upon both latitude and temperature measurements.

Jackson's Latitude Temperature Index is expressed by the formula: $LTI = MTWM (60 \text{ minus latitude})$ where MTWM is the mean temperature of the warmest month. Using the LTI, one can predict the varieties of grapes able to be ripened in a given wine district. Thus, districts with an LTI of below 190 should ripen Gewürztraminer, Müller-Thurgau, Pinot Gris, Pinot Blanc and Chardonnay; those with an LTI of 190–270 should ripen Pinot Noir and Riesling; those with an LTI of 270–380 should ripen Cabernet Sauvignon, Sauvignon Blanc, Chenin Blanc and Sémillon; and those with an LTI of over 380 should ripen Palomino and Grenache.

This index, however, appears to over-estimate the ripening potential of wetter regions, where autumn rains can effectively abbreviate the growing season.

Rain

The frequent rainfall that characterises our maritime climate creates favourable growing conditions for an enormous variety of plants. Rain, however, is the villain of the New Zealand climate so far as making wine is concerned.

Heavy rains frequently descend on the wine regions during the ripening and harvesting periods of the year. Sometimes abundant rainfall is viewed by the winemaker as an asset; summer rains, for instance, enhance the low-alcohol, fruity elegance of German white wines. The vine, however, needs a dry autumn.

On deep, well-drained soils, vines prefer a winter rainfall of about 380mm, followed by another 300mm during the October-April growing season. From a low level in early spring, the water demands of the vine climb to a mid-summer maximum as the vine achieves its peak of

HEAT UNITS IN THE GROWING SEASON

Northland	1300–1400°C
Auckland (Henderson and Kumeu	1300–1350°C
Waikato	1250–1300°C
Gisborne	1250–1300°C
Hawke's Bay	1200–1250°C
Martinborough	1150°C average*
Nelson	1050–1100°C
Marlborough	1150–1250°C
Canterbury	900–1100°C
Central Otago	900–950°C

SOURCES: Jackson, D. and Schuster, D., *Grape Growing and Wine Making: A Handbook for Cool Climates*, Martinborough, 1981, pp. 46-47.
*Martinborough Winemakers Associaton.

HAIL-DAMAGED GRAPES, LEFT VULNERABLE TO FUNGUS PROBLEMS AND BIRDS.

RAINFALL		
	Annual	**Feb–April**
Northland	1600mm	280mm
Auckland		
(Henderson)	1500mm	360mm
Waikato	1100–1200mm	260mm
Gisborne	1000–1050mm	240mm
Hawke's Bay	750– 800mm	180mm
Martinborough*	750mm	160mm
Nelson	1000–1250mm	200mm
Marlborough	650– 750mm	140mm
Canterbury	600– 750mm	140mm
Central Otago	300– 380mm	100mm

SOURCES: Jackson, D. and Schuster, D.,
Grape Growing and Wine Making:
A Handbook for Cool Climates,
Martinborough, 1981, pp. 46–47.
Berrysmith, F., *Viticulture*, Wellington,
1973, p. 11.
*Martinborough Winemakers Association.

vegetative growth. As vintage nears in New Zealand, the best conditions are moderate rains in January followed by very light rain for the rest of the season.

Heavy rains late in the season can damage most grape varieties and cause severe losses. Downpours in the month before vintage dilute sugar levels and split the berries. In most districts high humidity and rainfall can combine in adverse years to cause problems with such wet-weather diseases as botrytis and downy mildew. Ripening is delayed and the bunches rot. Chemical sprays are fortunately now able to somewhat reduce some of these problems associated with autumn rains, but botrytis bunch rot remains a major cause of yield and quality loss.

In respect of rainfall, measured both on an annual basis and during the critical February-April ripening period, some areas of New Zealand are much more fortunate than others. By world standards the rainfall in Henderson and the Waikato is excessive. Gisborne and Nelson are borderline. Marlborough, Canterbury, Martinborough and, to a lesser extent, Hawke's Bay are all regions with lower autumn rainfall and hence less risk.

Frosts

Heavy frosts in early spring are hazardous for young vine growth. Temperatures below freezing damage the fruit-set and ruin the size and condition of the eventual crop.

Severe spring frosts occasionally occur in New Zealand. Screen frosts, recorded in ventilated screens about 1.2 metres (4ft) above the ground, are the most likely to damage the vine's shoots and buds. Auckland, Te Kauwhata and areas north are largely frost-free, but the risk increases in the south. Screen frosts afflict Gisborne in the spring on average about once every three years, Hawke's Bay and Blenheim every second year, Christchurch every year and Alexandra (Central Otago) twice yearly. Nowhere, however, in the major grapegrowing areas is the threat of frost so severe as to deter future expansion.

Meso-Climates

Winemakers often try to convince you that their own particular vineyards enjoy 'micro-climates' superior to neighbouring sites. The term they should use for such localised climates is 'meso-climate'; a micro-climate, strictly speaking, is the climate within and immediately around a plant canopy. Disregarding the propaganda element, it is true that local conditions of wind and rain, frosts and drainage, soils and exposure can greatly affect grape quality.

In regions considered generally unsuitable for grapegrowing, it is not uncommon to find small areas where local conditions of climate and soil combine to allow the vine to flourish. Factors present at the local level can result in a marked variation in heat readings between vineyards and the local meteorological station. The sunny, sheltered slopes of the vineyards at Geisenheim, Germany, are said to accumulate fifteen to twenty percent more 'degree days' during the growing season than the surrounding districts.

Planting vines on a sunny slope facing north considerably increases heat readings. Dr Helmut Becker, the eminent German viticulturist, has stressed that New Zealand 'should pay more attention to gently sloping land, rather than flat land, because the slopes allow for better drainage and higher concentration of sunlight and heat'. The tendency, however, has been to develop flat land that is easier to work and yields grapes in profusion. Apart from localised sites in Auckland and Te Kauwhata most vines have been planted on flat to gently undulating terrain. On the Gisborne plains, for example, the average gradient is about 1 in 2000.

In extremely marginal climates for winemaking such as Central Otago, attempts to establish vineyards will rely heavily on the discovery of sites with favourable meso-climates.

SOILS

The Germans have a saying that where the plough can go the vine should not. Usually, vines planted in rich soils and allowed to crop heavily yield mediocre wine. If the vines are stressed by being planted in relatively poor soil, the smaller crop will be concentrated in flavour and produce better wine.

The outstanding attribute of the soil in the most famous vineyards is its poverty. Vines flourish in chalk in Champagne, on slate in the Mosel and on sandy gravel in Bordeaux. Vignerons in Bordeaux delight in stating that if their soils were not the best in the world, they would be the worst. An extensive root system that thrusts far into the ground in pursuit of water and other nutrients enables the vine to perform well in soils where often nothing else will grow.

Immensely adaptable, the grapevine will grow in soils ranging from heavy clays to gravel sands of low or high fertility, deep or shallow. Bragato noted that 'the vine displays no epicurean instincts as regards soil but has been found to luxuriate in all classes . . .'

The least suitable soils for quality winemaking are heavy clays and shallow or poorly drained soils. Californian viticulturist Dr Harold Olmo claimed after a 1978 visit that heavy waterlogging of the soil in the months prior to harvest was causing excessive vegetative growth in New Zealand and preventing the berries from fully ripening. Olmo called upon viticulturists to plant more heavily in soils that can rapidly drain away excess water supplies. The most desirable soils are well drained, of low-to-moderate fertility, rich in the minerals that yield subtle nuances in the flavour of wine.

Drip irrigation systems are now a common sight in the vineyards of Martinborough, Marlborough and Canterbury. In these regions, characterised by their lower average rainfall and lighter-textured soils, summer droughts can cause the vines to suffer severe water stress; berry size (and thus yield) are reduced and fruit ripening is retarded.

Vineyard irrigation is a practice not without its detractors; in most French appellation contrôlée districts it is banned. Heavy-handed irrigation can promote excessive vegetative growth and enhance yields at the expense of fruit quality.

THE HEAVY CLAY SOILS IN THE HENDERSON REGION HAVE POOR NATURAL DRAINAGE.

FERTILE, ALLUVIAL LOAM SOILS ARE CHARACTERISTIC OF THE GISBORNE PLAINS AT POVERTY BAY.

POCKETS OF SHINGLY SOILS IN HAWKE'S BAY ARE MUCH SOUGHT-AFTER AS VINEYARD SITES. THE IRONGATE VINEYARD IS EXTRAORDINARILY STONY AND FREE-DRAINING.

DRIP-IRRIGATION SYSTEMS ENHANCE THE VITICULTURIST'S CONTROL OVER THE VINE'S WATER SUPPLY, BUT IT IS ESSENTIAL THAT WATER REQUIREMENTS ARE PRECISELY CALCULATED.

CANTERBURY SOILS ARE TYPICALLY LOAMY
SILTS WITH SOME SURFACE STONES, OVERLYING
FREE-DRAINING RIVER GRAVELS.

THE BEST MARLBOROUGH VINEYARDS ARE
PLANTED IN PEBBLY, ALLUVIAL LOAMS
OVER GRAVELLY, FREE-DRAINING SUBSOILS.

The need for irrigation in Marlborough first became clear, however, when many of the original plantings in the early 1970s perished during droughts. As vines mature and their root systems penetrate deeper into the subsoil, their reliance upon irrigation diminishes. Nevertheless, the irrigation systems are retained to maintain yields in very dry years – a sort of viticultural insurance policy.

The soil pattern of New Zealand is complex, varying with the parent rocks, the climate that weathers the rocks, the topography and the covering vegetation. Most Auckland vineyards are on heavy clay land that requires deep ploughing and tile-draining to reduce waterlogging of the soil. In Gisborne the poor natural drainage promotes high fertility. The lighter soils of Hawke's Bay range from shingle to alluvial sand to silt and clay loams. At Blenheim the stony soils absorb the sun's rays and allow water to penetrate deep into the ground. The tendency, until recently, to establish most vineyards on high fertility soils, particularly in Gisborne and Hawke's Bay, has overall enhanced grape yields at the expense of quality. Recently expanded plantings in the stonier soils of Marlborough, Canterbury, Martinborough and parts of Hawke's Bay have succeeded in reducing vine vigour and enhancing fruit quality.

CLIMATE AND WINE STYLES

Cool-climate grapegrowing countries such as New Zealand are blessed with natural conditions ideal for producing premium table wines. In any region the style of wine produced is largely determined by the composition of the grapes at harvest, which in turn is heavily influenced by the local climate. The more rigorous the climate, the more subtly intriguing the wine.

The wine industry in New Zealand has fully realised the country's climatic potential. The strong emphasis placed, not long ago, on producing fortified wine styles has declined. The industry's ambition is now to win acceptance as one of the foremost table-wine producers of the world. The climate and the soils are there to do it.

Debate often centres on whether New Zealand possesses a red or a white-wine climate. Some point to the similarities of climate between Hawke's Bay and the red and white wine-producing district of Bordeaux. Others have argued that New Zealand has a cool white-wine climate and cannot produce good reds.

New Zealand is currently producing outstanding white wines from several grape varieties and – suddenly – world-class reds from Cabernet Sauvignon and Merlot. The overall standard of the whites is higher, but the climatic evidence leads irresistibly to the conclusion that we can succeed, handsomely, with both.

VITIS VINIFERA

The outstanding species of *Vitis* is *Vitis vinifera*, a species almost solely responsible for European wines. Originating in the area of the Caspian Sea, *Vitis vinifera* has been cultivated for at least five thousand years and featured prominently in the ancient agricultures of Phoenicia, Egypt, Greece and Rome. During the modern era of exploration and colonisation *Vitis vinifera* travelled as seeds, cuttings and rooted plants west to the Americas and south to South Africa, Australia and New Zealand.

Vitis vinifera is by far the most important wine species around the world. Despite their vulnerability to insect pests and fungous diseases, *vinifera* grapes without exception form the basis of all fine wines. Twenty-five years ago only one-third of vines grown in New Zealand were *vinifera* varieties; today they dominate plantings to the extent of over ninety-eight percent.

VITIS LABRUSCA

The profusion of wild-growing grapevines in the New World led the early explorer Leif Erikson to call his discovery 'Vineland' — or so legend has it. The first European settlers in America found several native species flourishing. *Vitis labrusca,* known in America as the 'fox' grape, is the most important.

Despite the assertive, unpleasant flavour of their wine, *Vitis labrusca* and other American species have played a vital role in modern viticulture. The wild-growing American vines developed a powerful resistance to both the endemic threat of phylloxera and the severe climate of the mid-Atlantic states. After phylloxera crossed the Atlantic eastwards last century, the European vineyards were reconstructed with classical *vinifera* vines grafted on to phylloxera-resistant native American rootstocks.

THE HYBRIDS

French grape breeders also made countless crossings of *vinifera* and American species, seeking to create new vines that could produce good wine and yet still grow on their own roots in phylloxera-infested soils. However, despite the labours of the vine breeders Seibel, Baco, Oberlin and others, the ideal hybrid never eventuated. Vines that were highly resistant to pests and disease yielded poor-quality grapes; if the wine proved satisfactory the vines proved vulnerable. And as the problems associated with grafting suitable phylloxera-resistant American rootstocks on *vinifera* vines were solved, the phylloxera-resistant qualities of the hybrids – often suspect – became obsolete.

The major hybrid varieties in New Zealand were imported by Government Viticulturist Charles Woodfin in the late 1920s. Among the more prominent were Baco 22A and Baco No. 1, Oberlin 595, Gaillard Gerard 157 and numerous Seibels. Some hybrids acquired local names, for instance 'Seibouchet' and 'Tintara' for Seibel 5437.

In New Zealand wine circles 'hybrid' has now become a rather dirty word. The grapes when picked are often high in acid and low in natural sugars. Owing at least partly to the presence of methyl anthranilate, the unpleasant flavours of their American parents are often easily detectable in hybrid wines. In Europe the planting of all except a few hybrids has been prohibited, and in New Zealand plantings have all but disappeared in recent years. Recent progress by European vine breeders may yet reverse this, since new-generation hybrids show such desirable characteristics as bunch-rot tolerance, while also producing wines indistinguishable from *vinifera* wines.

THE GRAPES

*O*rdinary wines were long produced in New Zealand without special consideration of the merits of different grape types. Only recently have the winemakers fully appreciated that excellent wine can be made only from a limited range of premium grape varieties. Good wine comes from good grapes.

Although several thousand varieties of grapes have been recorded worldwide, fewer than twenty are grown in any large quantity in New Zealand. Grapes belong to the genus Vitis (the Latin word for wine). There are dozens of grape species classified in the genus and almost all are useless for winemaking.

Grape varieties can loosely be divided into table (eating) and wine types. Apart from the Muscat varieties and Chasselas, few grapes are well suited to both table use and winemaking. The large, pleasantly flavoured berries of the table varieties typically yield wine that is dull and thin. By contrast, the small-berried varieties used in the best wines seem all seeds and skin when you eat them.

The older hybrids nevertheless made some positive contributions to New Zealand viticulture. When few New Zealanders were interested in table wines those hardy, high-yielding vines made winemaking far more economic than cultivating the shy-bearing *vinifera* varieties. Hybrids once dominated the vineyards, comprising sixty-six percent of total plantings in 1960; now they comprise less than two percent. The best hybrid wines offered sound, straightforward drinking.

MÜLLER-THURGAU.

VINEYARD SURVEYS

Every five years between 1960 and 1980, and again in 1983, the Ministry of Agriculture and Fisheries conducted a survey of New Zealand vineyards. The most up-to-date survey, conducted by Lincoln College late in 1986 in the wake of the grapevine-extraction scheme, like its forerunners reveals drastic changes in the varietal composition of our vineyards.

In 1960 the total vineyard area of 388 hectares was most heavily planted in Albany Surprise (sixty hectares), Baco 22A (forty-five hectares) and Seibel 5455 (twenty-nine hectares); these were all hybrid or *labrusca* varieties, offering no scope to the winemaker in pursuit of quality.

By 1965 Baco 22A (sixty-eight hectares) had outstripped Albany Surprise (sixty hectares) to become the main grape variety in New Zealand. Palomino, the Spanish sherry grape, moved into third position with fifty-eight hectares.

The rush of hybrid and *vinifera* plantings in the late 1960s showed up in the survey conducted in 1970. Palomino topped the list with 243 hectares, heading Baco 22A, at 217 hectares still in its ascendancy, and Müller-Thurgau rising from obscurity to third place with 194 hectares.

In 1975 Müller-Thurgau emerged well on top, at 649 hectares far ahead of Palomino (338 hectares) and the resilient Baco 22A (208 hectares). Other major plantings included, in fourth place, Cabernet Sauvignon (179 hectares), Seibel 5455 (129 hectares), Chasselas (126 hectares) and Pinotage (106 hectares). Plantings of Chardonnay and Pinot Noir were also rising.

Vine plantings more than doubled between 1975 and 1980, from 2351 to 4853 hectares. The 1980 vineyard survey also revealed that an astonishing fifty percent of all vines planted were less than two years old, and not yet bearing. Müller-Thurgau had maintained its ascendancy with a 200 percent increase in plantings to 1819 hectares – thirty-eight percent of the total vineyard area. Chenin Blanc (289 hectares) and Gewürztraminer (247 hectares) had enjoyed a rapid emergence.

Then Cabernet Sauvignon rose, between 1980 and 1983, from the relative obscurity of sixth place, to become New Zealand's second most heavily planted vine, pushing Palomino into third place, just ahead of Chardonnay.

The accuracy of the latest, 1986 survey was hamstrung by a poor response rate: only sixty-five percent of wine companies and seventy-nine percent of grapegrowers belonging to growers' associations returned the survey questionnaire. Its authors claimed the survey still included over ninety-one percent of all planted vines, but clearly the figures shown in the table opposite are conservative.

The survey does prove, however, that Müller-Thurgau has retained its predominance and still, as in 1983, accounts for over thirty-one percent of total plantings. Chardonnay has moved past Cabernet Sauvignon and is now clearly New Zealand's second most extensively planted variety. Both Sauvignon Blanc and Riesling have risen sharply in importance since 1983, unlike the sherry grape, Palomino, which plunged from third to ninth place.

NATIONAL TOTAL AREA OF PLANTED VINES

	1986		1983	
	Hectares	**% of Total Plantings**	**Hectares**	**% of Total Plantings**
Müller-Thurgau	1232	31.4	1873	31.9
Chardonnay	394	10.0	402	6.8
Cabernet Sauvignon	308	7.9	414	7.1
Sauvignon Blanc	254	6.5	200	3.3
Chenin Blanc	245	6.2	372	6.3
Riesling	234	6.0	148	2.5
Muscat varieties	234	6.0	331	5.5
Gewürztraminer	156	4.0	284	4.8
Palomino	137	3.5	408	6.8
Pinot Noir (including 'Gamay Beaujolais')	110	2.8	296	5.0

Other varieties covering at least fifty hectares are Sémillon (eight-seven hectares), Sylvaner (eighty-three hectares), Chasselas (seventy-three hectares) and Merlot (fifty-five hectares). The 1986 survey also records the smaller plantings of Pinotage (forty-eight hectares), Reichensteiner (forty-eight hectares) and Flora (forty-two hectares).

Overall, in late 1986 surveyed vines covered about 3914 hectares.

THE VARIETIES

BREIDECKER (NOT ILLUSTRATED)

Breidecker is a crossing of Müller-Thurgau with the white hybrid Seibel 7053. It is named in honour of Heinrich Breidecker, the nineteenth-century German winemaker at Kohukohu in the Hokianga.

Although Breidecker displays the typical hybrid resistance to rot, its wine is bland and unmemorable: tasted blind, it is usually mistaken for a rather ordinary quality Müller-Thurgau. A handful of varietal wines have been marketed – by Soljans, Larcomb, Hunter's, Matua Valley – but the grape is principally of value as a blending variety. Plantings are limited.

1986 plantings: 20 hectares

BACO 22A

Baco 22A was once a common hybrid but has now almost vanished. It was primarily used in cheap quaffing white wines, in a role similar to Seibel 5455 for bulk reds.

The vine is a cross between a coarse *labrusca* variety called Noah and Folle Blanche, one of three grapes used in the production of Cognac. Baco 22A features prominently in the vineyards of Armagnac, where it is used for making brandy, and in other countries where adverse weather conditions demand a stalwart vine. In New Zealand the grape was concentrated in Auckland and to a lesser extent in Gisborne.

Baco 22A won popularity in New Zealand for its impressive cropping abilities, up to twenty tonnes per hectare, and its resistance to wet weather. The grapes ripen in April, late in the season, which is a disadvantage, but this is offset by their ability to hang well on the vine until fully ripe. The berries are medium-sized with tough, transparent whitish-yellow skins.

Trials to assess the brandy-making potential of Baco 22A achieved promising results, but the quality of its table wine ranges from harsh to ordinary. The wine is often excessively acid with a detectable *labrusca* coarseness. Nevertheless, many people found the wine acceptable and the best versions, such as earlier vintages of Babich Dry White and Collard Private Bin Dry White, attained good flavour in a straightforward, no-fuss style.

1986 plantings: 9 hectares

CHARDONNAY

Oak-aged, complex, with deep and superbly sustained flavours, the Chardonnays of Burgundy and the New World – California, New Zealand and Australia – rank among the greatest dry white table wines of all. In New Zealand, plantings of this currently most fashionable of all grapes have outstripped those of every other variety except Müller-Thurgau.

Chardonnay used to be commonly referred to as Pinot Chardonnay, but it is not a true Pinot. The clones imported in the late 1920s never grew well, being infected with leaf-roll virus, and the vines languished, raising doubts – now proved unfounded – as to whether the variety was the same vine as the classic Chardonnay of Burgundy.

Although new virus-indexed clones promising a better vineyard performance have just become available, as recently as 1984 vine improvement committees around the country were still unable to locate commercial blocks of Chardonnay ideal as sources of new vine material. According to viticultural scientists Dr Richard Smart and Allan Clarke, this was 'a rather sorry state for such a potentially important variety'. Between 1982 and 1985, however, six new Chardonnay clones were imported.

The clone most commonly planted at present, imported from California, is relatively low-yielding because of its characteristically poor grape 'set', which produces the 'hen and chicken' (large and small berries) effect. According to Richard Smart, 'winemakers regard the presence of small berries as an advantage in making fine wines. Much to their chagrin, Californian winemakers now realise that this clone widely planted in New Zealand was discouraged from planting in California'.

Chardonnay vines are now established in all the major wine regions, notably in Gisborne, Hawke's Bay and Marlborough. The variety adapts well to a wide range of soil types and climates.

Early bud burst renders Chardonnay vines vulnerable to damage from spring frosts in colder regions. The grapes ripen mid-season in small bunches of thick-skinned, yellow-green berries harbouring high sugar levels (hence the rich alcohol typical of its wine). Yields, although moderate, are consistent at seven to ten tonnes per hectare.

New Zealand Chardonnays are medium to full-bodied, with fruit flavours ranging from crisp apples and lemons, through to the stone fruit – peaches and apricots – flavours of very ripe grapes. As superior fruit comes on stream and winemakers experiment with varying periods of skin contact, different yeasts, fermentation temperatures, wood fermentation, types of oak, barrel sizes, length of wood maturation and malolactic fermentations, the standard of our Chardonnay is improving virtually from one vintage to the next.

Styles produced range from fresh, unwooded wines like earlier vintages of Montana Gisborne Chardonnay through to mouth-filling, multi-faceted styles like Morton 'black label' Winery Reserve. Any list of top wines must include Coopers Creek Swamp Road, Kumeu River, Selaks Founders, Babich Irongate, Collard Rothesay and Hawke's Bay, Delegat's Proprietor's Reserve, Villa Maria Barrique Fermented, Cooks Private Bin, Morton Winery Reserve, Brookfields, Te Mata Elston, Vidal Reserve, Hunter's . . . but this list is by no means fixed.

1986 plantings: 384 hectares

CHASSELAS

Variously known as Chasselas, Golden Chasselas, Chasselas d'Or and Chasselas Doré, Chasselas is widely cultivated overseas as a table grape. As a wine grape it achieves some prominence in cool-climate regions, where its low-acid, early-ripening qualities are of value. In Switzerland Chasselas is the major grape variety and its wine is also known in Alsace, the Loire, Germany and Austria.

Chasselas until recently was one of New Zealand's principal white-wine grapes, but lately plantings have shrunk rapidly and virtually disappeared from all regions except Gisborne.

Maturing early, at about the same time as Müller-Thurgau, Chasselas produces about fifteen tonnes per hectare of large, greenish-yellow, low-acid grapes.

As a white table wine, Chasselas has a light bouquet and pleasant, low-acid flavour. Soft and fresh when young, it is easily mistaken for Müller-Thurgau in a blind tasting. When aged, it sometimes develops a fuller, earthy flavour in a light white-burgundy style.

The sales response to Chasselas wines marketed as varietals was slow in New Zealand and increasingly the wine is sold under brand and generic names. The grape is also often used as a base in sparkling wines and as an ideal low-acid variety for blending purposes.

1986 plantings: 73 hectares

CHENIN BLANC

Although a relative newcomer to the New Zealand wine scene, Chenin Blanc is a major variety in France. There, in the middle Loire, the vine yields fresh, fruity white wines such as Vouvray, typically with an acid finish in cooler years. Chenin Blanc also produces soft, full, easy-drinking wines in California and South Africa.

In New Zealand the wine industry is divided on the merits of this vigorous variety, which is now extensively planted in Hawke's Bay, Gisborne, the Waikato and, to a lesser extent, Marlborough.

Although Chenin Blanc ripens early in warm climates, in New Zealand it tends to ripen late, with penetrating acidity. Yields are high for a premium variety, at twelve to fifteen tonnes per hectare. Nevertheless, the grapes are vulnerable to wet weather and to botrytis. Some growers have recently discarded their vines and replanted with other varieties.

Chenin Blanc makes distinctly peachy, medium-bodied, fruity wine in New Zealand with more substantial body and flavour than Müller-Thurgau. As a varietal wine it is usually made slightly sweet to balance the high acidity. As a blending variety, it is a very useful match for such lower acid grapes as Müller-Thurgau and Chasselas.

Corbans established this variety as a premium wine with their delicious 1976 and 1977 vintages, made from Tolaga Bay grapes. More recently, the mantle of New Zealand's outstanding Chenin Blanc producer has passed to Collard, who have succeeded with both late-harvest medium and dry styles.

1986 plantings: 245 hectares

FLORA (NOT ILLUSTRATED)

Flora is a crossing of Gewürztraminer and Sémillon, developed by Dr Harold Olmo of the University of California. His goal was to breed a new grape able to retain spiciness and freshness (which Gewürztraminer cannot) in California's warmer districts. However, although Flora has enjoyed success in Mendocino, in the warmer areas its wine tends to flab.

In New Zealand, Flora is predominantly established in Gisborne, with lesser plantings in Marlborough. Matua Valley, which has marketed it as a varietal, made a well-spiced, broad-flavoured wine.

In the light of Gewürztraminer's stunning performance in New Zealand's cool climate, Flora's future role seems likely to be restricted to that of a blending variety.

1986 plantings: 42 hectares

GEWÜRZTRAMINER

The highly aromatic and spicy Gewürztraminers of Alsace are among the most distinctive white wines in the world. New Zealand, too, handles this grape with marked success.

Pronounced Ge-vertz-truh-meen-uh, with the stress on the 'meen', the name of the wine is sometimes shortened to Traminer. 'Gewürz' means spicy. In Germany it was customary to call the wine Gewürztraminer if it was spicy, Traminer if it was not. In Alsace the current practice is to label all the wines Gewürztraminer.

In New Zealand, Gewürztraminer has proved stunning in our cool-climate growing conditions. It had an inauspicious debut: in 1953 the Department of Agriculture imported a strain known as Roter Traminer which, after McWilliam's established a plot at Tuki Tuki, bore poorly and produced disappointing wine. As a result many winemakers became convinced that Gewürztraminer could not successfully be cultivated here.

Healthier vines have recently been planted in most districts with most champion wines, so far, emerging from Gisborne. Pockets in Auckland are also enjoying success and Marlborough-grown Gewürztraminers have improved in leaps and bounds in the past three or four vintages.

On the vines the grapes are easily identified by their distinctive rosy colour; pink and white berries are often found nestling in the same bunch. This vine is notoriously temperamental, ripening its grapes easily in New Zealand with plenty of sugar and fragrance, but highly susceptible to adverse weather during flowering – which can dramatically reduce the crop – and also vulnerable to powdery mildew and botrytis. To plant a vineyard exclusively in Gewürztraminer is a risk, one that few local viticulturists would contemplate.

The best long-term producer here has been Matawhero, typically drier and more flavour-packed than most. Villa Maria has clearly emerged at the lead of the crowded field of competition entrants with its marvellous reserve bottlings.

1986 plantings: 156 hectares

GREY RIESLING (Trousseau Gris)

This grape is not a Riesling at all, but is a French variety, grown in the Jura, called Trousseau Gris. In California, where it is encountered both as Gray Riesling and Chauché Gris, it produces only pleasant vin ordinaire.

Grey Riesling has been grown commercially for a decade in New Zealand, although many vines were uprooted in 1986. In Auckland, where it used to be viewed as a potential replacement for Müller-Thurgau, the vines grow strongly, cropping thirteen tonnes per hectare of dull, reddish-tan grapes. (To avoid colour transfer, the juice is immediately separated from the skins after picking.) The berries ripen early, with higher acids and sugars than Müller-Thurgau.

Matua Valley has pioneered this variety in New Zealand and more recently Cooks, Babich, Esk Valley, Collard, Lincoln and Pleasant Valley entered the field. Most have been rather ordinary, slightly sweet wines, with body somewhere between Müller-Thurgau and Chenin Blanc. The wine lacks interest in its first twelve months, then with age the flavour builds up and the distinct slightly earthy varietal character appears.

1983 plantings: 44 hectares
1986 plantings: not recorded

MUSCAT VARIETIES

Muscat varieties form a large, instantly recognisable family of white and red grapes notable for their almost overpowering musky scent and sweet grapy flavour. The vines grow all over the Mediterranean and in the New World wine regions, yielding a diversity of styles ranging from delicate dry whites in Alsace through to sweet Asti sparklings in Italy and, most commonly, sweet fortified wines such as those of Portugal and Australia.

Muscat Dr Hogg, an old English table grape, is by far the most common Muscat variety cultivated in New Zealand, although small patches of Muscat Canelli and Early Muscat also exist. Over half of all plantings are in Gisborne, with the rest virtually confined to Hawke's Bay and Marlborough.

The vines crop well in New Zealand, producing large fleshy berries with a pronounced Muscat aroma and flavour. Sometimes, following the German practice, Muscat is blended with Müller-Thurgau to add aroma to the wine; it also appears in 'Asti' type sparklings, in sweet fortified Muscats, and recently in light-bodied, fruity, sweetish varietal white wines.

Muscat dominates the overall style, although not the grape composition, of Montana's justifiably popular, gold award-winning Bernadino Spumante. By contrast, the still Muscat Blancs of Selaks, Babich, Matua Valley, Esk Valley and others never aroused interest among consumers and have largely vanished from the shelves.

1986 plantings: 234 hectares

MÜLLER-THURGAU

In New Zealand two styles of white wine often carry the stamp of the Müller-Thurgau grape – one pale straw in colour, light-bodied, with a delicate scent and crisp dry flavour; the other softer and more mouth-filling, tasting distinctly fruity, with a refreshing balance of sugars and acids.

Müller-Thurgau is often called Riesling-Sylvaner, in the belief that the variety is one of many crossings between the true Riesling vine and the Sylvaner. In fact the genetic origins of this grape have not been established beyond all doubt. To avoid assertions about the vine's ancestry, the Germans wisely prohibit the use in official circles of any name other than Müller-Thurgau.

The vine was bred late in the nineteenth century at Geisenheim in Germany, by Professor Hermann Müller, a native of the Swiss canton of Thurgau. Müller-Thurgau was originally regarded as a bulk producer of low merit. Later, growers unable to ripen Riesling grapes on less favoured sites discovered that the new vine could produce large quantities of attractive wine, with less susceptibility to weather conditions. The early-ripening Müller-Thurgau offered growers the prospect of a reasonable crop every year, and in poor years better quality wine than Riesling.

According to German viticulturist Dr Helmut Becker, 'no other variety has ever spread so rapidly in so few decades . . . up until 40 years ago, opponents wanted to strictly prohibit it. Now the critics of this strain are subdued, but not yet silent'.

The drawback is that Müller-Thurgau as a wine cannot match the body, intensity of flavour, or longevity of Riesling. German Müller-Thurgaus are described by one authority, S.F. Hallgarten, as 'mild, aromatic and pleasant with a slight Muscatel flavour'. In Dr Becker's view the wines are 'elegant, palatable, harmonious and mild, although Riesling drinkers often find them too mild'. Clearly, the Müller-Thurgau lacks the greatness of Riesling.

Nevertheless in 1985 the vine ranked, in terms of acreage, as the number

DR HERMANN MÜLLER, WHO IN 1882 WROTE:
'HOW IMPORTANT THE RESULT OF . . . A UNION,
COMBINING THE SUPERB CHARACTERISTICS OF
THE RIESLING GRAPE WITH THE RELIABLE
EARLY MATURING QUALITIES OF THE SYLVANER,
COULD BE FOR SOME WINE-PRODUCING AREAS'.

one variety in Germany, covering 25,292 hectares − twenty-five percent of the total vineyard area. Müller-Thurgau has made least impression in the most famous regions, especially in the Rheingau.

Elsewhere, Müller-Thurgau has spread to other cool winegrowing regions such as Austria and Switzerland, Hungary, Alsace, Liechtenstein and England. In the 1930s Government Viticulturist Charles Woodfin imported the vine into New Zealand.

The commercial value of Müller-Thurgau became apparent much later, when the demand for white table wines escalated in the 1960s. Then the vine spread rapidly, prized for its early ripening ability and high yields. A rush of plantings in the early 1970s rapidly established Müller-Thurgau as New Zealand's leading grape variety. In 1975 almost one-half of all vines aged one to four years were of this single variety. The wine industry had gone overboard for Müller-Thurgau, and plantings since then have expanded to over 1232 hectares, constituting over thirty-one percent of the total vineyard area and yielding up to forty-five percent of the national grape crop.

Müller-Thurgau grows vigorously in New Zealand and on most soils − it prefers moist, fertile soil to dry stony ground − yields good crops of ten to twenty tonnes per hectare. The berries, yellow-green and flecked with small brown spots, ripen early, and Müller-Thurgau is generally the first variety to be picked. The grapes are susceptible to wet weather at vintage and to fungous diseases, although careful spray programmes reduce the risks.

Müller-Thurgau does not usually achieve very high sugar levels on the vines (hence its low alcohol wine). During ripening the fruit loses acidity rapidly; this is often corrected by the addition of tartaric acid at the crusher.

Müller-Thurgau is well-established in all the major regions except Auckland. The vines crop most heavily on the more fertile East Coast soils and less economically in the Waikato. Distinct regional wine styles are beginning to emerge: Gisborne-grown Müller-Thurgaus (the most common) are light, grapy, very floral and forward; Hawke's Bay versions display a good balance of ripe fruit and crisp acidity; the Marlborough wines are more earthy and Alsatian in style.

New Zealand Müller-Thurgaus vary from dry to very sweet. As a dry wine Müller-Thurgau tends to lack body, needing slight sweetness to broaden the palate and deepen the flavour. Most Müller-Thurgaus are therefore backblended with a small amount of unfermented grapejuice to produce an elegant, fruity style that is very similar to most German commercial white wines and often better.

The name Müller-Thurgau on the label usually − but not always − implies that the wine has been made slightly sweet. Wines labelled Riesling-Sylvaner are generally drier. It is advisable to read the small print.

The best New Zealand Müller-Thurgaus are of a high standard. Among a wide array several wines stand out as having been consistently satisfying − Robard and Butler, Delegat's, Babich, Collard, Montana Marlborough and Hunter's.

Nevertheless most of our Müller-Thurgau is simply clean, straightforward wine − good vin ordinaire. Hence, increasing amounts of Müller-Thurgau are emerging as bulk wine in casks and carafes.

Müller-Thurgau offers good short-term cellaring prospects. In the first six months the wines are typically fresh and lively, highly aromatic and grapy in flavour. With age a more interesting, developed character emerges. Sweeter versions − until recently always freeze-concentrated, but of late naturally botrytised styles have emerged − occasionally acquire an oily consistency and a honeyed perfume reminiscent of the finer German whites.

1986 plantings: 1232 hectares

PALOMINO

Palomino is the leading New Zealand 'sherry' variety. The grape is traditionally used to produce the famous sherries of the Jerez region of Spain and at first glance would appear ill-suited to New Zealand's cooler climate.

The vine was largely unknown in New Zealand until its ability to produce very large crops was demonstrated at Te Kauwhata in the early 1950s. Thereafter the vine spread rapidly through all the wine districts. Palomino emerged by 1970 as the main grape variety in the country, with its heaviest concentrations in Auckland and Hawke's Bay. It still ranks today among New Zealand's ten most important grape varieties – just.

The Palomino vine grows with much vigour, yielding twenty to thirty tonnes per hectare of large, thick-skinned, fleshy yellow-green grapes that make good eating. The grapes ripen mid to late season with a relatively low acidity and without the high sugars achieved in warmer climates. Palomino withstands wet weather reasonably well, but if there are persistent rain and high humidities as vintage approaches, the grapes are susceptible to botrytis.

Palomino grapes feature in the better New Zealand sherries, dry and sweet, and the best of these are reminiscent of their Spanish counterparts. Dry sherries such as Montana Pale Dry and Flor Fino, Collard Extra Dry, Babich Flor Fino and Pacific Pale Dry are all excellent drinking, as are mature sweeter styles like Totara P.B. Cream and P.B. Brown sherries.

1986 plantings: 137 hectares

PINOT GRIS

1986 plantings: 12 hectares

Pinot Gris belongs to the Pinot family of vines and is cultivated in Central Europe, Germany and various regions of France. In Alsace – where it is also known as Tokay d'Alsace – Pinot Gris produces good wine, dry, full-flavoured and flinty.

Although Bragato praised the variety in 1906 ('in the far north [it] bears heavily and produces an excellent white wine'), Pinot Gris later fell out of favour with most growers because of its tendency to crop erratically. Today plantings are concentrated in Hawke's Bay and Canterbury.

The vines grow with moderate vigour, bearing an average crop of seven to ten tonnes per hectare of small, thin-skinned, greyish-blue berries. The grapes mature early with fair acidity and high sugar levels.

Cooks Pinot Gris and Mission Tokay d'Alsace kept the Pinot Gris flag fluttering in the early 1980s: the Mission wine typically slightly sweet and full-bodied, the Cooks version drier and more delicate to taste. Brookfields, and especially Dry River, have lately proved just how concentrated and savoury a wine Pinot Gris can be persuaded to yield in this country.

REICHENSTEINER

1986 plantings: 48 hectares

Created by Dr Helmut Becker, Reichensteiner is a crossing of Müller-Thurgau with the French table grape Madelaine Angevine and the Italian Caladreser Fröhlich. Issued by the Geisenheim Institute in 1978, it has swiftly achieved solid support in the vineyards of Germany – largely in the Rheinhessen – and England.

Ripening early, about the same time as Müller-Thurgau, it enjoys slightly higher acidity and must weights and also, due to its looser bunches, less rot.

Reichensteiner wine shares the fruitiness and mildness of Müller-Thurgau and displays good sugar-acid balance. In New Zealand, where plantings are confined to Gisborne, its role is principally that of an anonymous blending variety, although it has the potential for late-harvest styles – as delectably demonstrated by Corbans Noble Reichensteiner 1985, a raisiny, botrytised sweet wine harvested with a sugar level equal to the trockenbeerenauslese class in Germany.

RIESLING (Rhine Riesling)

Riesling is the greatest and most famous grape variety of Germany. Although surpassed now by Müller-Thurgau in acreage terms, Riesling is still dominant in the best areas – the Rheingau and the Mosel. There, its wine is strongly scented, the flavour a harmony of honey-like fruit and steely acid. Riesling also performs well in Alsace, Central Europe, California, Chile, South Africa and Australia, and recently this grape has made its presence felt in New Zealand.

The proper name of the variety is Riesling. In New Zealand it is often called Rhine Riesling to avoid the confusion that could arise out of the common spoken practice of abbreviating Riesling-Sylvaner (Müller-Thurgau) to Riesling. A recent trend, led by several boutique producers, to call their 'Rhine Riesling' wines Riesling is to be encouraged; this clearly implies that all Müller-Thurgaus should be called precisely that, and that the use of the name 'Riesling-Sylvaner' should be phased out.

Obtaining a reasonable yield from Riesling has long been recognised as a difficulty in New Zealand. Bragato declined to recommend the vines of this variety, 'being only fair bearers'. The 1975 vineyard survey revealed the scarcity of Riesling vines in the country; eight hectares in Hawke's Bay and half a hectare in Auckland. Since then planting has gathered momentum, especially in Marlborough, where almost half of the vines are now concentrated.

Riesling is a shy bearer, yielding only six to eight tonnes per hectare. The grapes ripen late in the season but hang on well, resisting frosts and cold. In Marlborough, where it has enjoyed the most eye-catching success, it is one of the last white varieties to be picked, and in Germany it is said every vintage is a cliff-hanger.

This variety needs a long slow period of ripening to fully develop its most intricate flavours. Thus the finest Rieslings tend to be grown in cooler regions enjoying long dry autumns – Canterbury and Central Otago are outstanding prospects.

In poor years, when the fruit harbours a low level of sugar and high acidity, the wine tends to be unappealingly sharp and thin, but given a good summer and settled autumn, a fragile, luscious wine emerges of unparalleled elegance and perfume.

Noble rot, a beneficial form of *Botrytis cinerea*, can transform Riesling grapes in the vineyard. In cool, moderately dry growing conditions, this fungus covers the translucent, yellow-green surface of the berries, extracting moisture without causing the fruit to collapse. Shrivelled, the grapes intensely concentrate their aroma and flavour constituents, yielding succulent, honey-sweet wines.

Most Riesling needs two years to achieve a satisfactory level of development: a further spell in the cellar builds up the often breathtaking attributes of its full maturity. Corbans (including its Robard and Butler and Stoneleigh labels), Montana Marlborough, Collard, Te Whare Ra, Hunter's, Delegat's, Millton, Coopers Creek, Weingut Seifried and Rongopai are all consistently rewarding.

1986 plantings: 234 hectares

SAUVIGNON BLANC

Sauvignon Blanc is rated behind only Riesling and Chardonnay as one of the world's noblest white-wine varieties. In Bordeaux, where it is widely planted, traditionally it has been blended with the more neutral Sémillon, to produce dry white Graves and sweet Sauternes. But in the regions of Sancerre and Pouilly Fumé in the upper Loire Valley, the Sauvignons are unblended and here the wines are assertive, cutting and flinty, in a style readily recognisable as cool-climate Sauvignon Blanc.

Sauvignon Blanc, although a vigorously growing vine, yields only a moderate crop of five to ten tonnes of small, yellow-green berries per hectare. The grapes ripen mid to late season, harbouring adequate sugars and a high level of acidity. Viticulturists have to combat two problems, however: the vines are tough-stemmed, making the bunches difficult to harvest mechanically, and in wet weather the grapes are prone to split, causing rot.

The vine is a relative newcomer to New Zealand vineyards. Matua Valley pioneered plantings at Waimauku in the early 1970s. Montana later established the variety commercially in Marlborough: their much praised Marlborough Sauvignon Blanc 1980, with several gold medals now under its belt, at nine years old is still in sound condition.

Sauvignon Blanc has rapidly emerged as the fourth most widely planted variety in the country. Marlborough is the principal growing region, followed by Gisborne and Hawke's Bay.

Two distinct methods of handling Sauvignon Blanc are practised in New Zealand wineries. By far the most common involves bottling the wine directly out of stainless steel tanks. These wines, placing their emphasis

squarely on the grape's tangy, piquant varietal character, are most often labelled as Sauvignon Blanc.

By contrast, those labelled as Fumé Blanc tone down Sauvignon's natural ebullience by maturing, and occasionally fermenting, the wine in oak casks. The result is a broader, potentially more complex wine, more costly to produce.

The pungent, 'nettley' bouquet of Sauvignon Blanc, traditionally described as gunflint – the smell of sparks after a flint strikes metal – leaps from the glass with a forcefulness some criticise as unsubtle. Others adore its distinctiveness. The flavour ranges from a sharp, green capsicum character – stemming from a touch of unripeness in the fruit – through to a riper, fruity gooseberry style and, finally, to the tropical fruit (peaches and apricots) overtones and lower acidity of very ripe fruit.

Many vineyards have proven themselves capable of producing top-flight Sauvignon Blancs. Outstanding labels include Selaks Sauvignon Blanc (and Sauvignon Blanc/Sémillon blend), Montana Marlborough Sauvignon Blanc, Kumeu River Sauvignon Fumé, Te Mata Cape Crest Sauvignon Blanc, Cloudy Bay Sauvignon Blanc, Coopers Creek Fumé Blanc, Morton Estate Winery Reserve Fumé Blanc, Corbans Fumé Blanc, Hunter's Sauvignon Blanc and Fumé Blanc, Villa Maria Reserve Sauvignon Blanc, Delegat's Proprietor's Reserve Fumé Blanc and Rongopai Sauvignon Blanc.

This variety seems assured of great prominence in the future.

1986 plantings: 254 hectares

SÉMILLON

Sémillon gives rise to a diversity of styles ranging from the fine dry whites of Graves and Australia to the sweet, late-harvested wines of Sauternes and Barsac. Sémillon imparts softness to its blend with Sauvignon Blanc in Graves, and in Sauternes, infection of Sémillon grapes with *Botrytis cinerea* brings a distinctive, 'noble rot' character to the best wines. Although in Europe the variety is invariably blended with other grapes, Australia makes excellent varietal wines from Sémillon, especially the soft, complex 'white burgundies' of the Hunter Valley.

The commercial plantings of Sémillon in New Zealand have yielded promising – although confusing – results. The vines, which display vigorous growth, yield moderately high crops of ten to seventeen tonnes per hectare. Their tough-skinned, greenish-yellow berries ripen slightly later than Sauvignon Blanc, with good weather resistance.

This last quality is very surprising, especially in New Zealand's often humid growing conditions, because the compact grape cluster typical of Sémillon usually renders it highly vulnerable to bunch rot. The clone widely planted in New Zealand – UCD2 – grows much looser bunches. This has led to some doubts about the correct naming of this variety, but French, American and New Zealand authorities have stated the name is probably correct. All the University of California (Davis) clones of Sémillon were imported in 1986 in an endeavour to establish the true identity of New Zealand's vines.

Sémillon is usually an ideal, softer and milder, blending partner for Sauvignon Blanc. In such cool-climate regions as the state of Washington, Tasmania and New Zealand, however, its wine can display a strident grassy aroma and higher acidity that is strikingly reminiscent of under-ripe Sauvignon Blanc. Riper wines, like de Redcliffe's 1985 and 1986, have lacked this aggressiveness and been better for it. Delegat's Proprietor's Reserve and Villa Maria Reserve are other top labels.

That Sémillon is also a useful, flavour-packed blending variety has been well demonstrated by Babich Fumé Vert (Sémillon, Sauvignon Blanc and Chardonnay), Coopers Dry (Chenin Blanc and Sémillon) and Selaks Sauvignon Blanc/Sémillon.

1986 plantings: 87 hectares

SYLVANER (NOT ILLUSTRATED)

Sylvaner, in the first half of this century Germany's most important grape variety, is still widely planted in the Rheinhessen, where it produces pleasant, rather unobtrusive wines, most of which are marketed as Liebfraumilch. The vine is also – decreasingly – common in Alsace, and in Austria and Switzerland, and has recently been established in New Zealand.

Here it grows with moderate vigour, with an average to high yield and harvest date lying between Müller-Thurgau and Riesling. It is susceptible to wet weather at harvest. Hawke's Bay has the greatest concentration of vines, followed by Gisborne and the Waikato.

Few varietal Sylvaners have been put before the public: the best have been Weingut Seifried's delicate and fruity wines. Most of the national crop of Sylvaner is being pressed into service for blending, due to its rather neutral flavour.

1986 plantings: 83 hectares

CABERNET FRANC

Cabernet Franc, a happier vine in cooler regions than Cabernet Sauvignon, looks poised to become one of New Zealand's more important red wine varieties. It is much valued in Bordeaux, particularly in St Emilion where, under the name of Bouchet, it is the grape primarily responsible for the esteemed Château Cheval Blanc. Cabernet Franc is also widely planted in the middle Loire and in north-eastern Italy.

The vine was established here early this century and 'succeeded well in the northernmost parts of the colony. Unfortunately, it seems to be subject to *coulure* [failure of the vine flowers to develop] in southern districts' (Bragato, 1906). Its suitability for cooler climates is based on the fact that it buds, and thus ripens, earlier than Cabernet Sauvignon, with slightly heavier crops. Virtually unknown for several decades, small pockets have recently been planted, principally in Hawke's Bay and Gisborne, and also in Auckland.

Cabernet Franc's wine is more genial than that of Cabernet Sauvignon, lower in tannin, acids and extract, with an instantly appealing aroma variously described as raspberries, violets and pencil shavings. By coupling a degree of the strength of claret with the suppleness of Beaujolais, Brajkovich (Kumeu River) Cabernet Franc 1987 first demonstrated this variety's ability to make a delicious varietal red in New Zealand.

More importantly, as part of the *encépagement* (varietal make-up) of vineyards such as St Nesbit, Coleraine, and Goldwater, it will aid winemakers in their pursuit of Médoc-like complexity.

1986 plantings: 15 hectares

CABERNET SAUVIGNON

The full-flavoured, complex red wines of the Cabernet Sauvignon grape, together with the vine's successful adaptation to a diversity of grapegrowing environments, have created for this variety a worldwide reputation as the finest red-wine grape of all. In New Zealand, as elsewhere, the best red wines often reflect the superb winemaking qualities of Cabernet Sauvignon.

Cabernet Sauvignon – often abbreviated to Cabernet – has a long history in New Zealand. It seems that the vine first arrived with Busby or with the French settlers at Akaroa. Last century the vine was well known in New Zealand and in 1906 Bragato pronounced it to be 'one of the

best varieties grown here . . . the wine produced is of an excellent quality'.

Nevertheless, interest in Cabernet Sauvignon slumped during the wasted years of cheap 'plonk' manufacture. The current revival dates from the early 1970s, when Cabernet Sauvignon came to be regarded as the ideal grape to upgrade the overall standard of red wines. The vine spread rapidly through all the major wine regions; in 1975 nearly eighty percent of all Cabernet Sauvignon vines in New Zealand were less than five years old. Cabernet Sauvignon now is firmly established as our most popular red-grape variety, constituting almost eight percent of the national vineyard.

In cool climates Cabernet Sauvignon ripens late in the season. Despite some susceptibility to fungous diseases, with proper spray protection the grapes hang well on the vine. Often labelled a shy bearer, Cabernet produces between six and twelve tonnes per hectare of small, blue-black tough-skinned berries tasting astringent even when fully ripe. In New Zealand the grapes are usually picked last, in April and even May, with high levels of acid and tannin.

In New Zealand Cabernet Sauvignon yields wine that is generally superior to that obtained from any other red variety. Nevertheless, the best reds are always made from ripe fruit and New Zealand Cabernets can emerge from poor seasons tasting thin and green. Also, many Cabernet Sauvignon vines have recently had to be replanted because they were from diseased stock. The new virus-indexed plantings coming into production are producing wines of a much higher standard.

Cabernet Sauvignon performs best in the warmer summer temperatures of the North Island. Plantings are most widespread in Hawke's Bay, where the grape yields fragrant, sturdy wine of a richness and complexity unrivalled by any other region. Auckland, in dry years, can also produce full-bodied, although often slightly herbaceous, wines (improved trellis design promises to reduce this). The Cabernet Sauvignons grown in Gisborne's fertile soils have veered towards blandness. In Marlborough – the second most heavily planted region – they are often rather *too* cool-climate in style, lacking the strength and opulence of optimally ripened fruit. In Canterbury Cabernet Sauvignon will not adequately ripen – St Helena's leafily astringent Port Hills Claret 1986 underscored this point. Wherever they are grown, Cabernet Sauvignon vines yield the best wine when grown in dry soils, which avoid late-season vegetative growth.

At their best, New Zealand Cabernets display the cool-climate characteristics of lightness of body (compared with warmer regions) and true, intense varietal flavour. Aged for one to two years in small oak, the wines are able to develop a style and subtlety similar to Bordeaux, although lacking the heavy French tannin.

By itself, Cabernet Sauvignon can be too austere for some palates and a search is currently underway for varieties to blend with Cabernet Sauvignon to produce a softer style. Pinotage has been used with only moderate success. Merlot, blended with Cabernet Sauvignon in Bordeaux and California, and recently established here, and Cabernet Franc, offer better prospects.

Scores of New Zealand Cabernets have fuelled my enthusiasm for this grape. Three memorable wines that are still personal favourites are McWilliam's Cabernet Sauvignon 1970, Nobilo's Cabernet Sauvignon 1976 and Babich Cabernet Sauvignon 1978; all three possessed the lovely, sustained flavour and delicacy of style that identifies the finest New Zealand reds.

Recent vintages, however, are bolder, deeper hued and more tightly tannic than anything seen in the 1970s. Three reasons for this are the vastly superior fruit coming on stream off virus-improved vines, the far more abundant employment of new oak casks for maturing that fruit, and the series of Indian summers experienced in 1983, 1985 and 1986.

Cabernet Sauvignons or Cabernet Sauvignon blends in the vanguard of premium New Zealand reds include Villa Maria Reserve, Cooks Private Bin Fernhill, Delegat's Proprietor's Reserve, Matua Valley, St Nesbit, Brookfields, Te Mata Awatea and Coleraine, Ngatarawa Glazebrook and Goldwater.

1986 plantings: 307 hectares

MERLOT

One of the most aristocratic of all red-grape varieties, Merlot has also been one of the most under-appreciated. In Bordeaux its plantings are double those of Cabernet Sauvignon – although most wine lovers swear the reverse is true.

To the Cabernet Sauvignon-based reds of the Médoc and Graves, Merlot imparts richness and softness. Merlot truly comes into its own in St Emilion and Pomerol, where a typical vineyard is planted two-thirds to Merlot with the rest to Cabernet Franc. It also grows in Italy, Switzerland, Eastern Europe, Chile and California, and in the late 1970s became established in New Zealand.

Its early – compared with Cabernet Sauvignon – budding and flowering can be a problem in cooler regions prone to spring frosts. Poor set is a common problem, reducing yield severely. The vine displays moderate vigour, producing eight to ten tonnes per hectare of blue-black, loose-bunched berries, harbouring less tannin and more sugar than Cabernet Sauvignon. Ripening is slightly earlier than Cabernet Sauvignon.

New Zealand's cool climate appears ideal for Merlot, where it can slowly build concentrated flavours over a lengthy ripening season. Hawke's Bay has emerged as the foremost growing region, having over one-half of all plantings, ahead of Auckland. It is thus far little seen in Marlborough.

Merlot has a dual role in New Zealand red winemaking. As a straight varietal – Château Petrus, the great name of Pomerol, is the outstanding example – its floral, plummy bouquet and soft, mouth-filling flavour are instantly appealing; it can be consumed much younger than Cabernet Sauvignon. Collard and Babich were available for a few years as varietal labels, but the key player now is Kumeu River Merlot/Cabernet, where the predominant fragrant, supple Merlot makes its presence well felt.

Merlot is more widely used to add its characteristic fullness and ripeness (hinting at sweetness) to the mid-palate of Cabernet Sauvignon. A host of Cabernet/Merlots are now lining the shelves, drawing their inspiration from the great Médoc reds.

1986 plantings: 55 hectares

MEUNIER (Pinot Meunier)

Meunier – also commonly known as Pinot Meunier – is the principal grape variety of the Champagne region of France.

In New Zealand, Meunier was the mainstay of the early wine industry. Government Viticulturist S.F. Anderson wrote in 1917 that: 'Fully two-thirds of the vines grown for winemaking in the Dominion are of this variety. It is the hardiest of all our wine-producing grapes. It is the most regular and consistent cropper, contains the largest amount of saccharine . . . [and] ripens well within our grape season. . .' According to Bragato, Meunier produced 'a good crop of high class wine'.

Meunier lost its lead position because of degenerative virus diseases which sapped the vines' strength and reduced the quality of their grapes. Some plants survive, especially in Hawke's Bay, but for many years Meunier has been confined to a role as a low-acid variety suitable for blending. It is rare to find the wine marketed as a straight varietal – Brookfields is the only recent exception – and reds from this historic grape have tended to lack colour and flavour depth.

1983 plantings: 8 hectares
1986 plantings: not recorded

PINOTAGE

Pinotage is a black South African grape variety, obtained by crossing Pinot Noir with a vine known in South Africa as Hermitage, but which is really the more humble Cinsaut grape of French and Algerian origin. Its breeder, Professor A.I. Perold, was endeavouring to create a softly-flavoured red grape of higher yield than the shy-bearing Pinot Noir.

As a commercially grown wine variety Pinotage is unique to South Africa and New Zealand, where it yields soft, rounded reds that are often underrated.

Pinotage was established in New Zealand during the late sixties and early seventies, during the rush to replace hybrids with *vinifera* material. The vine grew prolifically, ripening reasonably early with good yields of medium-sized, thick-skinned berries. The variety was widely planted in Auckland, because of its ability to withstand humid conditions, to a lesser extent in Gisborne and the Waikato – and more recently in Marlborough, where today over half of its plantings are found.

Pinotage has had a rather turbulent career in New Zealand. Once heralded as a premium variety capable of producing the 'great New Zealand red', it has since been much criticised. Some claim that Pinotage is coarse in the mid-palate and the wine has failed to impress such overseas authorities as John Avery and Len Evans.

The criticism has derived partly from the fact that many so-called Pinotage wines used to include substantial amounts of hybrids, ostensibly to improve the wine's colour. A straight Pinotage is much more worthwhile. Also, the quality of the wine has varied with the clone and the extent of virus infection.

A well-made Pinotage is a soft, burgundy-style wine, less tannic than Cabernet Sauvignon, peppery, with a pleasant berry-like flavour and smooth finish. On several occasions, when the variety has looked in danger of eclipse as a prestige red. Nobilo has scored a gold medal at the national wine competition. The company regularly vies with Montana for top honours with this grape. Pinotage, says Peter Hubscher, Montana's production manager, is the most underrated grape variety in the country.

Corbans 1964 Pinotage was the pioneer of commercial New Zealand Pinotages. In March 1985 I tasted that wine as a venerable twenty-one-year-old, still alive, its palate now drying out, but proof of the variety's ability to mature well in the long haul.

Pinotage is now also appearing in the quaffing-wine range, to the overall improvement of our carafe and cask reds. The production of rosés from Pinotage is another trend: the wines are light-bodied, fresh, pinkish, varying from dry to sweet and make excellent lunchtime drinking.

1986 plantings: 48 hectares

PINOT NOIR

Pinot Noir is one of the great red-wine varieties, singlehandedly responsible for the majestic, soft and mouth-filling reds of Burgundy. It is also of pivotal importance in Champagne, where it is prized for its body and longevity. But the vine is notoriously temperamental in its choice of residence and has not readily adapted to regions beyond northern Europe. In Oregon – where Pinot Noir is by far the most widely planted variety – wines of intriguing scent and elegance have emerged, but elsewhere in the United States and in Australia its wine has usually lacked real distinction.

Bragato observed in 1906 that Pinot Noir 'ordinarily bears well and yields a nice wine'. The vine is a challenge to viticulturists, however, being vulnerable to spring frosts and also very prone to rot. It ripens ahead of Cabernet Sauvignon, producing low yields of seven to ten tonnes per hectare of small berries of varying skin thickness.

Although the first vines in New Zealand were virus-infected, healthier vines have been available since the early 1970s. Several clones are being cultivated, including Bachtobel, the higher-yielding 10/5, and the clone wrongly called 'Gamay Beaujolais' (here and in California) which has now been positively identified as Pinot Noir.

A reasonably early ripener, Pinot Noir is especially well suited to coolish climates, where the grapes are able to hang on the vines for extended periods, picking up the most subtle scents and flavours. Plantings are currently well spread across Marlborough, Hawke's Bay and Gisborne, but the climatic indices would suggest that Martinborough, Marlborough and Canterbury have the crisper, more marginal ripening conditions in which Pinot Noir thrives.

Nobilo set the early pace with some superb Huapai-grown Pinot Noirs in the 1970s. Later Babich at Henderson and St Helena in Canterbury shared the top show honours. The most silky, deep-scented Pinot Noir ever made in this country, however, is Martinborough Vineyards 1986.

1986 plantings: 110 hectares

SEIBELS

These are red and white hybrid varieties, now almost vanished, but once popular for their heavy crops of weather-resistant grapes.

The white grapes such as Seibel 5408 and 5409 were never much grown in New Zealand. Many of our bulk reds, however, used to include substantial proportions of the black varieties Seibel 5437 and 5455.

Seibel 5437

Also known as Seibouchet and Tintara, Seibel 5437 was renowned for its brilliant-coloured purple-red juice, useful for blending with wines lacking in colour intensity, such as virused Pinotage.

The long, dark-blue grapes ripen in mid-season with high acids and an aggressive hybrid flavour.

Seibel 5455

Known also as Cinqua and Moya, Seibel 5455 is one of the more highly regarded hybrids grown in France as a bulk-wine producer.

The grape ripens in mid-March in New Zealand with very heavy crops of small, tough-skinned dark blue berries. The variety was principally grown in Auckland and also in Hawke's Bay and Gisborne.

The fruit when fully ripened is capable of making a suprisingly pleasant red wine, with a soft, quite fruity flavour. Seibel 5455 was usually found in New Zealand as the base material for cheap reds, sometimes blended, sometimes not. The moderate hybrid flavour is not sufficiently pronounced to be offensive. A few wines, usually produced from selected pickings, deservedly attracted attention, most notably earlier vintages of Abel's Reserve Dry Red and of Collard's Private Bin Claret.

1986 plantings: 11 hectares

SHIRAZ

Shiraz is the principal black grape of the Rhône Valley of France and is also heavily planted in Australia. In the Rhône it is called Syrah and sometimes in Australia, Hermitage. Regardless of the name of the vine or the location of its vineyard, Shiraz typically yields robust, richly flavoured reds, peppery in character and with a heady perfume.

Shiraz has a long history in New Zealand. Bragato was a fervent supporter, declaring in 1895 that 'The Hermitage will, in your colony, give heavy yields and wine of first quality . . . [it] should compose at least one half of the vineyard . . .' Good wines were made, but in many areas the grapes failed to ripen, lacking sugar and colour, and remaining overly acid. S.F. Anderson wrote in 1917 that Shiraz was being 'grown in nearly all our vineyards [but] the trouble with this variety has been an unevenness in ripening its fruit'.

After decades of eclipse, Shiraz is being re-evaluated. New clones and virus-indexed vines show an improved ripening performance. A few blends have appeared, notably Matua Valley Cabernet/Hermitage and Collard Pinotage/Cabernet/Shiraz. In both these wines Shiraz had a real impact, adding deep colour, fullness to the mid-palate and a soft finish. Nevertheless, this variety has traditionally flourished in much warmer grapegrowing climates and the future of Shiraz in New Zealand remains uncertain.

1980 plantings: 1 hectare
1986 plantings: not recorded

THE SEASONAL CYCLE
IN THE VINEYARDS

In winter the vines rest, building their resources for the burgeoning of growth which will take place much later in the year. The vineyards soon lie barren and silent, the vines dormant and bared to the winter rains. Now is a useful period for cleaning up the vineyard – for clearing debris away from drains and the ends of rows, and for replacing posts and wires.

In June, pruning begins and dominates vineyard activity through to the end of August. Left alone, the vines would spread along the ground and climb vigorously, pouring energy into vegetative growth, to the detriment of the fruit which will come later. Through trellising and pruning, the viticulturist is able to achieve greater ease of cultivation and produce a superior crop. In New Zealand, most vines are planted about two metres apart in rows three metres wide and trained along trellises varying between one and 1.7 metres in height.

The art of pruning requires a knowledge of the needs of different varieties as well as swift judgement of the strength of each individual vine. If too few buds are left on the canes after pruning the crop will be small and shoot growth too strong; if too many remain, although the crop will be heavy, the vine may be unable to ripen all its fruit. Pruning is thus a critical opportunity for the grower to influence the size and quality of his crop. A Gisborne study of the response of Müller-Thurgau vines to pruning levels varying between twenty and 120 buds per vine, found that yields soared in tandem with the increased bud numbers from twenty-one to forty-six tonnes per hectare, but as the yields increased, sugars declined.

Cane pruning is the most popular system in New Zealand. Between two and four canes are chosen to carry the new season's growth, each having ten to twenty buds. A few spurs, carrying several buds, are also retained to provide the fruiting canes for the following season. Once the pruner has decided on the correct balance the canes are cut – often these days using pneumatic or electrically operated secateurs – bent to the wire and tied in place. The bearing arms are laid along the bottom wire and later the new season's foliage will be trained above.

Spur pruning is another, less popular system whereby fruitful one-year-old wood is simply reduced to numerous spurs, each carrying two to six buds. Although many growers in New Zealand doubt the long-term cropping ability of spur-pruned vines, experimental vines in the Matawhero district showed no drop in yield and gave a saving in labour costs of over twenty-five percent.

'Minimal pruning' is a relatively new, cost-cutting system already adopted by some growers in Marlborough. It was developed in Australia, after surprised observers noted that Sultana vines left unpruned for many years still produced large crops of reasonable quality each year.

Vines minimally pruned are trained along two wires, one at the top of the post and the other about twenty-five centimetres below it. All growth is wrapped around these wires. The tops of the vines are never touched; pruning is simply a skirting operation, performed by a mechanical cutter bar about half a metre above the ground.

Although minimal pruning is cheaper and gives heavier crops, in New Zealand's moist conditions it could easily lead to excessive canopy growth and resultant drops in fruit ripeness; the Marlborough growers report their grapes do mature later. This technique thus appears likely to find favour only in vineyards specialising in bulk grape production.

The peaceful routines of vineyard labour are fixed by the passage of the seasons, each of which has its own special appeal. Perhaps the most spectacular is autumn, after the harvest, when green turns to gold and russet, making bold patterns of colour over vine-covered landscapes. The viticulturist's year really begins with the first cold spells in autumn, when the vines are green and still active and the bunches have been gathered in. Then the weather cools further, and in a flaming shower of crimson, yellow and rust-brown, the leaves drop from the vines.

FLAMING LEAVES IN THE BABICH VINEYARD AT THE PEAK OF AUTUMN.

IN WINTER, PRUNERS REMOVE NINETY PERCENT OF THE PREVIOUS SEASON'S CANES.

ABOVE RIGHT: THE REMAINING CANES ARE TWISTED AROUND THE WIRE AND TIED SECURELY AT THE END.

ANTHONY IVICEVICH OF WEST BROOK WAGING WAR ON FEATHERED VANDALS; UNCHECKED BIRDS CAN STRIP ROWS OF VINES TOTALLY BARE OF FRUIT.

When spring comes, sap rises and nudges fragile buds out from the gnarled canes that have protected them through winter. Shoots and flower-clusters emerge, and tiny leaves unfurl. Several weeks later the flowers 'set' as small, hard green berries. This is a critical period in the viticultural calendar because grapes, which are self-fertilising rather than insect-pollinated, are highly vulnerable to adverse weather at flowering. A poor fruit set, caused by wet, windy weather or cold temperatures at flowering, is a direct cause of a reduced harvest later in the season. From now until the vintage the vines need constant care.

To arrest weed growth the vineyards are cultivated several times during the growing season. Kikuyu grass, paspalum, blackberry and other weeds create pockets of stagnant air conducive to disease, and compete with the vines for moisture and nourishment. The strip of earth directly under the vines is therefore either sprayed with herbicides, hand-hoed, or ploughed with a manoeuvrable hydraulic blade attached to the side of a tractor.

In spring, cover crops such as lupins and clover, which supply the vines' nitrogen needs, are turned under. Soil which was ploughed onto the vines in autumn in order to channel winter rains away from the roots, is now cleared away. The rows are disced until the earth is well broken up and aerated. Chemical spray programmes commence too, and continue through to the harvest.

The sprays protect the vines against fungous diseases and insect pests such as oidium, black spot, botrytis, downy mildew and mealy bugs. Since the sprays protect the vines, rather than eradicating the pests, up to ten to fifteen applications may be necessary during the season to shield new growth and replace sprays washed away by rain.

Birds are another menace. Sparrows, blackbirds, starlings, mynas and thrushes feast on the ripening grapes, splitting the skins and paving the way for an onslaught of fungous diseases. Winegrowers use a variety of defences: wire netting, scarecrows, alternative 'lure' crops, kites, shotguns, raucous motorcycles, bird-repellent sprays and compressed air explosives.

An insecticide called Mesurol has been much used to combat birds over the past decade. Any bird unlucky enough to peck at a few treated grapes experiences throat irritation, gastric upset and even difficulty in flying. After wines exported to Canada in 1985 were found to have unacceptably high levels of the insecticide, Mesurol was withdrawn from New Zealand spray schedules. The outcome, according to Debbie Reid, formerly Villa Maria's viticultural expert, will be that bird damage worsens.

Botrytis

Botrytis is the worst problem for the viticulturist. Late in the season warm, wet weather encourages grapes to swell up with moisture and split open. Botrytis, which appears as a grey, fluffy mould on the leaves and bunches, causes the grapes to rot on the vines. Fine dry autumn weather can allow botrytis-infected grapes to develop an intense concentration of flavour and sweetness. In New Zealand's frequently wet autumns, however, botrytis can severely damage the grapes, oxidising the juice and tainting the flavour of its wine.

The culprits causing botrytis infection are the tiny spores produced each spring by over-wintering micro-organisms called sclerotia. To first establish its foothold, botrytis needs damaged plant tissue: the mass of dead flower caps and aborted flowers and berries produced during flowering and berry set. These dead parts, which are easily ravaged by botrytis, provide the springboard from which the fungus later launches its onslaught on the developing bunches.

Other fungi and yeasts also multiply in the presence of botrytis-infected fruit, as do acetic-acid bacteria and fruit flies. If adverse weather proves especially persistent, the even worse condition of sour rot can occur which is difficult in the extreme to control. A combination of heavy rain and high humidity during the final stages of ripening can literally overnight collapse whole bunches. The loss of a big portion of the harvest – the Auckland region suffered a twenty to thirty percent crop loss in 1979 – is the unhappy result.

Quality-orientated winemakers are now starting to refuse to accept excessively botrytis-infected fruit. Warwick Orchiston observed in 1985 that Vidal 'reject the crop in the field when the percentage of rot exceeds seven percent. Juices obtained from grapes with five percent rot show definite musty flavours'. Such unpalatable flavours are due to the botrytis-produced enzyme laccase, which is resistant to SO_2 (sulphur dioxide) and causes reduced keeping qualities in wine. Browning of white wines and colour instability in reds are major effects.

Several factors have accentuated the botrytis problem in recent years. The switch in plantings from the hardier hybrids to thinner-skinned *vinifera* varieties is one cause; another is the pursuit of riper grapes – botrytis is more active where sugar levels are high; another is the additional tissue damage caused by mechanical pruners.

To combat botrytis growers rely heavily on the use of specific fungicides in sprays, particularly the dicarboxymides: Ronilan, Rovral and Sumisclex. A danger here is the discovery in West Auckland vineyards in 1981 of strains of botrytis resistant to these fungicides. Precisely timed and – perhaps unexpectedly – fewer fungicide spray applications are recommended.

Although viticulturists more often than not are forced to contend with wet rot, dry autumns, especially in southern districts, can arrest the spread of botrytis infections. This can lead to a shrivelling of the bunches – 'noble rot' – and the production of nectareous sweet white wines. This immensely desirable form of *Botrytis cinerea* appears spontaneously in vineyards in France, Germany, Hungary, South Africa, California, southern Australia and New Zealand. One prerequisite is that the fruit must be healthy and ripe. Long dry spells before the harvest or – more precisely – damp, misty mornings followed by fine days around twenty to twenty-five degrees Celsius and cool nights, create the ideal environment for the development of noble rot. Occasional light breezes encourage its spread, and humidity should not rise above sixty percent if the berry skins are to stay intact.

The fungus transforms the bunches, not only their appearance – they become ugly – but also the balance of their juices. The botrytis, which

BOTRYTIS IS THE MOST DAMAGING WET-WEATHER ROT IN NEW ZEALAND VINEYARDS.

CHEMICAL SPRAYS ARE USED TO COMBAT A RANGE OF VINE DISEASES, BUT SPRAY RESIDUES CAN ALSO INTERFERE WITH FERMENTATION AND CONTRIBUTE OFF-FLAVOURS TO WINE. A SET PERIOD MUST BE ALLOWED TO ELAPSE BETWEEN THE FINAL SPRAYING AND HARVEST.

COLOUR CHANGES IN RED-WINE GRAPES ARE PARTICULARLY NOTICEABLE IN THE RAPID GROWTH PHASE PRIOR TO MATURITY. CABERNET SAUVIGNON GRAPES, SHOWN HERE, RIPEN LATE IN THE SEASON.

forms a fluffy coating over the berries – and falls away if you touch it – thrusts tiny filaments through the grape skins and feeds on the interior. The skins are wrinkled and some of the organic acids are metabolised. Through dehydration the grape sugars and extractives become highly concentrated – perfect for making sweet wine.

Inevitably these 'noble rot' wines are expensive: each vine at Château d'Yquem, the illustrious Sauternes vineyard, is said to yield about a single glass. But the wines produced from nobly rotten musts have a thrilling bouquet, treacly and honeyed, with a concentrated, creamy palate, heavy with sweetness. Increasingly in New Zealand our leading sweet whites are showing the beneficial impact of botrytis, at the expense of the once predominant freeze-concentrated styles.

Rongopai, Te Whare Ra and Millton are the leading trio in this field but, as Geoff Kelly has written, more and more of our winemakers appear to be catching the bug.

In summer the vines reach their peak period of growth. The tangled canes are trimmed back, tucked and tied. Leaf removal around the fruit zone, by hand or machine, to open up the fruit to maximum sunshine, has recently become common. As ripening proceeds, a waxy white 'bloom' of yeasts – traditionally responsible for the natural fermentation of grapejuice into wine – develops on the skins of the grapes. Soon, as the bunches approach their optimum level of ripeness, the harvest can begin.

When grapes ripen, two crucial changes occur. The amount of sugar is progressively enriched and the natural acids decline. Prior to the main ripening period, which begins a few weeks before the vintage, the grapes grow rapidly, yet remain hard and acid. At the point of 'turning' – the real beginning of the ripening period – black varieties develop colour and white grapes change from green to their characteristic white or yellow.

The berries soften and the changes in sweetness, acidity and flavour gather momentum. Sugar, almost nil at the point of 'turning', is swiftly built up in the leaves and transported to the fruit. Acids fall, the greener malic acid more steeply than the soft tartaric acid. In the very last stages of ripening these changes decelerate. For a few days, when the berries are at their maximum size, sugar enrichment is slow, and on cooler days may even waver, the sugar retreating back into the stalks.

To set the precise day on which the harvest should start, winegrowers traditionally relied on the ratio of sugars and acids in the grapes. These are the two major constituents of grapejuice and two of any wine's primary taste factors. For several weeks before the vintage, therefore, berries are randomly selected from the top, middle and bottom of bunches on both sides of the vines and analysed for their sugar and acid contents.

Grapes are often picked with an eye to obtaining the best possible yield. A growing trend, nevertheless, with premium varieties, is to delay the harvest in order to achieve higher sugar levels, even at the cost of weight loss through the evaporation of water in the fruit or increased risk of bunch rot.

Two relatively new factors now being closely monitored by growers who are seeking optimum fruit maturity are levels of pH and flavour composition. (pH is a measure, based on hydrogen ion concentration, of the acidity or alkalinity of a solution.) The desired pH level of about 3.3 in grape musts contributes to a clean fermentation and to a longer life in the bottle. This increased winemaking emphasis on pH itself places additional emphasis on careful vineyard husbandry – too high a pH is directly related to excessive fruit shading.

Assessment of grape flavour is also moving to the fore. Dr Rainer Eschenbruch – formerly of the Te Kauwhata Research Station, now a partner at Rongopai – has argued that grapejuices should be sensorily evaluated to pinpoint the precise time of harvest, and such juice tastings are becoming an integral part of grape-quality assessment.

HAND-HELD REFRACTOMETERS ARE COMMONLY USED FOR FIELD ANALYSIS OF FRUIT RIPENESS BEFORE THE HARVEST. AFTER A DROP OF JUICE HAS BEEN PLACED ON THE REFRACTOMETER GLASS AND THE LID CLOSED, THE SUGAR LEVEL REGISTERS DIRECTLY ON THE SCALE.

Another, more objective technique involves close tracking of the flavour compounds, called monoterpenes, which are largely responsible for the development of varietal character in grapes. Gewürztraminer character, for instance, is dominated by geraniol and nerol and that of Muscat is principally linalool. These 'terpene' levels rise as the bunches mature.

The vintage is the most demanding part of the winegrower's year. Considerable skill is needed if the grapes are to be picked at the right moment and arrive at the winery in sound condition. Large wineries now provide a regular field service to all their grapegrowers in the form of visits and sampling of fruit for maturity determination. In New Zealand the vintage, the first, vital step in the making of the new season's wine, usually begins late in February and lasts until May.

Only fifteen years ago the entire grape supply was picked by hand, in the traditional manner. The arrival of the first mechanical harvester in New Zealand in 1973, however, soon forced the hand-pickers into retreat.

Hand-pickers now survive only in the smaller or steeper vineyards, or where meticulous fruit quality, with minimal berry damage, is sought. The grapes, cut from the vines in bunches, are left in boxes under the vines for other vineyard workers to collect. These boxes are then either poured into cavernous, tractor-towed trailers in the field or simply stacked on a flat trailer and sent to the winery. Speed is crucial, especially for white varieties. If the grapes are delayed in the vineyard or roughly handled, the juice of any berries with broken skins can oxidise and lose the more delicate aromas and flavours. The wine suffers accordingly. To eliminate such oxidation, the grapes are occasionally crushed and destemmed in the field, and then pumped into a sealed tanker under a layer of inert gas – such as CO_2 or nitrogen – before despatch to the winery.

HAND-PICKERS REMOVE WHOLE BUNCHES FROM THE VINES, BUT THE MECHANICAL HARVESTERS LEAVE THE STALKS INTACT, ALTHOUGH STRIPPED.

MECHANICAL HARVESTERS HAVE NOT ENHANCED THE TRADITIONAL ROMANTIC IMAGE OF THE VINTAGE, BUT THEY HAVE SLASHED PICKING COSTS.

HAND-PICKERS WIELDING SECATEURS CUT THE RIPENED FRUIT IN BUNCHES FROM THE VINES AND THEN DROP THEM INTO BOXES UNDER THE ROWS, READY TO BE COLLECTED BY A TRACTOR-DRAWN BIN OR TRAILER.

Mechanical harvesting has destroyed much of the traditional conviviality and social atmosphere of the vintage. Nevertheless, its economic advantages are beyond dispute. One machine can harvest grapes at the same rate as seventy to eighty hand-pickers. Ross Goodin – owner of New Zealand's largest contract vineyard at Te Kauwhata – calculated for the 1985 vintage that hand-picked grapes cost $78–$217 per tonne to harvest and machine-harvested grapes only $28–$50 per tonne, depending on the variety. The speed of the mechanical harvesters, which can operate twenty-four hours a day, also allows the grapes to be left longer on the vines and so achieve a more advanced stage of maturity.

The harvesters straddle the vines and lumber up and down the rows, beating the grapes off with fibreglass rods. The fruit is then carried by flat, cleated belts or revolving buckets to a large hopper being towed by a tractor in an adjacent row. Any leaves and twigs are separated by a blower and discarded on the ground.

Not all is plain sailing: Warwick Orchiston, then the winemaker at Vidal, recently made reference to 'burst hydraulic hoses of harvesters gushing oil over the fruit . . . also secateurs, rocks, parts of vineyard machinery, wood and staples [are] . . . shaken by machine harvesters from the tops of vineyard posts and collected with the fruit'. En route from the vineyard to the crusher, 'truck tarpaulins, divider door clamps and bolts' had also been harvested.

After the harvesting machine has passed, some grapes lie strewn on the ground. Since individual berries rather than whole bunches are removed, the bare stalks are still attached to the vines.

After the vintage it is time for the cold days of autumn, seemingly barren but nonetheless full of promise, to set in again.

Dr Richard Smart – New Zealand's viticultural guru – in 1985 summarised the land and personnel resources devoted to viticultural research. He listed a scientist (himself) and a technician located at Ruakura Agricultural Research Centre, Hamilton; two technicians based at Te Kauwhata Viticultural Research Station; one part-time technician in Hawke's Bay and another in Gisborne. Experimental vineyards at their disposal included those of Te Kauwhata (8ha), Rukuhia, near Hamilton (1.2ha), Lawn Road, Hawke's Bay (0.2ha) and Manutuke, Gisborne (1ha).

This clear emphasis on North Island research has not impressed many Marlborough, Nelson and Canterbury growers (although valuable research is performed at Lincoln College and the Marlborough Research Centre). A 1987 survey, conducted by Ross Bradding, then a Management Studies student at the University of Waikato, showed that although ninety percent of Auckland growers were happy with the division of research between Ruakura, Te Kauwhata and the regions, growers elsewhere all wanted more regional research. Fifty-eight percent of Marlborough growers felt that MAF's viticultural advisory officers were 'no use at all'; only fifteen percent of North Island growers thought so.

Industry participation in research is primarily channelled through VORAC, the Viticultural and Oenological Research Advisory Council, which comprises representatives of the DSIR, MAF, Health Department, the Grape Growers' Council and the Wine Institute. VORAC was set up in 1981 to co-ordinate research activity, administer research funds and, ultimately, to work towards becoming a fully fledged independent research body. A lack of industry funding, however, has hamstrung its efforts to direct viticultural research. The Wine Institute and the Grape Growers' Council in 1987 agreed to form a new committee, Wine Growers of New Zealand, to address their research needs.

A funding crisis currently threatens to undercut New Zealand research programmes. Richard Smart wrote in 1986 that although 'in relation to its size, the New Zealand viticultural industry is well supported by research . . . this resource allocation is under constant threat, particularly when export performance and potential is used as a criteria by research administrators'. Viticultural research cost around $320,000 in 1987.

Research is currently largely funded by the Government but, in keeping with the Government's cost-recovery measures, MAF funding is being reduced by 37.5 percent by 1990–91. This has led viticultural researchers to investigate the possibilities of selling grapes grown at Te Kauwhata, or leasing land, or charging royalties on trellising systems, or pursuing private consultancy work. According to Mark Kliewer, professor of viticulture at the University of California, Davis, who in 1987 reported on New Zealand's research needs, 'a compulsory mandatory levy [set as a percentage of the grape crop value] where the entire industry contributes has historically been the only successful way for funding research'.

RESEARCH

Formal research into viticulture and winemaking was from the beginning the responsibility of the Department of Agriculture. The Department, now the Ministry of Agriculture and Fisheries, still retains responsibility for viticultural field work in the grapegrowing regions. In 1981, however, responsibility for oenological research passed to the Department of Scientific and Industrial Research (DSIR).

TE KAUWHATA

The Te Kauwhata Viticultural Research Station has vitally influenced the development of the commercial wine industry. Practically every grapevine in the country has at one stage or another originated from Te Kauwhata. The station, nevertheless, has often encountered intense criticism from winemakers.

Vines were first planted at Te Kauwhata in 1897 on land described by a contemporary observer, Gerald Peacocke, as 'an expanse of poor clay hills, interspersed with a succession of miserable-looking rush swamps'. The site was originally considered by the Department of Agriculture to be suitable only for growing wattle trees. Vines were eventually established not in the belief that Te Kauwhata was an ideal location for a viticultural research centre but in order to demonstrate the agricultural possibilities of that region. The department recorded in 1899 that 'a small area has been set aside as an experimental nursery . . . If these vines and fruit trees do well it will serve as an object lesson to surrounding settlers'.

The vines, including Shiraz, Chardonnay, Cabernet Sauvignon, Pinot Noir and Riesling, thrived. Peacocke related that 'the way the vines throve on this originally unsuitable-looking land surprised everyone. Not only did the vines grow, but they bore and ripened heavy crops of grapes . . .' This success led to the erection of a small winery completed in time for the 1902 vintage.

Three years later, under Bragato, there was 'a splendid vineyard of 18 acres, a nursery of two acres and a modern cellar', complete with 3000 gallons of wine. Special trainloads of visitors journeyed from Auckland to inspect progress including, in 1902, Assid Abraham Corban.

The flourishing research activity at Te Kauwhata was cut short by the spread of sympathy for prohibition. A slump in official support, followed by Bragato's departure in 1909, led to the station's viticultural efforts being restricted to essential vineyard maintenance. Experiments ceased.

The revival of interest in winemaking after World War One, coupled with the declining economic importance of wattle bark (a source of tannin for treating hides), led eventually to the resumption of research work at Te Kauwhata. In this period Charles Woodfin imported the new hybrid varieties and planted them out on trial. Then at the worst period of the Depression the National Expenditure Commission recommended that the station should be sold ('A saving of £350 would result'). But there were no buyers.

The Te Kauwhata station took full commercial advantage of the shortage of wine during World War Two. Official policy was to produce and sell sufficient wine to cover the station's operating costs. The cellar was upgraded and the vineyard extended; apple wine was made and water used to stretch the wine supply. Little emphasis was given to research.

A CORNER OF THE RESEARCH VINEYARD AT TE KAUWHATA, SHOWING THE STATION'S PROXIMITY TO LAKE WAIKARE.

After the war a much-needed change of direction was made. Commercial wine production was scaled down and resident scientific officers, such as Denis Kasza, conducted various research projects. These, however, were performed more on individual whim than as part of a properly controlled research programme. Explicit recognition of the shifting emphasis in Te Kauwhata's activities came in 1965 when control of the station was transferred from the Horticultural to the Research Division of the Department of Agriculture.

In the 1970s scientific staff, including a viticulturist, an oenologist and a microbiologist, conducted studies in vine spacing and trellising, vine nutrition and disease control. Basic data was collected on varietal yields and ripening patterns. Experimental wines – 150 in 1976 – were made to evaluate different varieties and to combat winemaking problems.

None of this saved Te Kauwhata from frequent and quite forceful criticism. One sore point with winegrowers was the station's physical isolation from the traditional wine areas at Henderson and Hawke's Bay. Because of this remoteness, research performed at Te Kauwhata often had to be duplicated in the major wine districts. Such delays caused considerable frustration to winemakers anxious to identify and establish promising new vines. To overcome this problem, evaluation trials are now established in all the principal wine regions simultaneously with those at Te Kauwhata.

The station has also been attacked for selling its wine to the public in direct competition with the commercial wine industry. From Romeo Bragato's era onwards Te Kauwhata acquired a reputation for producing good wine. For decades its commercial wine supply was sold out on a pre-order system before release.

The Wine Manufacturers' Federation charged in 1954 that Te Kauwhata was 'gathering the vulgar propensity of a commercial winery'. Te Kauwhata, however, never produced more than three percent of New Zealand's total wine output – the real competition lay more in the field of quality. This issue was finally resolved in 1975 when the station ceased bottling wine for public sale.

THE YEAR 1902 MARKED THE FIRST VINTAGE AT TE KAUWHATA VITICULTURAL RESEARCH STATION.

Another plunge in the rollercoaster history of Te Kauwhata was narrowly averted in 1980. The Ministry of Agriculture and Fisheries proposed to close the station down – to save funds – and transfer the basic vine collection to a site near Ruakura. The Wine Institute vigorously opposed the Department's plan, and won. However, as the Institute later confirmed: 'Tensions created by the attempts by MAF to dispose of the Te Kauwhata Research Station took a long time to cool'.

Te Kauwhata subsequently was retained and upgraded, its viticultural operation still under MAF direction, but its winemaking research under the control of the DSIR.

The vinification unit at Te Kauwhata is fully equipped for experimental and small-scale winemaking. For many years it was headed by Dr Rainer Eschenbruch, now at Rongopai. Deep in the original cellars, enormous open concrete vats and old wooden casks still stand side by side. More modern equipment includes upright stainless steel fermenters, each holding one tonne of grapes, ideal for microvinification, and twenty-litre glass carboys housed in a temperature-controlled room, each linked to a supply of inert gas. Of late, MAF and the DSIR have invested heavily in upgrading facilities, including the construction of a new laboratory and office complex.

Each year the DSIR undertakes about 150 microvinifications at Te Kauwhata using experimental fruit. These wines are subjected to sensory evaluation by commercial winemakers and wine judges, whose scores are rigorously computer-analysed for consistency.

The relatively low profile of winemaking research at Te Kauwhata, as opposed to the acclaimed viticultural research, partly reflects the wealth of winemaking expertise now present in the ranks of the wine industry itself. The industry's own technical professionalism has been boosted by the formation in early 1985 of the New Zealand Society of Viticulture and Oenology, whose stated objective is to 'promote the dissemination of technical information in viticulture and oenology and related sciences for the benefit of the grape and wine industries in New Zealand'.

RICHARD SMART

Dr Richard Smart, New Zealand's viticultural sage, has hammered home a central message to winemakers here since his appointment in January 1982 as Scientist (Viticulture) at Ruakura: the standard New Zealand vine trellis, by promoting excessively dense foliage growth, is causing undue shading of the fruit at the expense both of crop yields and wine quality.

Smart is respected by his viticultural colleagues as a world authority, particularly in the area of vine-canopy management – a subject which achieves its greatest relevance in highly vigorous growing situations such as those found in most New Zealand wine regions. Formerly Dean of the School of Oenology and Viticulture at Roseworthy Agricultural College, South Australia, he chose to pursue his career in New Zealand because here, he says, he had the opportunity to devote himself to fulltime research, as opposed to his part-time teaching load in Australia. Smart also praises the research facilities here.

Richard Smart was chairman of the organising committee that brought the Second International Symposium for Cool Climate Viticulture and Oenology to Auckland in early 1988. He is down-to-earth and has a penchant for factual accuracy. He is 'the best thing that has happened to the New Zealand wine industry in my lifetime', two leading winemakers told me.

According to Richard Smart, there are three principal areas of viticultural research needed in New Zealand: vine improvement, variety evaluation and grapevine physiology and management.

DR RICHARD SMART, A DISTINGUISHED AUSTRALIAN VITICULTURAL SCIENTIST, IS ABSORBED IN THE UNRAVELLING OF NEW ZEALAND'S VITICULTURAL POTENTIAL.

VINE IMPROVEMENT

At the core of the current viticultural research programme lies an endeavour to upgrade the basic quality of New Zealand grapevines (what the scientists call 'planting material'). The object of this ongoing work on vine improvement is to enable growers to have unrestricted access to 'high health, genetically superior and correctly named' vines.

The problem with existing vineyards, the majority of which were established during the planting boom of the 1970s, is that high-quality cuttings were then often in short supply. The vines, haphazardly sourced from established commercial vineyards, are now displaying widespread virus diseases and also – because most growers chose the cheaper option of not grafting onto resistant rootstocks – the debilitating effects of phylloxera.

The MAF vine-improvement scheme got off the ground in 1982 against the backdrop of intensifying phylloxera problems in Gisborne. The writing was clearly on the wall for those growers – the majority – who had not yet replanted with grafted vines. Smart realised that 'if we missed this opportunity to provide the industry with high health . . . material, then the opportunity would not arise again for two to three decades'.

The major components of vine-improvement research are:

Development of a Vine Register

Until recently there was no comprehensive list of grapevines imported into this country over the years. Smart and his colleagues have retrieved importation records dating back to 1954 – when quarantine started – and also secured details of vine imports since 1900 from the Department of Agriculture's annual reports.

The computerised register that has emerged from these labours records full details on each variety – its source, importer, clonal and virus status and other comments. Currently the list stretches to about 1000 items including 600 imports that cannot be traced to any existing vine – they have been lost.

Once this system was developed, researchers were able to pinpoint precisely which vines were, at that stage, already in the country and which ones needed to be imported.

Search for Early Vine Introductions

Many settlers imported vines last century, most prominent of the very early ones being Marsden, Busby and Pompallier. The importance today of those early imports is that probably they were less infected with viruses than imports made after 1900, and thus represent a potentially valuable source of healthy breeding material.

About seventy-five old vines have been collected since public appeals were launched in 1984. Many are *labrusca* plants – hardy survivors in the wild – but some venerable *vinifera* vines have also been unearthed. One of these is a Meunier vine, apparently virus-free, planted no later than the 1860s by French missionaries; another is an unidentified black variety from Lake Hayes, believed to have been transported to the area by goldminers in the 1860s. Early importations of Sémillon by Joseph Soler of Wanganui have also been discovered, together with Chasselas vines introduced by French settlers at Akaroa.

Naming Problems

In 1982 Richard Smart despatched twelve rootstock samples to the world-famous French ampelographers Paul Truel and Pierre Galet. (An ampelographer specialises in the identification and description of grape species and varieties.) Smart was subsequently informed of five likely naming errors.

As Smart says, the problems of variety naming are easily overlooked, because unless you have a trained person hunting for them, they usually do not come to light. But correct identification of grape varieties is particularly important in countries such as New Zealand, where varietal labelling of wines is so common. There are clear legal implications for any wineries perpetuating the use of grapevine misnomers when, as in New Zealand, accurate varietal labelling is required by law.

Doris Zuur, a Swiss student at Waikato University, recently completed the arduous but extremely valuable task of positively identifying most of the grape varieties growing in New Zealand. Of the 436 varieties Zuur studied in the national vine collection at Te Kauwhata, 4.2 percent were wrongly named and 20.3 percent had ampelographically unacceptable synonyms. The most serious commercial misnomer she discovered was the widely planted 'Gamay Beaujolais', now positively identified as a Pinot Noir clone.

Zuur has also proposed the elimination of the use of several confusing variety synonyms, both in the vineyard and on labels. Thus Riesling would displace Rhine Riesling, Meunier would displace Pinot Meunier, Trousseau Gris would displace Grey Riesling. A direct result of her research is that the Health Department's 1983 list of grape variety names acceptable for use on labels is to be updated to eliminate errors.

Zuur's simple grapevine identification key, designed to help growers correctly identify the plants in their vineyards, should also further her goal of ensuring that the right grapes end up in the right bottles.

DORIS ZUUR'S LENGTHY AND VALUABLE THESIS, 'AMPELOGRAPHIC STUDIES OF NEW ZEALAND GRAPE VARIETIES', ARGUES COGENTLY FOR THE NEED TO CHANGE SOME OF THE NAMES APPEARING ON NEW ZEALAND WINE LABELS. HERE SHE COMPARES VINE LEAVES TO AN AMPELOGRAPHIC TEXT – A CATALOGUE IDENTIFYING THE DIFFERENT CHARACTERISTICS OF GRAPE VARIETIES.

Virus Diseases

Viruses have sapped the strength of vines in New Zealand and overseas, reducing yields and preventing ripening.

Seven virus diseases have been recorded in New Zealand. 'Leaf roll' virus – the main problem – is easily recognised by its distinctive downward roll of the leaf margins, coupled with premature autumn colouring of the leaves. Other debilitating viruses include 'fan leaf' and 'corky bark', and as recently as 1986 a virus disease previously unknown in New Zealand, 'Rupestris stem pitting', was discovered.

These viruses appear to have originated from the original vine collections at Te Kauwhata. Some rootstocks used in the war against phylloxera in the early years are now known to have been symptomless carriers of virus diseases. Most of the country's vines have been propagated from these early Te Kauwhata plants and the viruses have simply been passed down from one generation to the next.

It has thus become crucial for the future health of New Zealand's vineyards to detect infected plants and ensure they are no longer used for propagation purposes. In 1983, 230 varieties and clones in the country's old collections were surveyed for their incidence of virus diseases and a high proportion showed virus symptoms. Virus testing was introduced and by 1985 fifty-seven vines showed 'leaf roll' infection and three 'corky bark'.

A major virus-elimination programme began in 1983 at Ruakura and at the DSIR laboratories at Palmerston North and Mt Albert. Using thermotherapy and tissue culture, 123 different varieties and clones were treated, and then planted in late 1984 at the Rukuhia National Foundation Vineyard near Hamilton. This collection is expected to be the source of certified virus-free planting material in the future.

The final outcome of these procedures must be better wines. Professor Mark Kliewer has categorically observed that 'the virus eradication programme in California has done more to improve productivity and quality of vineyards than any other single area of research'. A survey of healthy and badly virused Cabernet Sauvignon vines at Henderson has shown how far viruses can weaken a plant's performance. The healthy vines, cropping twice as heavily, ripened their fruit two weeks earlier with superior skin colours, lower acids and a twenty percent increase in sugar levels.

VIRUSES WEAKEN THE VINE, REDUCE THE CROP, RETARD RIPENING – AND CAUSE PREMATURE AUTUMN COLOURING OF THE LEAVES. THESE VINE LEAVES SHOW SYMPTOMS OF LEAF-ROLL VIRUS.

Clonal Selection

Elimination of viruses offers one way to improve our vineyards. Clonal selection offers another.

Sometimes vines of the same variety, planted side by side, show different characteristics. Often one is visibly superior to the other, with a heavier crop, finer fruit quality, or both. The selection and propagation of these individual clones – or strains – is called clonal selection.

As a general rule, the European wine countries improve their vineyards by upgrading their established varieties. Through a painstaking selection of vines over many years, a clone may be obtained that is outstandingly well adapted to a particular area. The Germans, for instance, claim since 1920 to have improved by clonal selection the yield of Riesling vines by up to 400 percent.

A clonal-selection programme for Müller-Thurgau, Chardonnay, Gewürztraminer and Cabernet Sauvignon got off the ground in New Zealand in 1982. After three years spent observing their yield and fruit composition in the vineyard, up to twenty-eight clones of each of the four varieties were planted in Hawke's Bay and Auckland for ongoing evaluation. The first recommendations are due in 1992.

Vine Imports

The most rapid and effective way to upgrade our vineyards is to import new clones of the most important classic varieties. Drawing on the broad range of European and American clones – carefully selected for their fruit quality, yield, virus freedom and disease resistance – gives viticulturists here far more planting options than having to rely on the modest lineup of clones currently in the country.

Richard Smart and Allan Clarke (a viticultural specialist based at the DSIR's Mt Albert Research Centre) have been working on a major vine-importing programme since 1982. According to Smart, previous efforts have been 'haphazard and not always done with knowledge of what was in the country and its virus status, and what was needed'. The range of clones of commercially popular varieties was not up to scratch; for instance, despite its pervasive vineyard presence, only two clones of Müller-

Thurgau had been imported. Many vines had been lost. One clone of Riesling had been imported on four separate occasions. Only half the range of rootstocks was available in 1982 as was clearly documented as having been available in 1905.

Between 1982 and 1985 Smart and Clarke co-ordinated the importation of many vines including six Chardonnay clones, four Sauvignon Blanc clones, three Pinot Noir clones plus such hitherto unavailable varieties as Petit Verdot (a very late-ripening Médoc grape giving dark, spicy wine) and Gamay Noir (the true Gamay grape of Beaujolais fame). These vines are all quarantined for two or three years before they are distributed.

Vine Distribution

Having located healthy vines, it is vital to build a distribution system that ensures growers have ready access to this improved material.

The New Zealand Vine Improvement Scheme was established in 1983. Co-ordinated by Allan Clarke, it is modelled on a highly successful grower self-help system developed in South Australia. Each region – including Central Otago – has its own committee which organises the establishment of source blocks of improved vines and also distributes buds from them.

The Vine Improvement Scheme has already begun to distribute upgraded planting material – by 1985 the first of a range of new rootstocks had been released – and these committees are now playing a central role in guaranteeing that commercial growers have access to quality vines.

Phylloxera

Almost a century after Romeo Bragato's identification of phylloxera and his sound advice on its treatment, New Zealand is still highly vulnerable to the pest. The phylloxera aphids attack by swarming over the roots and sucking on the vine's sap. Tumours develop on the damaged roots and the vine weakens and eventually dies.

Phylloxera was discovered in Hawke's Bay in 1964, negating a long-standing belief that the aphid was confined to areas north of the Waikato. The pest was found in 1970 in Gisborne and by 1982 about ninety percent of all Gisborne vineyard blocks was afflicted. A study by Doug King and John Meekings of the spread of phylloxera in three Gisborne vineyards found that the percentage of infested vines soared from twenty-two percent in 1982 to forty-one percent in 1983 and seventy-four percent in 1984.

In January 1984 phylloxera was detected on the roots of three weak vines in Marlborough. A survey two months later of fifteen other Marlborough vineyards found no further sign of the dreaded pest, but the rigorous confinement measures since adopted – including the replanting and spraying with insecticides of the infected block and meticulous cleaning of machinery – will only delay, rather than prevent, the inevitable spread of the disease in Marlborough.

Infested nursery material is the most likely cause of the spread of phylloxera in this country. According to G.H. Buchanan, an Australian entomologist whose study 'Grape Phylloxera in New Zealand' was published in 1982, the development of the newer planting regions in Gisborne, Marlborough and parts of Hawke's Bay took place with nursery material sourced from Auckland and the Waikato. 'Nursery material, including rooted vines, has been allowed to move from infested areas to new, uninfested areas provided it was subjected to a lindane-oil dip. Given the pressures of the enormous demand for planting material caused by the rapid expansion of New Zealand's viticulture, it would not be surprising if some nursery procedures were inadequately supervised or executed.'

The plants most vulnerable to phylloxera are *vinifera* varieties growing on their own roots. Some native American *labrusca* vines have strong resistance to the aphid and are used widely throughout the world as phylloxera-resistant rootstocks on which to graft the classic *vinifera* vines.

New Zealand's recent problem with phylloxera arises because its newer viticultural regions have been developed overwhelmingly with ungrafted vines. Most growers have sought to avoid the higher costs involved in planting grafted plants, and have opted for the easier alternative of simply establishing cuttings on their own roots. The 1983 'Hartevelt' Committee concluded that planting decisions had 'been influenced by relative prices of around three dollars for grafted [vines] and around thirty cents for own-rooted, and the tax advantages of later upgrading from own-rooted to grafted as a 'maintenance expenditure' qualifying for immediate full write-off . . .'

Most of our vines – eighty-three percent in 1980, declining to fifty-nine percent by 1986 (with a further 7.8 percent of vines being of unknown grafting status) – are ungrafted.

Mercifully, in view of the widespread presence of phylloxera in New Zealand, it appears to cause – in the short term, anyway – less severe damage here than in hotter, drier regions. Buchanan found phylloxera damage in New Zealand to be less severe than in Victoria, partly because of this country's cooler temperatures (giving a more gradual phylloxera population growth).

Phylloxera-damaged vines are highly susceptible to water stress. During the 1982–83 growing season in Gisborne, when December–February rainfall totalled only nineteen millimetres, vine vigour dropped dramatically in many vineyards. The following season, when rainfall over the same period totalled 208 millimetres, most vines staged a readily visible health comeback.

Phylloxera can even, through its devigorating effect on vines, enhance fruit ripeness. Damaged vines in a recent New Zealand study produced a crop one degree brix (a measure of the sugar level in grapejuice) sweeter than grapes off unaffected vines – but their yield was down by over ninety-nine percent.

Ultimately, replanting with grafted vines is the only answer.

A VINE SHOWING STRESS SYMPTOMS DUE TO PHYLLOXERA ATTACK.

VARIETY EVALUATION

Wine Grape Evaluation

Performance testing of new grape varieties has not been accorded high priority by New Zealand viticultural scientists until recently, owing to the widespread feeling that the future of the New Zealand industry would be based upon improved clones of the classic varieties already established here.

Now the industry's compelling need to develop a new source of low-cost bulk grapes – to combat the challenge of cheap wines from Australia under CER – has encouraged researchers to look closely at a new breed of German hybrids which yields superior wine to the old French hybrids. By using these new disease-resistant hybrids in combination with minimal pruning, Richard Smart has calculated that growers could conceivably lower costs of grape production by up to forty percent. Labour and chemical costs drop sharply.

A new variety-evaluation programme commenced in 1983. First, six vines of each new variety are planted at Te Kauwhata for limited fruit and wine analyses. Promising varieties are then evaluated in the various regions, on several rootstocks, before larger plantings are made to permit more commercial-scale evaluations.

Rootstock Evaluation

Viticulturists initially became interested in grafted plants as a means of combating phylloxera. Later it became obvious that rootstocks can also influence the size and quality of a vine's crop.

Rootstocks display wide variations in their resistance to phylloxera, affinity with different varieties, adaptation to various soil types and ability to promote yields. It is important, therefore, to match a variety with the right stock and the stock itself to the local soils and climate. New Zealand has traditionally been overly dependent on the single rootstock Mourvedre × Rupestris 1202.

This stock became popular both for its ready adaptation to Henderson's clay soils and as an early stock capable of bringing grapes to a reasonable level of ripeness before the onset of autumn rains. The problem, however, is that powerful rootstocks such as 1202 produce heavy vegetative growth at the cost of full ripening of the fruit.

Recently, New Zealand winemakers have started to switch away from 1202 in favour of weaker stocks, capable of bringing the grapes to a more advanced level of maturity. According to the 1986 vineyard survey, plantings of 1202 (now in second place) have been outstripped by S04, a moderate-to-vigorous rootstock which likes well-drained soils of lower fertility. Devigorating stocks will be more commonly used in future to reduce foliage growth.

The previous availability of phylloxera-resistant and virus-free rootstocks has been very limited. Most commercial stocks – except 1202 – have been more or less infected with viruses, although not with 'leaf roll'.

A further complication for growers to worry about is the strong evidence now emerging of the existence of different biotypes (or strains) of phylloxera in different countries, including New Zealand. In the past, New Zealand has selected rootstocks largely on the basis of European evaluations of their phylloxera-resistant qualities. Local research has now investigated the impact of local phylloxera biotypes on different rootstocks.

ROTBURGER (SYNONYM ZWEIGELT BLAU) IS HARDY AND EARLY RIPENING. IN AUSTRIA – WHERE IT IS THE THIRD MOST POPULAR RED GRAPE – ACCORDING TO WINE COMMENTATOR JANCIS ROBINSON, 'THE WINES IT PRODUCES . . . ARE DESIGNED TO APPEAL TO THE AUSTRIAN PALATE. ITS YIELD IS DESIGNED TO APPEAL TO THE AUSTRIAN GROWER'.

GRAPEVINE PHYSIOLOGY AND MANAGEMENT

Shading

Dr Smart and his research colleagues have cogently demonstrated that the conventional system of training grapevines here is far from ideal. Our natural growing conditions of high – often too high – fertility promote exuberant vine growth, which on the restrictive standard New Zealand trellis leads to the formation of densely leafed canopies creating high levels of shade. The negative effects of shade on vine yield and wine quality are well documented. According to Smart, apart from securing healthy vines 'the principal problems affecting the quality of the wine-grape harvest in New Zealand are those of within-canopy shading'.

An ideal vine canopy should have one to two layers of leaves. In thicker canopies, the interior leaves receive less than one percent of the ambient sunlight, which is insufficient for photosynthesis to occur. Also, the proportions of 'red' to 'far-red' light are reduced in the canopy, affecting anthocyanin and phenol synthesis. Only the outside leaves are able to contribute significantly to photosynthesis; those in the heart of the canopy, which frequently turn yellow and drop off, are a potential source of botrytis infection.

Shading at the canopy centre has negative implications for both crop size and quality. The shading of fruit buds lowers bud fruitfulness; heavy canopies usually display a higher percentage of non-fruitful shoots. Heavy shading also harms wine quality by lowering sugar, phenol and anthocyanin levels in the fruit, while raising such undesirables as malic acid and potassium (leading to higher pH). Colour development in red grapes is retarded and, because shaded bunches dry more slowly after rain – owing to the lower levels of sunlight and less wind penetration – botrytis is also encouraged.

The remedy for this plethora of problems caused by too dense vine canopies, says Smart, is canopy division, 'that is, a dense canopy is divided into two separate curtains. The curtains and shoots within the curtains should be far enough apart so that they do not cause excessive shade . . . by spreading the canopy one can maintain good fruit and leaf exposure as well as high yield. This is the reason for a worldwide resurgence of interest in studies of grapevine-training systems'.

A REDUCTION OF THE PROBLEM OF FRUIT SHADING PROMISES RIPER, HEALTHIER GRAPES FOR WINEMAKERS TO PROCESS. NOTE HOW THE HEAVY AND LIGHTER VINE CANOPIES AFFECT THE FRUIT'S EXPOSURE TO SUNLIGHT. ABOVE, A DENSE CANOPY WITH NO FRUIT VISIBLE AND NO GAPS FOR SUNLIGHT TO PENETRATE. BELOW, A FRUIT ZONE WITHOUT SHADING, OWING TO WIDE SPACING BETWEEN THE SHOOTS, AND LEAF PLUCKING.

Trellising

Trials conducted on five training systems at Te Kauwhata showed that the smallest crops and lowest quality fruit came from the standard New Zealand trellis. Using Gewürztraminer vines – a variety ideal for this type of trial because of its characteristic leafiness and high fruit pH levels – the trial showed in 1984 that divided canopies significantly reduce juice pH, and in 1984 and 1985 that divided canopies can double yields over the standard trellis while achieving equal sugar levels.

The Geneva Double Curtain trellising system exposes the fruit at the top of the canopy, with the shoots positioned downwards in two separated curtains of foliage. The 'U' trellising system, a modification of Alain Carbonneau's 'U' trellis, developed for Cabernet Sauvignon in Bordeaux, has two sloping curtains, this time with the fruit at the bottom. A 1987 study by David Crawford, 'Economics of New Trellis Systems', demonstrated that the profitability of cultivating the notoriously shy-bearing Gewürztraminer variety could be greatly enhanced by the extra yields gained by converting a standard trellis to a 'U' or 'GDC' trellising system.

The spotlight, however, has most often been played on Smart's Te Kauwhata Two Tier system (TK2T). A trellis system capable of being

THE STANDARD NEW ZEALAND TRELLISING SYSTEM, WITH THE FRUIT ZONE HAVING BEEN EXPOSED TO THE SUNLIGHT BY LEAF PLUCKING.

installed in existing vineyards without too many alterations, it involves two curtains of foliage, one positioned above the other, with a gap of about twenty centimetres between them. Careful and swift summer pruning is needed to prevent the two canopies intertwining.

Although harvesters can be adapted to the TK2T system, and it is claimed to maintain grape sugars while reducing juice pH, in 1986 Smart wrote that further experiments were necessary before any positive recommendations could be issued for commercial adoption of the TK2T.

The 'Scott Henry' system is another form of the TK2T, named after the Oregonian who invented it. It is conveniently installed on the standard New Zealand trellis, needing only the addition of a pair of movable foliage wires. A two-tier canopy is achieved by wrapping the bottom canes loosely during pruning and later rolling the canes through ninety degrees so the foliage grows downwards. The drawback for larger vineyards is the precise timing needed: shoot positioning must be started and completed soon after flowering, not too early (shoots will break off at the base) and not too late (when tendrils have bound the canopy together).

Smart has suggested growers should try the Scott Henry system on a limited basis. Ross Goodin, of Waikare Vineyards at Te Kauwhata, ran commercial trials and found the Scott Henry system to be 'practical to develop from the standard trellis, with some advantages in pruning, tucking and picking. Improved-quality grapes were produced, especially as regards freedom from rot'.

Another exciting trellis trial is being conducted at Rukuhia Horticultural Research Station near Hamilton. Experiments with Cabernet Franc have shown that a new system, the Ruakura Twin Two Tier (RT2T), can triple yields over the standard trellis while preserving or even enhancing wine quality. This system, currently being developed as a steel structure, is being evaluated in the United States and Australia as well as in New Zealand.

THE TE KAUWHATA TWO-TIER TRELLISING SYSTEM, SHOWING LEAF-PLUCKED GEWÜRZTRAMINER VINES. THE FINAL COMMERCIAL VERDICT ON THIS SYSTEM HAS NOT YET BEEN GIVEN.

CHAPTER THREE

Winemaking in New Zealand

WHITE WINES

The wine grape is unique: most fruits can be made to produce an acceptable alcoholic beverage, but only a few classic grape types can yield wine of real distinction.

Grapes are the usual and most natural source for making wine. Ripe grapes contain an unusually high level of sugar, sufficient to produce by fermentation the level of alcohol necessary in wine. The yeasts needed to activate the fermentation are conveniently located in the 'bloom' on the surface of the berries. Grapes are also more juicy and possess more complex flavours than other fruits, and it is these qualities which have made 'wine' synonymous with 'grape wine'.

The basic potential of a wine is set by its fruit quality. Beyond this, the skill of the winemaker and the quality of his or her equipment become important. With modern technology, it is more likely that the potential inherent in the fruit can be carried forward into the finished wine. Recent research into the finer details of juice handling, fermentation and aging has brought new winery methods and equipment. An outstanding example is refrigeration, a late arrival on the New Zealand wine scene but now widely used to stabilise wine, hold back unfermented grapejuice and control fermentation.

Many of the old established wineries in New Zealand were slow to appreciate the advantages of modern technology, because ancient traditions of peasant winemaking stood in the way. Most wineries were technically ill-prepared when public demand switched from heavy dessert to white table wines. It is a fortunate irony that New Zealand's late development of interest in wine science has allowed the wine industry to avoid other countries' mistakes and to adopt only the established best. The present level of sophistication of our wine technology compares well with overseas regions.

Before entering into the particulars of white and red winemaking it is useful to know the general techniques that are common to both:

The transport of the fresh-picked fruit from vineyard to winery can itself help to make or mar the quality of the eventual wine. Juice flowing from damaged berries, or freed by the successive tipping of the grapes from the harvester into tip trailers and then into trucks, can be oxidised after only one hour.

Depending on the variety and its condition, the type of harvester, the frequency of tips and the proximity of the winery, 'juicing' levels can range from ten to thirty percent of the grapes' juice contents. Should the journey from the vineyard to the crusher be lengthy – Gisborne or Hawke's Bay to Auckland is very common – juicing levels can soar even higher.

Prolonged transport of truckloads of grapes, often in warm autumn temperatures, demands adequate fruit protection. Sulphur-dioxide is thus added to the fruit at the harvester in the vineyard, rather than waiting until the fruit arrives at the crusher.

After their removal from the vines, white grapes are crushed as soon as possible, because white-wine juices are highly vulnerable to oxidation and browning, and if too much time elapses between picking and crushing the risk of spoilage increases. If you detect browning in a finished wine, it indicates that most of the delicate fruit flavours have been lost through oxidation.

Without oxygen many bacteria and fungi are unable to grow and spoil wine – although others function anaerobically – so that when making white wine it is essential to keep the juice away from air. The main problem caused by aeration is oxidation, which leads to a loss of fruit character. In cellars where wine has been made for a long time, there can be a multitude of spoilage yeasts and other micro-organisms present in the air and on equipment, eager to seize on the sugar and alcohol ingredients in wine. If they succeed, the wine develops unwanted surface yeast growths plus off-flavours and odours. Formation of acetic acid – the main spoilage indicator in wine – is an ever-present danger. To avoid spoilage, wine must be isolated from the air, in full vessels, and protected under layers of inert gas such as carbon dioxide and nitrogen.

CRUSHING

Crushing simply involves bursting the skins to free the juice for its fermentation. Contrary to romantic belief, crushing is no longer achieved by vineyard labourers prancing gleefully on the new season's fruit. Although one or two companies initiate crushing operations in the field, usually the intact grapes are emptied at the winery into a receiving hopper. Then the fruit, splitting under its own weight and with the juice beginning to run, is pulled by a large archimedes screw through into a de-stemming device.

Since grape stalks harbour a great deal of tannin that could make the juice too astringent, hand-picked grapes are detached from their stalks during crushing. Mechanical harvesters, of course, leave the stalks on the vines.

SULPHUR-DIOXIDE

Crushed grapes are called 'must'. At this stage, in order to inhibit the yeasts and bacteria present in the juice and to prevent oxidation, sulphur-dioxide is added.

Sulphur-dioxide has been the main preservative used in winemaking for centuries. Added to wine, SO_2 rapidly changes to sulphurous acid (H_2SO_3) which has a special capacity to absorb oxygen. White wines lacking sufficient sulphur-dioxide are prone to oxidise and develop a coarse, sherry-like character. SO_2 is also utilised to sterilise casks, bottles and corks.

Grapes consist of three basic elements: the 'bloom' on the surface of the skins, carrying yeasts and other micro-organisms; the skins, which contain colouring and flavouring substances; and the inner pulp and juice, which consists basically of water and sugar along with acids and other flavour components. For the winemaker the skins and the juice are the items of real interest.

Good wines are not easily made. Nevertheless, the myriad tasks of a modern winery are simply elaborations of a basic process.

When grapes are crushed, the yeasts present on the skins enter the juice and convert the grape sugars into alcohol and carbon dioxide. The seething of the juice during fermentation is caused by the evolution of CO_2 as a gas. When the sugar supply is exhausted, the wine is made and the yeasts sink to the bottom of the tank. The newly made wine is then pumped off its sediment, clarified, stabilised, and either bottled immediately or stored away in casks and tanks to await bottling or to mature.

ABOVE LEFT: UNLOADING A TRUCK-LOAD OF GRAPES AT MONTANA. TO GUARD AGAINST LOSS OF FRUIT QUALITY DURING THE JOURNEY FROM HARVESTER TO CRUSHER, SULPHUR-DIOXIDE IS USUALLY SPRINKLED OVER THE GRAPES IN THE VINEYARD.

AN AVALANCHE OF GRAPES DESCENDS INTO THE HOPPER. FROM HERE THE SPLITTING FRUIT IS PULLED BY A LARGE ARCHIMEDES SCREW THROUGH INTO THE CRUSHER.

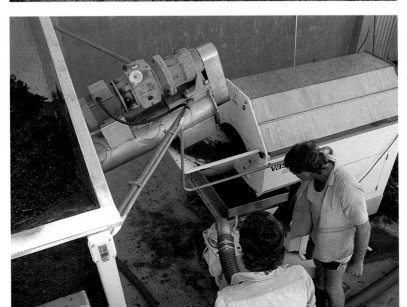

ON THE JOURNEY THROUGH THE CRUSHER, HAND-PICKED FRUIT IS DETACHED FROM THE STALKS, HERE CLEARLY VISIBLE ON THE GROUND.

The problem is that even low concentrations of sulphur-dioxide can impart a pungent, off-putting odour to wine. It is crucial to strike the right balance. New Zealand regulations set maximum levels of between 200 and 400 parts per million, depending on the residual sugar content.

JUICE SEPARATION

The journey through the de-stemmer removes the stalks and crushes the grapes. Superior quality 'free-run' juice can then be recovered by draining the must inside a tank with a slotted false side, or from under the press before squeezing the skins.

Further juice comes in stages from the mechanical pressing of the grapes. The Willmes bag press, for example, uses compressed air to swell a rubber bag in its centre, which presses the skins and pulp against a perforated outer shell. Another, the multi-stage continuous press, gives the winemaker close control over the separation of juices from a large volume of grapes. The first stage yields free-run juice, the second applies a gentle pressure, and a hard pressing makes the final extraction.

With each pressing the quality of the juice deteriorates. Free-run juice, the most delicate, is often fermented separately to make the top wine. Subsequent pressings contain higher levels of tannin and suspended solids and are more vulnerable to oxidation. The last pressing, which dries out the skins, yields juice usually considered suitable only for fortified wine production. Occasionally, some of this more robust juice is blended back into the free-run juice to boost the flavour.

FIELD CRUSHING IS RELATIVELY RARE, BUT CAN PREVENT POTENTIAL FRUIT SPOILAGE BY LOWERING THE TIME BETWEEN PICKING AND CRUSHING TO AN ABSOLUTE MINIMUM.

AFTER THE FREE-RUN JUICE HAS BEEN DRAINED OFF, THE REMAINING MASS OF SKINS, PIPS AND PULP IS STILL SATURATED WITH JUICE. TO RECOVER THIS COARSER JUICE, THE RESIDUE IS PULLED THROUGH INTO A PRESS.

DRY GRAPE RESIDUE BEING DISCARDED FROM A CONTINUOUS PRESS AT BABICH, AFTER THE JUICE HAS ALL BEEN REMOVED.

Although it is usual to make a swift separation of white-wine juice from the skins, this is not a hard and fast rule, as the period of contact depends on the style of wine being made. Where the goal is a light, delicate white or a white wine produced from black-skinned varieties, the juice is removed immediately. If a more substantial style is sought, a trend emerging in New Zealand is to allow, say, between four and twelve hours of skin contact, in an effort to step up the colour and flavour of the finished wine. Another alternative is to ferment the juice briefly on the skins, before removing the skins and continuing to ferment the juice alone.

CLARIFYING THE JUICE

After pressing, the juice contains a turbid accumulation of organic matter – particles of skin and pulp and broken-down yeast cells. These are prone to produce off-flavours (especially hydrogen-sulphide) during fermentation. Fermenting a clear juice is more likely to produce sound wine.

Sometimes the must is allowed to settle for a day or two after pressing and then it is pumped off the sediment. In New Zealand, a centrifuge is more often used to reduce the handling time. The centrifuge – looking like a cream separator and operating on the same principle – employs centrifugal force to throw the solids to the outer reaches of spinning discs, and the polished juice goes down the centre.

Then sugar and acid levels are adjusted, where necessary, to prepare the juice for its fermentation.

CRUSHED AND PRESSED GRAPES AFTER SEPARATION FROM THE JUICE. THIS RESIDUE IS DISCARDED.

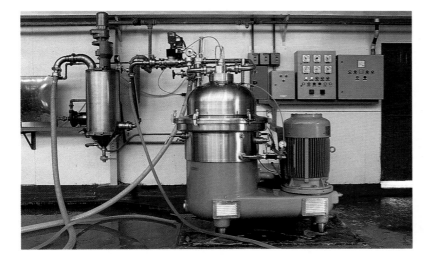

CENTRIFUGES ARE NOW COMMONLY USED IN LARGER WINERIES TO CLEAR THE MUST AFTER PRESSING AND PRIOR TO THE FERMENTATION.

SUGAR

Sugaring in New Zealand wine was once a controversial issue. Winemakers in the past have undeniably made much use of sugar relative to the gallonage of wine produced. For the 1967–68 season, for instance, Frank Thorpy calculated that the wine industry used nearly four pounds of sugar for every gallon of wine.

More of this 'Chelsea sunshine' was used to produce alcohol than for sweetening. When there is insufficient sugar in the juice to achieve through fermentation a stable level of alcohol (nine to eleven percent) in the finished wine, the winemaker usually adds a sugar and water solution, which dilutes the juice, but is more practical than adding crystal sugar. Sugar added to the must before fermentation has little discernible effect on the flavour of wine.

More recently the fruit has come on stream from new, earlier-ripening varieties and from healthier vines of established varieties, so that the natural sugar content of the grapes has risen. Nevertheless 'chaptalisation' (raising the level of sugar in musts) will always be needed in poorer years. New Zealand is hardly unique in this: all the cooler wine regions in 'lesser' vintages find it essential to supplement their low natural grape sugars. In Germany, for example, winemakers often add sugar to the must: up to fifteen percent for the lowest grade, Tafelwein, and up to ten percent in the middle category, Qualitätswein. Superior (Qualitätswein mit Prädikat) wines are by law not allowed to be chaptalised, although that does not necessarily prevent its occurrence.

ACIDITY

Acidity is vital to the colour, preservation and flavour of white wines. In its correct balance, acid imparts the desirable qualities of freshness and firmness, but too much acid leaves the wine sharp and sour. Temperate regions such as New Zealand often harvest grapes with a high natural acidity, sometimes too high.

Various options are available to the winemaker to de-acidify a high-acid must before the fermentation, including the simple addition of $CaCo_3$, known as 'chalking'. High and low acid musts can also be blended togther. Well-ripened early varieties may even arrive at the winery deficient in acidity, and here tartaric acid will be added to prevent the finished wine tasting flabby.

A crisp and lively acidity is normally one of the more engaging and instantly recognisable hallmarks of New Zealand whites.

WATER IN WINE

Adding water, which is the most obvious way to reduce acidity in wine, used to be only too well known in New Zealand. 'Oenological amelioration' was the official jargon for the practice of adding water to wine (or more accurately grapejuice) in an effort to improve its quality, and it was illegal in New Zealand until 1980. Nevertheless its use was unofficially tolerated, since it enabled winemakers to combat low sugars and high acids and reduce the coarse flavours of hybrid wines. Even government agencies were deeply involved in the practice of wine amelioration (or adulteration – it depends on your point of view). During the Second World War, for instance, the Department of Agriculture sanctioned the addition by winemakers of up to one-third water to their wines.

Wine watering, although rarely discussed outside industry circles, was routine procedure in most wineries. In 1971 an analysis by the DSIR found that about eighty percent of the sixty-eight white wines had been watered. A later study of 123 white wines entered in the 1977 National Wine Competition revealed a big improvement: the percentage of samples illegally diluted with water had dropped to twenty-seven percent.

Cask wines and fortifieds were nonetheless still heavily adulterated. In 1979 a Health Department investigation into the quality of cask wines found that half of those surveyed had 'indisputably' been stretched, some of them by more than fifty percent. In the same year the issue was brought to a head when Montana Wines introduced into the market casks of 'Brother Dominic'.

'Brother Dominic' was packaged and labelled like wine, and with massive promotion soon captured a lucrative slice of the bulk wine market. In terms of the Food and Drug Regulations, however, 'Brother Dominic' was an 'alcoholic beverage' made with limited assistance from grapes. The product aroused the ire of competing wine companies and the ensuing scrap soon riveted the attention of the media on the question of water and wine.

The Government hastened to change the regulations on winemaking prior to the 1980 harvest. On the grounds that a total ban on wine-watering would be impractical, the previous prohibition against water addition was dropped. Under the new regulations, all table wines were now required to contain a minimum eighty percent of grapejuice, and the juice level in wines named by grape variety or labelled as 'premium' or 'private bin' had to reach ninety-five percent. This allowed winemakers to add up to twenty percent water (where necessary) to table wines to aid de-acidification, chaptalisation and other winery procedures such as racking and fining.

To legalise what had once been illegal struck some critics as an odd way to reduce the water content of New Zealand wine. The paradox was resolved, however, by the Health Department's intention to firmly enforce the new rules. In reality the threat of official action resulted in a substantial reduction in use of the water-hose.

Since that period, riper fruit has come on stream from new and improved grape varieties. Following a 1983 tightening of the regulations, water may still be added to table wine, solely for the purpose of incorporating additives, in a proportion up to fifty millilitres per litre of wine (Australia limits water addition to thirty millilitres per litre of wine). This ninety-five percent minimum grapejuice level for *all* table wines has ensured that future vintages genuinely deserve to be called wine.

PIVOTAL TO THE SUCCESS OF THE WHOLE WINEMAKING PROCESS IS, OF COURSE, THE WINEMAKER. GERMAN-BORN NORBERT SEIBEL – SEEN HERE WITH HIS OWN LABEL – FASHIONED OUTSTANDING RIESLINGS AND GEWÜRZTRAMINERS FOR CORBANS AND HAS RECENTLY INTRODUCED SUBSTANTIAL IMPROVEMENTS AT PLEASANT VALLEY.

YEASTS

Yeasts are single-celled micro-organisms that grow and multiply during fermentation, using the sugar in the juice as a source of energy. Yeasts occur naturally on grapeskins and are also present in cellars, in the air, and on equipment.

Viticultural scientist Dr Jack Parle investigated the yeasts responsible for the natural fermentation of wine in New Zealand. The species of most interest to winemakers, *Saccharomyces cerevisiae*, is present only in small numbers. *Kloeckera apiculata*, the dominant type, yields a low level of alcohol and imparts an unpleasant flavour to wine. Yeasts such as this can also ruin wine by producing acetic acid and hydrogen-sulphide.

Since some yeasts have these bad fermentation characteristics, most wineries inhibit natural yeast growth by adding sulphur-dioxide to the must after crushing, and later initiate the fermentation with a selected 'pure' wine yeast.

'Cold fermentation' yeasts are now widely used in New Zealand. These yeasts are better able to tolerate high levels of sugar, alcohol and carbon dioxide during fermentation, the bouquet is improved, and the wine tends to be more constant in character and quality. By selecting individual yeast strains, the winemaker is also able to influence the secondary flavours produced during fermentation.

A mutant yeast recently developed in New Zealand has been hailed as a bacteriological breakthrough of worldwide significance. Successfully trialled in 1988 at Coopers Creek, *Schizosaccharomyces malidevorans* II swiftly lowers the sharp malic acid in unfermented grapejuice, thus allowing more drinkable and better-balanced wines to be made in cooler seasons.

FERMENTATION

After inoculation with a selected yeast culture, the first bubbles of CO_2 gas appearing in the juice signal that fermentation has begun.

The process of fermentation is essentially the conversion of sugar to alcohol and so of grapejuice to wine. The basic reaction can be shown thus:

Sugar + Yeast → Ethyl Alcohol + Carbon Dioxide + Energy.

Alcohol is the primary end product – New Zealand prescribes an upper limit of fifteen percent alcohol by volume for table wines – but other taste components also emerge that have a bearing on the final flavour of the wine. And as the acids in the wine combine with the alcohol, the elements that comprise the bouquet develop.

Usually the wine is fermented through to dryness, although sometimes the winemaker will act to stop the fermentation so as to retain a little residual sweetness.

Until about twenty years ago most New Zealand wineries used open fermenting vats made of wood or concrete. Wood, an easy material to shape, was the usual means of wine storage for our pioneer winemakers, and for them a knowledge of coopering was essential.

A BATTERY OF WINE-FERMENTATION TANKS AT CLOUDY BAY. VISITORS ARE OFTEN STRUCK BY THE PERVASIVE USE OF STAINLESS STEEL IN NEW ZEALAND WINEMAKING. ITS POPULARITY STEMS FROM THE FACT THAT, UNLIKE COPPER OR IRON, STAINLESS STEEL DOES NOT REACT CHEMICALLY WITH WINE.

Later, wooden vats were replaced by concrete vats lined with a neutral surfacing material. Open concrete vats coated with polyurethane are still seen, but they are rarely used today for the fermentation of white wines; to avoid the loss through air contact of elements crucial to the development of the bouquet and flavour, almost invariably white wines are fermented in enclosed stainless steel tanks.

During fermentation pressure builds up inside the tanks from the evolution of CO_2 gas. Wines fermented in a sealed tank often retain a small amount of CO_2 after bottling – leaving a 'spritzig' tingle in the mouth.

Cold Fermentation

An uncontrolled, hot fermentation is prone to yield a spoiled wine. Overseas, control over the build-up of heat during fermentation is sometimes achieved by fermenting wine in cool underground cellars. Until twenty years ago in New Zealand, however, the fermentation was slowed by simply adding heavy doses of sulphur-dioxide.

Corbans introduced cold fermentation techniques to New Zealand in the 1960s. It was apparent immediately that white wines which were fermented at a low temperature were noticeably more fragrant and fuller in flavour than those made by traditional methods. Cold fermentation allowed the winemaker to trap some of the aroma and flavour components that would otherwise escape with the gas.

Today it is customary to ferment white wines at 15°C or below. Sometimes water is passed through coils immersed in a fermentation tank or allowed to spill down the outside of the tank. Usually more sophisticated refrigeration methods are used. A coolant is run through a pipe spiralled between the inner and outer jackets of the tank, the heat generated during fermentation is dissipated and the ferment slows from a few days to three weeks or more.

WATER-COOLED TANKS. LOW TEMPERATURES (10–15 DEGREES CELSIUS) ARE ESPECIALLY IMPORTANT FOR WHITE WINES, DURING BOTH FERMENTATION AND STORAGE.

THIS 'ROTARY DRUM VACUUM FILTRATION UNIT'
IS USED FOR FILTERING THE LEES, THE
SEDIMENT AND WINE LEFT IN THE BOTTOM OF A
TANK AFTER THE MAJORITY OF THE WINE HAS
BEEN RACKED OFF – PUMPED AWAY INTO
ANOTHER STORAGE VESSEL.

CLARIFICATION

After the fermentation there is usually no sugar left. The yeasts are now inactive and gradually sink to the bottom of the tank where, with other sediment, they are known as 'lees'. At this stage the new wine is essentially unstable. Clarification involves the removal of these remaining solids in the wine by centrifuging – usually in larger wineries – racking, fining and filtering.

Racking is the removal of a wine from its lees by pumping it from one container to another. The first racking takes place as soon as possible after fermentation, to prevent off-flavours – especially that of hydrogen-sulphide – developing through the decomposition of yeast cells.

Although most of the solid material in a new wine settles naturally in the lees, a fine haze of proteins and yeast particles tends to remain in suspension. Fining materials such as bentonite (a type of clay) and gelatine are sometimes used as a kind of net to draw the suspended solids to the bottom of the tank.

Fining, a time-honoured method of clarifying wine, is now usually used in conjunction with advanced filtration processes. Filtration is the removal of particles by pumping wine through progressively finer filter pads. Compared with the traditional combination of racking and fining, filtration allows the winemaker to clean the wine rapidly and more efficiently.

The danger is that excessive fining and filtering can rip out the body and flavour of a wine along with its waste materials. This problem is particularly acute in such countries as New Zealand that produce naturally lighter wines. Sediment found in a bottle can often be a positive indication that the wine has its flavour and aging components intact.

Occasionally crystals of salts of tartaric acid can be seen in a bottle; this acid becomes insoluble in the alcohol produced during fermentation and tends to precipitate out as the wine matures. The wine in this case comes to no harm but sales may do, so to prevent this happening most companies chill the wine before bottling to reduce the solubility of the tartrates. These precipitate out and the wine is filtered and bottled cold. 'Cold-stabilised' wines are unlikely to throw any deposits in the bottle.

AGING

The young wine can now either be stored to mature or be promptly bottled.

A heavy majority of white wines made in New Zealand spend only a few months in steel tanks before bottling. Wood aging of whites is treated at the end of this outline of the techniques of white winemaking.

SWEETENING

Traditionally New Zealand's sweeter white wines were sweetened simply by adding cane sugar. Unfortunately, sugar added as a sweetener late in the winemaking process imparts a cloying, slightly sickly, artificial flavour to wine.

Natural grape sugars blend in much more harmoniously. The two techniques – 'back-blending' and 'stop-fermentation' – now used to produce most of the better medium whites, both involve the capturing of a natural sweetness.

Back-blending is the addition of unfermented or concentrated grapejuice to a wine prior to bottling. The technique was launched commercially in New Zealand in 1974, by Montana with Bernkaizler (now Benmorven) Riesling-Sylvaner.

The style immediately caught on, and has since been responsible for a vast improvement in the standard of out sweeter whites. Müller-Thurgau responds especially well to back-blending. Made in a dry style this variety can be rather thin and sharp; back-blending relieves this austerity and brings out the elegance inherent in the fruit. Wines that have been back-blended are generally more full-bodied – since grapejuice is weightier than wine – lower in alcohol and, of course, sweeter.

Stop-fermentation is a more complicated process that requires the fermentation to be interrupted. The wine is chilled to a temperature that renders the yeasts inactive before all the grape sugars have been converted to alcohol. The yeasts are then removed by centrifuging and sterile filtration; the resulting wine is slightly sweet and often contains trapped CO_2 along with the residual sugar. Hence the slight tingle on the tongue of many stop-fermented whites.

Some luscious, more expensive sweet white wines are produced in New Zealand by a third method – freeze concentration. By freezing out a proportion of the natural water content of grapejuice, a rich, extremely sweet juice can be obtained that, when fermented, can produce wine of great intensity. Freeze-concentrated wines look set to gradually decline, however, in the face of the recent emergence of genuine late-harvest styles (see *Botrytis cinerea*).

BOTTLING

Generally white wines are ensconced in bottles within a few months of the harvest. Light, delicate wines need little time to mature. By early bottling the winemaker is also able to preserve the fresh grapy character that appeals so strongly to many New Zealanders.

To ensure sterility, everything with which the wine comes into contact during bottling – hoses, bottling-lines, corks and bottles – must be sterilised. Final checks are made for spoilage and stability. At no stage must the wine be exposed to air.

A SIMPLE, HAND-OPERATED, SIPHON FILLING MACHINE IN USE AT NGATARAWA.

WINE CASKS

Wine casks have snowballed in popularity during the 1980s, emerging as by far the most common form of packaging for quaffing – as opposed to premium bottled – wines. At the peak of the 1985–86 discount frenzy, up to seventy-nine percent of all New Zealand table wine was sold in the ubiquitous wine cask, also called bag-in-box, softpack and – condescendingly – château cardboard.

A bag-in-box is just what the name conveys – a heat-sealed, plastic foil bag housed in a cardboard carton. Its dispensing device is a spout with a press-on tap. A filling machine creates a vacuum in the bag, fills it with wine and secures the tap.

The benefits of wine casks to wine drinkers include the reduced risk of breakage; reduced storage space (by comparison with an equivalent amount of bottled wine) and, because the bag collapses without admitting air when its wine is served, excellent keeping qualities once the cask is opened.

The chief drawback is a result of the permeability of plastic films to gases. The shelf-life of cask wine is only about nine months – hence the dates stamped on their bottoms. A higher residual level of free sulphur-dioxide is needed to counter the inroads gradually made by oxygen into the wine.

Carafe wines have of late been bogged down in a marketing 'no-man's land' between premium bottled wines and cheaper wine casks.

CASK PRODUCTION LINES – AS SEEN HERE FOR CARIBBEAN COOLER AT MONTANA – ARE HIGHLY EFFICIENT AND AUTOMATED IN A BID TO SLASH PRODUCTION COSTS.

A LOAD OF NEW OAK BARRELS ARRIVING AT
CLOUDY BAY. WOOD FLAVOURS IN WINE ARE
NOT CHEAP – IN 1988 A NEW, 500-LITRE FRENCH
OAK PUNCHEON COST AROUND $1200.

BARREL MATURATION

It would be an extraordinarily unresponsive wine drinker who could stroll between tiers of barrels of maturing Chardonnay or red wine, each cask emblazoned with such evocative cooperage names as Seguin Moreau, Demptos, Dargaud or Jaegle, and not be captivated. The sight, smell and taste of oak are integral parts of the romance and technology of New Zealand wine today.

Wood aging of white wines has snowballed in popularity this decade. The obvious candidate is Chardonnay. The great majority of New Zealand Chardonnays now display the complexity to be gained from oak maturation. Many Sauvignon Blancs – labelled as Fumé Blanc – Sémillons, Chenin Blancs and 'white burgundies' also received wood treatment, for periods ranging from three months to a year.

Although reds designed for everyday drinking are often merely aged in stainless steel and bottled about a year after the vintage, almost any red with an aspiration to quality has a spell in oak. As a rule, the more full-flavoured reds – Cabernet Sauvignon, Merlot and Cabernet Franc – spend the longest time in small casks; in New Zealand this is usually between one and two years.

Originally, casks were regarded simply as convenient containers in which to store wine. Coopering appears in rock carvings in ancient Egyptian tombs dating from around 2690 BC and by the first century BC barrels were commonly used for wine storage.

Barrels are based on the principle of the double arch and thus have enormous strength. They are also a form of wheel and easily shifted. Many types of timber have been employed to fashion casks, because any problems with permeability and undesired extractives can be countered by lining the vessel with paraffin. Hence not only oaks but also kauri, redwoods, eucalyptus, red gum and other woods have been pressed into service for barrels.

This century, however, the development of stainless steel and other relatively inert and impervious tank linings has led to the demise of wooden containers as the principal vessels for bulk wine storage. But it has also been much more universally appreciated that certain timbers, notably oak, can give a stunning lift to the quality of the wines they house.

Three reactions distinguish the maturation of wine in wooden containers from the simple storage of wine in impermeable vessels: the steady evaporation of alcohol and water through the side of the cask; the slight inroads made by oxygen into the wine also through the side of the cask; and the extraction of substances from the wood into the wine.

The most visible process during barrel aging is the slow absorption of some of the wine by the wood and its subsequent evaporation. According to Louis Pasteur, cold and humid cellars can reduce evaporation losses to only one or two percent per year, but the rate of evaporation can also soar to nine percent in too warm and too dry wineries. He put the average annual loss of wine by evaporation at four to five percent.

Wine resting in barrels is also gradually oxidised, not only by evaporation losses – and racking – but also by the slight penetration of air into the barrel through the pores of the timber. In small casks – with their higher wood surface to volume of wine ratio – aeration is much more rapid than in larger containers.

Even more central to the barrel maturation process are the oak-derived compounds that can enhance the sensory qualities of wine. The layer of wine next to the interior surface of the barrel builds up a high level of tannoids extracted from the oak. This extraction is aided by the oxygen present which effectively acts as a solvent. The compounds formed at the interior surface are slowly diffused throughout the wine.

In addition to the oak tannins which enhance the flavour, longevity and colour stability of wine, aromatic substances are extracted from the wood, such as vanillin (which tastes like vanilla). Related phenolic components, colour and resinous substances are also extracted. One recent study of oak shavings led to the identification of one hundred and eighteen different compounds.

The reasons for the ascendancy of oak over other timbers in coopering are not hard to pinpoint. Quite apart from the sensory considerations of smell and flavour, oak timber is strong and yet bendable and thus eminently workable. A cooper will also tell you that the structural features that make certain types of oak perfect for 'tight' cooperage are their medullary 'rays'. Rays are strips of cells which run radially through the tree, conducting sap across the grain. The rays in oak trees are unusually wide, representing about twenty to thirty percent of the wood, by comparison with only about fifteen percent in other hardwoods. These large rays enhance the strength and flexibility of oak and also its impermeability.

Which type of oak is best? This is an issue much debated in wine circles, but there are a multitude of conflicting opinions and there is not a great deal of experimental data. Oak of French origin, however, is by far the most popular in New Zealand.

The regional characteristics of French oak are largely influenced by soil and climate. Nevers oak, which is almost exclusively used for the maturation of red and white Bordeaux, is named after the *département* of Nevers. This gently undulating region of rich, moist soils grows fine-grained oak timber. According to Les Tonnelleries de Bourgogne – an association of Burgundian coopers – Nevers oak is ideal for maturing Cabernet Sauvignon and other full-bodied red varieties, plus Pinot Noir and Chardonnay. Nevers contributes body and a buttery, slightly citric flavour to wine.

Limousin oak comes from the *département* of Haute-Vienne, a rough and hilly region of poor sandy soils. Here the trees are stocky – growing as much laterally as vertically – and yield coarse-grained timber much used in Cognac production and more recently in Californian Chardonnays. Limousin has the widest grain of all French oaks and thus wine housed in it has a more rapid rate of evaporation and oxidation. It also perfumes and flavours wine speedily and imparts more colour than other oaks. Vanilla and lemon are the characteristic flavours bestowed on wine by Limousin oak.

OAK STORAGE AT MORTON ESTATE. TRADITIONALLY THE 'COOPER' SHAPED AND ASSEMBLED THE STAVES WITH THE 'HOOPER' ADDING THE FINISHING TOUCHES.

Nevers and Limousin are the two principal French oaks encountered in New Zealand wineries. Allier, Tronçais, Bourgogne and Vosges are other famous French forests lending their names to casks now starting to be experimented with here. Other European oaks are Yugoslav and German (the latter known for its mildness).

A cheaper alternative to the French timber is American oak. Oak grows in North America from southern Canada to the Gulf of Mexico but is not selected there on a regional basis as it is in Europe. American oak tends to contribute more of the colour and flavour of oak to wine than does French oak, but less extract and tannin. American oak-aged wines have a pungent, sweeter, more vanilla-like oak flavour, which experienced tasters can easily pick. Californian winemakers in general prefer French oak.

Few native New Zealand timbers have proved to be of value for winemaking. Totara has been widely used for tubs and vats; Te Kauwhata in 1937 reported 'full satisfaction' with both tawa and silver beech as cheaper substitutes for oak. Neither wood found widespread commercial support.

Apart from the type of oak used in coopering, the size, degree of 'toasting', and age of an individual barrel all influence the finished wine too. Smaller casks affect wine more rapidly than large, owing to their higher surface-to-volume ratio. The fact that small barrels holding 190 to 250 litres are the size most commonly used around the world for maturing reds is believed to be partly the result of the search for the optimum aging effect; not just the fact that such casks can be comfortably lifted by two men or rolled by one.

The smaller the barrel size, the greater the cost of maturing each litre of wine. Another problem is that wine changes more rapidly in small cooperage, making quality control more difficult. *Barriques*, with a 225-litre capacity, are nevertheless universally used in Bordeaux for red and white wines (but have only been seen in New Zealand in any quantity in the past few years). Hogsheads carry 300 litres. By far the most commonly used barrel in this country is the puncheon, which, with a 500-litre capacity, is the most economic of the smaller barrel sizes.

'Toasty' is an adjective which has shot into the vocabulary of New Zealand wine buffs in the past few years. French coopers, almost without exception, use a fire to bend oak staves into the shape of a barrel. Over the years various châteaux have called for their barrels to be held on the fire for varying lengths of time – up to forty-five minutes – to produce different 'toasting' levels. Wineries can now order casks with up to five different levels of toasting; from a light toast (a minimum firing just to bend the staves) through to a heavy toast (where the barrel is heavily charred).

The firing of the barrel alters the oak's chemistry which in turn means different sensory products are extracted by the wine matured inside. Studies have revealed that the extraction of aromatic aldehydes from oak is dramatically increased by charring up to 200°C. The higher the char level, the more 'smokiness' in the wine.

As barrels age, their contribution of aromatic compounds and oak extractives to wine diminishes. A panel of trained tasters was reported to be still able to pick the difference beween French and American oak-aged wines after three years, but it was anticipated they would have been struggling after four years. Between four and six years is the normal useful life of a barrel as regards oak extraction, but older barrels are still useful for storage.

One valuable way to prolong the effective life of a barrel is to remove one of the barrel heads and then shave the inside of the staves. By this removal of fatigued wood – and the usual build-up of tartrate deposits – a fresh surface of oak is exposed to the wine, from which a new supply of extractives can be gained.

An unromantic, but cheap, way to secure some of the flavouring effects of oak is to simply immerse oak chips in wine. The drawback here is that the absence of the controlled oxidation afforded by barrels prevents the usual extraction of important compounds from the wood. Oak chips cannot rival proper aging in barrels, but wine flavoured in this way is usually better than if it has enjoyed no wood influence at all.

BARREL FERMENTATION

'Oak fermented' is a phrase that more and more often surfaces during discussions of the production methods of this country's foremost Chardonnays and Fumé Blancs. What precisely is involved?

Barrel fermentation is an ancient practice which largely fell out of favour this century with the arrival of new materials, most importantly stainless steel, which could both lower the cost and enhance the reliability of fermentation. White Burgundy, however, has always been barrel fermented – the top vineyards in new barrels – and in New Zealand, despite the burdens of added time, effort and expense, barrel fermentation has come into vogue.

The appeal of barrel fermentation for winemakers is that it leads to superior integration of wood and wine. Barrel-fermented Chardonnay has a soft, nutty oak character; on the nose and palate it can be hard to discern where the fruit and oak elements start and end. By contrast, young stainless steel-fermented, wood-matured wines usually display clearcut, separate, fruit and wood characters that lack the overall integration achieved in barrel-fermented styles.

The fermentation can begin either in stainless-steel tanks and, once underway, be transferred to the casks, or it can commence in the wood.

Once fermentation begins, it pursues a characteristic temperature curve. There is little danger of the temperature rising beyond 30°C, owing to the inhibiting effect of the tannins leached from the oak on yeast activity. The barrels, however, can only be filled with juice to about a three-quarter level, otherwise the juice may boil over as fermentation peaks.

Maximum frothing is the signal that most of the fermentation is over. The next step is to top up all the barrels with unfermented juice held back in tanks, or fermenting juice from another barrel. Each barrel should be full by the time the fermentation has run its course.

The yeast is now left to settle for a day or two before it is re-suspended by stirring the contents of the barrel. Regular stirring of the yeast over the next couple of months serves a triple purpose: it ensures the ferment is completed to full dryness; it reduces the danger of hydrogen-sulphide spoilage; it encourages the pick-up of yeast-related flavour complexity. Finally the wine is pumped off its lees, the level of sulphur-dioxide is adjusted, and the wine may then be put back into the cleaned barrels for further aging.

Another increasingly explored winemaking technique is to put white wines through a secondary, bacterial malolactic fermentation in the barrel. The Burgundians use this technique both to enhance complexity – via the creation of traces of acetic acid, acetaldehydes, etc. – and lower acidity. Another option is to put only a part of the final blend through the malolactic fermentation.

An analysis by Bob Campbell of forty-seven 1986 vintage local Chardonnays, published in *Cuisine* magazine, unearthed the fact that fifty-five percent had been at least partially oak-fermented. It is clear that the practice of barrel fermenting our top Chardonnays is here to stay.

A SAMPLE OF FERMENTING WINE BEING DRAWN FROM THE CASK AT ST HELENA. WOOD FERMENTATION IS A LABORIOUS PROCESS, BUT ENCOURAGES MORE RAPID BALANCING OF THE FRUIT AND OAK FLAVOURS IN WINE.

RED WINES

The preparation of red wines departs from that of whites in two crucial ways. First, fermentation takes place with the skins in contact with the juice; secondly red wines are much more often matured in oak for long periods before bottling.

An accomplished winemaker can stamp his or her individual style on a quality red in a way that is less often possible with a white. Red wines are more robust and flavoursome than whites, so that in a way the processing of red wine is hedged about by fewer precautions; oxygen for example, in small amounts, has a highly beneficial effect on reds. You could say the making of white wine depends a lot on science, while making reds depends more on art.

Red wines are made from so-called 'black' grapes which in reality are of varying shades from deep blue to purple. The juice itself is usually pale, while the skins contain the colouring material and other components vital to the fuller character of a red wine. Fermenting the juice on the skins thus gives red wine its full colour and flavour.

FERMENTATION

Red wines are fermented in open containers as well as stainless steel tanks, since oxidation is less of a problem.

During fermentation the evolution of CO_2 gas causes the skins to rise to the surface and form a dense cap. If this layer of warm, dry skins remains unbroken, air and acetic-acid bacteria may be trapped, resulting in off-flavours and a high level of volatile acidity in the wine; colour extraction will also be impeded if there is a barrier of CO_2 gas between the juice and the skins. Therefore the cap is periodically mixed with the juice by plunging the skins under by hand or by drawing off the juice below the cap and pumping it back over the skins.

Red-wine fermentations are usually warmer than whites; 20°C to 30°C is ideal to ensure a generous extraction of colour. As the ferment seethes along, the alcohol draws out the colour from the skins and the juice gradually turns red. Tannin from the pips and skins dissolves into the juice, contributing body, flavour and aging potential to the wine. Depending on the amount of colour and tannin desired, the yeasts will have consumed at least half of the natural sugars before the fermenting juice is removed from the skins.

THE BUBBLES OF CARBON-DIOXIDE GAS IN THIS RED WINE FERMENTATION AT CORBANS' TARADALE WINERY INDICATE THE YEASTS ARE STILL ACTIVE AND THE FERMENTATION STILL ALIVE.

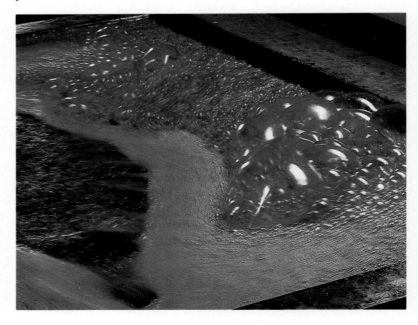

Choosing the right moment to draw off the part-wine is important. Few consumers age their reds these days and light, early maturing styles are most in demand. So to reduce tannin levels, most winemakers cut down on the period of skin contact. When sufficient colour has been picked up, the juice is drained from the skins and completes its fermentation alone. Pressed wine can later be blended back as required.

Carbonic Maceration

Another fermentation technique called carbonic maceration – or by its French name, *maceration carbonique* – is ideal for producing soft, fragrant and fruity reds. Beaujolais is the classic example.

Instead of being immediately crushed, whole berries are piled inside a fermenting vessel. The weight of the upper layers crushes the fruit below, which commences a normal fermentation, giving off carbon dioxide which blankets the intact fruit on top. Here, enzyme activity triggers an individual fermentation within each berry, extracting both colour and flavour from the inner skins.

Handling red grapes this way minimises oxidation and extraction of tannins. The ensuing wines are supple and fresh, ready for consumption early but do not usually respond well to bottle aging. Leading labels among New Zealand's 'nouveau' styles are Neudorf Young Nick's Red and Lincoln Beaujolais.

Malolactic fermentation

A major aspect of the making of red wine is the malolactic fermentation. This secondary fermentation – based on the bacterial conversion of malic acid to lactic acid and carbon dioxide – occurs in dry red wines after the initial alcoholic fermentation; a young red held on its lees with a low sulphur-dioxide level will usually 'go malolactic'.

New Zealand red wines gain immensely from this process because the wine becomes more palatable: malic acid imparts a harsh, sour taste to wine, whereas lactic acid is a soft, warm acid that enhances red wine. There is also a decline in total acidity – an advantage with most cool-climate wines. Biological stability is a third factor: a dry red which has not undergone a malolactic fermentation may later have it in the bottle, producing a gassy wine with sediment and an unpleasant 'nose' (a sort of poor man's sparkling Burgundy).

Many leading red-wine regions – France, northern Italy, the cooler zones of Australia – regard the malolactic fermentation as a desirable, indeed essential part of the red-winemaking process. Other warmer areas with lower natural acidity in their wines – southern Italy, most of Australia – prefer to avoid it. New Zealand falls into the first group.

A 1984 survey of New Zealand winemakers by Dr Susan Rodriguez found that ninety-three percent favoured a malolactic fermentation in their reds. Half the winemakers reported their malolactic fermentations started spontaneously; the others inoculated with a bacterial starter culture. Major reasons given for desiring a malolactic fermentation were lowered acidity, stability and increased complexity.

Methods of clarification, stabilisation and bottling for red and white wines are almost identical. Apart from the difference in the fermentation process, the principal way in which the making of red wine differs from the making of white wine lies in the method and length of maturation before bottling and release. A spell in oak barrels is much more common for red than for white wines.

ROSÉS

Rosés vary in colour from pink to a slightly tawny shade like an onion skin. The wine should be light and fruity, straightforward in its appeal, and above all refreshing.

Rosés are prepared in much the same way as whites. The best method is to allow red grapes a short period of skin contact during, or prior to, the fermentation, then to separate the skins and finally ferment the juice alone. The precise time the juice spends on the skins – routinely one or two days – holds the key to the wine's colour.

Other techniques include mixing red and white wines together. Oak aging is still uncommon since rosés are usually sold young.

'Lolly-water' was the old catch-cry for thin hybrid rosé wines with cane-sugar sweetness. But today a new breed of New Zealand rosé has appeared, drier and from such classic grapes as Pinot Noir, Cabernet Sauvignon and Pinotage. Leaders in the field include Collard Rosé of Pinotage and Cabernet rosés from Corbans and Te Mata. All are crisp and lively with good flavour; very appealing wines.

SPARKLING WINES

New Zealand has the potential to produce world-class sparklings. The country's basic wine style – crisp and delicate – is ideally suited to sparkling wines.

A major hindrance in the past has been the shortage of suitable grapes. The Champagne region of France, which like New Zealand frequently has difficulty fully ripening its grapes, uses Pinot Noir, Meunier and Chardonnay to produce the crisp acid dry whites on which Champagne is based. Current efforts in New Zealand using Chardonnay and Pinot Noir are starting to give our top sparklings a long-overdue lift.

Winemakers in New Zealand use three methods to place bubbles in wine. The most common technique, used in the medium-priced sparklings, is called bulk fermentation, or 'Charmat', after the Frenchman who developed it.

Here the bubbles are derived from a secondary fermentation carried out in a sealed tank. Yeasts and sugar are added to a dry base wine, and a proportion of the gas which is generated in the ensuing fermentation and trapped inside the tank, is bound to the alcohol. To achieve a sweet or dry style the winemaker simply halts the fermentation at the appropriate stage.

The wine is bottled cold. More bubbles are retained, because CO_2 is more soluble at low temperatures, and the reduced pressure makes for an easier bottling operation.

A great many excellent Spanish, French, German, Italian, South African and Australian sparkling wines are made in this way. The most popular sparkling in New Zealand, Penfold's Chardon, is bulk fermented. No gas is artificially introduced and the bubbles linger briefly in the glass after pouring.

The cheapest sparkling wines are 'carbonated'. Here the base wine is chilled inside a sealed tank and CO_2 gas is simply pumped into it. Pressure builds up in the wine as the temperature returns to normal after bottling.

The drawback with this technique is that the gas fails to combine with the alcohol (there is no secondary fermentation) and the CO_2 remains in the wine as large undissolved bubbles. These race out of the glass when the wine is poured.

METHODE CHAMPENOISE

'How it puns and quibbles in the glass,' wrote George Farquhar about Champagne in *Love in a Bottle*, published in 1699. 'Methode Champenoise' is the traditional, labour-intensive and costly production method pioneered in the Champagne district of France but now part of the recipe of all of the world's outstanding sparkling wines. Here the bubbles are derived from a secondary fermentation that occurs not in an enclosed tank but in the bottle itself.

Pinot Noir, Chardonnay and Meunier are the key grapes in true Champagne, usually picked in a slightly underripe condition in that northerly region's cool climate. In New Zealand the same varieties – except Meunier – have also come to the fore: Montana's Lindauer relies principally upon Pinot Noir, whereas the first release of Morton Estate Methode Champenoise was a seventy percent Chardonnay (for lightness and delicacy) and thirty percent Pinot Noir (for fullness of body) blend. Often the fruit is picked early here when the acids and pH are in optimum balance, with less emphasis on sugar levels. The goal is a firm base wine of fairly high acidity; low-acid wines made into sparklings tend to be flabby.

Following the primary fermentation of the base wine in stainless-steel tanks, sugar and yeasts are added. Next the wine is ensconced in very strong bottles ready for its secondary fermentation. Only enough sugar is added to ferment out when the wine reaches its desired pressure; too much sugar would generate too much gas and the bottles would explode.

At the end of the secondary bottle fermentation – lasting six weeks to several months – the yeast cells decompose, conferring a yeasty character on the wine, which is welcomed as an essential quality factor. The bottles are now stacked on their sides, with the yeast sediment staying in contact with the wine, for a maturation period of two to three years.

Then the bottles are laid head down in special 'riddling' racks in which the bottles are frequently shaken and tipped so that the yeast is gradually shifted from the sides of the bottle down to the cork. Small batches are still riddled by hand – each bottle of the first Vidal Brut was hand-riddled thirty times – but for large-scale production automatic riddling racks – gyropalettes – are now used, which settle the yeast sediment by means of an automated sequence of vibrations.

BOTTLES HEAD DOWN IN THE RIDDLING RACKS AT GIESEN. USUALLY ONLY THE CROWN SEALS (LOWER) ARE USED UP TO THE DISGORGING STAGE, BUT PLASTIC CORKS ARE SUBSTITUTED IF THE CROWN SEALS DO NOT HOLD WELL.

THE GYROPALETTES IN CELLIER LE BRUN'S SUBTERRANEAN CELLARS ACCOMPLISH AUTOMATICALLY WHAT TRADITIONALLY TOOK LONG HOURS OF WRIST-WRENCHING LABOUR.

'Disgorging' follows, where the bottle-neck is frozen solid to allow the cork and sediment plug to be removed without the loss of too much wine. Finally the bottle is topped-up and sweetened with a liqueur of brandy and sugar, corked – with a proper 'Champagne' cork – and wired.

A modern, and less costly, method for producing bottle-fermented sparkling wine is called 'transfer'. Rather than being laboriously disgorged, after its bottle fermentation the wine is transferred into pressurised stainless-steel tanks, where it is settled, filtered and – if necessary – sweetened in bulk, before being re-bottled.

Prior to 1980 only one or two winemakers had experimented with bottle-fermented sparklings: Mission and Selaks had pioneered the method with unspectacular results. Now, however, Montana, Selaks, Cellier Le Brun, Morton Estate and Vidal all have successful 'methode champenoise' wines vinted from Pinot Noir, Chardonnay or a blend of both – and more are in the wings.

EVERY FOUR HOURS, ON AN AUTOMATIC COMPUTERISED CYCLE, THE GYROPALETTE SHIFTS INTO A NEW POSITION, GRADUALLY SHAKING THE YEAST SEDIMENT DOWN INTO THE NECK OF THE BOTTLES.

SHERRIES

A ndré Simon, wine author and legendary founder of the Wine and Food Society, gave a candid opinion on the 'sherries' and 'ports' he tasted in New Zealand in 1964. 'Very few of the dessert wines can claim to belong to the quality wine class,' he wrote in *Wines of the World*, edited by Simon in 1967. 'They are sweet, spirity, without any trace of bouquet or breed.'

Locally produced sherry first achieved popularity in New Zealand after the First World War. By the time of Simon's visit, sherries and ports dominated sales, and they still retain a significant seventeen percent share of the market. Nevertheless it is hard to enthuse about the majority of these wines.

The heart of the problem is that New Zealand's climate is ill suited to produce sherry or port or any other fortified wine style. The best fortified wines come from hot countries – Portugal, Spain, South Africa, Australia – where the grapes achieve a high natural level of sweetness. These plentiful sugars produce a natural lusciousness and strong alcoholic content in the wines. New Zealand winemakers have been forced to compensate for the lesser ripening of their grape material with heavy additions of cane-sugar for sweetening, and as a result our fortified wines tend to lack the fruit character of true sherry and port; most are simply neutral fortified wines.

DRY SHERRY MATURING IN WOOD AT CORBANS' TARADALE WINERY.

The alcohol content of sherry, or port, in New Zealand must by regulation lie between fifteen and twenty-three percent. Until 1981 these wines had to be fortified with spirit distilled from wine made in New Zealand, but in practice a distillation 'wash', made from fermented grapeskins, pips, pulp, sugar and water was often distilled to produce fortifying spirit.

The Distillation Act was amended in 1981 to allow the fortification of wine with spirit derived from non-vinous sources. Today the winemakers' stills are rarely fired up. Almost all dessert wines are fortified with whey alcohol made by the New Zealand Dairy Company: although this has a more neutral flavour than grape spirit, it is markedly cheaper.

In the past many so-called 'sherries' and 'ports' were made from grape-skins, yeasts, sugar and water with only minimum help from grapejuice.

A 1980 amendment to the Food and Drug Regulations reduced this adulteration by prescribing a sixty percent minimum grapejuice level for dessert wines. This level took into account the diluting effects of such additives as fortifying spirit and liquid sugar for sweetening.

Old sweet sherries can nevertheless be surprisingly good. The best emerge after many years' aging in barrels with a rich, full, mellow character that has often won high accolades from wine judges. Totara has recently been the leading specialist in this style.

Now that New Zealand has also perfected the 'flor' technique, a few dry sherries of outstanding quality have been developed. 'Flor' is Spanish for flower; in Spain the flor yeast 'flowers' as a creamy substance on the surface of sherry in a cask, imparting a nutty, yeasty flavour.

Sometimes in New Zealand flor sherries are made by this traditional method, although here the base wine has to be artificially inoculated with a flor yeast, whereas in Spain this occurs naturally. Larger wineries such as Montana use an alternative 'submerged flor' technique. This involves pumping flor yeast, and oxygen, into the sherry under pressure. The result is a faster and more pungent pick-up of flor character. Top versions – particularly Montana Pale Dry Sherry – are notably reminiscent of their Spanish counterparts and fine wines in their own right.

PORT

In the past the standard of New Zealand port has paralleled that of sherry. Port used to be a concoction derived from the black skins which remained after a red wine had been made. Sweetened with heavy additions of cane sugar and sometimes flavoured, such wines bore little resemblance to the famed dessert wines of the region surrounding Oporto in Portugal.

Port is properly made by fermenting red grapes on their skins until most of the sugar has been consumed. Then the fermentation of the sweet part-wine is halted by running it off the skins and fortifying to about eighteen to nineteen percent alcohol by volume. After fining and filtering, the wine is transferred to oak barrels for its vital maturation period in wood.

Ruby ports are bottled young, within a couple of years, and display a distinct ruby colour combined with a soft, fruity, relatively fresh flavour. Tawny ports show the effects of longer oak aging with a tawny-brown appearance and a more mature, complex palate.

The end result should be a rounded, fruity, not overly sweet wine. Two of the most consistently bemedalled ports at recent competitions, Babich Reserve Port and Collard Tawny Port, both lean towards the Portuguese style of port, being fruity and fairly dry. Pleasant Valley Founders Port is a rare, fifteen-year-old treat, sweet and nutty.

Vintage ports, based on Cabernet Sauvignon and made for cellaring, are an important emerging wine style. Prominent among early releases are full-bodied, dark and flavoursome ports from Matua Valley, Cooks, Babich, Corbans and Lincoln. A number of these, lacking the sheer fruit intensity and robust tannin of the remarkably long-lived Portuguese vintage ports, have pulled up short in the bottle after less than five years.

CHAPTER FOUR

The Principal Wine Regions

Winegrowing is a strongly localised occupation. Hawke's Bay and Poverty Bay account for almost two-thirds of the national vineyard area. If these provinces are added together with Auckland, Marlborough and the Waikato, ninety-eight percent of vines are found to be concentrated in five provinces. Scattered holdings also exist in Northland, Bay of Plenty, Wanganui, the Wairarapa, Wellington, Nelson, Canterbury and Central Otago, but there is no viticulture on a commercial basis elsewhere.

At various stages of our history, nonetheless, grapevines have been planted, with or without success, over most parts of the country. Bragato in 1895 encountered vines growing in Central Otago, Akaroa, Nelson, the Wairarapa, Hawke's Bay, Bay of Plenty, Wanganui, the Waikato, Auckland and Northland. Such a widespread scattering of early grape-growing and winemaking reflected the isolated, far-flung nature of the first settlements. Although, ideally, considerations of climate and soil should have been uppermost in selecting areas to establish vines, in fact it was the influence of cultural traditions and the availability of cheap land which played leading roles in the early location of the industry in New Zealand.

The early exploitation of the Auckland region was due to the scale of the available market and the presence of Dalmatians and others eager to make wine, rather than to any climatic or physical advantages. Hawke's Bay, with ideal natural conditions for grapegrowing, was sufficiently distant from Auckland to compete for markets in the south. Auckland and Hawke's Bay thus remained the two centres of New Zealand wine for more than a half century. Then in the 1960s, when it became obvious that extensive new plantings would be necessary to cater for the rising demand for table wines, vineyards spread beyond the traditional grape-growing zones into Taupaki, Kumeu, Mangatangi and, above all, Poverty Bay.

Poverty Bay, although sharing some of the climatic advantages of Hawke's Bay, is isolated by rugged terrain from the major wine markets. However, Corbans, Cooks and Montana encouraged contract growers there to establish sizeable areas in vines. The answer lay in the fertility of the Gisborne Plains soils; Auckland and the Waikato produce an average yield of eight and a half tonnes per hectare of *vinifera* grapes; Poverty Bay yields seventeen and a half tonnes.

The more recent move into Marlborough by Montana, Corbans and Penfolds was in pursuit of another objective. Crops there are relatively light at eight to ten tonnes per hectare – but scientific analyses had shown that the region is ideal for premium cool-climate table winemaking.

The recent flowering of viticulture in Canterbury and Martinborough has been the outcome of similar searches for new regions possessing natural advantages of climate and soil. Site selection is the most crucial decision of all when establishing a new vineyard. New Zealand winemakers are paralleling a common trend overseas by shifting to cooler climate zones. The search for riper and cleaner fruit has led many newcomers to the industry to avoid the higher rainfall areas of West Auckland, the Waikato and Poverty Bay in favour of the long dry belt extending down the east coast of both islands from Hawke's Bay through the Wairarapa and Marlborough to Canterbury.

With the pronounced variations in soil and climate from Northland to Central Otago, the challenge now facing winemakers is to sort out the best grapes for each region and then to produce the style of wine which fully captures the potential inherent in the fruit. Back in 1896 Whangarei vinegrower Lionel Hanlon stressed this point at a Conference of Australasian Fruitgrowers held in Wellington. 'As has been the case in other countries, so doubtless it will be the case here, that each district will produce one class of wine which will surpass all others in point of excellence . . . The absurdity of every man who has an acre or two of vineyard manufacturing so-called port, sherry, Bordeaux, Burgundy, Chablis, Tokay etc., need not be discussed. It cannot too forcibly be impressed upon the future winegrowers of New Zealand the great importance of each district producing a class of wine of definite type.'

It seems that New Zealand winegrowing is going in the direction indicated by Hanlon. It is true that sound reasons often exist for blending together grapes from a variety of regions, and it may not always be economically feasible to produce small batches of regional wines, but regionalism is nevertheless a strong trend.

Certain local strengths are already apparent; Auckland in Cabernet Sauvignon and other classic reds; Gisborne in Gewürztraminer and Chardonnay; Hawke's Bay in Cabernet Sauvignon, Merlot, Chardonnay and Sauvignon Blanc; Martinborough in Pinot Noir and Gewürztraminer; Marlborough in Sauvignon Blanc and Riesling; Canterbury in Riesling and Pinot Noir.

The formation of Hawke's Bay Vintners in 1979 offered further evidence of the growing emphasis on regional identification – all wineries in the district agreed to jointly foster Hawke's Bay's image as an area which produces quality wines. In 1983, the Winemakers of West Auckland started adopting the same aims. Of late the winemakers of Marlborough, Canterbury and Martinborough have also banded together to promote their regional identities.

THE WINEMAKING REGIONS
Areas in vines 1986

NORTHLAND
8 ha.

AUCKLAND
221 ha.

WAIKATO
206 ha.

BAY OF PLENTY
2 ha.

POVERTY BAY/
EAST CAPE
1425 ha.

HAWKE'S BAY
1032 ha.

NELSON
30 ha.

WAIRARAPA
21 ha.

MARLBOROUGH
934 ha.

CANTERBURY
35 ha.

CENTRAL OTAGO
8 ha. (estimated)

TOTAL AREA 3922 ha.

Note
The 1986 Vineyard Survey's figures slightly underestimated actual plantings.

According to the Wine Institute, by 1988 vine plantings totalled approximately 6000 ha, with most recent plantings concentrated in Marlborough.

NORTHLAND

The northernmost region of New Zealand stretches out over 500 kilometres of rolling hill country. Its climate is almost subtropical, with warm humid summers, mild winters and abundant rainfall. Northland's main occupation is pastoral farming, yet from the Kaipara Harbour in the south to Ruawai in the north, there are currently nine licensed winemakers.

Northland was the cradle of New Zealand wine: here Marsden planted the first vines and here, too, Busby made the first wine. After 1840 and the Treaty of Waitangi, however, the region was exploited mainly for its magnificent kauri forests and later for its gum. Descendants of Dalmatian gumdiggers and the sons and daughters of more recent Dalmatian arrivals almost alone have preserved the winemaking traditions of Busby. Few depend on their vines for a living; with a total of eight hectares under vines, in fact, the region has a mere 0.2 percent of New Zealand's vineyard area. Only a rivulet of wine flows in Northland; the vineyards, averaging less than one hectare, are the smallest in the country and their wine is mostly sold locally. Hillside, Te Hana, Château du Brak, Continental and Bryladd are not household names in the rest of New Zealand – or even in Northland for that matter. The Antipodean is another story altogether.

The wines, predominantly sweet and fortified vin ordinaire, are reminiscent of the national wine style twenty years ago.

Continental

The largest grower in Northland is Continental Wines at Otaika, just south of Whangarei, with over five hectares under vines. This vineyard was established in 1964 by Mate Vuletich who, as his widow relates, was born under a grapevine on the family vineyard in Yugoslavia. Vuletich originally planted Baco 22A and Niagara vines, but more recently plots of Cabernet Sauvignon, Pinot Noir, Chardonnay, Gewürztraminer and Müller-Thurgau have been established.

Today the founder's son Mario (37) is the only full-time winemaker in the North. In a small well-equipped winery, about 2000 cases of wine are annually produced, all sold at the gate. Although ports and sherries still form part of the range, Mario Vuletich's 'personal goal is to make two top reds, Pinot Noir and Cabernet Sauvignon'.

My bottle of 1986 Pinot Noir, despite its bronze medal, was not distinguished. However, a Continental Riesling-Sylvaner I tasted in 1987 showed clearcut varietal character, and Graeme Barrow, Northland's resident wine writer, has found the Müller-Thurgau to be 'clean and fruity'.

The Antipodean

The Antipodean blazed onto the wine scene in 1987 like a comet, fuelled by a highly effective publicity campaign. By mid-1988, however, much of the early excitement had faded.

This tiny winery is the brainchild of brothers Petar and James Vuletic, Auckland lawyers who are distant relatives of the Vuletich family at Northland's Continental Wines. At their Matakana winery, near Leigh – an area renowned for its plentiful sunshine – the brothers set out to fashion a single red wine of fine quality.

In Petar Vuletic's words: 'The idea of making a great wine in the tradition of the Bordeaux first growths was conceived by my brother and I, while we were both still in our teens. It was discussed with our father who advised us that if we were ever to do this, we were to go to a particular area north of Warkworth and there establish a vineyard on a particular farm which he first observed in 1928.'

Their two-hectare vineyard, planted in 1979, lies on a steep, north-west-facing clay slope, only two kilometres from the ocean. Apart from the

assistance of bird-shooters and hand-pickers at vintage, the Vuletics have performed the myriad vineyard and winery tasks themselves at weekends.

The Antipodean is a blend of approximately sixty-five percent Cabernet Sauvignon, thirty percent Merlot and five percent Malbec, varying according to the season. The fruit, lightly pressed in a basket press, is then fermented in totara vats (a link with the 1950s and 1960s, when the Vuletic family made wine on Auckland's North Shore). Only wild, natural yeasts are used in a bid to build more complexity and individuality into the wine.

After maturing in new, thin-staved Seguin Moreau barriques for eighteen to thirty months, The Antipodean is filled into a mix of half and normal-sized bottles, magnums and a few five litre rehoboams. The total annual output amounts to a few hundred cases only.

Described by Jancis Robinson in the *Evening Standard* as a 'carefully hyped' wine, The Antipodean was lined up by the Vuletics with a cluster of celebrated Bordeaux reds for the benefit of the influential London wine press. Their reaction was divided. Writing in *Wine* magazine, Robert Joseph praised the 1986 and 1987 vintages for their 'complexities of long-lasting spicy-plummy flavour often missing in New World wines and ripe roundness rarely encountered in New Zealand reds'. Philip Morrice, writing in *Decanter* magazine, also declared that 'beyond greatness comes perfection. This is what has been achieved with The Antipodean 1987'.

By contrast, Jane MacQuitty of *The Times* clearly prefers Te Mata's Coleraine Cabernet/Merlot. 'What separates the thousand cases of Coleraine Cabernet/Merlot every year from The Antipodean and the rest is its intensely ripe exuberant fruit flavour, a characteristic not yet found in the other mostly leaner and less luscious New Zealand Cabernets.' Jancis Robinson also reported tasting The Antipodean 1985 alongside twenty-five other top young New Zealand reds 'and, tasting blind being the ultimate test, I'm afraid it did not stand out'. I too found the 1985 vintage an anti-climax – although scented and soft, its colour revealed premature aging and it lacked both the fruit intensity and tautness of structure of a top claret-style red.

The final verdict on The Antipodean has yet to be written. Indeed, in mid-1988, James Vuletic's application to the High Court in Auckland to terminate his partnership with his brother – the result of 'a personal falling out' – left the fledgling winery's future highly uncertain.

BYPASSING MOST OF THE LOCAL WINE PRESS, THE VULETICS LAUNCHED THE FIRST THREE VINTAGES OF THE ANTIPODEAN IN LONDON. THE SUBSEQUENT HYSTERIA – WHICH PROVED SHORT-LIVED – CULMINATING IN THE SALE AT AUCTION OF A REHOBOAM OF THE ANTIPODEAN 1985 FOR $5100, REVEALED MUCH ABOUT THE ESSENTIAL IMMATURITY OF THE NEW ZEALAND WINE MARKET.

KUMEU/HUAPAI/ WAIMAUKU

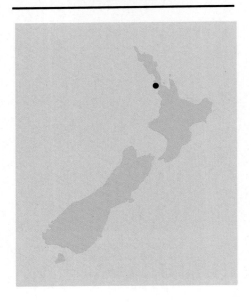

From Waimauku in the north-west to Riverhead in the east and southwards to Taupaki, this region surrounding the rural townships of Kumeu and Huapai boasts several noted wineries: Matua Valley, Nobilo, Coopers Creek, Kumeu River and Selaks have all contributed to the area's strong reputation.

The current rebirth of interest in Auckland viticulture is to a large extent concentrated here. The local climate, according to meteorologists, is one of the best for table winemaking in Auckland, with the district's distance from the Waitakere Ranges giving a lower rainfall than at Henderson. The signs of success are everywhere: in the aesthetically delightful buildings at Matua Valley and Coopers Creek; in the burgeoning of vineyard restaurants at Abel and Co., Selaks and Matua Valley; and, most importantly, in the wines themselves. Many are ranked among the country's best.

In 1960 Kumeu-Huapai accounted for a mere nineteen percent of all plantings in the Auckland province; by 1975 the figure had soared past fifty percent. Henderson winemakers of the 1960s, wishing to expand to meet increasing demand, faced a serious problem in the lack of cheap, reasonably large blocks of land in Henderson. Their options were threefold: to purchase the new grapes from contract growers, to relocate their wineries, or to buy new vineyard land away from their company headquarters.

With land at Henderson between 1965 and 1970 valued at $4500 per hectare, and land at Kumeu selling for only $1500 per hectare, expansion soon shifted to the Kumeu-Huapai area. Old established companies were able to plant new vineyards only fifteen kilometres away from their existing wineries.

Many companies – Delegat's, Lincoln, Soljans, Collard, Cooks, Corbans and others – established new vineyards here (some later pulled out). Others, such as Nobilo and Kumeu River (formerly San Marino), have an extended history in the district. Matua Valley and Abel and Co. are relatively recent arrivals who chose to base their entire operations here.

Fledgling wineries are still emerging while one or two older ones decline. The latest newcomer is Limeburners Bay, lying to the east in Hobsonville Road. David Papa has also injected new life into Papa's Estate, in Station Road, Huapai, and been rewarded with some promising reds.

Markovina, a small winery in Old Railway Road, Kumeu, although still in business has of late been quiet. Glenburn Wines, a THC Trophy-winning sherry and port specialist, owned by the Jelas family of Riverhead, closed its doors in 1984. This followed hard on the heels of the 1983 closure of Peter's Vineyards, in Nixon Road, Taupaki, home of a popular, although exceedingly light, Pinot Noir.

It should be emphasised that the majority of the wines produced here are made from fruit trucked in from more southern districts, notably Gisborne and Hawke's Bay. However, confidence in the quality of local grapes is soaring: Kumeu River wines are exclusively produced from local fruit and Matua Valley are expanding their Waimauku vineyards.

Rationalisation is underway in the vineyards as the winemakers single out the grape varieties most adaptable to the region's humid summers and heavy clay soils. Plantings of Gewürztraminer, Chenin Blanc, Müller-Thurgau, Chasselas and Grey Riesling have slumped in popularity. Red grapes are now predominant in the Auckland region: Cabernet Sauvignon is the leader, with Pinot Noir and Pinotage also making the list of top five grape varieties. Palomino (only a shade behind Cabernet Sauvignon), Chardonnay, Sémillon, Merlot and Sauvignon Blanc are also well entrenched.

Further exploring the theme of 'horses for courses', winemakers here are also experimenting with new and healthier clones of existing varieties, use of devigorating rootstocks, 'grassing down' to reduce waterlogging of the soil, improved trellising techniques and other methods to upgrade their fruit quality.

The outcome has been some outstanding wines, both red and white. Red wines stand out as the best: Nobilo's Huapai Cabernet Sauvignon, early Abel and Co. reds, Kumeu River Merlot/Cabernet (plus Villa Maria's Reserve labels based on Kumeu fruit). Auckland's high summer and autumn temperatures and ample sunshine are clearly well-suited to ripening the later-maturing red varieties. In such warm, dry vintages as 1985 and 1986, the Cabernet Sauvignon, Cabernet Franc, Merlot, Pinot Noir and Pinotage-based reds from West Auckland can rival the country's best.

Although relatively recent, Kumeu River's successes with Chardonnay and Sauvignon Blanc, and Collard's successes with Chardonnay and Sauvignon Blanc at their Rothesay vineyard in Waimauku, all point to this region also possessing potential for the production of dry, full-bodied white wines.

Family-owned Dalmatian enterprises are still a vital influence here.

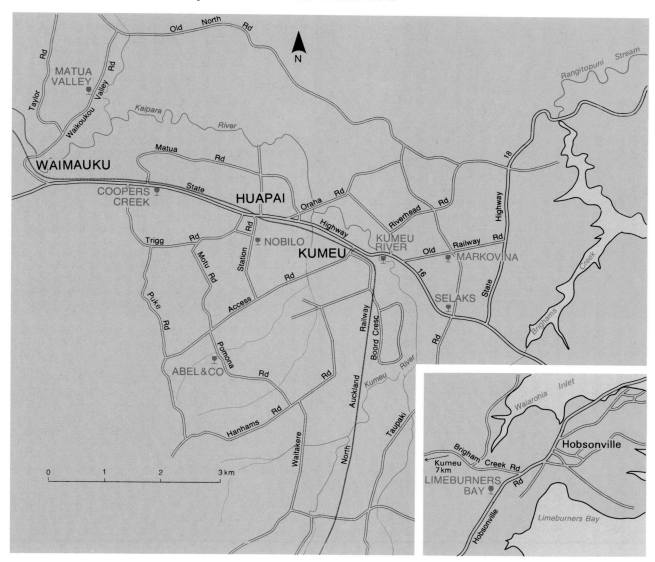

Abel and Co.

The reputation of Abel and Co., a winery that once had a prestige label, was eroded following the early death of its founder, Malcolm Abel, but some of the recent signs have been encouraging.

Malcolm Abel, a soft-spoken winemaker who died in 1981 at the age of thirty-eight, owned the only winery in the country that then specialised entirely in a single wine style. Abel, after purchasing a four-hectare block in Pomona Road, Kumeu in 1970, erected a chalet-style winery and started buying in grapes. His first commercial release, Reserve Dry Red 1974, scored well in wine competitions, and silver awards for the 1975 and 1976 vintages soon established Abel and Co. as a leading 'boutique' winery.

In the belief – shared with Nobilo – that Kumeu is red-wine country, he chose to concentrate on dry red table wines. To preserve the area style, grapes for the company's wines were drawn almost entirely from the surrounding locality. Two lines were regularly offered, Reserve Red and Pinotage. Both were always highly drinkable, reflecting the benefits of well-ripened fruit.

DAN SOUTHEE HAS REDIRECTED ABEL AND CO.'S PRODUCTION AWAY FROM THE INITIAL CONCENTRATION ON RED STYLES TO EQUAL EMPHASIS ON WHITE AND RED WINES. THE EARLY MAGIC CREATED BY MALCOLM ABEL HAS YET TO BE FULLY RECAPTURED.

Recollecting, while writing this, the presence of one last bottle of Abel Reserve Red 1979 in my cellar, I brought it upstairs and pulled the cork. 1979 was a washout of a vintage and yet here, by no means cracking up, was a red-brown, soft red, mellow and fragrant. What would Abel have achieved with more experience under his belt and with quality fruit to work with?

After Malcolm Abel's death – only a short time after his move into wine-making on a full-time basis – the winery was sold to two science graduates then in their mid-late twenties, Danny Southee and Robert Schroder. Southee, a B.Sc. graduate in microbiology from Otago University, viewed the opportunity to buy an already set-up small winery as one unlikely to be repeated. He and his mother duly sold their family retail wine outlets to plough money into the winery. Still only thirty-two, Southee jokes that his greying hair is directly attributable to the wine industry's demanding workload.

Following Robert Schroder's withdrawal from the venture in 1985, Southee formed a new partnership with George Beck, who handles the winery's administration and on-site retail activities.

Abel and Co. draws most of its red grapes from Auckland and most of its white grapes from Gisborne. Southee has pulled out the original Pinot Noir vines planted by Malcolm Abel in the two and one-half hectare hillside vineyard behind the winery – the rootstocks were unsatisfactory and also Southee does not see Pinot Noir as an ideal variety for Auckland – and replaced them with Cabernet Franc and Merlot. At another small, leased vineyard down the road he has planted mostly Chardonnay vines.

Other red grapes are drawn from Dysart Lane (off Pomona Road), Taupaki (the 'Gamay Beaujolais'), Hobsonville and Awaiti in the Hauraki Plains. Chardonnay and Riesling are purchased from Gisborne.

Southee makes his wine in a compact, triple A-frame winery with a rough-sawn timber exterior and orange-tile roof. He is an innovative winemaker who, as he put it in a winery newsletter, has 'endeavoured to launch onto a path very much individualising our wines'. This has not been without a price, as Abel and Co. wines oscillate slightly in quality.

Beaujolais Nouvelle Zélande is a winery specialty. It is fermented in small, 1000-litre vessels, using equal quantities of whole bunches and crushed fruit. The wine is bottled immediately and marketed in May, six months ahead of French Beaujolais.

Although having the character and strength of a true red, it has tended to lack the suppleness and fragrance of a top Beaujolais. It does, however, fulfil the winery's stated ambition to 'introduce more people to red wine and make that introduction less of a trauma. Rushing into large Cabernets and complex Pinot Noirs is quite frightening for most New Zealanders'.

Southee ferments his reds at warmer temperatures than are customary elsewhere; this extracts more intense colour from the skins but also sometimes contributes a noticeable whiff of volatile acidity. His Pinotage is a notably bold red, full in extract, very ripe-tasting and soft.

A trio of Cabernet Sauvignons are also produced. Those labelled Limeburners Bay and Awaiti are traditional, wood-matured styles, whereas the Pomona Cabernet is a non-wooded wine, designed to serve as an introduction to reds.

Two styles of Chardonnay have been seen, one barrel matured, the other barrel fermented. (Southee is using Nevers oak quarter-barriques, with a tiny capacity of only fifty litres each, in his search for maximum flavour complexity.) A Gewürztraminer and Rhine Riesling round out the range.

Abel and Co. wines are sold by mail order and through retailers in Auckland and Wellington. The winery restaurant, 'High Jinks', opens for lunch seven days per week.

Dan Southee says happiness is 'making my five thousand cases of wine each year and paying my bills – it's a lovely life'. Malcolm Abel, his ashes buried beneath a gum tree in the vineyard he gave birth to, would surely approve of that sentiment.

Coopers Creek

Many talented winemakers in employed positions dream of one day fashioning wine under their own label. Setting up a new winery, however, is a formidable challenge, because wine production – embracing the fields of viticulture, oenology and management – is a business of extraordinary complexity.

Coopers Creek is tucked unobtrusively away alongside the main road beyond Huapai. A striking sales-administration-hospitality centre has recently been erected and here, four years after their first vintage, partners Randy Weaver and Andrew Hendry created one of this country's most sensational Chardonnays. In mid-1988, however, Weaver announced his withdrawal from the partnership and returned to the United States.

Weaver and Hendry first crossed paths at Penfolds in Henderson during the late 1970s. Hendry, born in Wanganui, later educated in Auckland, is a tall, soft-spoken, forty-two-year-old accountant, relaxed in manner and brimming with wit. A well-respected spokesman for small-scale winemakers on the Wine Institute's influential executive committee, Hendry is the financial brain guiding Coopers Creek and also controller of its marketing operations.

Randy Weaver, an Oregonian, first arrived in New Zealand in 1973 aged twenty-seven. With him came his wife Phyllis and an infatuation with wine born during the time he lived in that intensely wine-conscious city, San Francisco.

Armed with a master's degree specialising in viticulture and oenology, from the University of California, Davis, Weaver worked for Montana in Gisborne, before returning to California and a lengthy spell with the giant Paul Masson winery.

ANDREW HENDRY AND HIS WIFE CYNDY HAVE NOW EMERGED AS THE PRINCIPAL SHAREHOLDERS IN COOPERS CREEK, FOLLOWING PARTNER AND WINEMAKER RANDY WEAVER'S DEPARTURE FROM THE PARTNERSHIP IN 1988.

Still intrigued, however, by New Zealand's outstanding natural winemaking potential, and also excited by the desire to do something different from his United States wine colleagues, Weaver came back to New Zealand to work for Frank Yukich, his old boss at Montana, now owner of Penfolds. Hendry was then Penfolds' company secretary and financial controller.

Confident in their own abilities, and harbouring strong reservations about Yukich's ambitious growth plans for Penfolds, the two decided to gradually set up their own small winery. Hendry quietly resigned in order to purchase land and to organise the formation of a limited liability company, involving both grower-partners and other investors. Two weeks later, Yukich got wind of Weaver's future plans and fired him.

Over the next two years, Randy Weaver served as a consultant to several wine companies, while also organising the planting of his own company's vineyards and finally, in 1981, the erection of the Coopers Creek winery. The name, Coopers Creek, he says, was taken from an old local map.

The home vineyard of three hectares alongside the winery is planted in Cabernet Sauvignon and Merlot vines. From here, although Coopers Creek produces largely white wine, will flow its Cabernet/Merlot blend. Coopers Creek's path was for a long time blocked by the local council, which adamantly refused to allow the new winery – but not the older ones – to process grapes grown outside the district.

Weaver was even forced to make his 1983 vintage at six different wineries. This issue was finally resolved, after the partners lowered their projected production ceiling to comply with the local body's demands, but not before Hendry and Weaver had marketed a special 'Fighting Fund' label to publicise their drawn-out battle.

From the first vintage, Coopers Creek wines found favour with Auckland's restaurateurs. By selling directly to the restaurants, the winery keeps a share of the margins normally picked up by merchant distributors. The restaurants gain a closer relationship with their supplier. Mail order sales have also from the start been a crucial part of the winery's distribution strategy.

Following a sustained courtship of the Australian market, export sales have also blossomed to the point where Melbourne now rivals Wellington as Coopers Creek's second largest market, behind Auckland.

This company's declared intention is to produce wines that are, above all else, *food* wines. The very highest awards once seemed to elude it, until the 1985 Gewürztraminer scored a gold medal at that year's National Wine Competition. But the range is uniformly full-bodied and dry.

A scan through my tasting notes, compiled since 1982, revealed a strong personal enjoyment of these satisfying, robust, long-flavoured wines from Coopers Creek.

The Gewürztraminer in most vintages is dry, robust, rounded and ripe, showing an impressive flavour intensity without being overpoweringly spicy. More 'Alsace' in style – meaning earthy and more austere – than the average New Zealand Gewürztraminer, the solid alcohol, satisfying dryness, and rounded varietal character add up to an excellent food wine.

Coopers Creek Fumé Blanc is a consistent, deep-flavoured dry wine with a penetrating leafy bouquet. Made from Gisborne fruit, with oak fleshing out the whole, this is a complex, balanced, rich wine with a long finish.

Coopers Dry is one of those rare and delightful wines where both the name and price undersell the merits of the wine itself. In this marriage of Chenin Blanc's body and fruitiness with Sémillon's crisp, grassy characteristics, in its youth the Sémillon holds the upper hand, with the Chenin asserting itself more fully as the wine matures.

Two styles of Chardonnay are marketed. The Hawke's Bay Chardonnay, following extended skin contact and warm fermentation of unclarified juice in stainless steel, is matured in new and once-used Nevers oak barrels. The result is a powerful, dry, 'oatmealy' style, firm and austere.

Swamp Road Chardonnay is the undisputed jewel in the Coopers Creek range. Congratulating them on their precise honesty in labelling, the Australian wine writer James Halliday then urged: 'why not change the name of the road?'

Swamp Road Chardonnay is made from fruit grown by Fenton Kelly in Swamp Road, in the Omaranui Valley in Hawke's Bay. Oak fermented, the wine then rests on its lees for two months, before being racked for a further three months aging into new Nevers oak hogsheads. At its best – as in 1986 – it is an arrestingly mouth-filling, succulent, complex wine with layers of peachy, fig-like and oak flavours. The colour is light gold, the bouquet oaky and yeasty. Its overall richness and long, trailing finish have stamped this as one of the country's leading Chardonnays.

Kumeu River

Kumeu River – under its earlier name, San Marino – was one of the first wineries to establish such classical grape varieties as Chardonnay and Pinotage, and also enjoyed an early reputation for hybrid quaffing wines such as its Kumeu Dry Red. Owned by the ebullient Mate Brajkovich, one of the most prominent and popular personalities in the wine industry, the winery has recently emerged from a flat patch in the 1970s to capture high respect as a serious, innovative producer of table wines.

The winery and vineyard are sited on the main highway, one kilometre south of Kumeu. Early Dalmatian settlers tended vines on the property for several decades before the Brajkovichs' arrival. Martin Lovich, who first occupied the property around the turn of the century, is believed to have made wine from Isabella fruit, and Stanko Jurakovich, who followed in 1915, made a sherry and port. When nineteen-year-old, Dalmatian-born Mate Brajkovich and his father bought the property in 1944, along with seven hectares of pasture, they acquired a fermenting vat, barrels and a half-hectare of Isabella and Albany Surprise vines.

Shortly after the war Brajkovich began planting hybrids and then, in the 1950s, Pinotage and Chardonnay. (Aged in old brandy casks, the Chardonnay invariably came out more alcoholic than when it went in.) The strong impact of this winery on the Auckland wine scene of the 1950s and 1960s owed much to its legendary hospitality: the poets Denis Glover and Rex Fairburn, heart surgeon Douglas Robb and soft-drink manufacturer Harold Innes were all frequent visitors.

Several family members are today involved in the daily operations at Kumeu River: Mate, who was awarded an OBE for his services to the wine industry and the community in 1985; his wife Melba; their son Michael, who now controls the winemaking; and his younger brother Milan, who, with a degree in chemical engineering under his belt, is now learning the ropes of winemaking.

Michael Brajkovich (28) is a quiet, handsome man who has inherited every centimetre of his father's towering physical presence. After training with distinction at Roseworthy College, South Australia, he returned to his family vineyard ('Nobody asked me to stay in Australia,' he told *Wineglass* magazine, tongue-in-cheek) before spending the 1983 vintage at Château Magdelaine, a leading *premier grand cru* of St Emilion. Here he developed not only a behind-the-scenes appreciation of Bordeaux winemaking techniques, but also, he says, the conviction that a small-scale New Zealand winery had more to learn from the French about handcrafting wines of individuality and finesse than from the Australians or Californians.

Brajkovich works exclusively with Kumeu fruit. On the rise across the highway from the winery, ten hectares of Cabernet Sauvignon, Cabernet

Franc, Chardonnay and Sauvignon Blanc vines have been trained on U-shaped trellises. Only a kilometre away – as the crow flies – the Brajkovichs also own an eight-hectare block of Merlot vines planted by Corbans in the early-mid 1970s. Kumeu growers Fred Rakich and Charlie Bazzard also supply Chardonnay, Pinot Noir and Müller-Thurgau.

Convinced that Kumeu can produce fruit of outstanding quality, Brajkovich points to how planting on hill sites improves drainage; to the merits of 'grassing down' between the rows as a way to reduce waterlogging of the soil; to the enhanced fruit ripeness he achieves using the U-trellis system; and to the superior fruit selectivity of hand-harvesting. His wines support his conviction. Perhaps more than any other individual, Brajkovich through his outstanding trio of Chardonnay, Sauvignon Fumé and Merlot/Cabernet wines has resurrected West Auckland's reputation as a quality wine region.

The winery, with its annual crush of 240 tonnes, in reality is much larger than it looks from the front. Should you step through the rear of the vineyard shop, you will be standing in the original, concrete-walled winery erected by Mate in the 1940s. Nearby rests a century-old barrel once owned by Heinrich Breidecker, still housing port.

Brajkovich's wines have been marketed under four labels: Kumeu River (the premium range), Brajkovich (the middle range), San Marino (now the bottom-end range) and Temple Hill (for a distributor). Many wine lovers have commented on the wines' sheer drinkability; as Michael Brett, of the *Auckland Star* summed it up: 'the contents of the bottle seem to evaporate before one'.

Three whites – Sauvignon Fumé, Chardonnay, and Dry Müller-Thurgau – and three reds – Merlot/Cabernet, Pinot Noir and Cabernet Franc – lie at the heart of the range. All, with the exception of the Dry Müller-Thurgau, are modelled on classic French wine styles.

Brajkovich has adopted a white-winemaking technique common in France but rare here. Instead of crushing and de-stemming the grapes

MATE BRAJKOVICH, FLANKED BY HIS SONS MICHAEL (LEFT) AND MILAN. MATE HAS THE CHARISMA, MICHAEL THE ANALYTICAL, INNOVATIVE WINEMAKING PROWESS, WHILE MILAN IS STILL LEARNING.

before pressing them, the bunches, stalks and all, go straight into the press. This method gives very clear juice which settles rapidly, he says. Both the Sauvignon Fumé and Chardonnay are also at least partly oak-fermented and then undergo a malolactic fermentation to enhance their drinkability and complexity.

Bottled in a Bordeaux-shape bottle, the Sauvignon Fumé is usually a splendidly ripe, full, rich-flavoured wine, demonstrating well the Sauvignon Blanc variety's ability – when fully ripened – to be stylish rather than strident. Brajkovich is aiming for a 'tropical fruit' rather than an 'herbaceous' style.

The Chardonnay is also excellent, soft and nutty in a Meursault-reminiscent style. Its ripe fruit flavour, yeastiness from the barrel ferment, and soft, sustained finish are attributes also found in the Sauvignon Fumé – and thus, one discerns elements of an emerging house style.

Although overshadowed by the Sauvignon Fumé and Chardonnay, the Dry Müller-Thurgau is also very good – beautifully poised, slightly off-dry and more flavoursome than most.

Kumeu River is perhaps best known for its Merlot/Cabernet, a red which has developed through three labels from a straight, varietal Merlot to a Cabernet/Merlot and, finally, the Merlot-predominant blend. Brajkovich sees a parallel between the success of Merlot in St Emilion's heavy soils, where it ripens two weeks ahead of Cabernet Sauvignon, and Kumeu's own needs.

The wine shows more suppleness and charm than a straight Cabernet Sauvignon, yet retains complexity and flavour depth. The bouquet is plummy and smoky, the colour a bold cherry red. This is a distinctive wine, with the medium body and firm structure of claret, coupled with ripe and berryish flavour.

The Pinot Noir is fermented on its stalks in a bid for added flavour. The result, at two years old, is a tight, rather closed red, crying out for a spell in the cellar to allow its varietal fragrance and soft elegance to emerge.

By contrast, the Cabernet Franc is delectable in its youth. Fruity, yet with solid extract and an underlying firmness, this wine tastes exactly like a grape should that often is employed to soften and pacify Cabernet Sauvignon. Jancis Robinson's description of the wine this variety produces in the Loire – 'a sort of claret Beaujolais' – rings equally true of Brajkovich's strong, fruity red.

Limeburners Bay

It is not hard to predict that after a grapegrower supplies premium Cabernet Sauvignon fruit to two different wineries, then witnesses them both waltz off with gold medals, his thoughts might turn to making and marketing the wine under his own label. Limeburners Bay winery, owned by forty-four-year-old Alan Laurenson and his Danish wife Jetta, lies several kilometres to the east of Kumeu and Huapai in Hobsonville Road. This is the youngest winery in the region.

Alan Laurenson is an affable, stocky man, raised in the King Country, who learned aspects of viticulture when employed by Barry Soljan, before recently settling into his full-time winemaking career. Jetta is a cartographer who has also studied horticulture; she designed the winery and its labels and also oversees the vineyard.

Erected in time for the 1987 vintage, their compact timber winery features a barrel storage area, laboratory and tasting room downstairs, with an upstairs office. Production, already running at a level of 3500 cases, should climb eventually to around 5000 cases per year.

The meticulously tended two-hectare vineyard adjacent to the winery is planted entirely in red grapes: eighty-five percent Cabernet Sauvignon, ten percent Merlot and five percent Cabernet Franc. On these gently sloping loam clays, the Laurensons harvest about twelve tonnes per hectare of ripe fruit in late April. They also draw white grapes – Chardonnay, Sauvignon Blanc and Müller-Thurgau – from Gisborne.

While awaiting the erection of their own winery, the Laurensons arranged for another winery to make their wine for them, which subsequently embroiled them in a period of 'nightmarish' disputes. Since 1987, however, all their wines have been processed at the new winery. Should the quality of the dark, marvellously fragrant and complex Limeburners Bay Cabernet Sauvignon 1984 be recaptured, their reds will be much sought-after.

The 1987 Chardonnay scored an auspicious silver medal at that year's Air New Zealand Wine Awards. This is an earthy, full-bodied wine, 'oatmealy' from its partial fermentation in heavily toasted puncheons, and extremely soft. A Müller-Thurgau is included in the range as an affordable wine for consuming anytime.

The unusual name of this winery merits an explanation. Limeburners Bay, lying nearby on an upper reach of the Waitemata Harbour, is where a pioneer settler, Rice Owen Clark, finding his land to be overly sour, burned shells for lime.

ALAN AND JETTA LAURENSON'S LIMEBURNERS BAY WINERY IS THE LATEST ARRIVAL ON THE WEST AUCKLAND WINE SCENE. THE 1984 LIMEBURNERS BAY CABERNET SAUVIGNON WILL BE A TOUGH ACT TO FOLLOW.

Matua Valley

One of the most innovative wineries in New Zealand – perhaps the leading success story of the past decade – lies north-west of Huapai, about four kilometres from the village of Waimauku in the tranquil Waikoukou Valley. Here the Hunting Lodge Restaurant, in a house near the winery built in 1868, serves country-style food, emphasising lamb, beef and game.

Matua Valley – named after the original vineyard in Matua Road, Huapai – is controlled by the Spence brothers, Ross (45), who trained at the wine faculty of Fresno University of California, and Bill (37), who studied agriculture at Massey. They have winemaking in their blood: a grandfather emigrated from Dalmatia and their father Rod Spence for several decades ran a small Henderson winery – Spence's – now best remembered for its Royal Blend Sherry. Adrienne, Ross' wife, works fulltime for Matua Valley, and members of the Margan family, who now have a fifty percent shareholding, also sit on the board.

The venture began in a leased tin shed in Swanson, near Henderson, with the brothers holding down full-time jobs elsewhere and producing their wine in the evenings and at weekends. The first show entries won immediate acclaim and there were silver medals for successive vintages of Matua Valley Burgundy, a soft, flavoursome red then vinted from hybrid grape material. The spectacle of these two part-time winemakers outperforming the major established wineries in the hybrid red class won for the company an enthusiastic early following.

ROSS (LEFT) AND BILL SPENCE. THEIR DOWN-TO-EARTH APPEARANCES MASK TWO OF THE SHARPER MINDS IN THE INDUSTRY.

The tin shed lasted three vintages until an expired lease forced a change of premises. The present vertical-timbered, corrugated-iron roofed, octagonal winery, which crushes about 650 tonnes of fruit annually, was still being built during the first vintage in 1978. In 1987 two much needed offices were added – before then, incredibly, they coped without any office at all.

A great deal of Matua Valley's runaway success can be attributed to the partners' acute awareness of the importance of public relations. The brothers themselves are popular personalities, extroverted and informal, with boundless energy. The more and more sophisticated packaging of their wines, their obvious appreciation of architecture, their vineyard restaurant, their habit of flying wine writers to the vineyard by helicopter, their declared intention to stage jazz concerts in the winery grounds: all demonstrate a sure sense of public relations. The outcome is that their wines enjoy an extraordinarily high profile.

The present octagonal winery at Waimauku is designed to handle 40,000 cases of wine a year. In the twenty-five hectare, undulating estate vineyard on sandy loam soils are extensive plantings of Pinot Noir, Chardonnay and Sauvignon Blanc, together with smaller plots of Cabernet Franc and Merlot. The Spences have a great deal of faith in West Auckland as a red-wine region: the heat and sunshine are right, the clay soils ideal; rain is the only bugbear, they say. They also draw Cabernet Sauvignon, Chardonnay, Sauvignon Blanc and Gewürztraminer from Hawke's Bay, and Chardonnay, Müller-Thurgau, Gewürztraminer and Chenin Blanc from the Gisborne region.

Matua Valley produces a broad array of interesting and often high-quality wines. Among the dozen or so white wines, the Judd Estate Chardonnay, Chablis and Fumé Blanc are probably the best known labels.

Judd Estate Chardonnay is the company's flagship white wine. Based on fruit grown in Maurice Judd's Gisborne vineyard, this wine is fermented in new Nevers oak barriques, then rests on its lees for a couple of months prior to bottling. Sold very young, in its youth it has a light buttercup hue, a deep, oaky bouquet and figgy/oatmealy palate crying out for bottle age.

The big-selling Chablis is a pale straw, medium-dry style, clean and pleasantly fruity. Here Müller-Thurgau, Chasselas and Chenin Blanc deliver straightforward, fresh flavours with a touch of sweetness to broaden the commercial appeal.

The Fumé Blanc, confusingly, is not wood-aged. Produced from Waimauku fruit, the wine has varied over the years, but has settled of late into a crisp, tangy style with moderate, grassy Sauvignon Blanc character. It is overshadowed by the Reserve Sauvignon Blanc, a more subtle and complex style made from riper fruit matured in oak puncheons.

One of the best value-for-money wines in the Matua Valley range is the strong-flavoured, firm Chenin Blanc/Chardonnay. In this distinctive blend the juicy, pineappley Chenin Blanc flavour comes to the fore early, balanced by steely acidity, with the Chardonnay asserting itself more fully as the wine matures.

Other Matua Valley white wines include Müller-Thurgau and Gewürztraminer (both have enjoyed top medal success); Rhine Riesling, Grey Riesling – they are the only winery reporting buoyant sales of this variety – and a sweet, freeze-concentrated Late Harvest Muscat.

A winery specialty is the dry, earthy Pinot Noir Blanc. Made from the white juice of black grapes, removed from the skins after only brief contact, this wine sports a pale pink, 'blush' tinge. Oaked for a short period, it is full-bodied and flavoursome, with hints of red-wine strength and character.

Matua Valley's range of red wines is dominated by its outstanding Cabernet Sauvignon. Occasional early vintages stood out – the 1977 vintage at five years old developed into an exquisite wine, and several early blends of Cabernet/Hermitage were appealing – but the excellent 1985 lifted the label into the vanguard of this country's reds. A lovely, scented red, it much impressed the great Bordeaux authority, Edmund Penning-Rowsell, who praised its 'very big colour, rich nose and real depth of flavour. At £8.50 it is obviously not cheap, but less than a French wine of comparable quality'.

The 1986 has consolidated and built on the reputation of its predecessor. Hawke's Bay fruit from the Smith vineyard was blended with twenty percent Auckland fruit, which enhanced the bouquet, says Ross Spence. The wine was then matured for one year in a mix of new and one-year-old barrels. The outcome is a bold, voluptuous red, rather tighter in structure than the 1985 and yet hugely enjoyable in its youth.

Nobilo

Renowned for its Müller-Thurgau and respected for its trio of reds – Cabernet Sauvignon, Pinotage and Pinot Noir – Nobilo in the late 1970s was one of the leading wine companies in New Zealand, with a proud success record in competitions. Then the Nobilo star waned, owing both to intensifying competition and to the release of several red wines not up to previous expectations. Sales of its enormously popular Müller-Thurgau suffered during the discount war of 1985–1986, causing severe financial problems, which culminated in the sale of large chunks of land, plus the laying-off of staff. Now Nobilo is on the comeback trail.

At twenty-four, Nikola Nobilo arrived in New Zealand in 1937, from the island of Korcula in the Adriatic Sea. (Legend has it that the first Nobilo to step ashore on Korcula was a seafarer who met two ugly sisters whom none of the villagers would wed. He took one of them as his wife, settled on the island, and for centuries the family tended vines and made wine for the local market.) A stonemason by trade, it is thus natural that Nikola (Nick Nobilo Snr) and his wife Zuva planted vines near the main highway just north of Huapai in 1943, while also tending chickens, cows and grapefruit trees.

The Nobilo operation was transformed in the 1960s when Nick Nobilo Jnr joined the company. Gilbey-Nobilo, formed in 1966, saw Gilbey's of England taking up a substantial shareholding, and providing the funds for an ambitious expansion programme based on classical grape varieties. When Gilbey's withdrew in 1974 – a move forced by shareholding transfers in Britain – Nobilo was established with the vineyards and wood-aging facilities necessary to produce fine wines.

The reconstructed company, formed in 1975, brought the Nobilo family into partnership with distribution agents Nathans and the PSIS – a liquor interest later acquired by Wilson Neill – plus the Development Finance Corporation. One outcome of these financial changes was a loss of overall financial control by the Nobilo family.

It is pleasing to record, however, that in the wake of the industry's 1985–1986 price war Nobilo has re-emerged as one of the country's largest family-owned vineyards. By selling off surplus land, the family was able to buy out – at 'the right price', it says – all three partners.

Throughout the winery's ownership history members of the Nobilo family have retained charge of the daily operations. The swarthy, good-looking Nick Nobilo Jnr (45) is the chief executive who, in his other role as executive winemaker, actively participates in the vintage between February and May each year. Steve Nobilo (48) concentrates on marketing (including sales) and Mark (40) on viticulture. Malcolm Harre is also a key staff member, having worked here as assistant winemaker for over a decade.

Until a few years ago Nobilo company policy was to concentrate on red wines, in the belief that the Huapai area is especially suited to their production. A major replanting and expansion programme between 1981 and 1986 saw white grapes phased out of the home vineyards and their extension to fifty-two hectares of red varieties. The plan was to draw all white varieties from the East Coast.

Now white wines have moved much closer to centre stage in the Nobilo operation. The Huapai vineyards have been reduced from fifty-two to only sixteen hectares. Only red varieties are grown here: Cabernet Sauvignon, Merlot and Pinotage (which Nick Nobilo champions as 'the most successful grape variety in the Auckland region'). Cabernet Sauvignon fruit is also drawn from Hawke's Bay and Marlborough. White grapes are now drawn from all around the country. Gisborne growers supply Müller-Thurgau, Chardonnay and Gewürztraminer; Hawke's Bay growers supply Sauvignon Blanc and Chardonnay; Marlborough growers supply

Sémillon, Sauvignon Blanc and Chardonnay. The Nobilos are also looking at Martinborough as a future source of fruit.

Of the white wines, Nobilo's Müller-Thurgau is deservedly popular. Made from Gisborne fruit, this is a charmingly fruity, mild wine with low alcohol and soft acidity. Among the industry's market leaders, it stands out for its appealing delicacy; fruitiness and a gentle sweetness are the lingering impressions. Ask Nick Nobilo why his Müller-Thurgau is such a huge seller – when scores of rival Müller-Thurgaus are crowding the shelves – and he points to the fact that it was the first in its field, to its consistency over the years, and to the high quality of his fruit. A dry version, labelled Riesling-Sylvaner, has also been released.

The industry's glamour white grapes, Chardonnay and Sauvignon Blanc, are now coming to the fore. Back in the 1970s – although the vines were of an inferior clone and virused – Nobilo's Pinot Chardonnay was one of New Zealand's foremost white wines. Now four Chardonnays are marketed, three of them single-vineyard wines.

Dixon Chardonnay has enjoyed the highest profile. Controversy surrounded the excellent 1985 vintage when, having won the Decanter Trophy for the wine with the highest export potential at the Air New Zealand Export Competition in London, it subsequently crashed to no award at the 1986 National Wine Competition. Produced from Gisborne fruit and wholly barrel-fermented, it is a mouth-filling, nutty, complex style.

Of the other single-vineyard Chardonnays, Tietjen Chardonnay is two-thirds barrel-fermented and the Tombleson Chardonnay, although given a conventional stainless-steel fermentation, is barrel-matured. There is also a commercial Chardonnay blended from a range of vineyards.

THE PUBLICITY SPOTLIGHT IS USUALLY PLAYED ON CHIEF EXECUTIVE NICK NOBILO (CENTRE). MARKETING MANAGER, STEVE (RIGHT), AND VINEYARD MANAGER, MARK, ARE ALSO MEMBERS OF THE FAMILY TEAM AT NOBILO.

Sauvignon Blanc appears in two styles. The first, labelled as Sauvignon Blanc, is a fresh, non-wooded, slightly sweet wine; the second, labelled as Sauvignon Blanc Fumé Style, is a much more pungent, wood-fermented wine. Nobilo also blends Sauvignon Blanc with Cabernet Sauvignon to make an unusually deep-flavoured Rosé.

The Gewürztraminer, made from Gisborne fruit, is held on the skins for eight to ten hours to accentuate its spicy varietal flavours. To produce a medium-dry style, the fermentation is stopped with about ten grams per litre of sugar remaining.

In selected years – 1976, 1981, 1983 – very small quantities of sweet whites have been produced. Müller-Thurgau and Gewürztraminer grapes were left on the vines in 1983 until they started to dehydrate, then hand-picked and fermented in old wood. The outcome was intensely sweet white wine.

Classic Hills is another label under which Nobilo has lately released a solid range of varietal and blended white wines.

Overall, the finest achievement of this vineyard is the Huapai Cabernet Sauvignon – at its best a complex wine, showing a lovely balance of fruit and oak flavours. The 1976 vintage was one of the best New Zealand reds of the decade. The fruit, harvested at the end of April, was field-crushed, fermented on the skins and then aged for two years in French oak puncheons. Opened in 1987, the wine was still superb – perfumed, deeply coloured, with subtle flavours very reminiscent of red Bordeaux.

Although the 1978 had a similar character, the 1979 to 1982 vintages proved disappointing. This flat spot, says Nick Nobilo, was due to the debilitating, worsening effects of viruses in the vines they had planted a decade earlier. Since then, healthier fruit has come on stream and recent vintages of the Huapai Cabernet Sauvignon have been steadily returning to form. A Marlborough Cabernet Sauvignon, bolder and more complex than most Marlborough reds, has also been marketed.

Although other wineries are releasing fine Cabernet Sauvignon, Nobilo's Pinotage has fewer rivals. The 1976 and 1978 vintages still linger in the memory as full reds with soft, peppery flavours reminiscent of the Rhône wines of France. Both the 1983 Huapai and Te Karaka (Gisborne) labels captured golds, and recent vintages from Huapai have been back in the Nobilo tradition of intense, stylish reds.

Nobilo produce their Pinot Noir by a partial carbonic maceration fermentation. Crushed and uncrushed bunches are fermented together in stainless steel for one week before being pressed and fully fermented out. Following a malolactic fermentation the wine is matured in French oak barrels for about eighteen months.

The 1976 and 1978 were outstanding, with a penetrating and true Pinot bouquet and a combination of big fruit and tannin, very like French Burgundy. Opened on its tenth birthday, the 1976 was superb. More recent releases, from vintages in the mid-1980s, have been enjoyable although not fully recapturing their standard of a decade ago.

Château Valley was brought out to help convert white-wine drinkers to red. Described by Nick Nobilo as 'halfway between the fruity Beaujolais style of Piat d'Or and the fullness of the more gutsy Jacob's Creek', it is a raspberryish red, low in tannin, with a soft, sweet finish. The grapes used are a company secret.

Pursuing an idea first embodied in his memorable 1976 Private Bin Claret, Nick Nobilo is presently developing a new, but similar, blended red from estate-grown Cabernet Sauvignon, Pinotage and Pinot Noir. Called Concept, it is held at the winery for five years before release.

With its stained-glass windows and Nobilo-crested carpets, the Nobilo 'château' – the administration and vineyard sales building – is a most handsome environment in which to sip your wine.

Selaks

Selaks is an old-established family vineyard nestled on gently undulating land in Old North Road, Kumeu. Its reputation hinges largely on its masterful Sauvignon Blancs, penetrating, nettley wines of pure, intense varietal characters.

Marino Selak, another emigrant Dalmatian, arrived in Auckland in 1906. After many years on the northern gumfields, he planted vines, fruit trees and vegetables at Te Atatu. The year 1934 marked the first Selak vintage in New Zealand.

Mate Selak, then seventeen, made a similar trek from his homeland to join his uncle Marino in 1940. Times were tough. Mate recalls writing to every hotel in Auckland in 1949, offering his wines for sale. Some wrote back, politely declining; others have yet to reply. The vineyard gradually expanded, becoming one of the first to specialise in table wines. But in the early 1960s the north-west motorway sliced through the small vineyard.

In 1965 Mate Selak re-established the company at Kumeu, with the first vintage there in 1969. Recently, Selaks – run by the warm-hearted Mate (66) and his two sons, Ivan (37) and Michael (27) – has become solidly established at the quality end of the market.

The company's ambitions were hindered up to the early 1980s by a shortage of quality grape material other than the Müller-Thurgau variety. Selaks were forced to rely heavily on Gisborne grapes. However, the company has replanted the four-hectare home vineyard in Sémillon and Merlot and at Riverhead, on land sloping down to Brigham's Creek, a twelve-hectare vineyard has been established in Riesling, Pinot Noir and Chardonnay; the first plantings came on stream in 1983. Selaks also buy fruit from Auckland, Gisborne and Marlborough and have recently planted a new, twenty-hectare vineyard in Marlborough, based on Sauvignon Blanc, Sémillon and Chardonnay.

MICHAEL SELAK (CENTRE) – FLANKED BY HIS FATHER MATE AND WINEMAKER DARRYL WOOLLEY – HAS, AT THE AGE OF ONLY TWENTY-SEVEN, ALREADY ASSUMED CONTROL OF THE DAILY OPERATIONS AT SELAKS.

A labour of love for Mate Selak since 1956 has been his determination to produce a good methode champenoise sparkling wine. The wine, once called Champelle but now labelled Methode Champenoise, caused many headaches in its development stages, including problems with oxidation and clarification and the perils of exploding bottles. The year 1971 marked the first commercial release.

One early drawback was the use of Chasselas as the base wine. However, seventy percent Pinot Noir and thirty percent Chardonnay are currently used and in my recent tastings the wine has revealed mature-tasting fruit with plenty of yeastiness and flavour depth, although some bottles show a more sustained bead than others. An insulated tunnel has even been built in an effort to duplicate the unvarying cool temperatures of the chalk cellars of Champagne.

In 1983 Selaks was joined by a young Australian winemaker, Kevin Judd. His arrival was soon followed by a marked lift in the quality of wine bearing the Selaks label. Since Judd's 1985 departure for Cloudy Bay, Darryl Woolley has made the wine. An Australian in his thirties, Woolley worked under Tim Knappstein at Enterprise Wines in the Clare Valley, and then under Norbert Seibel at Corbans' Gisborne winery, before taking over the winemaking responsibility at Selaks.

Twenty-five thousand cases of wine flow each year from Selaks unadorned concrete-block winery. Production has dropped in recent years from 600 to 400 tonnes – with the axing of carafe and cask lines – but will rise as the new Marlborough plantings come on stream.

Over many years, Selaks have built up a loyal following for their White Burgundy. Aged in American oak, with an almost imperceptible touch of residual sweetness, the fruit used in the blend has steadfastly been kept a secret.

Despite the promise of both the Brigham's Creek and Gisborne Rhine Rieslings, they unfortunately, like other New Zealand Rhine Rieslings, have yet to win a strong consumer following. The wines made from Brigham's Creek fruit have slightly more body, flavour and acidity, according to the Selaks. They also produce a good Müller-Thurgau from Gisborne fruit, which is sweetened with Muscat juice.

Selaks Sauvignon Blanc is pungent and deep-flavoured: a classic cool-climate Marlborough Sauvignon Blanc. The wine rests its case on its pure, crisp fruit flavour, softened by a whisker of sweetness; it is not oak-aged. The 1984 vintage placed first in a much publicised tasting of Sauvignon Blancs from around the world, organised by the British magazine *Decanter*. In New Zealand competitions, this and subsequent vintages have built up an illustrious track record.

The Sauvignon Blanc/Sémillon, a sixty/forty blend which is both cold fermented and matured in Nevers oak puncheons, is equally outstanding. Here the grassy undercurrent of Sémillon, plus the wood treatment, create a more austere, steely style which needs bottle aging to unleash its full complexity. There is also a wood-fermented straight Sémillon, stalky and bone dry.

In most years since 1983 Selaks have marketed a top Chardonnay and Cabernet Sauvignon under their Founders label. This label is reserved for wine judged to be outstanding: when, as happened in 1984 with Cabernet Sauvignon, the fruit is viewed as not up-to-scratch, the label does not appear.

Selaks Founders Chardonnay is made from ripe Gisborne fruit, fermented and matured for twelve months in new Nevers oak puncheons, both heavily and lightly toasted. In its youth it is yellow, oaky and fat, needing three years to round out. The standard Chardonnay is also made from Gisborne fruit, harvested earlier. Also wood-fermented, but only spending a total of four months in oak, this wine is more suitable for early consumption.

Selaks have also marketed a string of freeze-concentrated sweet whites, based on Müller-Thurgau, Sémillon and Riesling, or a blend of Riesling and Gewürztraminer. These are light in alcohol, fresh and appealing.

Overall, Selaks reds lack the distinction of their white wines. The company style tends towards soft, easy-drinking reds lacking depth and complexity. This holds true of both the Cabernet Sauvignon and Private Bin Claret – a Pinot Noir and Cabernet blend – which are made from Auckland and Gisborne fruit and aged only briefly in seasoned oak barrels. The Founders Cabernet Sauvignon, produced from Gisborne fruit matured in new Nevers oak puncheons, is more classy, responding well to several years bottle aging.

HENDERSON

In the shadow of the Waitakere Ranges are grouped several of the oldest wineries in New Zealand. Henderson, twenty kilometres west of Auckland city, has the largest cluster of wineries in the country. Strung out along Lincoln Road, Sturges Road and the floor of the Henderson Valley, all but one of the wineries are small or medium-sized. The oldest – Corbans and Pleasant Valley – were founded in 1902.

Here a flourishing Dalmatian community has imprinted its energetic, vinous way of life on the entire district. Although winemaking in New Zealand is no longer a Dalmatian preserve, here, numerically at least, they still prevail.

Generally, these Dalmatian vineyards began life as small mixed holdings of fruit trees, vines and vegetables. Dalmatian settlers who had lived on peasant farms in Dalmatia, typically saved funds on the northern gumfields and then looked for self-sufficiency. Cheap parcels of land were available for purchase in the Henderson-Oratia area and the large Auckland market beckoned.

Since 1960 these holdings have shifted towards specialisation in market-gardening, orcharding or winemaking. Also there has been a gradual shift of vine plantings away from Henderson itself. Back in 1960, eighty percent of Auckland's vineyards and orchards were in Henderson and Oratia. Later, the north-west motorway opened West Auckland up to the pressures of urban expansion and reduced the land available for viticulture. The surviving vineyards benefit from differential rating systems that significantly ease their rates burden, but some land values, especially those close to the Great North Road, soared too high to be kept in vines.

Between 1975 and 1986, vineyard areas in the Auckland region slumped from 750 hectares – thirty-two percent of the national area – to only 221 hectares or five percent of entire plantings. Major companies such as Montana and Corbans – the latter now prefers to expand into Gisborne, Hawke's Bay and Marlborough – no longer depend on Auckland as a source of grapes. And several smaller wineries – Western Vineyards, Spence's and Eastern Vineyards – have ceased production.

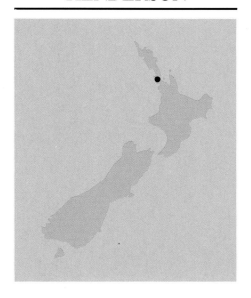

VINES HAVE FLOURISHED IN THE FOOTHILLS OF THE WAITAKERE RANGES SINCE THE END OF LAST CENTURY.

Henderson suffers from serious physical and climatic handicaps for viticulture. The rainfall, rising steeply from the city westwards to the Waitakeres, is far from ideal for winemaking. Auckland University scientists have recently claimed that moist low clouds which hang around the hills cause the area's unusually high rainfall by swelling the raindrops which descend through them from higher rainclouds. The plentiful rains, in association with high humidity, create ideal conditons for fungous diseases, especially during the critical February-April ripening period. The soils, too, are heavy, requiring deep ploughing and tile draining.

Because of this wet climate, the hardy, weather and disease-resistant hybrid varieties were always more popular in Henderson than elsewhere. Two decades ago Auckland had twice as many hybrids as Hawke's Bay, and in 1980 the presence of hybrid varieties (twenty-eight percent) was still way ahead of the national average (ten percent).

The 1986 vineyard survey revealed that bulk white wine grapes, like Müller-Thurgau and Chasselas, are only lightly planted in Auckland. Here is another reason for Auckland's relative demise as a grapegrowing area; most companies rely heavily on Müller-Thurgau as the basis for a variety of wine styles, and that variety crops relatively poorly in Auckland. Gisborne and Hawke's Bay produce far heavier tonnages.

Henderson may be in eclipse in terms of recent vineyard development, but in other respects the area remains vital to the wine industry. Although Auckland has only five percent of the national vineyard area, much of the wine is made there. The headquarters and bottling plants of most of the large and medium-sized wine companies in New Zealand are in Auckland, close to the largest market. An enormous amount of the country's wine output is transported to Auckland as fruit, as partly processed wine, or as finished wine ready for bottling.

The past five years have been notable for the closure of the large Penfolds winery and the lack of visible progress at such wineries as Mayfair, Mazuran, Windy Hill, Pechar's and Fino Valley.

Penfolds (NZ) was established in 1963 on a small property in Lincoln Road bought from the old firm of Averill Brothers, who had planted vines there in 1922. The new company was founded as a joint venture between Penfolds (Australia) and local brewers and merchants. In 1977 Penfolds (Australia) sold most of its shares to Frank Yukich, who in turn sold out to Lion Breweries in 1982. Following Montana's purchase of Penfolds in 1986, the Henderson winery was closed and its winemaking equipment and key staff integrated into Montana's operations.

A couple of decades ago Mayfair Vineyards enjoyed a strong reputation for its sherries, cocktails and liqueurs. But today the vogue for such products as Limbo Lime Gin, Rock'n' Roll and Blackberry Nip has vanished, leaving this small family winery in Sturges Road, run by the Ivicevichs, heavily reduced in output.

The Mazuran winery specialised in fortified wines for decades with outstanding success. It was founded in the late 1930s by George Mazuran, who in the 1950s embarked on a unique lobbying career designed to foster the sales of independent, family-owned wineries such as his own.

Ironically, the winegrowing bonanza that owed so much to his efforts passed his own company by. The Mazuran vineyard in Lincoln Road is small and the wines are hard to find. The range of products, concentrated on sherries and ports – some matured for up to twenty years – has barely changed for decades. The Mazuran style is almost unmistakable: these are big dessert wines, mellow, often sweet and syrupy, always rich.

George Mazuran died in 1982 and his wife Florence soon afterwards. Their daughter Patricia, who with her husband Rado Hladilo, ran the winery following her parents' deaths, herself passed away in 1987.

Windy Hill was founded by Milan Erceg – who died in 1988 – on the corner of Metcalfe and Simpson Roads in 1934. Although this winery has a reputation for good dry sherries and solid reds, Paul Erceg, the son of the founder, has until recently not been actively involved.

Pechar's, a small winery in Henderson Valley Road, was founded by Steve Pechar in 1971. Its wines are mediocre but inexpensive. Fino Valley is another basically undistinguished winery in Henderson Valley Road, run by the Torduch family. Back in the early 1970s, in roaring company at the winery on Saturday afternoons, Fino Valley Medium Dry Red served as my introduction to the world of wine.

Most recent viticultural research has been concentrated in the newer wine areas, so that considerable scope remains in Henderson for experimentation with new varieties, clones and rootstocks; who knows, this older wine district may yet provide further surprises. With four distinguished wineries – Babich, Collard, Corbans and Delegat's – retaining their operations here, the Henderson wine trail still has a multitude of vinous delights for the wine lover.

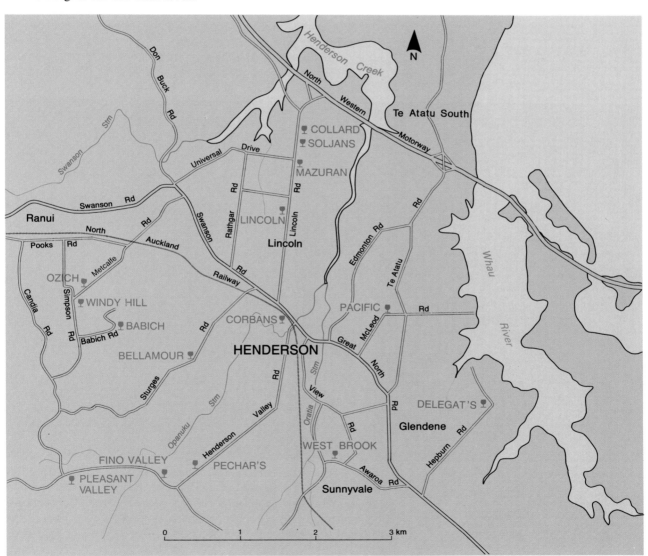

Babich

I must openly declare an interest here. In late 1975 I first ventured down Babich Road in pursuit of an outdoor job during the university holidays. Thirteen years later, now in the role of marketing manager, I am still threading my way each morning down that road to the Babich winery.

Babich is a classic example of the several medium-sized, independent wineries in New Zealand run by families of Dalmatian origin. It is run by two brothers, Peter (56) and Joe (47) who, since they divided up responsibilities over twenty years ago – Peter looking after the vineyards and administration, Joe making the wine – have had the great good fortune to get along perfectly with each other. Peter is a warm and gentle, but strong man, proud of his family's achievements and determined to safeguard them through his longstanding tenure of a seat on the Wine Institute's influential executive committee. Joe, a long-serving senior wine judge, has the 'tall and rangy good looks' described by Robert Joseph in *Wine* magazine. Their gracious sister, Maureen, works in the office and behind the vineyard counter.

Babich's ancestral home lies in the winegrowing area of Imotski. In 1910, as a boy of fourteen, Josip (Joe) Babich Snr left Dalmatia to join his three brothers toiling in the gumfields of the Far North. His first wine was produced in 1916. At Kaikino, on the last stretch of land leading to Cape Reinga, he grew grapes, trod them with his feet, and opened a wineshop.

PETER (LEFT) AND JOE BABICH – PICTURED WITH THEIR SISTER MAUREEN AND MOTHER MARA – HAVE STEADILY BUILT THEIR COMPANY INTO ONE OF NEW ZEALAND'S FOREMOST FAMILY-CONTROLLED VINEYARDS. THREE TIMES BETWEEN 1984 AND 1987 JOE BABICH'S WINES WON THE PRESTIGIOUS VINTNERS TROPHY.

The shift to the Henderson Valley came in 1919. On a twenty-four-hectare wilderness property, Joe milked cows, grew vegetables, established a small orchard – and planted classical Meunier vines. Ten years later Joe Babich wed another emigrant Dalmatian, Mara Grgic. Their lifetime of shared endeavour included the births of five children, and the steady expansion of the vineyard.

During the war, winemaking slowly became the family's major business activity. By the 1950s son Peter was at the helm, and the 1960s saw the emergence of Joe Babich Jnr as winemaker.

Until his death in 1983, Joe Babich Snr was one of the Grand Old

Men of the New Zealand wine industry. One of the most moving moments in his long, arduous life occurred in 1981, when he watched a container load of his wine set out for Europe, the continent he had left a lifetime ago. In some deeply satisfying sense the wheel of his life had turned full circle. Exports are now an integral and growing part of the Babich marketing strategy, notably to England but also to the United States and Australia.

About thirty hectares of grapevines now grow on Babich's loam-clay soils. These are supplemented each year by grapes bought from growers in the Gisborne, Hawke's Bay, Marlborough and Auckland regions. The Babich vineyard is predominantly planted with Cabernet Sauvignon, Pinotage, Pinot Noir, Chardonnay, Sauvignon Blanc, Gewürztraminer and Palomino vines. A prime source of quality fruit is the Irongate vineyard, planted in an old shingle bed of the Ngaruroro River, near the foothills bordering the western plains of Hawke's Bay. Twenty-five metres beneath the surface gravels runs the Irongate aquifer, from which this vineyard takes its name. The Chardonnay, Cabernet Sauvignon, Merlot and Cabernet Franc vines planted here yield light crops of ripe, deep-flavoured fruit.

Babich, with its annual production of about 60,000 cases, is the seventh or eighth largest winery in the country – larger than many realise. Over many years it has carved out a solid reputation for value-for-money pricing and reliable, often excellent, wines.

Immaculately clean, crisp, dry wines are the hallmark of Joe Babich's white wine style. Classic Dry, the popular label which has evolved from the older Dry White, is blended from several grape varieties to a crisp, unswervingly bone-dry style.

Dry Riesling-Sylvaner has long been one of Joe Babich's specialties, with the double gold, triple trophy-winning 1984 vintage so far the jewel in the crown. Delicate, floral and fractionally off-dry, it affords a welcome alternative to what I view as our increasingly obsessive focus on Chardonnays and Sauvignon Blancs. Its Müller-Thurgau stablemate is also based on Gisborne fruit but made in a sweeter, more fruity style.

Both the Gewürztraminer and Rhine Riesling tend to be light, delicate and fragrant in style – pleasant commercial wines without any claims to greatness.

Sauvignon Blanc first entered the Babich range in 1986. Two styles have been marketed since then, both made from Hawke's Bay grapes, both dry. The one labelled as Sauvignon Blanc is a full-bodied, non-wooded wine with the accent squarely on its tangy green capsicum-like fruit character. The Barrel Fermented Sauvignon Blanc underpins the variety's naturally piquant flavour with oak, creating a potentially more complex wine, demanding longer bottle age.

Fumé Vert (smoky-green) is a blend of Sémillon, Sauvignon Blanc and Chardonnay, with a bare hint of sweetness which nicely balances the thrusting, herbaceous flavour of the predominant Sémillon.

Babich Chardonnay has won respect for its quality/price juxtaposition. This is a dry, full-bodied wine made from Auckland and Gisborne fruit enhanced by several months' maturation in Nevers oak puncheons. With each vintage since its debut in 1982 the wine has become bolder and more mouth-filling, as Joe Babich comes to grips with the intricacies of Chardonnay production.

Irongate Chardonnay is the winery flagship. This is a rich, intense wine in the classic Chardonnay mould, both fermented and matured in new Nevers oak puncheons. It appeals to me for its flavour strength and toasty complexity; at twelve percent alcohol it is stylish rather than overwhelming. It has carved out a distinguished track record in competitions: the 1985 (at the National Wine Competition), the 1986 (at the International Wine and Spirit Competition, London) and the 1987 (at the Air New Zealand Wine Awards) have all won gold medals. Both the 1985 and 1987 were also recipients of the Vintners Trophy, awarded to the Best Current Vintage Dry White Table Wine.

Babich is also deeply entrenched in the red wine market. Joe Babich Snr set the early pattern with his hybrid Dry Red and Vintara Red, which in the 1950s were reputed to be among the few drinkable local reds.

The Pinotage/Cabernet is another Babich specialty, now spanning twenty vintages. This is a soft, fruity red wine, blended from seventy-five percent Pinotage, twenty-five percent Cabernet Sauvignon. Most vintages reach top form at three to five years old.

The Pinot Noir, like the Pinotage/Cabernet sourced from estate-grown fruit, has helped build West Auckland's reputation as a distinguished red-wine producing region. The 1981, 1983 and 1984 all scored gold medals and were pleasingly full of elusive Pinot Noir varietal characteristics, with more colour depth and body than the later 1985 and 1986 vintages. Only the 1981 vintage, however, has matured well over a span of several years in the bottle.

The Cabernet Sauvignon, bearing its distinctive black label, from its origins in 1976 until 1984 was made solely from Henderson fruit. The style was medium-bodied, with medium-full colour depth and a pleasantly oaky palate. By far the pick of the bunch was the unusually ripe and scented 1978 vintage, which reached its peak around 1985.

The duo of gold medals awarded to Babich Hawke's Bay Cabernet Sauvignon 1985 and Hawke's Bay Cabernet/Merlot 1985 followed hard on the heels of the decision to commence drawing fruit for red wine from Hawke's Bay. Made from magnificent fruit grown in an old-established vineyard, both wines were matured in Nevers oak puncheons for a year, the Cabernet/Merlot exclusively in new barrels. Where the Cabernet/Merlot is a voluptuous red with mouth-encircling flavours, the 100 percent varietal Cabernet Sauvignon is a slightly leaner, more tannic wine, structured along the lines of classic claret. This, beyond doubt, is the best Cabernet Sauvignon yet from winemaker Joe Babich.

Babich also market a full range of sherries and ports. The dry Palomino Sherry is a company mainstay, but the most distinguished fortified wine is the rare Reserve Port, an excellent old tawny.

Mara Babich, now in her mid-eighties, still strolls across to the winery for a chat each day. The family influence is powerful at Babich, the source of its strength. There is little room to doubt that the winery will celebrate its seventy-fifth anniversary in 1991 or its centenary in 2016; one of Peter's sons, David, is already immersed in winemaking studies at Roseworthy College in South Australia.

Bellamour

The launch of the Bellamour label in 1987 signalled that a renaissance was planned for the winery once called Balic Estate, and before that, Golden Sunset. In August 1988, however, Bellamour was placed in receivership.

A pioneer firm, Golden Sunset was founded in 1912 by Josip (Joseph) Balich, a Dalmatian who had deserted from the Austrian army (the 'h' was later dropped from the family name to avoid confusion with Babich). Balich planted his vines at night, by candlelight, after a hard day's labour in the Corban vineyard. The Model T Ford in which Joseph Balich toured the area selling his invalid port – warmly recommended for medicinal purposes – has long been displayed at the winery in Sturges Road.

Until a few years ago, under winemaker Vic Talyancich, Balic produced a great deal of sparkling wine; the most popular was Balic Asti Spumante.

But the table wines had generally fallen one or two steps behind the rest of the industry. Following Vic Talyancich's departure from the company, but prior to the release of the first wines under the Bellamour label, a couple of plain cask wines were marketed – a 'blush' wine, Tiger Lily; and a medium white, Tramtrack Rieslerr – followed by a range of excellent bought-in wines, notably a lovely Hawke's Bay Rhine Riesling 1985 and Gisborne Gewürztraminer 1985.

Diana Balich (44) is Joseph Balich's grand-daughter and one of the few women ever to head a New Zealand winery. Soft-spoken, she has a deep interest in the history of West Auckland and has wanted to inject 'some romance and culture back into the industry'.

The home vineyard, stretched out behind the winery, has contracted since lesser varieties were pulled out a couple of years ago; 2.5 hectares are planted now in Pinot Noir and Cabernet Sauvignon. Bellamour has drawn its fruit principally from Hawke's Bay, including Chardonnay, Sauvignon Blanc, Chenin Blanc, Müller-Thurgau, Riesling and Gewürztraminer.

Bellamour, which Diana Balich says means 'the look of love', was chosen as the name for the new venture to symbolise both 'the love, care and attention . . . essential in the making of premium quality wines' and 'the natural beauty of the winery buildings and the sixty-five acre [26ha] property of vineyards, rolling grasslands, picnic and lake areas'. Plans were announced to build Bellamour into a popular tourist centre.

In the old brick and wood winery erected prior to the Depression, after the original winery burned down, Bellamour aimed to produce twenty-five to thirty thousand cases of wine each year. Fortified wines, sparklings and wine casks were all axed. The premium range of varietals was marketed under a Limited Release label, featuring a series of striking impressionistic paintings, and the commercial bottlings carried an Estate Selection label featuring a picture of the winery.

From Bellamour's 1987 debut – made by winemaker John Baruzzi, who has since departed – I tasted a solid, moderately full Chenin/Chardonnay, a restrained Gewürztraminer, a crisp and green-grassed Sauvignon Blanc and an elegant, squeaky-clean Rhine Riesling looking capable of many years' development.

DIANA BALICH IS ONE OF ONLY A HANDFUL OF WOMEN WHO HAVE HEADED A NEW ZEALAND WINERY.

149

Collard Bros

Collard Bros first burst into prominence by scoring five silver medals at the 1972 national wine show. At that stage, most members of the wine trade had not even heard of the vineyard.

The founder, J.W. Collard, who bought the present property in Lincoln Road in 1910, called it Sutton Baron after the village in Kent where traditionally his family had grown hops and fruit. The first vines were planted in response to the urgings of Mrs Collard's brothers, the Averills. From 1946 until 1963, when Penfolds took over the Averill winery, Collard wines were made there.

Today this small, well-respected company is administered by Lionel Collard (67); the winemakers are his two sons, Bruce (39), a senior national wine judge, and Geoffrey (36), who worked in the Mosel for three years on a Rotary exchange scholarship. Lionel is often found behind the vineyard counter, but his sons are shy men, according to Lionel, preferring to let their wines speak for themselves – which they manage to do most eloquently.

The home vineyard, just off the north-west motorway, is planted in Cabernet Sauvignon, Cabernet Franc, Merlot, Sémillon, Riesling and Gewürztraminer vines. Grapes used to be bought exclusively from Auckland growers but are now also drawn from Te Kauwhata, Hawke's Bay and Marlborough.

In response to intensifying urban pressures, in the early 1980s Bruce and Geoffrey purchased a large property in the Waikoukou Valley, close to Matua Valley. Here, in the Rothesay vineyard of sixteen hectares, they have planted Chardonnay, Sauvignon Blanc, Gewürztraminer, Riesling, Cabernet Sauvignon and Cabernet Franc vines. The soils are heavier here than in the home vineyard at Henderson and although the two plots have similar ripening patterns, the Rothesay fruit has the edge in quality, they have found.

Although hybrids have now been completely phased out of the Collard vineyard, the company used to handle them well. The Private Bin Dry White, vinted from Baco 22A, had a full aroma and clean sharp taste; Len Evans, the renowned Australian wine man, was rapturous over the 1978: 'I'm impressed out of my mind by this wine. It is exceptionally clean, with lovely freshness, balance and harmony . . .' And the Private Bin Claret, produced from Seibel 5455 grapes, was usually a medium-bodied, firm red with only a bare hint of coarseness to betray its hybrid origins.

The company's reputation up to the early-mid 1980s was largely built by three varietal white wines: Müller-Thurgau (now dropped from the range), Rhine Riesling and Gewürztraminer. These were – and still are – often Germanic in style, for the Collards deliberately set out to reproduce Down Under the harmony and elegance typical of the best German white wines.

Collard Rhine Rieslings are regularly in this country's top drawer. Based on fruit drawn from the home vineyard, Rothesay, Te Kauwhata and Marlborough, from one vintage to the next different styles have emerged. Opened in early 1988, the full-bodied Alsace-style Te Kauwhata Dry 1985 displayed a wealth of classic citric Riesling bouquet and flavour of rare depth. By contrast, the 1987 Rhine Riesling, blended from Rothesay and home-vineyard grapes, is a medium style, epitomising this variety's unrivalled elegance when a hint of sweetness offsets its natural sharpness. The 1985 Botrytised and 1986 Marlborough Botrytised Rhine Rieslings are sweeter still – the 1986 wine May-harvested and stop-fermented at forty-eight grams per litre of residual sugar. Collard are proven masters of this delectable variety and the modest way they charge for it makes it one of this country's top value-for-money buys.

Collard Gewürztraminer, based on Rothesay and Henderson grapes, is a floral, rather restrained style, without the spicy rush of Gewürztraminers sourced from further south.

Lately the company has moved to develop a much broader range of dry white wines. The Private Bin White Burgundy, descended from the old Private Bin Dry White, is strong in body and flavour and cheap to buy. This blend of Chenin Blanc's fruitiness, Sémillon's pungent bouquet and crisp acidity, and Chardonnay's flavour and fullness is a happy one.

Collard has emerged as New Zealand's champion Chenin Blanc winery. The wines are produced from obviously very well-ripened Te Kauwhata (and formally Henderson) fruit, which is fermented to dryness and then partially matured in French oak puncheons. These are richly scented and deep-flavoured wines, redolent of tropical fruit salad.

The Sauvignon Blanc is made from Rothesay vineyard fruit and not handled in oak. It is dry and mouth-filling, flinty, less voluptuous than its Marlborough-grown counterparts, but a superb dinner wine.

Collard Chardonnays have built up an extraordinary track record in shows, a performance Lionel Collard attributes to his sons' winemaking skills and to their 'very careful handling of Chardonnay in new Nevers oak puncheons'. He is reluctant, however, to divulge any precise details about the winery's oak fermentation or maturation techniques.

Three Chardonnay labels have been marketed, all from different North Island regions and all reaching gold medal status. The Tolaga Bay, half aged in new Nevers oak, was a 'deliberately youthful, fresh, clean style'. The Hawke's Bay Chardonnay is a powerful wine with soft, creamy oak. From the Rothesay vineyard comes a firm, medium-bodied style with subtle lingering flavours.

For many years the established top Collard red was the Pinotage/Cabernet – the 1974 and 1978 both won golds. This was consistently a soft, pleasant wine, but a shade too light to be really outstanding. A couple of vintages of unblended Merlot, straight Cabernet Sauvignon and Cabernet Sauvignon/Shiraz blends have been seen; however, the top Collard red since 1980 has clearly been the Cabernet Sauvignon/Merlot.

A FIERCE INDIVIDUALIST, LIONEL COLLARD ALSO ENJOYS A DESERVED REPUTATION FOR HIS UNCOMPROMISING APPROACH TO ALL ASPECTS OF WINE QUALITY.

Resplendent in its Château Mouton-Rothschild-inspired series of labels designed by local artists, the Cabernet Sauvignon/Merlot has been consistently elegant and fragrant, but once again, until recently, a shade on the light side. 1986 marked a turning point. Blended from eighty percent Cabernet Sauvignon (from Auckland, Hawke's Bay and Marlborough), fifteen percent Henderson Merlot and five percent Cabernet Franc, this extremely ripe, deep hued, soft red is the first distinguished red wine from Collard.

On a lower plane, Collard also markets an excellent Private Bin Claret, featuring an unusual blend of Cabernet Sauvignon, Pinot Noir and Shiraz. This is ripe, soft, scented and outstanding value-for-money.

With an annual output of around 15,000 cases, Collard has now outgrown 'boutique' winery status. Company policy is nonetheless to stay reasonably small and progressively reduce its range of labels.

Corbans

IN MARLBOROUGH'S STONE-STREWN SOILS, SEVERAL HUNDRED KILOMETRES TO THE SOUTH OF THE ORIGINAL MT LEBANON PLANTINGS, CORBANS HAS ESTABLISHED ITS STONELEIGH AND SETTLEMENT VINEYARDS. THE EARLY RELEASES ARE NOW CHALLENGING MONTANA'S FORMER COMMERCIAL PRE-EMINENCE IN THE REGION.

For forty years, the adroit management of the Corban family ensured their domination of the New Zealand wine industry. From its humble beginnings as a one-and-a-half hectare vineyard founded by Lebanese immigrant Assid Abraham Corban at Henderson in 1902, the winery flourished through prohibition and depression and early established itself as a household name. But today the company is Corbans only in name, being a wholly owned subsidiary of Magnum Corporation Limited, itself a subsidiary of Brierley Investments Limited.

A.A. Corban, a stonemason from the village of Shweir on the flanks of Mt Lebanon, inland from Beirut, arrived in New Zealand in 1892. He travelled the goldfields and mining towns of the North Island peddling ornaments and fancy goods, then set up as a dealer in Auckland's Queen Street. Two years later, he sent for his wife Najibie and sons Khaleel and Wadier to join him.

The beginning of Corban's 'Mt Lebanon Vineyards' lies in the 1902 purchase – for £320 – of four hectares of Henderson gumland, complete with a small cottage and a few Isabella vines. His strong ambition to produce wine – a family tradition back in Lebanon – led Assid Abraham Corban to establish a small vineyard: Black Hamburghs for the table and such classic varieties as Chasselas, Hermitage and Cabernet Sauvignon for winemaking; no Albany Surprise – that, said A.A. Corban, was a vine suitable only for lazy winegrowers. At the first Corban vintage in the new country in 1908, the fruit was crushed by hand with a wooden club and an open hogshead used as the fermenting vat.

A small white brick building, still standing at the entrance to Corbans winery, bears testimony to the marketing problems A.A. Corban immediately encountered. West Auckland voted 'dry' in 1908, denying Corban the right to sell his wine directly from his cellar. A railwayman's cottage, standing only a few metres away across the railway tracks in a 'wet' electorate, was pressed into service as a sales depot until 1914, when the surviving white building was erected. This was later superseded by a sales outlet in Auckland city.

By 1916 son Wadier had assumed the duties of winemaker. At the New Zealand and South Seas Exhibition 1925–26, Wadier's Corbans port won first place. Khaleel took charge of sales, travelling the length of the country in an old Dodge van, building up a strong trade in tonic and restorative wines.

Although the arrival of a rotary hoe in 1934, and a caterpillar tractor soon after greatly eased the vineyard toil, by all accounts, until his death from a stroke in 1941, Assid Abraham Corban remained a patriarch in the Old Testament mould, and a strong believer in the virtues of hard work. Najibie, too, until her death in 1957 remained in close touch with all aspects of management.

When the wine boom began in earnest in the 1960s, Corbans' plantings leap-frogged from the Henderson Valley north to Riverlea, Kumeu and Taupaki, and later contracts were negotiated with growers in Auckland and Gisborne. Alex Corban, as winemaker, demonstrated a flair for technical innovation: pioneering the use of refrigeration, introducing the use of selected yeast cultures for fermentation in 1958, ushering in bulk fermentation of sparkling wines in 1962, and producing the first commercial releases of flor sherry, Riesling-Sylvaner (Müller-Thurgau), Pinotage and Chardonnay.

To reinforce the company's economic base, A.A. Corban and Sons admitted a nineteen percent shareholding by wine and spirit merchants. But when the challenge from Montana emerged in the late 1960s, the Corban family's own financial resources proved insufficient to pay for the huge expansion necessary if the company was to retain its ascendancy. Rothmans – later renamed Magnum Corporation – became a shareholder and steadily increased its influence; although Joe Corban (vineyards manager) is still actively involved in the firm, today the Corban family has altogether lost its financial control.

Corbans planted new vineyards at Gisborne in 1968 and three years later sited a second winery there. Subsequently plantings spread up the East Coast to Tolaga Bay, and also to Te Kauwhata.

Through the mid-1970s Corbans struggled to match the quality advances of its rivals. The phasing out of hybrids seemed slow and top white wines such as Chardonnay were consistently plain. The company's prestige was in danger of permanent erosion.

From 1980 onwards, however, there was a marked lift in wine quality, assisted by the arrival of German Norbert Seibel, a Geisenheim graduate with winemaking experience in Germany, France and South Africa.

Corbans' haul of silver medals for table wines at the National Wine Competition tripled between 1978 and 1980.

Rothmans, after gaining full ownership of Corbans in 1979, embarked on a multi-million dollar upgrading and expansion programme. New winemaking equipment was purchased and in 1980 the Stoneleigh and Settlement vineyards in Marlborough were planted in Chardonnay, Sauvignon Blanc, Riesling, Sémillon, Gewürztraminer, Cabernet Sauvignon and Merlot. Corbans' climb in prestige in recent years has been strongly assisted by the outstanding fruit coming on stream from these Marlborough vineyards.

In 1987 Corbans bought the assets of the ailing wine company Cooks/McWilliam's Limited for $20 million; both companies had already been subsidiaries of Brierley Investments Limited. Paul Treacher was appointed General Manager of the enlarged company, now holding about thirty percent of the market for New Zealand wine. Treacher was recently portrayed by his former colleague Bob Campbell as having 'boyish good looks [which] disguise a mature, yet adventurous and often aggressive approach to company management and marketing'.

CORBANS' GENERAL MANAGER, PAUL TREACHER (LEFT), AND CHIEF WINEMAKER, KERRY HITCHCOCK. THE 1987 RATIONALISATION OF BRIERLEY INVESTMENTS' WINE INTERESTS BROUGHT THEM TOGETHER.

According to Treacher, the acquisition of Cooks/McWilliam's 'represented an essential major rationalisation within the local winemaking industry . . . New Zealand winemakers have been hit by punitive wine taxes, serious oversupply of bulk grapes, the withdrawal of export incentives and the phasing out of tariffs and quotas on imports. Further pressures are expected to come on the industry, and it is essential that local large-scale winemakers become and remain as cost efficient as their counterparts abroad . . . The bringing together of Corbans and Cooks/McWilliam's will provide a much stronger base'.

Immediate restructuring brought the closure of Cooks' offices in Auckland and packaging plant in Mercer; about seventy staff lost their jobs. The Corban family homestead at the Henderson winery lives on as the company head office. The new giant – second only to Montana/Penfolds in scale – draws fruit from company-owned vineyards and contract growers lying up to 650 kilometres apart, from Te Kauwhata down through Gisborne, Hawke's Bay and Marlborough, to Canterbury. With a quartet of wineries – at Henderson (used for the final blending and bottling of all the wines crushed and fermented further south), Te Kauwhata, Gisborne and Napier – and temporary access to Cloudy Bay's facilities at Blenheim, the enlarged company is planning a decentralised approach to give its wines plenty of scope for regional variation.

Shouldering overall responsibility for Corbans' winemaking is Kerry Hitchcock (41) who served as Cooks' winemaker right from the first vintage in 1972. From Hitchcock the division of responsibility extends to senior winemakers installed in each of the four company wineries.

Corbans market a very diverse range of wine under the Corbans, Robard and Butler, and Stoneleigh labels (Cooks and McWilliam's labels are treated under Cooks). The Corbans label appears on fortified, cask and bottled table wines, including some outstanding 'private bin' wines made from Marlborough fruit. Robard and Butler is a range of overall high-quality, often high-alcohol, bottled table wines. Stoneleigh presents a range of commercially available bottled table wines from the Stoneleigh vineyard in Marlborough.

The whites first: Corbans' range of casks features a Marlborough Müller-Thurgau, St Amand Chablis, Traminer/Riesling, Gisborne Sémillon, Montel Sauterne (sic) and the popular Liebestraum, a medium blend of Gisborne-grown Müller-Thurgau, Chenin Blanc and – most recently – Riesling.

In the more exotic varietals, Corbans are demonstrating much ability with Gewürztraminer. These are medium-dry and fragrant wines with pungent spice.

Another success is Sauvignon Blanc, highlighted by the lovely refined Corbans Fumé Blanc, with its very ripe gooseberry fruit lifted by a restrained touch of oak. Marlborough-grown grapes are fermented and matured in Nevers oak puncheons for three months. The non-wooded Stoneleigh Sauvignon Blanc, a whisker short of full dryness, affords an interesting style contrast, more grassy and bracing.

Corbans has also demonstrated much ability with Riesling, in a range of styles from the flowery, medium Marlborough Rhine Riesling to the more austere, drier Robard and Butler Rhine Riesling – both have earned a cluster of gold medals. Corbans deserve credit for persevering with these delightful wines during an era when consumers have by-and-large failed to recognise their attractiveness.

A trio of Chardonnays appear under the Corbans, Robard and Butler, and Stoneleigh labels. Stoneleigh Chardonnay is a crisp, fresh style with citric fruit flavours, aged for three months in wood. Corbans Chardonnay, made from Marlborough fruit matured in new Nevers oak puncheons for five months, ranks as one of the foremost South Island Chardonnays; the delectably buttery 1984 vintage, awarded an Australian gold medal, was outstanding. The Robard and Butler Chardonnays, also from Marlborough grapes, are broad, soft wines, in their youth brimming with oak carpentry.

A rich, luscious 1980 Auslese set the precedent for several outstanding sweet white wines from Corbans. Especially memorable are the Noble Reichensteiner 1985, a deep amber, treacly wine made from rampantly botrytised Tolaga Bay-grown grapes, and the Noble Rhine Riesling 1986, a sweet, squeaky clean, nectareous wine fermented from Marlborough fruit harvested as late as mid-June.

For many years Corbans adhered to a policy of marketing a 'claret' rather than a Cabernet Sauvignon. The familiar Claret and Burgundy labels are still in the range, although now positioned more as quaffing reds.

The first release of Cabernet Sauvignon, 1976, was a bold, ripe-tasting red that scored a gold award. Vintages in the early 1980s then tended to lack intensity. Then came the dark-hued, soft Cabernet Sauvignon/Merlot 1983, another gold medal winner in which the Merlot made its presence well felt. By the late 1980s, smooth, silky Cabernet/Merlot blends had emerged as another winery specialty.

Velluto Rosso is a popular red, ideal for lovers of medium white wine

WITH FOUR WINERIES LOCATED AROUND THE NORTH ISLAND, CORBANS HAS NOW CLEARLY EMERGED AS NEW ZEALAND'S SECOND-LARGEST WINE COMPANY, WITH A STRONG MARKET SHARE ESTIMATED TO BE THIRTY PERCENT.

searching for a taste change. This light ruby, non-wooded blend of Pinot Noir and Cabernet Sauvignon is usually fresh and crisp – in many ways like a white wine – with simple raspberryish/strawberryish flavours and an upfront (38 grams per litre) sweetness.

The most memorable New Zealand port I've tasted of late is undoubtedly Corbans Cabernet Port 1983. Tolaga Bay fruit fortified with very old brandy, then matured in small oak hogsheads, has developed into a rich, fruity port of majestic concentration and depth.

Delegat's

Having earned recognition in the early-mid 1980s as a consistently fine producer of Chardonnay, Delegat's suffered severely during the industry's price war of 1985–86. With the support of Wilson Neill, its new substantial shareholder, it has now embarked on a period of consolidation.

This medium-sized winery tucked away in Hepburn Road, Henderson, was founded by Nikola (Nick) Delegat in 1947. Delegat first arrived in New Zealand in 1923 but later retraced his steps to Yugoslavia, before finally establishing a two-hectare plot of vines at Henderson. Today his son Jim Delegat (39) is the company head and his energetic and unfailingly cheerful daughter Rose (36) is the export sales director.

JIM DELEGAT (RIGHT) AND HIS TALENTED AND AMBITIOUS WINEMAKER, BRENT MARRIS. JIM'S SISTER ROSE IS ALSO INVOLVED, PLAYING A VITAL ROLE IN MARKETING.

Delegat's appeared to be content to produce sound, ordinary wines until the 1979 arrival of a young Australian winemaker, John Hancock, signalled a change of direction. Almost overnight, Hancock lifted the standard of Delegat's wines: the gold medal won by his 1979 Selected Vintage Riesling-Sylvaner was to be the first of a string of successes. Excellent Pinot Gris, Muscat Blanc, Chardonnay and Auslese Müller-Thurgau followed.

After a grim struggle during the industry's discount battle, Delegat's entered voluntary receivership in late 1985. A sharply reduced vintage was processed in 1986. Wilson Neill, the Dunedin-based company owning a large chain of retail liquor outlets, subsequently took a substantial interest, leaving the Delegat family with a reduced but still sizeable shareholding.

The move gave Wilson Neill a protected source of supply, paralleling the 'vertical integration' between Liquorland outlets and Corbans.

The company does not own vineyards. Fruit is purchased from Gisborne – Chardonnay, Riesling and Sauvignon Blanc – and Hawke's Bay – Müller-Thurgau, Gewürztraminer, Sauvignon Blanc, Chardonnay, Cabernet Sauvignon, Merlot and Cabernet Franc. From Lincoln Ellmer's vineyard at Te Karaka, in the hills above the Gisborne flats, superb Riesling and Sauvignon Blanc fruit is drawn.

Following John Hancock's departure for Morton Estate, Larry McKenna made the wine until he, in turn, joined Martinborough Vineyards. Brent Marris (26), a Roseworthy College graduate whose father grows grapes for Montana in Marlborough, took over the reins from the 1986 vintage. He is soft-spoken and ambitious, with a youthful passion for conversing about wine.

Delegat's market a two-tier range: a group of straight varietals which are nationally distributed, and the Proprietor's Reserve collection of 'pick-of-the-crop' wines, usually drier and more wood influenced.

Outstanding among the Delegat's lineup of white wines has been the Auslese and the Chardonnay. The Auslese of vintages between 1980 and 1985 was a lovely, low-alcohol sweet wine, fermented from freeze-concentrated Müller-Thurgau juice. 1986, however marked a turning point: the freeze-concentration technique has been discarded and now they use only botrytised Riesling fruit for the Auslese. Marris is searching for a more complex, naturally luscious style of sweet white wine.

The Chardonnays of the early 1980s ranked alongside Cooks and McWilliam's as the best in the land. Fat, with pungent – in retrospect almost overpowering – Nevers oak flavour, they reached a high point with the outstanding 1982 vintage, the champion wine at the 1983 National Wine Competition.

The 1984 and 1985 vintages were slightly eclipsed by their commercial rivals, but 1986 brought a stunning return to top form. Marris is less heavy-handed in his use of wood than some of his colleagues and more prepared to let his wines' ripe, bold fruit flavours assert themselves. He delights in exploring the intricacies of Chardonnay-making. His 1987 Proprietor's Reserve Chardonnay was painstakingly constructed from various percentages of tank and barrel-fermented wines, subsequently given a variety of maturation spells in oak, with a share of the base wines also undergoing a malolactic fermentation. The 1986 is an intensely succulent, peachy wine, with the accent squarely on the fruit and a complex backdrop of oak. A highly individual talent is at work here.

Both a Fumé Blanc and Sauvignon Blanc are made from Gisborne fruit, all drawn from the same vineyard. The non-wooded Sauvignon Blanc, which harbours a barely discernible hint of sweetness, tends to be crisp and grassy in cooler years while in warmer seasons achieving a ripe, fruit-salad spread of flavours. The barrel-fermented Fumé Blanc, under the Proprietor's Reserve label, shows a pungent Sauvignon flavour and oak complexity which has more than once carried it into the gold medal ranks.

Only two red wines are made here, both Cabernet Sauvignons. The commercial label is a relatively light Hawke's Bay wine, matured for one year in seasoned wood. The Proprietor's Reserve version is much more distinguished. Hawke's Bay fruit, matured for over one year in new Nevers oak puncheons, produced a dark, gutsy red in 1985 and a much more elegant, scented and soft wine in 1986. From 1988 onwards Merlot and Cabernet Franc have been incorporated in the blend.

If you visit the property, when you step into the concrete block vineyard shop with its exposed beams you are entering Nikola Delegat's original winery.

Lincoln

LINCOLN – (FROM LEFT) NICK CHAN,
WINEMAKER, PETER FREDATOVICH SNR, JOHN,
AND PETER FREDATOVICH JNR – HAVE A
DETERMINATION TO WIN ACCEPTANCE IN THE
PREMIUM BOTTLED-WINE MARKET, BACKED UP
BY A SOLID ARRAY OF VARIETALS.

Interesting moves are afoot at Lincoln. This medium-sized, family-owned winery in Lincoln Road – with a long-standing reputation for dry sherry – has embarked recently on a concerted drive into the varietal table-wine market.

Petar Fredatovich, the founder, worked in New Zealand as a stonemason for twelve years before acquiring the present property, then clothed in wattle trees and blackberry, in 1937. After clearing and stumping the land and planting a half-hectare vineyard on overhead trellising to accommodate the harvest, he then coopered his own barrels out of totara.

For three decades Petar's son Peter has been managing director of the company. Peter has now retired, aged 63, and responsibility for the company's operation has passed to his own sons, Peter Jnr (37), who handles administration, and John (34), who controls the vineyards. The Fredatovich 'clan' – including the founder's widow, Lukrica – all dwell within a couple of stone-throws of each other in houses bordering the home vineyard.

That vineyard of three hectares holds a mix of Cabernet Sauvignon, 'Gamay Beaujolais', Palomino and Shiraz, plus a few of the original plantings of Muscat vines. At Brigham's Creek, Lincoln also has a more extensive, loam-clay vineyard established in Merlot, Chenin Blanc, Sauvignon Blanc, Palomino and Muscat. The fruit from these holdings is augmented by contract grapes drawn from the Hawke's Bay, Gisborne and Marlborough regions.

Although Lincoln has traditionally produced a large volume of table wines, these were plain until the 1985 arrival of winemaker Nick Chan, the son of Gilbert Chan of Totara Vineyards, and a Roseworthy College graduate. Chan's initial wines were sound, although unspectacular, but lately the overall standard of Lincoln wines has improved under his stewardship from one vintage to the next. Drinking his wines, one gets the strong feeling that here is a qualified young winemaker learning the practical ropes of winemaking – fast.

The whites first: Lincoln Brigham's Creek White is apparently a big seller – and with its bountiful dry flavour, based on a blend of two-thirds Chenin Blanc and one-third Sémillon, and reasonable price, it fully deserves to be. I have also tasted an excellent, medium-dry Chenin Blanc Barrel Fermentation 1987, a yeasty, oaky style with an unusually broad, soft palate. Lincoln have chosen to persevere with Chenin Blanc in an unresponsive market and are producing some imaginative wines.

One of the finest ever Lincoln table wines was the 1986 Marlborough Gewürztraminer, a deep-flavoured beauty with luscious, ripe hints of raisins and honey. Its stablemate, the much sweeter and richly alcoholic 1986 Marlborough Gewürztraminer Ice Wine was equally superb.

Two Chardonnay labels have recently been marketed. Gisborne Chardonnay 1987 is a lightly oaked style with the accent on fruitiness. The 1986 Marlborough Chardonnay, by far the best Lincoln Chardonnay yet, emerged from nine months aging in Nevers oak barriques toasty and yeasty, although slightly leaner than the most outstanding 1986s.

Lincoln Brigham's Creek Red is, to quote Peter Fredatovich Jnr, 'a soft, easy red with very light oak handling, sold in its current vintage'. Blended from – in order of importance – Cabernet Sauvignon, Pinotage and Merlot, it is fresh and sappy in its youth, raspberryish and crisp. Here is an ideal luncheon red.

A Lincoln specialty is the charmingly labelled Beaujolais, tasting like a fresh light rosé. Produced using the carbonic maceration technique, it is marketed in mid-May, barely eight weeks after the grapes were harvested by hand, and six months ahead of the French.

Lincoln's premium fortified wines include the Palomino Dry and Oloroso sherries, a non-wooded Vintage Port from Cabernet Sauvignon, a seven-year-old Pioneer Port, an Old Tawny Port up to fifteen years old and, to cap them all, an Anniversary Show Reserve Old Tawny up to twenty years old.

Ozich

O zich is a traditionally low-profile winery that now bears watching. Sited at the top of Metcalfe Road, across the road from Windy Hill, it was founded by Mate Ozich, now in his late sixties, who brought his family to New Zealand in 1954. Since the first vintage in the 1960s, the vineyard on a north-facing slope behind the winery has grown to eight hectares, principally planted in Cabernet Sauvignon, Merlot, Breidecker, Palomino and black Seibel (for port) vines.

Mate's sons, Davorin (37) and Miro (35), who 'grew up in the nearby Babich vineyard', now run the winery, Davorin concentrating on winemaking and marketing, Miro on viticulture. The impact of Davorin, who holds an M.Sc. in biochemistry and in 1987 spent a couple of months working at Châteaux Cos d'Estournel and Margaux, will be intriguing to trace, for he has only recently joined the family winery.

Ozich wines are made in a small, concrete block winery, urgently in need of expansion. They carry two labels, St Jerome for table wines and Nova for fortifieds (Novak is one of the family vineyards in Dalmatia; after a printer inadvertently dropped the 'k' the shortened name stuck).

The Nova range features three ports: a predominantly Cabernet Sauvignon-based Vintage Port, a tawny Reserve Port and the popular Physician's Port, also a tawny style. There is a bone-dry Breidecker and a dark, gutsy Premium Red from Seibel hybrids. The highlight of the range, however, is the St Jerome Cabernet/Merlot 1986, a two to one varietal blend of estate-grown fruit matured for ten months in new Alliers oak barriques. An elegant, brick-red, light-bodied wine, ripe and with true Merlot suppleness, this is the pride and joy of the Ozich brothers, their promising 'first effort in the new direction we want to go'.

DAVORIN (LEFT) AND MIRO OZICH WITH THEIR FATHER MATE. ALTHOUGH THEIR WINERY IS STILL PRINCIPALLY A SOURCE OF FORTIFIED WINES, DAVORIN AND MIRO ARE KEEN TO MAKE QUALITY REDS.

Pacific

MILLIE ERCEG HEADS A LARGE WINERY PRIMARILY DEVOTED TO CASK-WINE AND COOLER PRODUCTION, BUT IS ALSO ENDEAVOURING TO CLIMB INTO THE RANKS OF THE PREMIUM BOTTLED-WINE PRODUCERS.

Pacific is a largish, family-owned winery, with an output much higher than most wine enthusiasts realise. Although its production focusses on cask wines and coolers, it is also endeavouring to win a footing in the bottled table wine market.

Mijo (Mick) Erceg, the founder who died in 1983 aged 75, arrived in New Zealand in 1929 at the age of fifteen, on the eve of the Depression. After several years' labour on gumfields, roads and the vineyards of other Dalmatians, he bought a small farm in McLeod Road, Henderson, and by 1936 had his own vines established.

Pacific entered into a marketing arrangement with Seppelt of Australia in 1967, and for several years Pacific wines appeared on the shelves under the Seppelt label. A range of 'Saint Stefan' wines followed and, more recently, several Pacific lines have been sold carrying the Monlouis, Michael's and Willowbrook labels.

Pacific has suffered in recent years from an unfortunate degree of instability, reflected in its rapidly changing parade of labels, winemakers and involved family members. Ivan Erceg, now in his mid thirties, who made the wine in the early 1980s, had studied malolactic fermentations and acidity in wine at graduate level, but his wines failed to stand out. He has since departed from the company. His talented brother Michael – holder of an American doctorate in mathemetics – has also recently withdrawn leaving their mother, Millie Erceg, as the driving force at Pacific.

Steve Tubic, a Waikato-born winemaker who worked at Corbans between 1979 and early 1986, before working the 1986 vintage at Pacific under the consultant, Norbert Seibel, has assumed sole winemaking responsibility from the 1987 vintage.

The concrete-block, fibrolite and timber winery backs onto the five-hectare estate vineyard, which is entirely planted in Cabernet Sauvignon and Merlot vines. This is the sole source of Pacific's fruit for red winemaking. White grapes are drawn from the Gisborne and Hawke's Bay regions.

Pacific coolers – Tropical, Wild Peach, Wild Cherry and Citrus – are popular, marketed both in casks and in bottles. A trio of table wines in casks are also widely encountered: the dryish Chablis, medium-dry Bernhoffen and medium Chalenberg.

Bottled table wines are released in two tiers. There is a range of standard varietal wines plus a Reserve lineup bearing distinctive diamond-shaped black labels. The overall standard of these bottled wines since the 1986 vintage has ranged from sound to excellent.

That last adjective is especially true of the breakthrough wine for Pacific in its bid to become a quality producer – its Reserve Gewürztraminer 1986, originally marketed as Willowbrook Gewürztraminer. This wine, fashioned by Norbert Seibel, captured gold medals at home and abroad and has been followed by a very good 1987.

Sauvignon Blanc has a pervasive presence in the Pacific range, appearing under a straight Sauvignon Blanc label, tangy and grassy; a Reserve Sauvignon Blanc label, less piercing and more ripely fruity; and a Reserve Fumé Blanc label. Other whites made include Rhine Riesling, Chardonnay and a Reserve Sauterne (sic) blended from freeze-concentrated Riesling and Muscat.

Oak-aged for eight months, the Cabernet Sauvignon is brick-red, light and fruity – best drunk young.

Fortified wines remain part of the range, with both the Reserve Tawny Port and Private Bin Pale Dry Sherry having over the last few years carried off gold medals.

Pleasant Valley

P leasant Valley has the dual distinction of being not only the oldest surviving Dalmatian vineyard in Henderson, but also the oldest winery in the land under the continuous ownership of the same family.

Stipan Jelich, the founder, arrived in Auckland in 1890 at the age of twenty-two. After five years' labour on the northern gumfields he bought, at five pounds an acre, thirty-two hectares of hill country in the Henderson Valley. His first crop of grapes, Black Hamburghs, fetched him less on the Auckland markets than the charges of the carrier and auctioneer. By 1902, winemaking had emerged as a better source of income, and from then until Stipan Jelich (Stephan Yelas) retired in 1939, the vineyard served as a model of the fruits of peasant stubbornness: the land was turned over by spade; the vines, tied to manuka stakes, were hand-hoed, and sprayed from a knapsack mounted on the back. During Stipan's working life, not even a horse helped to ease the toil.

Yelas' son Moscow long ago introduced more modern vineyard techniques, replacing manuka stakes with wire trellises and knapsack sprayers with machine sprayers. Until his death in 1984, Moscow, although semi-retired, still made the wine while his son, Stephan, concentrated on viticulture.

STEPHAN YELAS, ASTRIDE AN ANTIQUATED CORKING MACHINE. HIS WINES UNDER THE PLEASANT VALLEY LABEL ARE DELIVERING OUTSTANDING VALUE FOR MONEY.

Around 1980 the cellars were quiet, even sleepy; much of the grape crop was sold to other companies and the wines were not widely seen beyond the winery. The top range, bearing the inscription 'Château Yelas', occasionally won bronze medals and some bottles sold at the vineyard were extraordinarily old: in 1981 a 'Royal Bin' Pinotage from 1973 was available.

Output consisted predominantly of Amoroso Sherry, White Moscato – a fortified wine based on Niagara grapes – and Sauternes. No table wines, even reds, were wood-aged: according to Moscow Yelas this process was too costly and instead, to encourage a slight oxidation, his reds were given additional rackings. His Hock, Pinotage and Fino Dry Sherry were sound, honest wines, lacking delicacy but good value at very cheap prices.

Now, under the guidance of Stephan ('Steppie') Yelas (41), Pleasant Valley has embarked on the comeback trail. The arduous task of hauling this historic, run-down winery from the 1960s into the late 1980s is bringing out an intensity of commitment in Stephan which promises to slowly restore the reputation Pleasant Valley enjoyed in its heyday twenty-five years ago.

The five-hectare home vineyard on rolling clay soils is planted in old Pinot Noir and Muscat, and recently established Cabernet Sauvignon,

Pinotage, Merlot, Chardonnay, Müller-Thurgau and Reichensteiner vines. Another two-hectare company vineyard at Riverhead supplies Sémillon, Grey Riesling and Dr Hogg Muscat fruit. Premium white varieties such as Sauvignon Blanc, Chardonnay and Riesling are also bought from Gisborne and soon, Marlborough.

The original kauri winery is still used for barrel storage. The winery is marvellously atmospheric, full of dark nooks and crannies, old concrete fermentation tanks, old corking machines and – everywhere you look – aged barrels housing ports and sherries decades old, many of them unopened and untasted since Moscow Yelas died. His son has inherited a treasure trove of venerable old fortified wines.

From 1986 until mid-1988 Pleasant Valley wines were produced under the guidance of Norbert Seibel, formerly chief winemaker at Corbans (who also markets a small amount of wine under his own label, Seibel Wines, and plans his own winery at Waikanae). Seibel's successor at Pleasant Valley is Roseworthy College-trained New Zealander Peter Evans (26). About 7000 cases of wine are made annually.

Like many wineries, Pleasant Valley markets a two-tier range of table wines: the premium range is called Pleasant Valley, the lower range Valley. Valley Dry Red and Medium Red are both non-wooded blends of Cabernet Sauvignon and Pinot Noir; Valley Dry White and Medium White are both blended from Müller-Thurgau and Chenin Blanc. The winery's best seller is still a non-vintaged Sauternes, sold in bottles and carafes 'not to yuppies but to middle-aged people and pensioners', Stephan says.

The premium Pleasant Valley lineup includes a barrique-aged Fumé Blanc (the company is now purchasing new oak for its top wines), Sauvignon Blanc, Rhine Riesling, Sémillon, Chauché Gris, Müller-Thurgau, Cabernet Sauvignon, Pinotage and Pinot Noir. My tastings of the 1987 Rhine Riesling and Fumé Blanc, and the 1986 Sémillon and Pinotage, show these to be uniformly clean, carefully crafted wines with clear-cut varietal characters, currently much underrated by wine lovers.

Of Pleasant Valley's traditional range of fortified wines, the jewel in the crown is the amber-brown, nutty-sweet Founder's Port, an almost liqueur-like, fifteen-year-old tawny style with an illustrious record in recent show judgings.

Soljans

Soljans, traditionally one of the best small Henderson dessert winemakers, has recently branched out with a sound lineup of white and red varietal table wines.

The founder, the late Frank Soljan, arrived in New Zealand in 1927 at the age of fifteen. Today, the block of fruit trees and vines he planted in Lincoln Road in 1937 is still a combined orchard and vineyard, run by his sons Tony (44), the winemaker, and Rex (45), who cultivates the impeccable vineyard.

A scene of rare beauty, Black Hamburgh table grapes trained along overhead trellises, greets visitors to the Soljans winery in summer. At Riverlea a second vineyard has been planted in Müller-Thurgau, Breidecker, Sauvignon Blanc, Palomino and Cabernet Sauvignon vines. Premium white varieties such as Chardonnay, Gewürztraminer and Sauvignon Blanc are also bought from Gisborne.

Soljans produces several thousand cases of wine annually, most of it sold directly to the public in the original winery, built before the Second World War, which serves today as the vineyard shop. Here cheerful Tony Soljan, an influential figure in the wine industry as a long-term spokesman for small-scale vineyards, can often be found on Saturdays dispensing the fruits of his labours.

This winery has long been respected as a sherry producer and Soljans' top offering, the Pergola Sherry, emerges after many years in small oak barrels as a full, rich dessert wine. The Reserve Sherry, younger and matured in larger totara casks, is also a sweet, dark-brown dessert wine, a shade lighter than the Pergola Sherry: both are fine examples of this wine style.

Of the table wines, the sales success story so far is the Henderson Spumante, a clean and sweet sparkling wine with a full Muscat bouquet and fruity flavour. For no-fuss occasions Soljans produce a Dry White and a Moselle, from a blend of Müller-Thurgau and Breidecker, and there is also a Dry Red, from non-wooded Seibel fruit.

The premium range of table wines includes Sauvignon Blanc – 'perhaps the pick of the bunch so far', says Soljan – Chardonnay (aged in French oak barriques for three months), Gewürztraminer and Cabernet Sauvignon (aged in barriques for nine months). These are all clean, soundly made wines. A Müller-Thurgau and a fresh, appealing, medium-dry Breidecker round out the range.

Soljans gives visitors a rare opportunity to pick up bottle-aged white table wines – when I called, four-year-old Chardonnay and three-year-old Sauvignon Blanc were lining the shelves. Another asset is the popular sheltered picnic area, a tranquil resting place in the midst of lawns, apple trees and overhead-trellised vines.

TONY SOLJAN'S IRREPRESSIBLE GRIN AND MELLOW OLD SHERRIES HAVE WON FOR HIS SMALL VINEYARD A VERY LOYAL CLIENTELE.

West Brook

West Brook – until recently called Panorama – is a small, family-operated winery in the residential Awaroa Road area of Henderson.

Tony Ivicevich and his father Mick arrived in New Zealand from their native Dalmatia in 1934. After only one year, the present property had been purchased and planted in trees and grapevines. By 1937 the first port and sherry were on the market, sold for one shilling and sixpence in beer bottles without labels.

Tony (67) has now retired and the winery is run by his son Anthony (39) with assistance from his wife Susan, and his mother. An uncle helps run the vineyard.

The two-hectare home vineyard behind the concrete-block winery is planted principally in Cabernet Sauvignon, with a small plot of Merlot. Premium white varieties are bought from Henderson and Gisborne and soon, from Marlborough.

The level of production is not high and the wines are not widely encountered. Panorama is the label still appearing on fortified wines and on the bottom end of the range table wines – Chablis, Moselle and Sauternes.

The new West Brook label – which features a mill and waterwheel similar to those once found in the area – is reserved for the best bottled table wines. These include a dry, non-wooded Sauvignon Blanc, a medium Rhine Riesling, Müller-Thurgau, Sémillon, a Chardonnay made from Henderson and Gisborne fruit, matured in new oak, and a Cabernet Sauvignon from Henderson fruit, aged in American and Limousin oak casks. My pick of the range is the Gewürztraminer, pungent in bouquet and firmly spicy from one vintage to the next. Anthony Ivicevich prefers his Chardonnay.

Ivicevich is currently looking closely at the possibility of employing a winemaker and lifting his production to supply 'trade' outlets. His goal is to put more and more emphasis on making mid-price varietal wines, solid in quality but affordable too.

ANTHONY IVICEVICH – FACING THE FUTURE WITH A NEW IMAGE AND A SOLID RANGE OF VARIETAL TABLE WINES.

AUCKLAND

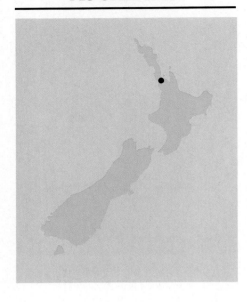

BRYAN MOGRIDGE, MONTANA'S GENERAL
MANAGER, HAS CARVED OUT A HIGH-FLYING
CAREER FOR HIMSELF IN THE WINE INDUSTRY.
HE FORMERLY HEADED CORBANS AND ALSO
CHAIRS THE WINE INSTITUTE.

Montana

Montana early in its expansion announced an ambition which was extraordinary for the wine industry: to produce not only the most but the best wine in the country. In a dramatic burst nearly two decades ago, it overhauled the traditional market leaders, McWilliam's and Corbans, and at present commands a hefty forty percent plus share of the market. The range of products is sound throughout and several, notably the Marlborough Sauvignon Blanc and Marlborough Rhine Riesling, must be rated among New Zealand's top wines.

With company-owned and contract vineyards and a giant of a winery at Marlborough, contract vineyards and a large winery at Gisborne and contract vineyards in Hawke's Bay, Montana is a vastly fragmented operation. It is treated here in the Auckland region, where it first emerged and still bases its major bottling and warehousing facility and head office.

Ivan Yukich, founder of this giant company, arrived in New Zealand from Dalmatia as a youth of fifteen. After returning to his homeland, he came back to New Zealand in 1934, this time with a wife and two sons. After years devoted to market gardening, Yukich later planted a fifth-hectare vineyard high in the Waitakere Ranges west of Auckland, calling it Montana, the Dalmatian word for mountain.

1944 saw the first Montana wine on the market. Under the direction of sons Mate – the viticulturist – and Frank – winemaker and salesman – the vineyard grew to ten hectares by the end of the 1950s. The company then embarked on a period of expansion unparalleled in New Zealand wine history. To build up its financial and distribution clout, Montana joined forces with Campbell and Ehrenfried, the liquor wholesaling giant, and Auckland financier Rolf Porter. A new 120-hectare vineyard was established at Mangatangi in the Waikato and by the late 1960s contract growers at Gisborne were receiving guidance and financial assistance. A new Gisborne winery began operating by 1972 and a year later Montana absorbed the old family firm of Waihirere.

Although production was booming the company at this stage earned a reputation for placing sales volume goals ahead of product quality. The launch-pad for Montana's spectacular growth was a series of sparkling 'pop' wines – Pearl, Cold Duck and Poulet Poulet – which briefly won a following. For those with a finer appreciation of wine the company somehow managed to produce an array of classic labels.

The real force behind Montana's early rise was Frank Yukich. He early perceived the trend away from sherry to white table wine and was the first to adopt aggressive marketing strategies. Then, in 1973, the giant multinational distilling and winemaking company Seagram obtained a forty percent share-holding in Montana, contributing money, technical resources and marketing expertise. The same year, Montana made an issue of 2.4 million public shares. Seagram's investments, shareholders' funds and independent loans together provided $8 million over the next three years for development purposes.

Next came the pivotal move into Marlborough. As Wayne Thomas, then a young scientist in the Plant Diseases Division of the DSIR has related: 'In March 1973, Montana under the guidance of its founder and managing director, Mr F.I. Yukich, planned and intended to undertake a major vineyard planting programme in New Zealand . . . Although plenty of suitable land was available in both the Poverty Bay and Hawke's Bay regions, my own impression was that it was too highly priced for vineyards . . .

'I gave the subject of alternative vineyard areas in New Zealand considerable thought and . . . then phoned Mr Frank Yukich and suggested that . . . he should consider the possibility of establishing vineyards in the Marlborough region as it had all the necessary criteria on the surface to make it successful . . .

'[Later] Mr Yukich rang, requesting that I have suitable authorities in the Viticulture Department at the University of California, Davis, confirm that the Marlborough region would be suitable for growing wine grapes . . . Confirmation was duly obtained from Professors Winkler, Lider, Berg and Cook. . .'

The first vine was planted in Marlborough on 24 August 1973: a silver coin, the traditional token of good fortune, was dropped in the hole and Sir David Beattie, then chairman of the company, with a sprinkling of sparkling wine dedicated the historic vine.

Montana then moved swiftly to rectify its quality problems. The standard of the 1974 and subsequent vintages soon lifted the company into the ranks of the industry's leaders.

Still pursuing the mass market, the company now shifted its emphasis to non-sparkling table wines. Bernkaizler Riesling (now called Benmorven) began to open up a huge market for slightly sweet white wines later developed with Blenheimer – by far New Zealand's biggest selling wine.

Frank Yukich severed his ties with Montana in 1974, after several disputes with Seagram. Soon after, the company also severed its link with the old Yukich vineyard at Titirangi. The twenty-hectare vineyard site and substantial winery was unsuited to further development and the company chose instead to expand elsewhere. The old winery was dismantled and most of the equipment sent to Blenheim.

Montana's costly move into Marlborough contributed to the company's depressed financial condition from 1974 to 1976. But the subsequent recovery represents a major business success story. After two years of losses, Montana showed a small profit in 1975–76 and by 1978 had paid its maiden dividend. Profits in the year ending 30 June 1983 totalled $6.4 million.

In late 1985 Corporate Investments Limited took control of Montana, by adding Seagram's 43.8 percent stake to its own already substantial shareholding. Seagram pulled out when the industry's fortunes turned sour: in the year to 30 June 1986 the company recorded a loss of almost $1.6 million. Corporate Investments, a company listed on the stock exchange, is principally owned by its chairman, Peter Masfen, who has served as a director of Montana for fifteen years. In late 1987 Corporate Investments secured a 100 percent shareholding in Montana and then de-listed the company from the stock exchange.

Following its acquisition of Penfolds Wines (NZ) Limited in late 1986 from Lion Corporation Limited, Montana has moved back into the black, posting a $5.14 million profit for the year ending 30 June 1987. Penfolds will be retained as a separate trading identity, marketing a range of North Island-sourced wines having greater oak influence than has hitherto characterised Montana's range.

General manager Bryan Mogridge, who jocularly told an Auckland newspaper he works in the wine industry 'because I like a glass or two', is a B.Sc. graduate who formerly headed Corbans. A distinguished chairman of the Wine Institute since 1985, Mogridge is a young man who displays the disciplined self-confidence of a born leader.

Under national production manager Peter Hubscher (45), Montana has been systematically gearing itself to repel the onslaught of Australian wines due under CER. 'Our whole strategy is planned to prevent us being swamped by the Australians,' says Hubscher.

In Gisborne, the Montana and former Penfolds wineries have been linked by pipelines. At the Riverlands winery a few kilometres on the

PETER HUBSCHER, MONTANA'S NATIONAL PRODUCTION MANAGER, IS DETERMINED THAT HIS COMPANY WILL WARD OFF THE POWERFUL CHALLENGE FROM AUSTRALIAN WINES ARISING FROM C.E.R.

seaward side of Blenheim, six towering 550,000-litre insulated tanks have been installed to store reserves of top-selling wines in optimum condition. The 'tank farm' here, of 200 separate tanks, has the capacity to store up to twenty million litres of wine. During vintage up to 500 tonnes of fruit avalanches in each day from contract vineyards and the company's own plantings covering 400 hectares at Brancott, Renwick, Fairhall and Woodbourne. The complex also features a cask-filling plant (producing 20,000 casks daily), a barrel hall, cooperage, offices and a retail shop.

From Blenheim and Gisborne much wine then rolls north in bulk rail tankers to Auckland for bottling. All finishing and maturing of bottled wines is carried out at the Glen Innes complex in Auckland. If you stroll around this expansive complex with Peter Hubscher, through a labyrinth of storage tanks and pulsating bottling lines, finally to a large wall-mounted photograph of Montana's sweeping Marlborough vineyards, your inevitable lingering impression is of the company's enormous scale.

In conversation Hubscher is eager to emphasise that Montana has hundreds of employees, including over thirty graduates. Although the spotlight inevitably falls upon such individuals as Masfen, Mogridge and Hubscher himself, the key to Montana's on-going success is the quality of its teamwork, he believes.

Accorded praise by many observers in earlier years as New Zealand's largest and best winery, Montana is facing more formidable competition today. The company has retained its successful track record with its Marlborough Rhine Rieslings and Sauvignon Blancs, but with Chardonnay and Cabernet Sauvignon, the most prestigious varieties, Montana has fallen slightly behind, reflecting its lack − until the recent takeover of Penfolds − of a vineyard foothold in Hawke's Bay.

VINES BATHING IN SUNSHINE IN MONTANA'S
VINEYARD AT RENWICK, MARLBOROUGH.

The company's policy is to supply the market, here and overseas, with large volumes of sound, often excellent, wines at affordable prices. It does this brilliantly. However, its pick-of-the-crop, bottle-aged wines, marketed under the Winemaker's Selection label, have not matched the quality of the top wines made by some of its smaller rivals. As Michael Brett of the *Auckland Star* put it: 'The company is not geared to produce small quantities of splendid quality wine even though their winemakers may itch to do so.' Having said that, one must also acknowledge that some of the commercially available wines from Montana are themselves of 'splendid quality'.

Oak has traditionally played a very minor role in Montana's range of white wines; instead the emphasis is on fruit intensity. 'If you use wood to give your wines more complexity they must be aged; this is not the case for most wines,' says Hubscher.

Montana's enormously popular Blenheimer is New Zealand's answer to Blue Nun. (In 1977 a *Sunday News* columnist wrote: 'They're going to call one of their best white wines "Blenheimer". Think again, fellas. That's awful.')

Blenheimer, despite the seeming implication of its name, is made mainly from Gisborne-grown Müller-Thurgau fruit. A mild, light-bodied, fruity wine, it carries twenty-five grams per litre of sugar in a medium style. Although understandably lacking the fragrance and fruit intensity of a top Müller-Thurgau, this is a perfectly acceptable, undemanding wine for occasions when wine is the backdrop to, rather than the focus of, conversation. It is a marketing triumph.

Since its market launch in 1981, Montana Wohnsiedler Müller-Thurgau has outstripped the sales of the thirty or so other competing brands of Müller-Thurgau. Gold medals for the 1983 and 1984 vintages underscored the company's strength in mass commercial wines. It is usually slightly sweet, delicately flavoured, flowery and fresh.

The popular Gisborne Chardonnay – with an annual output of 60,000 cases, by far the country's biggest-selling Chardonnay – has traditionally been a light, easy-drinking style, not quite bone dry. Peachy and soft, until recently it had no wood treatment, but now it is partially aged in American oak puncheons. Kaituna Hills Chardonnay is the private-bin label, made from Marlborough fruit aged in new Nevers oak puncheons. Those vintages I have tasted have been light-bodied, fresh and 'toasty', but lacking strength and depth.

Montana's range of Marlborough white wines has nevertheless fully justified the company's faith in the district. Since the first 1979 vintage, Montana's Marlborough Rhine Riesling has stood out – a fragrant, flowery, polished wine with abundant fruit flavour and crisp acidity. The 1982 vintage scored top in its class at the 1983 Australian National Competition in Canberra; the 1987 vintage scored a gold medal at the 1987 Air New Zealand Wine Awards. At three to five years old most vintages are awash with delectable, apple and pineapple fruit flavours.

Montana Marlborough Sauvignon Blanc is full of distinctive herbal varietal character. Unmistakably Sauvignon Blanc in its youth, with its assertive capsicum-like bouquet and flavour, after a couple of years' bottle age this dry wine develops a less pungent, more gooseberryish character, softer and lusher.

It is beyond doubt that this label has focussed more international attention on the soaring standard of New Zealand wine than any other. It is that rare combination: a world-class wine that is nonetheless freely available and affordable. In choosing the 1986 vintage as 'Wine of the Year' in his 1987 *Good Wine Guide*, London critic Robert Joseph declared that 'this remarkable New Zealand wine is not only a slap in the eye for all those producers of dull, over-priced Sancerre and Pouilly Fumé, it is also one of the most deliciously and unashamedly fruity dry white wines I have ever tasted'.

Montana has also marketed a second range of wines under the label Marlborough Valley. One of these, Marlborough Valley Sauvignon

ROWS OF MONTANA VINES MARCH FOR SEVERAL HUNDRED METRES ACROSS THE STONY WAIRAU PLAINS.

Blanc/Sémillon, has pure, ripe gooseberry fruit, with Sémillon's grassy hints adding flavour strength and firmness. Montana Brancott Estate Fumé Blanc, matured in French oak puncheons, is a third variation on the theme of Marlborough-grown Sauvignon Blanc.

Turning to the red wines, Montana's Cabernet Sauvignon led the range from 1973 to 1977, and then was superseded by the Marlborough Cabernet Sauvignon. Those early reds, made from Gisborne fruit, pioneered in New Zealand the production of quality red wine in large volumes. Generally fruity, straightforward Cabernet Sauvignons, they ranged in standard from the last, sharp and nondescript 1977, to the memorable red label 1973 reserve bin.

Montana's Marlborough Cabernet Sauvignon has been the pick of the company's range of Marlborough reds. A uniform style has emerged: medium-bodied, with plenty of Cabernet Sauvignon fruit and adequate tannin. However, their typically slightly vegetative bouquets and flavours, coupled with a lightness of mouthfeel, are *too* cool-climate in style to rival the premium reds of Hawke's Bay and Auckland. The private-bin Wairau Valley Cabernet Sauvignon has also been leafy and austere, lacking the ripe fragrance and flavour richness derived from optimally ripened fruit.

Montana's other varietal reds from Marlborough, Pinotage and Pinot Noir, are always appealing although – with the exception of the cherry-red, soft and supple 1983 Marlborough Pinotage – seldom memorable. The range of aged, private-bin Marlborough reds has been highlighted by a couple of vintages of Riverlands Pinotage and Mt Richmond Claret, both fragrant, mellow conversation pieces.

Fairhall River Claret is an everyday-drinking, rosy-hued blend of Pinotage, Pinot Noir and Cabernet Sauvignon grown in Montana's Fairhall vineyard. This is a medium-bodied, flavoursome red, showing little sign of oak, light tannin and a smoothness which suggests fractional sweetness.

Three sparkling wines are of interest. Bernadino Spumante is a blend of Gisborne grapes, including Dr Hogg Muscat, backblended to seventy-five grams per litre of sugar with unfermented Muscat juice. Muscat dominates the overall style, although not the grape composition. This sweet light sparkling, only nine percent alcohol, has built up a distinguished track record in show judgings.

Lindauer, launched in 1981 in brut (dry) and sec (medium-dry) versions, was this country's first widely released bottle-fermented sparkling. Predominantly Pinot Noir grapes are used to produce an impressive wine, showing plenty of fruit and sustained bubbles, although lacking the flavour development and pronounced yeastiness of classic French Champagnes. However, in early 1988 Montana announced it is linking with the Champagne house of Deutz to produce a new New Zealand 'methode champenoise' sparkling for sale in 1991.

If there is one Penfolds label Montana is sure to preserve, it is Chardon, New Zealand's favourite sparkling which bears a name equally reminiscent of Moët and Chandon, the Champagne house, and the Chardonnay variety. Chardon is produced from Gisborne grapes, backblended to seventy-five grams per litre of sugar with Muscat juice. The palate is fresh, crisp, low alcohol, and sweet, with clearcut Müller-Thurgau flavour. Its lightness and fruitiness have won it countless fans.

Recent releases under the Penfolds label include the Clive River range of varietals – low-priced and sound, although in the case of the Chardonnay, notably nondescript – and Hyland, a bottle-fermented sparkling of sustained bubbles and light sweetness.

Of Montana's small range of fortified wines, the flor Pale Dry Sherry is particularly outstanding.

WAIHEKE ISLAND

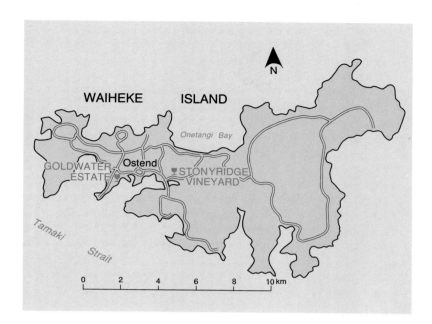

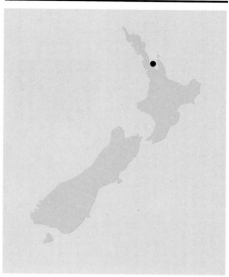

Goldwater Estate

KIM AND JEANETTE GOLDWATER PRODUCE DISTINGUISHED REDS BACKED UP BY A FLAIR FOR PUBLIC RELATIONS.

Rumours circulating several years ago about the establishment of new 'boutique' wineries on Waiheke Island met in most quarters with disbelief. Was not viticulture rapidly shifting away from the long-established Auckland region to Gisborne, Hawke's Bay and Marlborough? Few believed that outstanding red wine would soon be flowing from this sprawling island in Auckland's Hauraki Gulf.

Although the Goldwaters at Putiki Bay and Stephen White at Onetangi are pioneering the new era of Waiheke wine, they are not the first vintners this island has attracted. Old, rambling hybrid vines and an aged road sign pointing to 'The Vineyard' are tangible reminders of the Gradiska family winery, which produced both fortified and a trickle of table wines around the 1950s, until a series of personal tragedies overtook the family and winemaking ceased.

The next flush of viticultural enthusiasm came in 1978 when Kim Goldwater, now aged fifty – a former engineer and fashion photographer – and his wife Jeanette planted their first experimental vines in poor, sandy clay soils on the hillside overlooking Putiki Bay.

The Goldwaters, who were fuelled as students by Babich and San Marino dry reds, recall how they were later 'seduced by the Mediterranean lifestyle and especially the idea of serving wine with food every day'. French wines, however, says Kim Goldwater, are 'usually bloody awful, and so we thought that if we could do well here, we could knock them for six'. His winemaking ambition is 'to win international recognition for making one of the world's great wines'.

The prospects for making outstanding wines here are helped by the island enjoying a warmer and drier ripening season than vineyards on the mainland although, as in 1986, wet vintages do still occur.

Under the guidance of viticultural expert Dr Richard Smart, the Goldwaters have established a small two-hectare vineyard of classic Bordeaux varieties: Cabernet Sauvignon, Merlot and Cabernet Franc for red wine; and Sauvignon Blanc for white. Most of their vines are trained in a U-shape – uncommon here – designed to open up their centres to the sun and reduce leaf shading of the crop.

Vintage time draws a crowd of friends and relatives who pick the bunches by hand and then stay to celebrate the harvest. The new season's red wine is then fermented in stainless-steel vats, before being transferred into new French Nevers oak puncheons for a spell lasting up to two years. Neither cold-stabilised nor filtered, Goldwater reds can be expected to develop a crust in the bottle during aging.

A quartet of Cabernet Sauvignons has been released from the 1982 to 1985 vintages, all labelled as straight varietal wines. Each shared the Goldwater stamp of deep, near-opaque colour and a rich, distinctly herbaceous palate characteristic of Cabernet Sauvignons grown in cool-climate regions. For sheer intensity of flavour and obvious fruit ripeness, these wines have already staked out a position among this country's top-class reds.

From the excellent 1985 vintage, the Goldwaters have marketed a Cabernet/Merlot/Franc blend which has capped all its predecessors: Merlot, says Kim Goldwater, lends softness to the blend, balancing the more austere Cabernet Sauvignon; and Cabernet Franc imparts both colour and alcohol. My sample revealed a lovely marriage of fruit and oak flavours, and an overall complexity and stylishness which justified its high price tag. Six hundred cases only were released. The 1986 Cabernet/Merlot has been marketed as Nob Hill, a secondary label introduced for wines of less distinction.

By contrast with the compelling character of this winery's reds, most (the 1987 was an exception) Goldwater Sauvignon Blanc Fumés have been dry, wood-aged wines with understated varietal characteristics. A flavoursome dry rosé from Cabernet Sauvignon rounds out the range in enticing clear bottles.

A CORNER OF THE GOLDWATER VINEYARD, OVERLOOKING PUTIKI BAY.

Stonyridge Vineyard

Stephen White's presence at Stonyridge Vineyard, near Onetangi, since 1982 has reinforced the Goldwaters' belief in Waiheke's wine potential. The two vineyards share remarkably similar approaches to wine production.

White is a thirty-year-old Aucklander who, after taking a Diploma of Horticulture at Lincoln College, worked in vineyards in Tuscany and California, and at Châteaux d' Angludet and Palmer in Bordeaux before returning to New Zealand to pursue his high ambition: 'to make one of the best Médoc-style reds in the world'.

Searching for a vineyard site with high summer temperatures, low summer rainfall, a maritime influence (to boost night temperatures) and poor, free-draining soil, he found it on Waiheke. Stonyridge, named after a nearby hill quarry, lies slightly further inland than the Goldwater vineyard on clay soils, rich in magnesium. Kiwifruit failed here but over 200 olive trees have flourished.

The Stonyridge vineyard runs to two hectares of north-facing, predominantly Cabernet Sauvignon and Merlot vines, with smaller amounts of Cabernet Franc and Malbec. The vines are all trained in classic Bordeaux fashion, and the berries purposely kept small – giving proportionately more skins to their juice – in a bid to build deeper flavour into the finished wine

White and his partner Dr John McLeod, who brings administrative and scientific skills to the venture, are specialising, like Goldwater, in the production of claret-style reds. Equipment and winemaking techniques have been extensively derived from Bordeaux.

The several grape varieties are separately vinified. After each cask has been regularly tasted, the wines are selectively assembled with the top wine appearing under the flagship label, Larose (named after the many roses growing in the vineyard at Stonyridge). Lesser barrels and/or press wine are kept for the second-string label, Airfield (named after a nearby landing strip).

Stonyridge's maiden release consisted of 200 cases of 1985 Larose and sixty cases of 1985 Airfield Cabernet Sauvignon. The Larose was a highly promising start: a purplish-red, eighty percent Cabernet Sauvignon and twenty percent Merlot blend, with classic 'cigar box' claret bouquet and a firm, well-structured palate looking set to develop for several years. In colour and body the 1985 Larose was lighter than the corresponding Goldwater vintage. In its infancy, however, the much more powerful 1987 displayed an intense thrusting palate, deep blackberry hue and an overall weight and stylishness that promised to achieve great heights.

The Goldwaters and Stephen White look set to demonstrate an old truth on Waiheke: that small winemaking endeavours based on meticulous vineyard site selection, plus sound, no-compromise winery procedures, can produce wines of extraordinary merit and individuality.

STEPHEN WHITE AND HIS WIFE JANE – AMONG THEIR EARLY FRUITS IS AN UNUSUALLY DARK-HUED AND POWERFUL 1987 LAROSE.

SOUTH AUCKLAND

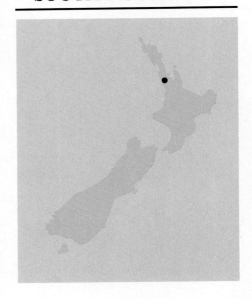

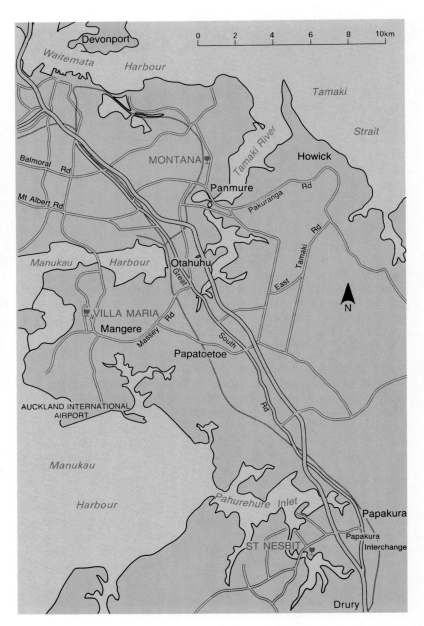

St Nesbit

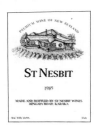

One of the most exquisitely fragrant and well-bred New Zealand reds I have ever encountered bore the label St Nesbit 1984. The release of this wine in 1987, with a gold medal under its belt, heralded the arrival of tax lawyer Dr Tony Molloy, QC, as a force to be reckoned with among this country's red-winemaking fraternity.

St Nesbit is a small winery tucked away on a southern arm of the Manukau Harbour in Hingaia Road, Karaka, only a couple of kilometres from Auckland's southern motorway. After buying a fourteen-hectare dairy farm here in 1980, two years later Molloy planted his two-hectare vineyard of Cabernet Sauvignon, Merlot and Cabernet Franc vines in Karaka's fertile, loamy soils. His passion is 'to set new standards of excellence in making New Zealand wine'.

Tony Molloy (44) is an outgoing, razor-sharp man, the owner of a study lined with a thousand and one books on the law and winemaking. These, including classic French-language winemaking texts, are well-thumbed, for he has pursued a carefully planned, analytical path into the winemaking arena.

Molloy is also a partly trained Catholic priest, but his theological volumes hold no clues to the identity of St Nesbit. In naming his winery, Molloy has chosen to canonise his late grandfather, a former New Zealand cricket captain, Nesbit Snedden.

For his debut 1984 vintage, Molloy was totally reliant upon bought-in fruit. Between 1985 and 1987 both home-vineyard and contract-grown grapes were processed. From 1989, however, the crush will be exclusively of estate-grown fruit. Molloy makes the wine himself, with the assistance to date of Dr Rainer Eschenbruch, Tom Van Dam and Mark Compton.

Molloy's roomy (600 square metres) winery started off, he recalls, as 'a new floor put in an old cowshed. Then we put a new cowshed over the floor'. Despite this modesty, the St Nesbit winery is in reality highly sophisticated.

Molloy has designed his own squat fermentation vessels which feature floating sealed lids. These hold the 'cap' of skins immersed in the fermenting juice – for maximum colour and flavour extraction – and also give greater flexibility of storage space. Only new barriques are used for maturation, principally Nevers with lesser amounts of Tronçais and American oak. On average the wine rests in casks for around eighteen months. To reduce evaporation losses through the staves, the outsides of the barrels are kept moist by an automatic sprinkler system.

Contrary to most peoples' preconceptions – based on the overall quality of the 1984 and 1985 vintages in New Zealand – the 1984 St Nesbit was superior to the 1985 which, although scented and bold, lacked the complexity of its predecessor. In explanation Tony Molloy points out that the 1984 matured for twenty-eight months in new casks whereas the 1985 spent only twelve months in one-year-old wood.

At the vineyard last year I tasted separately the components of the 1986 St Nesbit: individual glasses of Cabernet Sauvignon, Cabernet Franc and Merlot drawn from the barrels. All lived up to their varietal reputations: the Merlot was supple and fragrant, Cabernet Franc lighter-hued and fruity, Cabernet Sauvignon pungent and more astringent. Within a few years Petit Verdot, a variety currently on the comeback trail in Bordeaux, will put the finishing touches on Molloy's blend.

St Nesbit is a rarity in the New Zealand industry – a winery which chooses to specialise in the production of a single label. Output is planned to peak by the mid-1990s at around 4000 cases per year. The wine should be worth following.

TONY MOLLOY'S SUCCESSFUL ENTRY INTO THE WINE FIELD PARALLELS THAT OF MANY OTHER LAWYERS, IN NEW ZEALAND AND OVERSEAS, WHO HAVE BEEN SIMILARLY SMITTEN BY THE WINE BUG.

Villa Maria

Under the single-minded guidance of George Fistonich (48), a half-hectare vineyard near the Manukau Harbour in Kirkbride Road, Mangere, has grown to become the third largest wine company in the country.

The origins of Villa Maria lie in a tiny operation called Mountain Vineyards, which was run as a hobby by Dalmatian immigrant Andrew Fistonich. Fistonich worked on the gumfields, then later made a few bottles of wine for himself and friends before becoming a licensed winemaker in 1949. When illness slowed him down, his son George abandoned his career plans in carpentry, leased his father's vineyard, formed a new company, and bought a press, barrels and pumps from Maungatapu Vineyards at Tauranga. In 1961, Villa Maria Hock nosed out into the market.

The winery initially made its presence felt at the bottom end of the market. The slogan 'Let Villa Maria introduce you to wine' associated with the sale of sherries and quaffing table wines, created an image the company for years struggled to overcome. But in recent years Villa Maria

VILLA MARIA'S INDESTRUCTIBLE MANAGING DIRECTOR, GEORGE FISTONICH (RIGHT), WITH HIS CHIEF WINEMAKER, KYM MILNE.

has established an illustrious track record in wine competitions.

George Fistonich is a quiet man, almost impassive on the surface. Those who know him intimately, however, are always struck by his overwhelming passion for Villa Maria and the strength of his ambition. Villa Maria expanded rapidly through the 1970s – absorbing Vidal in 1976 – and early 1980s, emerging as a fierce rival of the largest wineries such as Montana, Corbans and Cooks. John Spencer of the Caxton group of companies was then a silent but substantial shareholder.

At the height of the wine industry's price war late in 1985, Villa Maria went into a much-publicised receivership. With its limited capital reserves, the winery was simply unable to survive in the heavy loss-making trading environment created by its larger rivals. George Exton, then managing director of Cooks/McWilliam's, told Auckland's *Metro* magazine that in his opinion Villa Maria 'destroyed themselves. They consciously went out to increase their market share. They went to the bottom end of the market, the bag-in-box end where there is no profit margin. It was a financial exercise that went wrong'.

'Everyone accepts that we were targeted,' responded Fistonich. The truth is that Cooks/McWilliam's executives made a number of public statements to the effect that New Zealand had room for only two major wineries – indicating their lack of sympathy for Villa Maria's plight. However, Villa Maria's heavy output of cask wines, in a market segment lacking consumer brand loyalty, was always an inherently risky strategy.

Following Villa Maria's successful reconstruction (see page 50) the winery is now jointly owned by the families of George Fistonich and Grant Adams, who is deputy-chairman of the investment company Equiticorp. All debts have been cleared and in early 1987 the new company even announced the purchase of the ailing Hawke's Bay winery Glenvale. Production overall has virtually been halved with a much heavier emphasis on bottled premium wines.

Villa Maria relies heavily on contract-grown fruit. Grapes are drawn from several North Island regions – Hawke's Bay, Gisborne (Sauvignon Blanc, Chardonnay, Müller-Thurgau and Gewürztraminer), Te Kauwhata and Auckland.

Auckland is now emerging as an increasingly important source of Villa Maria's intake of premium fruit. Cabernet Sauvignon is drawn from Brian Hetherington's vineyard at Kumeu and at Ihumatao, a peninsula bordering Auckland airport, Gewürztraminer, Chardonnay and Sauvignon Blanc are cultivated. To oversee this diversity of fruit sources, for several years Villa Maria has employed a full-time viticulturist.

George Fistonich has surrounded himself with a youthful team. Chief winemaker Kym Milne, for example, is only twenty-nine. Australian-born Milne graduated from Roseworthy College and then worked at Berri Estates for three years before joining Villa Maria in 1984. As chief winemaker, he has authority over the winemakers at Vidal and Esk Valley (Glenvale).

Villa Maria's top wines, marketed under a Reserve label, have of late enjoyed an unprecedented run of gold-medal and trophy-winning successes. Its Reserve Chardonnays, Gewürztraminers, Sauvignon Blancs, Cabernet Sauvignons and Cabernet/Merlot blends are indisputably among New Zealand's most outstanding wines.

Wines carrying the Reserve label are produced from the best fruit off selected vineyards and distributed in quantities of up to one thousand cases (and are thus scarce). The range of wines labelled as Private Bin is not in reality a private-bin range at all, for these wines are in ready supply. Almost all Villa Maria's cask wines are marketed under the Maison Vin brand and fortified wines are labelled as Old Masters.

Brookvale Riesling-Sylvaner is the company's biggest volume seller: this is a Gisborne-grown Müller-Thurgau, fruity and medium in the popular style. Well worth seeking out is Villa Maria Chenin Blanc, usually a dryish, mouth-filling and flavoursome wine, a sort of poor man's Chardonnay.

Now to the quartet of premium white varietals. Gewürztraminer has for a decade formed one of the pinnacles of the Villa Maria range (the freeze-concentrated Sauternes used to form the other). The Private Bin, commercial label has – notably in 1985 – shown flashes of outstanding form but more often this is a pleasant medium-dry wine. The Reserve Gewürztraminer, however, is another story. Made from local Ihumatao fruit, it has a lovely golden sheen and is a pungently perfumed and powerful wine.

Two Chardonnays appear, the show-topping Barrique Fermented wine plus the more easily located Private Bin Chardonnay, a blend of Gisborne and Auckland fruit aged for four months in French oak. With its peachy fruit and evident but not overpowering oak, this lesser label has been very sound.

It lives in the shadow, however, of the Barrique Fermented Chardonnay. The 1986 vintage, a rich, deep style with powerful wood influence, took the THC Trophy at the 1987 Air New Zealand Wine Awards as the champion wine of the show. Gisborne fruit grown in heavy clays was all barrel-fermented, with a small percentage also undergoing a malolactic fermentation. So bold is the style it needs at least two or three years bottle age for the fruit to fully unfold. The 1987 is in the same mould.

The commercial Sauvignon Blanc is a Gisborne-grown blend of ripe and early picked grapes. At its best – as in 1985 – it can be unexpectedly classy but usually this is an undemanding, dryish, lightly herbaceous wine. The Reserve wine is a wood-aged style, based on fruit from various regions: in 1987 Gisborne, in 1986 Te Kauwhata and Hawke's Bay. Here the accent is on fruit ripeness, reflected in the delicious 'fruit-salad' character in the bouquet and flavour.

Villa Maria's commercial Cabernet Sauvignons show obvious fruit ripeness and have plenty of stuffing. These, more and more, are Auckland-grown reds, matured in one to three-year-old casks for twelve months. In Kym Milne's words: 'the aim is for a full-flavoured, ripe Cabernet style with subtle oak character but soft and able to be drunk young'.

The Reserve Cabernet Sauvignon and Cabernet/Merlot are much more firmly structured and complex. Based on Kumeu fruit, they are matured for twelve to eighteen months in a mix of Nevers and German (which adds spiciness, says Milne) oak barrels. For depth of flavour and tautness of backbone these are deservedly ranked among this country's leading reds.

WAIKATO/ BAY OF PLENTY

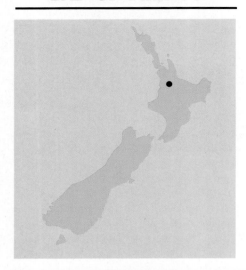

Because of the Land Wars in the nineteenth century, the Waikato, bounded to the east by the Coromandel Ranges and to the west by the Tasman, was settled by Europeans comparatively late. From 1880, however, the forests were cleared, swamps drained and dairy farms established. The foundation of the Government viticultural research station at Te Kauwhata in 1897 gave an early boost to grapegrowing and by 1986 growers had 206 hectares, or 5.3 percent of the country's total plantings, under vines.

Viticultural activity is still centred at Te Kauwhata, with the Cooks winery, the Government research station (see the Research section in chapter two), the small Rongopai and Aspen Ridge wineries and numerous contract growers – notably Ross Goodin, the president of the Grape Growers' Council, whose 100-hectare Waikare Vineyards is the largest contract-grower's vineyard in the country. Further afield at Mangatawhiri is the de Redcliffe winery and close to Thames lies the only Chinese-owned winery in New Zealand, Totara SYC.

Aspen Ridge is a very small winery near Lake Waikare, east of Te Kauwhata township. The company was established in 1963 by Alister McKissock – who also directed the Te Kauwhata research station from

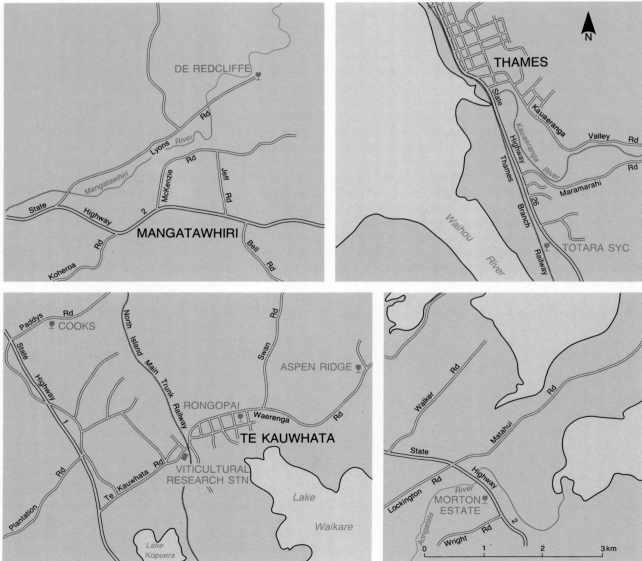

1963 until his resignation in 1966 – with the assistance of Nathan's liquor interests. Since Nathan severed their distribution link the wines have been hard to find and those I have tasted were plain. Aspen Ridge also markets a range of grapejuices and gourmet grape jellies.

Other tiny wineries with a local following are Vilagrad and Karamea. Vilagrad, sited in Rukuhia Road, Ngahinepouri, just south of Hamilton, was established by Ivan Milicich Snr in 1922. Pieter Nooyen and his wife, the third generation of the family, now produce a range of table and fortified wines, including a Cabernet Sauvignon, Pinotage, Müller-Thurgau and Gewürztraminer.

Karamea Pinot Noir 1985 raised a few eyebrows by scoring a silver medal at the 1987 Air New Zealand Wine Awards. Wallace Timbrell and his wife run this little winery located in Pirongia Road, Frankton, south-west of Hamilton. The several vintages of Pinot Noir I have tasted have been very light but have consistently captured true Pinot Noir varietal character. A Cabernet Sauvignon, Müller-Thurgau, Pinotage Rosé and Gewürztraminer/Breidecker blend fill out the range.

MOST VINEYARDS IN THE WAIKATO ARE PLANTED ON MILD SLOPES WITH CLAY SUBSOILS.

There are only a few wineries in the Waikato and a significant proportion – higher than elsewhere – of the grape crop is not even processed into wine. In 1980 the number of growers producing fruit for grapejuice outnumbered those who were producing it for making wine.

Despite the dominating presence of the Cooks winery, from 1975 the region's relative importance declined, as new plantings spread to the East Coast and to the South Island. Yields are lower than in the fertile Gisborne soils, and Te Kauwhata shares West Auckland's climatic disadvantages: although temperatures and sunshine hours are generally higher than in top European wine regions, the rainfall is higher too.

Cooks used to see Te Kauwhata as a potential premium red-wine district, a claim suggested by their own early Te Kauwhata Cabernet Sauvignons and Clarets, typically elegant light reds. Yet recent plantings have emphasised white-wine grapes, reflecting the stronger demand for these wines. In 1986, the major varieties in the Waikato were, in order: Müller-Thurgau, Chenin Blanc, Sauvignon Blanc, Cabernet Sauvignon, Sylvaner and Palomino.

Cooks

Following a 1967 proposal for the formation of a new wine company, Cooks burgeoned in the 1970s into a major force in the industry. Later the company became engaged in a grim struggle to survive. Following a sustained series of heavy losses and the merger of Cooks and McWilliam's in 1984, Corbans purchased Cooks/ McWilliam's in early 1987, thereby creating this country's second largest winemaking conglomerate, behind Montana. The Cooks label, however, has survived.

David Lucas – entrepreneur, retailer and the original driving force behind Cooks – noted the prosperity even of hybrid-producing wineries in the 1960s, and concluded that the planting out of *vinifera* vines should allow wines of superior quality to be made. Wrote Lucas in a widely circulated prospectus: 'The demand for wine of domestic production cannot be satisfied by present and known projected grape plantings. Additionally, about one-third of the present plantings are of poor-quality grapes or are used by winemakers unable to produce either a consistent or a quality wine. There is thus an inviting and profitable opportunity to establish a major new vineyard in New Zealand.'

Cooks, whose name was chosen for its power to evoke thoughts of age and respectability, was sited at Te Kauwhata, as advised by Californian viticultural expert Professor Petrucci, who was impressed by the close parallel between the heat summation readings of Bordeaux and Te Kauwhata. The closeness of the Government research station and the Auckland market also swayed Cooks' decision. Eighty hectares of easily undulating land was bought and in 1969 planting began.

Cooks a year later offered shares to the public, the first New Zealand winery to do so. Since then, a procession of big investors has included CBA Finance, Marac, Hawke's Bay Farmers Co-operative and Brierley Investments. But as the result of a number of failed labels – Clairmont, Spritzer, Blend No. 5 and 7 – and protracted involvement in heavy discounting, profits slumped from $1.1 million in the June 1982 year to a $721,817 loss in the June 1983 year.

THE COOKS WINERY GRACES THE SKYLINE AT TE KAUWHATA.

Hard on the heels of another $1.5 million loss in the six months to December 1983, Brierley Investments, then a fifty percent shareholder, embarked on a shake-up of the company. In a deliberate effort to become smaller, Cooks in 1984 halved its intake of grapes. Five of eight company directors left, and for the first time a realistic attitude was adopted towards pricing policy.

However, the company still posted heavy losses after the September 1984 merger with McWilliam's: $4.3 million in the 30 June 1985 year and nearly $3 million the following year. After the Corbans takeover in early 1987, the shell Cooks/McWilliam's organisation was restructured into an investment, rather than wine, company called Theseus Investments.

Cooks has often been labelled a 'space age' winery on account of its extensive use of electronic quality-control devices. The winery rises prominently on the Te Kauwhata skyline, flanked by a recently much reduced, four-hectare vineyard planted in Chardonnay and Sauvignon Blanc.

Over the years, the company strayed from the original concept of producing only premium-grade table wines. The flavoured wine, 'Party Pack', achieved the doubtful distinction in 1981 of being the cheapest wine-type drink on the market. Few people lamented the swift failure of the hock, lime and soda mix, 'Spritzer'.

Winemaker Kerry Hitchcock – now chief winemaker for Corbans – succeeded early with a red wine, Cooks Cabernet Sauvignon 1973, which won the champion THC Trophy in 1974. In the late 1970s the Cabernet Sauvignon lined overseas shelves and was absent from the local market. However, gold awards for 1983, 1984, 1985 and 1986 Private Bin Fernhill Cabernet Sauvignon have since enabled Cooks to partly restore its earlier dominance of the prestige Cabernet Sauvignon field.

Cooks P.B. Fernhill Cabernet possesses flavour and body on the scale of premium Californian and Australian reds. It is made from fruit grown in company-owned vineyards planted in stony, silty soils on the banks of the Ngaruroro River in Hawke's Bay. The wine spends between twelve and eighteen months in French, American and German oak casks, both new and once-used. In Kerry Hitchcock's view, the 1983 vintage is the finest so far, but even in lesser years this wine can be unexpectedly rewarding.

Cooks market a two-tier range. Top wines carry the words Private Bin with a gold slash across the label corner, whereas the more commercial releases, which were formerly called Premium Varietal with a red slash, are now labelled as Longridge. The Cabernet/Merlot and Cabernet Sauvignon appearing under the lesser label have also been bold and flavour-packed.

Cooks Chasseur is one of this country's top-selling white wines. This is a fruity, medium-sweet blend of Müller-Thurgau, Chasselas and Chenin Blanc, quite flavoursome, with definite Chenin Blanc fruitiness and a sweetish (twenty-eight grams per litre of sugar) finish.

Cooks used to market a very wide range of varietal white wines – Chenin Blanc, Müller-Thurgau, Sylvaner, Chauché Gris, Sauvignon Blanc, Pinot Gris, Gewürztraminer and Chardonnay – but in the mid-1980s many of these appeared instead under the McWilliam's colours. Beginning with the 1986 vintage, a lineup of middle-range varietal wines has reappeared, highlighted by a delicious Late Pick Rhine Riesling and a Dry Gewürztraminer loaded with spice.

Chardonnay from Cooks is a champion wine: the 1982, 1983, 1984 and Private Bin 1985 Chardonnays have all scored gold awards. The P.B. Chardonnay is based on either Gisborne or Hawke's Bay grapes, depending on the fruit quality each vintage (the first several vintages from 1980 were

TRISH JANE IS THE SENIOR WINEMAKER IN CHARGE OF THE COOKS WINERY AT TE KAUWHATA. KERRY HITCHCOCK, HOWEVER, HAS OVERALL RESPONSIBILITY FOR THE ENLARGED CORBANS GROUP'S FOUR WINERIES IN THE NORTH ISLAND.

all Gisborne-grown). The wine, barrel-fermented since 1986, spends nine months in a mix of American, French and German oak barrels.

A perfumed, powerful, 'sweetish' wood character has been a distinctive feature of Cooks' top Chardonnays, reflecting the impact of American oak aging. Early vintages, which peaked around three years old, vied with Delegat's and McWilliam's for top New Zealand honours with this variety. More recent vintages have sustained this high quality, although the label now has a host of rivals.

de Redcliffe

CHRIS CANNING (RIGHT) WITH HIS WINEMAKER, MARK COMPTON. CANNING'S GOAL, TO SHIFT DE REDCLIFFE INTO THE RANKS OF TOP PRODUCERS, HAS HITHERTO BEEN HINDERED BY THE COMPANY'S LACK OF A SPECIALIST WINEMAKER.

The first wines to carry the de Redcliffe label – blends of Cabernet/Merlot and Chardonnay/Sémillon – won for this beautiful isolated vineyard in the Mangatawhiri Valley a reputation for innovative winemaking.

Wellington-born Chris Canning (48) returned to New Zealand in 1975 after many years running an advertising agency in London and New York, having also tended vines in France and been part-owner of a vineyard in Italy. In a natural basin among the Hunua's bush-clad hills, Canning began in 1976 to plant his own vineyard: 'I wouldn't say it was a case of a man of destiny who had to make wine. The reason I bought the place was to escape [foreign] capital gains tax'.

Canning describes himself as a marketing entrepreneur who has focussed on the wine industry. His entrepreneurial talents – and those of his wife Pamela – have recently been demonstrated by the rise at de Redcliffe of the $8 million Hotel Du Vin, an accommodation and conference complex set amidst native trees which boasts a restaurant where the wine list changes daily. The hotel is aimed at Aucklanders who are 'forty-five minutes away by road, much less by helicopter'. De Redcliffe Group Limited, incorporating the vineyard, winery and hotel, was floated on the stock exchange in 1987, with Canning the majority shareholder.

In the estate vineyard, on river silts with a gravel base, ten hectares of Sémillon, Chardonnay, Cabernet Sauvignon and Merlot vines have been planted, bordered by the Mangatawhiri River. Pinot Noir did not succeed and this variety has been uprooted. Chardonnay, Sauvignon Blanc and Pinot Noir fruit is purchased from West Auckland, Te Kauwhata and Hawke's Bay.

Until the 1986 vintage de Redcliffe wines were crushed and fermented elsewhere but barrel-aged at the vineyard. Now the wines are crushed and fermented at the new on-site winery, bottled in Henderson and warehoused in Papakura. Responsible for the 15,000-case annual production is thirty-five-year-old Mark Compton, a Wellington-born B.Sc., who followed his three-year winemaking stint in Australia with a long period at Montana, overseeing bottling and the production of Lindauer.

According to Compton, before his 1987 arrival de Redcliffe wines were 'good solid commercial wines'; now he is pursuing higher extract levels and deeper flavours.

The Chardonnay/Sémillon is a dry, flavoursome wine, barrel-aged for one year, with the more assertive Sémillon tightly reined in by the fatter, rounder Chardonnay. There is also a crisply herbaceous unblended Sémillon, a dry and sustained Waikato wine, lacking the characteristic aggressiveness of this variety in New Zealand – and better for it.

The de Redcliffe range has recently expanded to include such uniquely named and packaged wines as White Lady and Coral Reef. The White Lady depicted on the label, who 'lives permanently with her head in the clouds and is unashamedly naked, yet is rapidly becoming the most popular guest at New Zealand dinner tables', is also featured in a stained-glass window at the winery; the wine itself is a sound dry white blended from Chenin Blanc, Chardonnay and Flora, made expressly to appeal to 'the average consumer'. Coral Reef is a blush (pink) wine blended from Pinot Noir – fermented off the skins – and Chardonnay.

Chardonnay has lately come to the fore at de Redcliffe. Mangatawhiri fruit is oak-fermented and about one-third of the wine undergoes a malolactic fermentation. Both the 1986 and gold-medal 1987 vintages are complex, yeasty and mouth-filling wines.

The silky Cabernet/Merlot is an elegant light red, matured for eighteen months in French oak. After a highly promising debut in 1980, several subsequent vintages lacked enough weight to be distinguished, but the latest releases show greater substance.

Morton Estate

Despite its location in the western Bay of Plenty, isolated from the principal wine regions, the young Morton Estate winery has carved out an elevated reputation, particularly for its Chardonnays. Traditionally the Bay of Plenty region has been of negligible winemaking importance, only two vineyards having previously existed here, at Maungatapu and Maketu.

In view of its founder Morton Brown's 'new boy' status within the industry, many winemakers have been impressed by how swiftly this winery made its presence felt. Morton Brown (42) is a former Woolworths trainee, Wellington car salesman and dealer who later invested in kiwifruit and recently also in asparagus and cherries. Finance and marketing are his forte. Brown describes himself as an entrepreneur, drawn to the wine industry because 'you are your own boss. We can set our own price, export it, sell it into the trade and at the door. There are no [marketing] licensing authorities'.

Brown erected his Cape Dutch-style, plastered concrete winery on State Highway Two at Aongatete, twenty-four kilometres on the Auckland side of Tauranga, in 1982. Then the highly talented and affable winemaker John Hancock, already something of a cult figure following his successful years at Delegat's, moved south to join him. Hancock (37) is a South

MORTON BROWN (RIGHT) AND HIS ASSISTANT WINEMAKER, STEVE BIRD. THE CHARDONNAYS, FUMÉ BLANC AND METHODE CHAMPENOISE HERE ARE ALL DISTINGUISHED, BUT THE FEW REDS HAVE NOT BEEN MEMORABLE.

JOHN HANCOCK, WHOSE RICHLY OAKED WHITE
WINES AND EXTROVERTED PERSONALITY HAVE
EARNED A HIGH PROFILE FOR MORTON ESTATE.

Australian who made fruit wines while a schoolboy, later graduated from
Roseworthy College, then worked for Lindemans and the Berri
Cooperative Winery before shifting to Delegat's in 1979. Now a company
shareholder, Hancock says he came to New Zealand for 'the chance to
make the 'newly discovered' cool climate white wines. Delicate,
flavoursome wines are the ultimate in style to me'.

In 1987 Brown sold Morton Estate Wineries Limited to Morton Equities
Limited, in return for a forty percent shareholding in the new company, and
then Morton Equities was floated on the stock exchange. In September 1988,
however, Mildara Wines of Australia gained control of Morton Equities.

At present the winery draws its grapes from the home vineyard of six
hectares, planted in Pinot Noir, and from contract growers in Hawke's
Bay (Chardonnay, Sauvignon Blanc, Gewürztraminer and Cabernet
Sauvignon) and Gisborne (Chardonnay). To guarantee a supply of fruit
to satisfy its burgeoning demand, in 1987 the company purchased a one
hundred-hectare block at Maraekakaho, near Hastings, and has planted
it in Chardonnay, Sauvignon Blanc, Pinot Noir and Cabernet Sauvignon.
A crushing plant will also be erected there.

The Morton Estate winery is very compact: the crusher, wall-mounted
drainer tanks and press are positioned within a few metres of each other
for maximum operating convenience. There is no warehouse because
bottled stocks are stored in a local coolstore. Above the temperature-
controlled 'Champagne' room is a fascinating barrel room, housing
hundreds of barrels from the Seguin Moreau, Demptos, Jaegle and
Dargaud cooperages.

Hancock loves to explore the intricacies of oak's effects on wine – and
his wines show it. Nevers oak is 'great', says Hancock, but because nearly
all other wineries are using it he is looking for something different.
Limousin oak he sees as too powerful for New Zealand's delicate fruit,
so he is placing a great deal of emphasis on Vosge and Allier oaks, which
are characterised by their slow extraction of oak substances. All the
different oak types are currently being evaluated for establishing long-
term preferences, but meantime the wines are blended together for sale.
A half hour with Hancock tasting Chardonnays undergoing a score of
different wood treatments is an experience never forgotten.

Since the first vintage, 1983, a broad range of wines has emerged,
uniformly well made. Only bottled table wines are made. Commercial
releases carry a grey label; the much rarer, Winery Reserve wines are often
termed 'black label'.

The grey-label Chardonnay is a company mainstay. Following the
elegant 1983 gold-medal wine, the 1984 was on a lower plane, but later
vintages have brought a welcome return to form. Hawke's Bay and
Gisborne fruit is eighty percent fermented in tanks, twenty percent in
barrels, then barrel-matured for six months. It emerges toasty, deep
flavoured and elegant, and is a roaring commercial success with over
10,000 cases snapped up in a short time each year. Its little brother, labelled
White Burgundy, is another Chardonnay given a 'little' wood aging.

Its big brother is the famous 'black label' Chardonnay, a style which
represents John Hancock's search for maximum complexity, by stamping
powerful oak on the best supporting fruit. Made entirely from Hawke's
Bay grapes, it is all barrel-fermented and rests for twelve months on its
lees in new French oak barriques. Part of the final blend also undergoes
a malolactic fermentation. The outcome is a robust, multi-faceted wine
of huge flavour, golden, oaky, and showing an overall richness that rivals
the premium white Burgundies it is modelled upon.

Another mainstay is Sauvignon Blanc, usually full of gooseberry and
lime flavours. Made from Hawke's Bay fruit, this is a non-wooded wine,

carrying a slight hint of sweetness. From time to time a Late Harvest Sauvignon Blanc appears, sweet, well-ripened and mellower.

Morton Estate Winery Reserve Fumé Blanc at its best is a stunning wine. Barrel-fermented since the 1986 vintage, it spends up to a year resting on its lees, emerging with ripe tropical fruit flavours intermeshed with French-reminiscent yeastiness and a rich oakiness.

A solid Gewürztraminer, an elegant dry Riesling-Sylvaner and a Müller-Thurgau round out the still white-wine range.

Bottle-fermented sparkling wines are another Morton Estate success. The debut, 1985 Methode Champenoise, captured a deserved gold award. Blended from seventy percent Chardonnay and thirty percent Pinot Noir, the wine displays an overall stylishness, flavour intensity and sustained bead that holds promise of great things in the future. The 1986 is all Chardonnay based – lighter, with greater delicacy – and the 1987 is a reversal of the 1985 blend: seventy percent Pinot Noir and thirty percent Chardonnay. Four riddling machines automatically turn the bottles every three hours to shake the sediment down into their necks, performing in a few days a task which would take several weeks by hand.

So far the red wines have not stood out – the 1984 Cabernet/Merlot lacked depth and the 1986 Cabernet Sauvignon is fruity but straightforward.

Rongopai

Rongopai burst unheralded on the wine scene in 1986 with a 300-case release of three botrytised wines at a standard – and at prices – that compelled widespread interest.

Rongopai – meaning 'good taste' or 'good feeling' – winery in Waerenga Road, Te Kauwhata, is the fruit of the labours of Dr Rainer Eschenbruch (49) and Tom Van Dam (34), who until recently were DSIR employees based at the Te Kauwhata research station. German-born Eschenbruch is a tall and angular, vastly experienced winemaker, holder of a Ph.D. from the Geisenheim Institute. After several years at Stellenbosch Farmers' Wineries in South Africa, he arrived in this country in 1973 to take charge of the programme of winemaking research at Te Kauwhata.

RAINER ESCHENBRUCH (RIGHT) AND TOM VAN DAM ARE BOTH COMMITTED TO UNRAVELLING THE WAIKATO'S WINE POTENTIAL. BOTRYTISED SWEET WHITES UNDER THE RONGOPAI LABEL HAVE BEEN OF STARTLING QUALITY.

Van Dam, a bearded, obviously thoughtful man, is an M.Sc. graduate who after starting work at Ruakura in 1978 ended up as the officer-in-charge at Te Kauwhata. He and Eschenbruch formed their partnership in 1982.

An old winery built by Thomas Hutchinson, who early planted a vineyard on the Rongopai block of land at Te Kauwhata, still stands on the property, its original concrete fermentation vats now empty. Another, recently renovated winery now used by Eschenbruch and Van Dam was built in the 1940s by Lou Gordon, who also operated under the name Rongopai. 1988 was the first vintage processed by the partners at their own winery; earlier crops were crushed at St Nesbit.

On loam-clay soils sloping gently to the north – earlier covered in Albany Surprise vines, which they promptly bulldozed – Eschenbruch and Van Dam have established a two-hectare vineyard of Riesling, Chardonnay and Cabernet Sauvignon vines, densely planted to lower the vines' vigour. They are developing another two-hectare vineyard nearby and also draw contract grapes from Ross Goodin's Waikare Vineyards.

Rongopai's fame hinges on its late-harvested, botrytised sweet whites, a style clearly traceable back to Rainer Eschenbruch's German origins. He also produced botrytised wines on an experimental basis at Te Kauwhata in 1981. (The reader can sense his controlled excitement in his 1984 paper which summarised the effects of harvest date and sugar levels on the quality of wines made from Reichensteiner. Early harvested grapes, picked on 23 February at 17.5 degrees brix and normal-harvested grapes, picked on 11 March, at 21.5 degrees brix, both yielded wines which tasted 'thin, empty, watery and coarse'. By contrast late-harvested grapes, picked another month later at almost 24 degrees brix, yielded wine with 'a very good extract content [which] tastes very full and presents itself as a Sauternes-type with a significant concentration of character'.)

To secure adequate crops of botrytised fruit, the partners at Rongopai have an arrangement with the local grower, Ross Goodin, whereby he is guaranteed a minimum payment for sound grapes and, for riper fruit, a bonus. Any loss – and a percentage of the crop has been lost over the years – is Rongopai's.

Rongopai's production – 1500 cases in 1987 – will steadily climb to an optimum level of 3000 cases. Dry styles are made: 1986 brought a strapping debut Chardonnay and 1987 the first Cabernet Sauvignon. The Sauvignon Blanc in favourable years is an absolutely distinctive Te Kauwhata wine, carrying all the hallmarks of ultra-ripe fruit: soft, rich, almost creamy intensity and a mellow, gooseberries-and-honey flavour. Here is one of the forerunners of a new style of New Zealand Sauvignon Blanc, worlds away from the once ubiquitous stalky/grassy style.

Of the sweeter whites, Rongopai Late Harvest Müller-Thurgau is light in body, but has lovely flavour concentration and a voluptuous fragrance. The Late Harvest Riesling is a golden, botrytised wine, medium-sweet and honeyish. But the highlight of this highly Germanic trio is undoubtedly the opulent Riesling Auslese, a perfumed and elegant Riesling enhanced by its thrillingly intense botrytis character.

Totara SYC

Ah Chan of Canton – 'Kumara Joe' to most people – planted in 1925 a small plot of Albany Surprise table grapes, together with kumara, to supply the Thames market. Stanley Chan, no relation of Ah Chan although from the same village in Canton, bought the tiny vineyard in 1950, and started winemaking. So began Totara SYC Vineyards, the country's only Chinese-owned wine company.

The name Totara SYC was derived from the Totara Valley – near the winery site just outside Thames – and Stanley Young Chan's initials. Stanley Chan's mother's family brewed and sold rice wine in their Canton shop; his father was a distiller before emigrating to Dargaville at the turn of the century. Today, this small, low-profile vineyard is run by one of Stanley Chan's sons, Gilbert (47).

The winery itself, surprisingly, presents to the visitor a Spanish facade with a curved archway. Canned water chestnuts and beancurds line the shelves in the vineyard shop.

Totara, says Gilbert Chan, is currently in 'a state of transition'. The winery bottled almost no varietal wines in the 1984, 1986 and 1987 vintages; all the company-owned vineyards at Thames and Kumeu were uprooted in 1986; Gilbert's brother Ken, until recently the managing director, has now withdrawn from active management. Although fruit has recently been bought from growers in the Gisborne and Hawke's Bay regions, much of this has been processed into cask wines. Gilbert Chan is now endeavouring to shift his production more decisively into premium table wines.

Until a decade ago, Totara's reputation hinged primarily on its fortified wines and sweet white table wines. A puzzlingly wide array of labels, too often claiming 'private bin' status, won limited respect. Yet although the company is not widely considered a producer of quality wine, it regularly tastes success in competition: in 1987, for instance, its P.B. Brown Sherry scored a gold award at the Easter Show Competition, and three sherries plus a 1987 Müller-Thurgau scored silver medals at the Air New Zealand Wine Awards.

Totara's strength in table wines has largely been confined to white wines, with the exception of a chunky, soft 1985 Cabernet Sauvignon. The wine that lingers most in the memory is the 1979 Riesling-Sylvaner – from a poor vintage, this displayed plenty of fruit and matured superbly. Chenin Blanc has also been well handled here – the 1978 gold-medal wine opened up amazingly full and fresh in 1987.

Totara Fu Gai is listed at many Chinese licensed restaurants; made purposely to accompany Chinese cuisine, this blend of Chenin Blanc, Müller-Thurgau and Muscat Dr Hogg makes fruity, slightly sweet, easy drinking.

Totara Valley – the label for the bottom range – includes a Dry White, Moselle, Sauternes and Rich Dry Red. Other table wines on sale in early 1988 included a Müller-Thurgau and dry Riesling-Sylvaner; a non-wooded P.B. Chardonnay; City of Sails (Müller-Thurgau backblended with Muscat); Aucklander (Müller-Thurgau); Big Red ('soft generous Australian style'); Carnelian (medium red); and Le Chef Red ('with attached mulled spices sachet').

Another feature of this winery is its liqueurs, including Kiwifruit and the coffee-based Totara Café, reminiscent of the Mexican product Kahlua but sold at a much lower price.

POVERTY BAY/
EAST CAPE

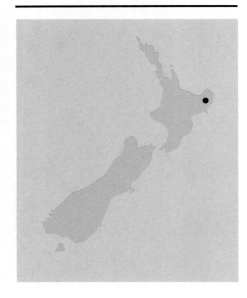

VINES SWEEP ACROSS THE GISBORNE PLAINS,
BEARING BOUNTIFUL CROPS IN THE DEEP,
FERTILE SOILS.

Gisborne is the wine industry's bread basket, the prime source of bulk grapes for its hungry cask production lines.

This non-glamorous image undoubtedly also stems from the relative paucity of fully self-contained wineries here; the Gisborne wine trail currently extends only to Matawhero and Millton. The up-market image of these two enterprising 'boutique' vineyards has tended to be over-whelmed by the broader picture of Gisborne as a 'plain Jane' region. Thus the tag 'carafe country' has been easy to apply.

Ponder, then, on what these wines have in common: Delegat's Selected Vintage Sauvignon Blanc 1986, Pacific Willowbrook Gewürztraminer 1986, Millton Rhine Riesling Medium Opou Vineyards 1987 and Villa Maria Barrique Fermented Chardonnay 1986. All were made from Gisborne-grown fruit and they all scored gold awards at the 1987 Air New Zealand Wine Awards. The Barrique Fermented Chardonnay even took the most sought-after trophy for the champion wine of the show.

A spread of gold awards like this, right across the prestigious Chardonnay, Rhine Riesling, Sauvignon Blanc and Gewürztraminer show classes, lead pointedly to the conclusion that Gisborne has had an undeservedly bad press.

The East Cape, dominated by the Raukumara Range, has only limited lowland areas suitable for viticulture. Grapegrowing is confined to the Poverty Bay flats around Gisborne, which form the largest of the coastal alluvial plains, and to smaller ones further north at Tolaga Bay and Tikitiki, and to the south near Wairoa.

Friedrick Wohnsiedler pioneered winemaking in Gisborne after a false start by Marist missionaries, who landed by mistake at Turanganui (Gisborne) in 1850 and there planted vines before departing for their original destination, Hawke's Bay.

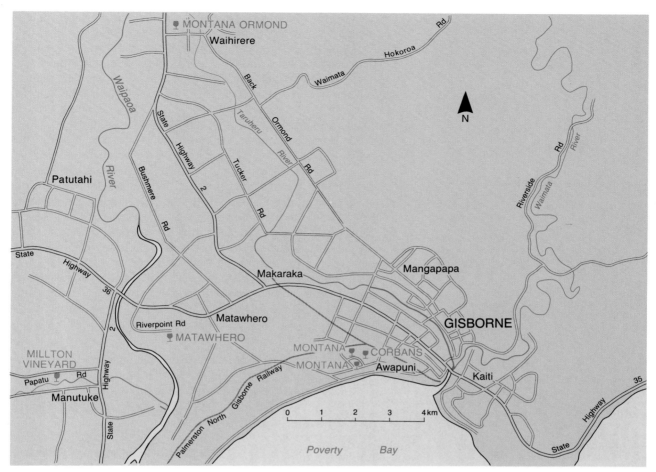

Wohnsiedler, born on a tributary of the Rhine, arrived in New Zealand around the turn of the century. When patriots laid waste his Gisborne smallgoods business during the 1914–18 war, Wohnsiedler moved out and onto the land, planting vines at Ormond in 1921. His first vintage, a sweet red, was labelled simply as 'Wine'.

When Wohnsiedler died in 1956, his Waihirere vineyard only covered four hectares. (His name lives on, of course, on the label of New Zealand's most popular varietal Müller-Thurgau, Montana Wohnsiedler.) In 1961, a rapid expansion programme began which, after a series of financial restructurings, saw the Wohnsiedler family eventually lose control. By 1973 Montana had completely absorbed Waihirere.

From a paltry acreage of vines supplying the old Waihirere winery, since 1965 viticulture has swept the Gisborne plains. Corbans and Montana between them have three large wineries in the area (not open to visitors), and by 1986 about 150 grapegrowers had between them one-third of New Zealand's total area in vines.

Gisborne is white-wine country. Müller-Thurgau, Chardonnay and Dr Hogg Muscat are – in that order – the region's three foremost varieties. Run your eye down a list of the ten leading grape varieties planted in Gisborne and you will not find a single red. Here the later-ripening red varieties tend to become swollen, at the cost of flavour and colour intensity: with the odd exception, Cabernet Sauvignon has not performed well in Gisborne.

The doubts over grape quality centre principally on the fact that although the vines get ample amounts of sunshine and heat, the highly fertile soils and plentiful autumn rains combine to produce both excessively dense vine-foliage growth and bumper crops. The rainfall during the critical

February-April harvest period averages seventy percent higher than in Marlborough, and thirty-three percent higher than Hawke's Bay.

In the past, this has encouraged growers to pick their crops as soon as an acceptable sugar level was achieved, in order to avoid bunch rot.

In a few devastating days in early March 1988, cyclone Bola dumped 300–600mm of rain on Gisborne, the equivalent of one-third to one-half of the region's average annual rainfall. Many vineyards were wiped out, their fruit submerged in water and their vines smothered in a sea of silt.

Selected vineyards, however, are now employing a variety of viticultural techniques to achieve fruit quality far above the norm. By shifting new vineyards up into the hill country; planting on less fertile clay soils; selecting devigorating rootstocks; planting more phylloxera-resistant vines (the bug has made rapid inroads into Gisborne's vineyards since its discovery there in 1970); planting new, improved clones; planting virus-free vines; plucking leaves to reduce fruit shading; later harvesting to advance ripening; and a range of other approaches, Gisborne viticulturists have of late been exploring more fully their region's fine wine potential.

Venture Vineyards is the newest label. Marshall Savidge, long established as a grapegrower in this region, has recently marketed a Chenin Blanc, Chardonnay and Cabernet/Merlot, all in very tight supply.

Matawhero

The reputation of Matawhero has spread far beyond this true 'boutique'-scale winery and its encircling vineyards. In a country which has earned much international praise for the standard of its Gewürztraminers, Matawhero has carved out a reputation second to none for its handling of this grape.

Company head Denis Irwin, in his early forties, is one of the great individualists of the New Zealand wine industry, a man whose prominence stems from his unique personal blend of innovative winemaking, entrepreneurial business style – and love of letting his hair down.

Matawhero's vineyards, surrounding the winery at the end of Riverpoint Road near Gisborne city, and at Manutuke, encompass over thirty-five hectares of Gewürztraminer and ten other grape varieties. Much of the crop is sold to larger wine companies, but Irwin has first choice of the available fruit.

In recent years Denis Irwin has spent the majority of his time across the Tasman. In his absence, Hatsch Kalberer, a thirty-three-year-old Swiss, assumed the day-to-day responsibility for running Matawhero. Kalberer is a tall, gentle winemaker who came to New Zealand because this is further than anywhere else from Europe's problems. He arrived at Matawhero in 1982 and liked the dryness of the wines: 'I can see myself growing old here,' he says with deep contentment.

So far, Matawhero's success has hinged primarily on Gewürztraminer. The Gewürztraminer is everything that wine of this variety should be: pungent, very aromatic, unmistakably spicy in taste.

The first vintage, 1976, was made in a converted chicken shed and scored a silver medal at that year's National Wine Competition. The 1978 scored a gold medal and when I last tasted it a couple of years ago it was still a thrilling wine. Over the years the style has fluctuated from dry to medium-dry but consistently the wines have captured intense Gewürztraminer flavour.

Ask Kalberer why Matawhero Gewürztraminer is so good, and he stresses Matawhero's soil quality; the viticultural techniques they have evolved over many years' experience with this notoriously fickle vineyard performer; and their decision to give naturally occurring, 'wild' yeasts free rein during the fermentation, rather than use the more conventional cultured yeasts. Kalberer is trying to simplify the winemaking process when elsewhere it has become more and more complicated.

Matawhero Chardonnay has also lately come to the fore and both the 1982 and 1983 vintages are full, mouth-filling styles, slow to mature. (The 1984 is of a lower standard.) Since 1986, the Chardonnay has been barrel-fermented and given a secondary, bacterial malolactic fermentation to enhance complexity.

Matawhero has now withdrawn from wine competitions but not before its 1983 Merlot scored a rare gold medal for a Gisborne-grown red. The 1986 Cabernet/Merlot, tasted from the barrel, was a bright, purplish wine of medium-full colour, lighter in body than its Hawke's Bay counterparts, but ripe and elegant.

A dry and satisfying Rosé, an Estate Red, Chenin Blanc, Sauvignon Blanc/Sémillon, Traminer/Riesling-Sylvaner and Chenin/Chardonnay flesh out the range.

MATAWHERO WINEMAKER HATSCH KALBERER HAS BEEN DENIS IRWIN'S LOYAL LIEUTENANT DURING HIS BOSS'S RECENT SOJOURN ACROSS THE TASMAN.

Millton Vineyard

Once suspended from a Christchurch private school for making blackberry wine in the prefects' study, James Millton (32) now runs, together with his wife Annie (31), Gisborne's newest winery in Papatu Road, Manutuke, sixteen kilometres south of the city.

Millton initially spent two years with Montana before leaving to pursue his wine career overseas. After working on a small estate in the Rheinhessen, he returned to a vintage with Corbans and then, after opting out of a Roseworthy College winemaking course, went to work on Annie's father's vineyard in Gisborne.

Now the Milltons' own vineyards have spread out over eighteen hectares of river flats in the Manutuke and Matawhero districts. On loam clays in Papatu Road they grow an assortment of white and red grapes; at the Clos du St Anne vineyard – along the road from Denis Irwin in Riverpoint Road, Matawhero – they have planted Chardonnay and Müller-Thurgau vines. Alongside their administration building – an old shearers' quarters – the Milltons erected a new coolstore winery in the summer of 1983–84.

THE MILLTONS GROW SUCH HERBS AS TANSY, WORMWOOD AND HYSSOP UNDER THEIR VINES IN A BID TO REPEL INSECTS AND ALSO TO FORCE THE VINES TO COMPETE FOR SOIL NUTRIENTS. THE NETTING PREVENTS BIRDS PLUNDERING THE FRUIT.

ELEGANTLY UNDERSTATED, DISTINCTIVE PACKAGING IS A HALLMARK OF THE MILLTON RANGE.

In the conviction that 'we are what we eat', the Milltons have set themselves the difficult task of making organically grown wines in commercial volumes without extensive reliance on pesticides and other chemicals. For health – and, they admit, economic – reasons, the Milltons are practising an 'integrated pest-management system' in their endeavour to reduce chemical usage in their vineyards. They spray as frequently as other wineries, but in place of chemical sprays use herbal preparations.

The Millton style of white wines is reflected in James Millton's words on his own 1985 Chardonnay: 'Crisp, refreshing and clean'. The Chenin Blancs are elegant, tart wines with plenty of distinctive peachy varietal flavour, rating well among New Zealand Chenins. In future, Millton plans two styles: a dry, barrel-fermented Chenin Blanc and a medium Reserve.

The Chardonnays have ranged in quality from the crisp, plain wine made in 1985 to the creamy, full-bodied Clos du St Anne 1986, a soft and appealing style which, however, lacks the steeliness of most Hawke's Bay Chardonnays.

Two Chardonnay labels are planned for the future – the standard line, to be barrel-fermented with partial malolactic fermentation, and the premium Clos du St Anne, which will utilise riper grapes and natural yeasts, and 100 percent malolactic fermentation.

Millton's fame, however, rests squarely upon its sweet, botrytised Rieslings. The 1985 Late Harvest Bunch Selection Rhine Riesling, a lovely, gentle, auslese-style wine, was awarded Millton's first gold medal at the 1986 Easter Show Competition. The Rhine Riesling Medium Opou Vineyards 1987 has also scored gold.

'Noble rot', the beneficial dry form of *Botrytis cinerea*, shrivels and concentrates Riesling grapes in the Millton vineyard. The outcome is intense, nectareous wine which is only consistently rivalled in this country by the outstanding sweet white wines of Rongopai and Te Whare Ra.

The Millton range also features a solid Classic Dry White (with a distinctly herbaceous, Sauvignon Blanc-derived tang), Fumé Blanc, Te Arai River Cabernet Sauvignon and Steinberg Müller-Thurgau.

Their display of dried flowers, house plants and old-English garden perennials is another drawcard – but that's another story.

HAWKE'S BAY

Hawke's Bay, one of New Zealand's pioneer winemaking districts which today still retains its traditional importance, also has the potential to become one of the world's great wine regions.

Here is located the oldest winemaking concern in New Zealand still under the same management – Mission Vineyards, established by the Catholic Society of Mary in 1851. The oldest winery still operating, erected in stages from the 1870s, can be found at the Te Mata Estate. In 1986, with 1032 hectares (or twenty-six percent of the national total), Hawke's Bay ranked second to Poverty Bay in the extent of its vineyards.

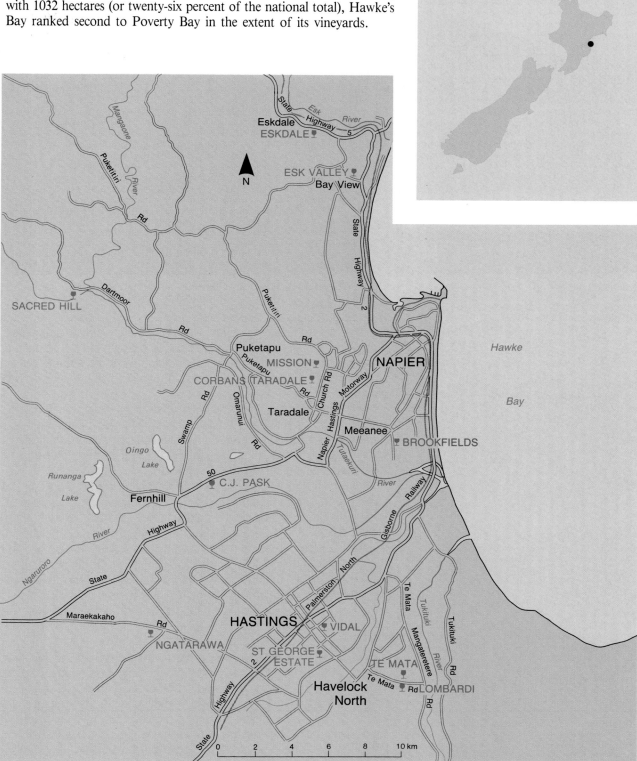

THE HILLS RISE IN THE WEST, THE PACIFIC COAST LIES TO THE EAST; BETWEEN ARE THE FERTILE, ALLUVIAL LOAMS AND SHINGLY POCKETS WHERE VINES FLOURISH.

The terrain of Hawke's Bay varies from the rugged inland ranges, the Ruahine and Kaweka, climbing to over 1600 metres, to the coastal Heretaunga Plains. In this sheltered environment, protected by the high country from the prevailing westerly winds, agriculture thrives: pastoralism, process cropping, orcharding and market gardening. And on the margins of the plains, at Taradale, Te Mata, Fernhill, Ngatarawa, Haumoana and in the Esk Valley, the favourably dry and sunny climate supports an easy growth of the vine.

Hawke's Bay is one of the sunniest areas of the country; the city of Napier, for instance, enjoys similar sunshine hours and temperatures to Bordeaux. In summer, anticyclonic conditions sometimes lead to droughts; such weather can produce grapes with high sugar contents and forms a key advantage for Hawke's Bay viticulture.

One drawback is that the easterly facing aspect renders Hawke's Bay vulnerable to easterly cyclonic depressions and their accompanying rainfall. Some of the heaviest rains ever recorded in New Zealand have descended on the region. In bad years such as 1979 and 1988, the vineyards of Hawke's Bay can be deluged with autumn rains. Nevertheless, in most years the autumn rainfall is markedly less than at Gisborne.

One of Hawke's Bay's prime viticultural assets is its wide range of soil types: the Heretaunga Plains consist mainly of fertile alluvial soils over gravelly subsoils deposited by the rivers and creeks draining the surrounding uplands.

The pioneer winemakers headed close to the lower hills of Hawke's Bay as the best sites. At the 1896 Conference of Australasian Fruitgrowers held in Wellington, Whangarei vinegrower Lionel Hanlon enthused: '. . . on the gently sloping limestone hills that are so characteristic of the [Hawke's Bay] district . . . may be found hundreds of ideal sites for vineyards. In some places the hills present the peculiar truncated appearance of the vine-clothed hills of the celebrated Côte d'Or district in France . . .' But recently most vineyards have been planted on the plains to secure higher grape yields.

A comprehensive regional study published in 1985 by the Hawke's Bay Vintners stated frankly that 'many soils on the Heretaunga Plains are quite wet and vines grow too vigorously, giving large yields of grapes with poor balance and insufficient ripeness [notably the areas of fertile silty loams having a high water table] . . . Other more freely draining shingle soils . . . may be too dry in the growing season which would limit proper canopy development for ideal fruit maturation. This is overcome with trickle irrigation'. About ten percent of the vineyards in Hawke's Bay, those planted in stonier soils, are irrigated.

Districts warmly recommended for viticulture by the regional study included the Taradale hills, Ngatarawa (warm, dry and promising to produce grapes 'of the highest quality'), river terraces along the Tuki Tuki and Ngaruroro rivers, and Havelock North.

Only in the past twenty years has viticulture reached significant proportions in Hawke's Bay: in the late 1930s, for instance, only twenty-five hectares of vines were grown in the province. Then in 1967 contract growing extended to Hawke's Bay. Where previously the established wineries had concentrated their plantings in the Esk Valley, Taradale and Haumoana areas, the arrival of contract grapegrowing opened up new sub-regions, notably the Fernhill-Korokipo district. By 1986 the vineyards of over one hundred grapegrowers stretched over a forty-kilometre belt running from the Esk Valley, at the north end of the plains, to Te Mata, in the south.

For decades the dominant force in the Bay was McWilliam's, with its dry white Cresta Doré, sparkling Marque Vue and red Bakano virtually household names. Founded in 1944, the New Zealand company was wholly Australian-owned until 1962, and grew rapidly until 1961 when it merged with McDonald's Wines to become the largest winery in the country.

McDonald's dated back to 1897. Bartholomew Steinmetz, a native of Luxembourg, had left his position as a lay brother at Mission Vineyards to establish his own two-hectare vineyard. A fourteen-year-old labourer called Tom McDonald began work there in 1921 and by 1926 had taken over the business.

DAVID (LEFT) AND MARK MASON OF THE FLEDGLING SACRED HILL WINERY – A FUMÉ BLANC WORTH TRYING.

Keen to increase production, Tom McDonald passed control to the Christchurch-based brewers and merchants Ballins in 1944 but stayed on as manager. McDonald, who retired from the post of McWilliam's production manager in 1976, and later chaired the Wine Institute from 1980 to 1982, for decades dominated the Hawke's Bay wine scene, a man of formidable intellect and genial company. On two occasions in the early

1980s when I spent an hour or two with him, he opened a bottle of McWilliam's Cabernet Sauvignon 1967, a deep-scented, mellow wine then of fading beauty. He died in 1987, aged seventy-nine.

Following a series of mergers and takeovers, the three former McWilliam's wineries in Hawke's Bay are now part of the Corbans empire. The old Faraday Street winery is to be phased out, with the crushing and fermenting complex at Pandora becoming Corbans' major facility in Hawke's Bay. The old McDonald's winery at Taradale has been retained as a Corbans hospitality centre.

Yet, although McWilliam's, with a famous series of Cabernet Sauvignons dating back to 1965 and several extraordinarily fine Chardonnays, early proved the province's ability to produce some superb table wines, vine plantings to 1980 almost eschewed these varieties. The 1980 vineyard survey revealed that Müller-Thurgau constituted half of Hawke's Bay vines – yet only McWilliam's, with their Late Pick Riesling-Sylvaners, had made wines of interest from this grape.

However, in the last decade much more widespread plantings have occurred of the aristocratic grape varieties most suited to Hawke's Bay's growing environment. The 1986 vineyard survey revealed that the six most important varieties planted here are, in order: Müller-Thurgau, Cabernet Sauvignon, Chenin Blanc, Chardonnay, Sauvignon Blanc and Muscat Dr Hogg (with lesser, but significant areas devoted to Sylvaner, Gewürztraminer, Palomino, Riesling and Merlot).

There are eleven wineries here, with Sacred Hill the latest arrival. The Mason brothers, David (30) and Mark (27), own a seventeen-hectare vineyard in Dartmoor Road, near Puketapu ('sacred hill'), which is planted in Sauvignon Blanc, Chardonnay, Gewürztraminer and Pinot Noir. They reserve the finest grapes for their own label and also buy in fruit. An old shed serves as their winery, which processed its debut vintage in 1986.

A lineup of four wines is planned: Fumé Blanc, Cabernet/Merlot, Chardonnay and Gewürztraminer. I have enjoyed two vintages of the pricey, one-third barrel-fermented Sacred Hill Fumé Blanc, both meticulously clean and full flavoured.

Brookfields

Peter Robertson, owner of Brookfields Vineyards, only a kilometre from the sea at Meeanee, is a highly articulate, seven-days-per-week winemaker who personally enjoys mouth-filling dry wine styles. His output of rich, full-bodied wines from Cabernet Sauvignon, Chardonnay and Sauvignon Blanc has recently earned high respect for the Brookfields label.

Traditionally a sherry specialist, Brookfields was founded in 1937 by Hawke's Bay-born Richard Ellis. The Ellis family retained ownership for forty years. Robertson (37) who grew up in Otago, is a B.Sc. graduate in biochemistry, whose interest in winemaking was aroused when employed as a student at Barker's fruit winery at Geraldine in the South Island. After spending a couple of years at McWilliam's in Hawke's Bay – working his way up from labourer to laboratory chemist – Robertson took over the old Ellis winery and three-hectare vineyard – then on the verge of closing down – from the founder's son Jack in 1977.

Until 1981, Peter Robertson had to rely principally on Müller-Thurgau and Chasselas fruit material; thus his wines were sound but not memorable. Now the silty-loam home vineyard stretching from the winery to the gate has been replanted with Chardonnay, Riesling, Gewürztraminer and Sauvignon Blanc vines. He also draws Cabernet Sauvignon from Tuki Tuki, Chardonnay from Fernhill, and Sauvignon Blanc from Ngatarawa, supplemented by a mixture of fruit from local Meeanee sources.

Robertson each year produces around 5000 cases of table wine in his compact, half-century-old winery, constructed of handmade concrete blocks. The winery's legacy of fortified-wine production still lingers on in the steady stream of customers who drive out for their 'fill your own' sherry, but Robertson's energies are much more absorbed by his tight array of red and white table wines.

In warmer vintages, Brookfields Chardonnay is on a grand, rather Californian scale, verging on fourteen percent alcohol. This fat wine, yeasty from its fermentation in new Nevers oak puncheons, has intensely peachy, rich fruit flavour. The second-string Chardonnay, labelled Chablis, made with lighter oak handling, can also be unexpectedly satisfying: 'This is the wine I drink at night,' says Robertson.

In its youth, Brookfields Sauvignon Fumé is full in body, dry and bursting with ripe gooseberryish fruit and plentiful oak – needing a couple of years to really settle down. It is smartly packaged in punted claret-shape bottles, like the white wines of Bordeaux, themselves partly based on Sauvignon Blanc.

Other white wines here include a solid Gewürztraminer and a medium-dry Tokay d'Alsace.

The duo of top reds are the Cabernet Sauvignon and Cabernet/Merlot. Brookfields 1983 Cabernet Sauvignon, one of the best Hawke's Bay Cabernets of that year, announced this winery's arrival as a serious red-wine producer, and that enticingly ripe and fragrant red has been followed by a string of equally successful Cabernets. Working with 'punchy ripe Hawke's Bay fruit', Robertson fashions deep-hued, weighty, flavour-packed reds, enjoyable early but also responding well to bottle age.

Broader and softer, the Cabernet/Merlot is a blend of approximately sixty percent Cabernet Sauvignon, twenty-five percent Cabernet Franc and fifteen percent Merlot. Robertson says Cabernet Sauvignon gives 'robustness' to the medley, Cabernet Franc 'fragrance' and Merlot 'softness'. This is the pick of the two top reds if you must broach one early.

PETER ROBERTSON – NOT THE SORT TO SOUND HIS OWN TRUMPET, HE IS, NEVERTHELESS, CONSISTENTLY MAKING SOME OF THE MOST ROBUST, DEEP-FLAVOURED WINES IN THE BAY.

Esk Valley

Ask any wine enthusiast two or three years ago to name the largest seven vineyards in the country, and few would have suggested Glenvale. Having occupied the number seven slot until the recent price war – by virtue of its growing output of table wine, both in casks and bottles, under the Esk Valley label – Glenvale subsequently retreated from its pursuit of the cheap cask market. But in early 1987 Villa Maria absorbed this old family winery.

Two brothers, Robbie Bird (34), who studied at the University of California, Davis, and Don (32), who spent time at Roseworthy College in Australia, ran the company until 1987. In 1933 their grandfather, Englishman Robert Bird, bought five hectares of land at Bay View north of Napier, planning to establish a market garden and orchard. But during the Depression the return for grapes of under twopence per pound soon encouraged Bird to enter the wine industry. In the original cellar, a tunnel scooped out of the hillside, early Glenvale wines were vinted using the humble Albany Surprise variety. His son – the second Robert – retired in 1979, opening the way to the top for the two brothers while they were still in their mid-twenties.

Glenvale's production had traditionally emphasised fortified wines; and in particular its Extra Strength Sherry had many fervent supporters. But in 1976 the release of two varietal table wines – Müller-Thurgau and Sonnengold (Chasselas) – marked the company's serious move into the table-wine market. Earlier Glenvale table wines had had a deservedly low image.

The far superior Esk Valley releases from the 1983 vintage were led by three silver-medal wines: Chenin Blanc, Chardonnay and Claret. Then came Esk Valley's marvellous 1984 Sauvignon Blanc, one of the first New Zealand Sauvignons to move past the stalky/grassy style – this is still a fine dry wine, rich in varietal character, ripe and mellow. Other premium bottled wines were reliable and competitively priced. The Bird brothers' undoing, however, was to over-expand in the highly price-sensitive cask-wine market. The two brothers have now left the winery.

Announcing the sale of Glenvale to Villa Maria in January 1987, Robbie Bird admitted that the industry price war 'knocked us for six, and we faced possible closure if we continued. We have decided to accept our rather large losses and hope that the winery will thrive under its new owner'. Villa Maria acquired the winery, its plant and stocks, plus the rights to the Esk Valley and Glenvale labels, but the Bird family retained its extensive vineyards. George Fistonich of Villa Maria declared that although the administration and marketing of the company – now renamed Esk Valley Estates – would be brought under the Villa Maria roof, the winemaking operation would retain its individuality. The strategy is to promote Esk Valley as a 'boutique' label.

Esk Valley produces about 60,000 cases per year, bottled on the premises but distributed from Villa Maria in Auckland. All table wines are marketed as Esk Valley but the Glenvale name survives on fortified wines.

The latest cluster of Esk Valley labels features a steely, wood-aged Chenin Blanc, a medium-dry Rhine Riesling, a dry Sauvignon Blanc, a backblended Müller-Thurgau and a Chardonnay matured in French oak barriques and German oak puncheons.

Building on Esk Valley's recent track record of chunky, ripe and soft Cabernets, a pair of claret-style reds has also lately emerged: a stylish, fruity, but taut Cabernet Sauvignon and a Cabernet/Merlot. A range of reserve labels is also planned.

HILLSIDES DENSELY COVERED WITH TIMBER RING THE ESK VALLEY WINERY. A 'BOUTIQUE' MARKETING STRATEGY IS PLANNED UNDER THE NEW REGIME.

Eskdale

On the Napier-Taupo road in the Esk Valley lies one of Hawke's Bay's smallest and most individual vineyards.

Kim Salonius (45) came to Auckland from his native Canada in 1964 to read for a degree in history. As a child he watched while his father made wine for home consumption from grapes brought north from California. Later, while advancing his medieval studies in Germany, his interest in winemaking was rekindled. By 1973 his first vines were in the ground.

Salonius adopts a low profile, does not advertise his wine or regularly participate in industry affairs, enjoys deep conversations with his customers and, he states, tries not to work more than four hours per day – which he says gives him the time to devour several books weekly.

Eskdale's sole source of fruit is the silty, four-hectare home vineyard between the winery and the road, planted in Cabernet Sauvignon, Chardonnay and Gewürztraminer. Pinot Noir was uprooted after only one vintage, 1981, succeeded. Salonius allows his grapes to ripen to very advanced levels before the pickers move in.

His small winery, with wooden trusses and stained-glass windows, looks every inch like a shrine to Bacchus. Salonius built it himself, using bricks and Douglas fir, placing his storage tanks underground to preserve the winery's beauty. A new storage and crushing facility has lately been erected. Everything is planned to last: 'This is home, I'll die here,' he says contentedly.

The Eskdale label usually indicates dry, wood-matured table wine of high interest. Only three wines are made. The Cabernet Sauvignon is a bold, chunky red with a ripe berryish flavour and pungent bouquet. Salonius' personal fondness for heavy red wines – he has enthused over a Rumanian Pinot Noir to me – affords an insight into his own red style.

The Chardonnays, matured in Nevers oak puncheons, one-third new each year, tend to be mouth-filling, golden and fat. The Gewürztraminer is a buxom style, pungent and spicy; about every third year a sweet, botrytised style emerges.

These wines display an individuality that can be quite absorbing.

KIM SALONIUS IS THE ONLY MEDIEVALIST AMONG NEW ZEALAND'S WINEMAKING FRATERNITY.

Lombardi

Italian traditions in winemaking are preserved at this small family-owned winery near Havelock North. In 1948 Englishman W.H. Green and his wife Tina planted a 1.2-hectare vineyard on a soldier's rehabilitation block in Te Mata Road. After Mrs Green, born in the Bay of Naples, turned to her grandparents in Italy for winemaking advice, 1959 brought the first Lombardi vintage.

Today the founders' son, Tony (36), a Massey University chemistry graduate, runs the winery. The three-hectare vineyard is planted in Müller-Thurgau, Muscats, Pinotage, Palomino and other varieties, and fruit is also purchased from Hawke's Bay growers.

Production is still centred on fortified wines; dry sherry is a strong seller. But the vineyard specialties are Italian-style liqueurs and vermouths. The vermouths range from Dry (white) to Vermouth Di Torino (medium red) and Vermouth Bianco (sweet white). The range of liqueurs – packing only a soft punch at just below twenty-three percent alcohol, the legal maximum – features Anisette (aniseed), Astrega ('Drambuie type'), Caffe Sport (coffee), Golden Drop ('Galliano type') and Triple Sec (orange).

Table wines sold at the winery include Hock, Riesling-Sylvaner, Moselle, Sauternes, Pinotage (a medium-dry rosé), Dry Red Seibel and a pair of sparklings – these are clean quaffing wines. Most of the output is sold at the gate and the Lombardi range is rarely seen beyond Hawke's Bay.

TONY GREEN – REPRODUCING IN HAWKE'S BAY THE WINE STYLES OF ITALY, HIS MOTHER'S NATIVE COUNTRY.

Mission

The Society of Mary, housed in a cluster of wooden buildings in the midst of lawns, trees and vines at the base of the Taradale hills, is New Zealand's only nineteenth-century producer of wines still under the same management. Its sizeable winery and vineyards – administered by the Greenmeadows Mission Trust Board – help fund the running of its Marist seminary, whose graduates staff parishes and educational centres throughout New Zealand and the South Pacific.

The present site is the last of several occupied by the Marist mission during its long history in Hawke's Bay. Father Lampila and two lay brothers, Florentin and Basil, after mistaking the Poverty Bay coast for their real destination, Hawke's Bay, planted vines near Gisborne in 1850. A year later they moved south and planted more vines at Pakowhai, near Napier. The story goes that in 1852, on a return visit to Poverty Bay, Father Lampila found the abandoned vineyard bearing a small crop of grapes, made a barrel of sacramental wine and shipped it to Napier. But the seamen broached the cargo, drank the wine – and the cask completed its journey full of sea water.

A Maori chief, Puhara, took the French missionaries under his protection at Pakowhai. The brothers taught and nursed the local Maori, and gardens and vineyards were laid out. After Puhara was killed, however, in an inter-tribal clash in 1857, the brothers were forced to move again, this time to Meeanee.

THE SOCIETY OF MARY IS COMMERCIALLY INVOLVED IN WINE PRODUCTION IN ORDER TO FUND THE MARIST SEMINARY.

PAUL MOONEY, THE WINEMAKER AT MISSION, MAKES A RANGE OF SOLID, ALTHOUGH RARELY INTENSE, WINES AT REALISTIC PRICES.

For several decades wine production at Meeanee was very limited, sufficient only to supply the brothers' needs for sacramental and table wines. A son of a French peasant winemaker, Brother Cyprian, arrived in 1871 to take charge of winemaking – but not until around 1895 were the first recorded sales made, mainly of red wine.

Two years later, local rivers burst their banks, flooding the Meeanee plains and inundating the Mission cellars. After deciding to shift to higher ground, the Society of Mary bought 240 hectares of the dead Henry Tiffen's land at Greenmeadows and established a four-hectare vineyard there. But not until 1910, after further disastrous floods, was the seminary itself moved to Greenmeadows; the wooden building was cut into sections and hauled there by steam engine. Fire almost destroyed the wine vaults in 1929, and thousands of gallons of wine were lost in the Napier earthquake of 1931, but of late nature appears to have made its peace with the Mission.

Until the end of the 1970s Mission wines, often mediocre and lacking depth, were hindered by a lack both of finance and of advanced winemaking equipment. To many consumers, a halo appeared to encircle bottles of Mission wine, yet medal successes were few. The improved industry-wide standards left the church authorities with a basic decision: to be left further behind, or to compete.

The result was a programme of major expansion, designed to lift both the production level and the standards of Mission table wines. $250,000 was allocated for winery equipment and vineyard improvements.

The 1979 vintage marked a turning-point in the standard of the Mission's wines. New labelling helped, but behind the more sophisticated marketing lay a leap forward in the flavour intensity. The Mission Sylvaner/Riesling-Sylvaner 1979, for instance (previously called Riesling Hock) was full-bodied and flavoursome; that year's Chasselas was a well-handled version of the variety, dry and surprisingly robust.

Credited with having guided the Mission's step up to premium varietal wines is Brother John, the winemaker from the 1960s until 1982. Brother John – who had learned the ropes of winemaking in Bordeaux – developed the Mission's bottle-fermented sparkling wine, Fontanella, which was phased out of the range a decade ago but in its day was much sought-after.

The cellars are staffed principally by lay brothers who also have other duties. Paul Mooney, a Waikato University B.Sc. graduate who trained under Brother John for three years, is the Mission's first lay winemaker. Warwick Orchiston (47) who recently joined the Mission after more than a decade at Vidal, has been appointed winery manager.

The winery itself is a utilitarian, corrugated-iron building. Its output, at around 40,000 cases, is that of a medium-sized winery by New Zealand standards.

Brother Osika, a Tongan who has spent sixteen years as a lay brother, heads the Mission's viticultural activity. In the twenty-hectare vineyard planted in silty soils at Meeanee in the late 1970s, Pinot Gris, Sauvignon Blanc, Merlot, Cabernet Sauvignon and Cabernet Franc are grown. In the twenty-hectare home block at Greenmeadows – lower cropping than at Meeanee – Müller-Thurgau, Chardonnay, Sémillon and Cabernet Sauvignon have been planted. Other grapes are drawn from growers in the Fernhill district.

A CORNER OF THE MISSION VINEYARD, NESTLED AGAINST THE BASE OF THE TARADALE HILLS. VINES HAVE FLOURISHED IN THE DISTRICT FOR OVER A CENTURY.

Following its burst of development in the late 1970s, the Mission has lately settled into a pattern of sound commercial winemaking. The Tokay d'Alsace (Pinot Gris) is uniformly full-bodied and medium-dry, extracting plenty of the distinctive peachy, earthy character of this variety. Of equal interest is the Sémillon/Sauvignon Blanc, one of the first blends produced in this country from these traditional partners in white Bordeaux. This crisp, piquant wine needs to round out for a couple of years in the bottle. Other tangy, herbaceous whites include a dry Sauvignon Blanc and a Fumé Blanc of high standard.

The Chardonnays have been enjoyable but workman-like. A new reserve Chardonnay, held longer in barrels, is designed to elevate the Mission's Chardonnay profile. There is also a White Burgundy, blended from Sémillon, Sauvignon Blanc and Pinot Gris, matured in large casks.

St Mary Riesling-Sylvaner is this vineyard's biggest selling line. Pleasantly fruity, it is a medium style, sweetened with Muscat Dr Hogg juice. It has recently been partnered by a Müller-Thurgau, vigorously flavoursome after the blending in of a touch of Sauvignon Blanc. Sweeter again is the long-popular Estella Sauternes, which also reveals the presence of Sauvignon Blanc.

The Mission red wines used to be distinctively light and pale, verging on rosés. The early Cabernet Sauvignons never approached McWilliam's standard, and the Pinot – made from old Meunier vines – was an ideal chilled luncheon wine.

Today the top reds are Cabernet/Merlot, a seventy percent/thirty percent blend matured for one year in new Nevers oak puncheons; Cabernet Sauvignon, given 'a touch of new oak'; and Reserve Claret, a Cabernet Sauvignon/Merlot blend, not wood-aged. These are light-styled, ripe and fruity reds, lacking real intensity.

Mission still enjoy a following for their fortified wines, including Marinella Sherry, Vintage Port and Altar Wine – a medium-sweet style 'vintaged in accordance with Church requirements'.

Ngatarawa

Alwyn Corban pursues an uncompromising approach to wine-making at Ngatarawa, based on dry, robust wine styles.

Ngatarawa, lying ten minutes' drive west of Hastings near Bridge Pa, is a partnership formed in 1981 between Corban and the Glazebrook family, of the 2400-hectare Washpool sheep station, who have owned the site of the present vineyard for over fifty years.

Alwyn Corban (36) a reserved and gentle personality, is the son of Alex Corban, the Wine Institute's first chairman. After capping his impressive academic record with a master's degree in oenology at the University of California, Davis, Corban spent a year at the Stanley Wine Company in South Australia, followed by four years at McWilliam's in Napier, before founding Ngatarawa with Gary Glazebrook. Glazebrook and Corban were introduced by Kim Salonius of Eskdale, a mutual friend.

The winery is based on a converted stables built of heart rimu and totara in the 1890s. While the building's soft exterior lines have been preserved – creating 'a winery that doesn't look like a winery' says Corban contentedly – the internal walls have been gutted to free up space for wine storage and a new concrete floor laid. Barely visible at the rear of the old 'stables winery', a new building has arisen to accommodate most of the winemaking equipment.

The Ngatarawa vineyards are in the 'Hastings dry belt', a recognised low-rainfall district. The three-hectare estate vineyard, on sandy loam soils overlying alluvial gravels – which dry out swiftly in summer – is where Riesling and Sauvignon Blanc are planted. A second, eight-hectare vineyard to the west is established in Chardonnay, Cabernet Sauvignon, Merlot and Cabernet Franc. Only a small proportion of the crop is purchased from other growers.

Ngatarawa's output is low: only 6000 cases annually. Undoubtedly the best known wine is the Stables Red, a Cabernet of bold and assertive flavours. All vintages thus far have displayed excellent fruit ripeness and soft tannins, making this one of the country's best reds for drinking in its youth. The style originated in 1982 – when Ngatarawa simply could not afford to mature it in wood – and proved instantly popular. The label is still 'balanced more towards fruit than wood', says Corban.

Glazebrook Cabernet/Merlot is the company flagship. A near-opaque, tautly structured red with a marvellously concentrated, spicy/leafy flavour, it is a classic claret style demanding several years' evolution in the bottle. Aged for one year in Nevers oak puncheons, it is only produced in the best years.

Corban's reserve stocks of barrel-fermented white wines can also be arresting – the Sauvignon Blanc Special Reserve offers a mouth-filling combination of Sauvignon and strong oak flavours, crying out for bottle aging. The more commercial Sauvignon Blanc is a limey, non-wooded, bone-dry style.

The Chardonnay here is robust and oaky. It is barrel-fermented in a mix of used and new Nevers oak puncheons, but overall Corban prefers using older casks for whites. Rather hard and unforthcoming in its youth, it too needs at least two years to blossom.

Having launched his Rhine Riesling as a dry, austere style, Corban has recently experimented by hanging his fruit much longer on the vines, with thrilling success. Ngatarawa Late Harvest Rhine Riesling – made in years favourable to the spread of dry *Botrytis cinerea* – is green-gold in hue, delectably sweet and nectareous, of an intensity equivalent to a German auslese or even beyond.

On a less elevated level, Stables Classic White is a solid wine, a shade off dryness, 'a blend of the noble varieties grown in the vineyard'. An Old Saddlers Sherry and Late Bottle Vintage Port, each matured in wood for several years, flesh out the range.

WITH HIS FAMILY BACKGROUND, IMPRESSIVE ACADEMIC RECORD AND SOME OUTSTANDING CABERNET/MERLOTS AND BOTRYTISED RIESLINGS ALREADY IN THE BOTTLE, ALWYN CORBAN IS A WINEMAKER WHOSE PERFORMANCE IS WORTH FOLLOWING.

C.J. Pask

CHRIS PASK – A GRAPEGROWER OWNING
EXTENSIVE VINEYARDS WHO HAS TURNED
TO WINEMAKING WITH INSTANT SUCCESS.

Pinot Noir of cherry hue, mouth-filling alcohol and the flavour of ripe strawberries first ushered this fledgling winery in Korokipo Road, Fernhill, into the limelight.

C.J. Pask winery is operated by Chris Pask (48) and his daughter Tessa. Pask, a burly former top-dressing pilot, has for sixteen years been a contract grapegrower, supplying fruit to several companies. Having each year turned out a couple of barrels of wine for his friends and relatives and, he says, being 'interested in adding value', he recently elected to move into commercial wine production under his own label.

Pask owns sixty hectares of vines, divided into three vineyards, one surrounding the winery at Fernhill and two others towards Ngatarawa. For his own label he naturally takes first pick of the fruit.

In his winery, a converted tractor shed with a mezzanine and other 'bits' added, Pask currently produces about 3000 cases per year. Apart from the robust and supple Pinot Noir – matured for six months in new Nevers barriques and puncheons – his range also features a couple of even more muscular claret-style reds.

The Cabernet Sauvignons and Cabernet/Merlot I have tasted ooze ripe fruit and rich alcohol on a notably grand scale. The taste delights of very ripe fruit are also evident in the cheaper label, Roy's Hill Reserve, a fragrant, soft blend of – in order – Merlot, Cabernet Franc and Cabernet Sauvignon.

The C.J. Pask lineup of white wines has also included a Chardonnay, a mediocre Crista Canelli made from Muscat Canelli grapes, an equally plain Roy's Hill Dry and a fresh, limey, much more successful Sauvignon Blanc.

Although still acquiring the skills of making white wine, Pask has got away to an auspicious start.

St George Estate

St George Estate is a genuinely boutique-scale operation on the corner of the Havelock North-Hastings highway and St George's Road, aiming to specialise in Cabernet/Merlot, Sauvignon Blanc and Chardonnay.

The company is a partnership founded in 1985 between winemaker Michael Bennett (49) and Martin Elliott (57), formerly proprietor of the Havelock North wineshop. Born in England, Bennett made 'vinho verde' in Portugal while trying to eke out a living as a freelance photographer before joining Villa Maria/Vidal for three years and then Te Mata between 1979 and 1984. Assured and amiable, he observes that each time he has shifted employment within the wine industry he has gone to a smaller-scale operation until eventually he 'will disappear altogether'.

On flat, silty soils in front of the winery, the three-hectare home vineyard – owned by Martin Elliott and leased to the company – is planted in Gewürztraminer, Muscat, Shiraz and Sauvignon Blanc. Premium Chardonnay, Sauvignon Blanc and Cabernet Sauvignon grapes are also sourced from Bob and Di Taylor's three-hectare vineyard at Haumoana, planted in light silts overlying river gravels.

The cosy, beautiful Cape Dutch-style winery, housing a restaurant, was built out of concrete blocks and timber by Bennett and Elliott themselves. The annual output, still very low at 2000 cases, is planned to gradually climb to a ceiling of 5000 cases.

The top wine here is undoubtedly the powerful Cabernet/Merlot. A giant of a red, it is near-opaque, full-bodied and forceful, high in extract and tannin, yet softened by the use of American rather than French oak puncheons. My other favourite wine is the barrel-fermented Chardonnay, which also displays the lifted aroma of American oak and a soft, creamy palate.

Other white wines in the St George lineup are a pungently aromatic, dryish, but very fruity July Muscat; a Müller-Thurgau; a solid Gewürztraminer; and a pair of Sauvignon Blancs, one an estate-grown wine made slightly sweet, the other, based on Haumoana fruit, dry. There is also a tart, dryish Farndon Riesling 1987, made from fruit grown at David Yates' vineyard in Farndon Road (which arrived by mistake at the St George winery 'due to a transport mix-up – which was fortunate for us if not for someone else').

Another St George specialty is the Rosé, based on an unusual blend of Sauvignon Blanc and Malbec – nearly dry, light but delivering plenty of flavour.

MARTIN ELLIOTT (LEFT) AND MICHAEL BENNETT – A SOLID LINEUP OF WINES UNDER THE ST GEORGE LABEL AND A COSY RESTAURANT IN WHICH TO ENJOY THEM.

Discussion of Te Mata invariably turns to the much-vaunted Coleraine Cabernet/Merlot and its slightly less well-known stablemate, the Awatea Cabernet/Merlot. In the past decade this historic winery, rejuvenated by John Buck and his partner, Michael Morris, has carved out an international reputation for its magnificent reds.

Bernard Chambers, a member of the wealthy landowning family that ran Te Mata Station, as a hobby in 1892 planted a hectare of vines supplied by the Mission brothers. The vines flourished, leading Chambers to convert a stable erected in 1872 into his cellar, to employ an Australian winemaker and, in 1896, to plunge into commercial wine production.

By 1909 the Chambers vineyard was the largest in the country, annually producing 54,000 litres of wine from the fourteen hectares of Meunier, Shiraz, Cabernet Sauvignon, Riesling and Verdelho vines. Commented the New Zealand *Journal of Agriculture* in May 1914: 'Mr Chambers' wines are principally hocks, claret and sweet, and are commanding a large sale'.

But from this peak, production declined and eventually during the Depression the vineyard went into receivership. A series of new owners failed to restore the vineyard's fortunes.

The revival of Te Mata's reputation began in 1974, when Michael Morris and John Buck, both established wine judges, acquired the run-down company. Morris, a Wellington accountant, is a non-working partner. Buck, the managing director, has enjoyed a high profile on his career path leading finally – and triumphantly – to the hills of Havelock North.

Buck loves the limelight – and performs brilliantly in it. 'I don't think I'm a person who has ever lacked self-confidence,' he admits. He is learned

Te Mata

JOHN BUCK – A REPUTATION FOR STYLISH REDS
AND EQUALLY STYLISH ARCHITECTURE.

('The lessons of wine are all there in the books and magazines'), short, sharp-witted and extroverted: in sum, the nearest equivalent this country has produced to that mercurial Australian wine man Len Evans.

After a two-year career in the UK wine trade, Buck returned to New Zealand in 1966. 'I drove up to Hawke's Bay, spent some time with Tom McDonald, was given a couple of Tom's Cabernets [which] were served up blind at a luncheon with a Château Haut-Brion, and I also got a thing called McWilliam's Tuki Tuki Rhine Riesling . . . I saw these wines and I thought, Ye God! There's actually some colossal potential here.' Buck was soon convinced that in Hawke's Bay, given the correct combination of site, soils and grape varieties, wines of world class could be made.

After an eight-year search for the right property, he and Morris purchased the old Te Mata winery; the cellars, built of brick and native timbers, were restored to their original condition and equipped with stainless steel tanks and new oak casks. For the new owners' first vintage, 1979 – an unusually wet one – the winemaker of that period, Michael Bennett, had to work with such limited fruit material as Chasselas, Baco 22A, Palomino and Müller-Thurgau. 'I really thought after that vintage, you know, if this is winemaking, what the hell am I doing here?' recalls Buck.

1980 brought a rapid change of fortune. 'We were fortunate to acquire the Awatea vineyard and it had a small block of old Cabernet on it. I guess we picked three or four tonnes off it and the moment we crushed those grapes we knew that our assertion as to the right variety to grow on these hills was correct.' Te Mata 1980 Cabernet Sauvignon then carried off the trophy for the best red at the 1981 National Wine Competition – a feat repeated by the 1981 vintage in 1982 – and Te Mata was on its way.

The winery markets its top wines whenever possible with a vineyard site designation. Coleraine Cabernet/Merlot, for instance, is sourced from John and Wendy Buck's own two-hectare vineyard called Coleraine, planted with a mix of varieties modelled on the Médoc: Cabernet Sauvignon seventy-five percent, Merlot twenty-two percent and Cabernet Franc three percent. The three-hectare Awatea vineyard – named after a passenger liner which plied the Tasman prior to World War Two – is an old Vidal vineyard, recently replanted by its owners, Bryan and Noela Austen-Smith.

Elston vineyard, the source of Te Mata's powerful Chardonnay, is established in tan-coloured gravels (or 'red metal') topped with sandy loams. Cape Crest, planted on a terrace overlooking Te Awanga, is another 'red metal' vineyard. For winemaker Peter Cowley (34), the answer to Te Mata's success lies here, in these vineyards sited up off the alluvial flats on well-drained, low-vigour soils sloping north. Cowley, an Auckland University B.Sc. graduate, gained a Roseworthy diploma and then worked with Larry McKenna at Delegat's before joining Te Mata.

Te Mata's red-wine production methods are 'slanted towards classical French winemaking', says Cowley. Cabernet Sauvignon, for instance, is hand-picked – ideally at 22.5 to 23.5 degrees brix – then destemmed and fermented for about one week in open stainless-steel fermenters. Every four hours throughout the warm fermentation, in which the temperatures climb to a maximum of 29–30 degrees Celsius, the cap of skins is plunged under by hand. Press wine is blended back as necessary and the wine undergoes a secondary malolactic fermentation.

The new wine is then matured for twelve to eighteen months in Seguin Moreau and Demptos Nevers oak casks, over one-half new each year. For greater ease of handling, the winery is gradually shifting from using puncheons to the smaller barriques. During its sojourn in wood, the wine is racked several times and is egg-white fined after nine months. After bottling, the recommended period of cellaring is between five and twenty years, depending upon the vintage.

These are big reds, sporting equally large reputations. Awatea Cabernet/Merlot in favourable vintages shows an extraordinarily bold colour, with a penetrating minty/leafy bouquet and long, intense palate. It might easily be mistaken for a leading Australian red from a cooler region.

Buck sees Coleraine as 'more fleshy' than the 'slightly firmer' Awatea. At, say, five years old Coleraine is miraculously scented with deep, powerful fruit and an overall tautness and complexity highly reminiscent of a fine Bordeaux. Undoubtedly Bernard Chambers would have approved of it.

The whites feature a slow-maturing, partly barrel-fermented Elston Chardonnay which, although formidable in its youth − bursting with fresh fruit, pungent oak and bold alcohol − at about four years old rounds out into a satisfying and notably 'complete' wine.

Of the pair of Sauvignon Blancs, Cape Crest and Castle Hill, the Cape Crest is steely with a powerful surge of gooseberry/lime flavours and tremendous body; Castle Hill is also full-bodied but less distinguished. There is also an oak-fermented Estate Reserve Sauvignon Blanc, in which the wood subdues the Sauvignon's varietal character, creating more of a white-burgundy style.

The Rosé also shows a breadth of flavour unusual in New Zealand rosés, finishing long and dry.

1987 brought the opening of Te Mata's new, Ian Athfield-designed headquarters. This plastered-concrete building, painted throughout in cool pastel shades, houses a boardroom and kitchen on the upper floor, with the offices, sales area and a tasting room at ground level. Below ground, in the 'library' of old wines, rest several wax-sealed, ullaged bottles of Te Mata wine dating from shortly after the turn of the century.

THE MUCH-PHOTOGRAPHED IAN ATHFIELD-DESIGNED COLERAINE, HOME OF JOHN AND WENDY BUCK AND THEIR FAMILY. THE WINERY IS ONLY A STONE'S THROW AWAY.

Vidal

KATE MARRIS, WINEMAKER AT VIDAL. SHE LIVES IN AUCKLAND, SPENDS THE VINTAGE IN HAWKE'S BAY AND COMMUTES TO HASTINGS REGULARLY THROUGHOUT THE YEAR.

Vidal is an old-established Hastings winery which, like Esk Valley at the far end of the Bay, is now an integral part of the Villa Maria conglomerate. Anthony Vidal, the founder, came to New Zealand from Spain at the age of twenty-two in 1888. After eleven years working with his uncle, Wanganui winemaker Joseph Soler, Vidal experimented with viticulture at Palmerston North before shifting to Hawke's Bay. In 1905 he bought a half-hectare property at Hastings, converted the existing stables into a cellar and planted grapevines.

The winery flourished; a new, three-hectare vineyard was established at Te Awanga in 1916 and, a few years later, another three hectares was acquired from Chambers' Te Mata vineyard. After Anthony Vidal's death, control of the company passed to his three sons: Frank, the winemaker; Cecil, who concentrated on sales; and Leslie, who supervised the vines. For decades the winery enjoyed a solid reputation. John Buck, now of Te Mata Estate, in 1969 stated in his book *Take a Little Wine,* that Vidal's Claret and Burgundy were 'the two finest, freely available dry reds on the New Zealand market'. Using Cabernet Sauvignon, Meunier and hybrid fruit, the brothers produced a Burgundy of 'style, good colour, body and balance' and a Claret 'lighter in body and more austere to taste'.

But after 1972, when Seppelt's of Australia acquired a sixty percent share of Vidal, standard lines were dropped, labels changed and the quality of the wine began to fall away. The slide continued under another owner, Ross MacLennan, from 1974 to 1976.

The steady restoration of Vidal's reputation began in 1976, after George Fistonich of Villa Maria bought the company. Vidal has retained its separate identity under management policy and the grapes, all contract grown, are drawn entirely from the Hawke's Bay region.

Following the recent departure of winemaker Warwick Orchiston – who had worked at Vidal since 1974 – for the Mission, Australian-born Kate Marris (26) has taken over the winemaking reins. A Roseworthy College graduate, Marris came to New Zealand in 1983 accompanying her returning husband-to-be, Brent Marris, who is now the winemaker at Delegat's. Kate Marris went straight to Vidal and, although based in Auckland, she works each vintage at the Hastings winery and also visits regularly throughout the year.

Vidal whites – notably Chardonnay, Gewürztraminer and Fumé Blanc – are appealing commercial styles. The Chardonnay, a tank-fermented, wood-matured wine, can be steely and closed in cooler years or ripe, buttery and soft in warmer vintages. There is also a Reserve Chardonnay, produced only in ideal years, which has recently built up a distinguished track record in competitive judgings. Marris finds Hawke's Bay Chardonnays to be consistently higher in acid and lower in pH than Gisborne Chardonnays and thus ideally structured for bottle aging.

Vidal Gewürztraminer is dryish and flavoursome, displaying more peppery/spicy varietal characteristics than used to be considered the norm for Hawke's Bay (the overall standard of the region's Gewürztraminers has improved sharply in recent vintages). The Fumé Blanc displays ripe gooseberryish fruit fleshed out with subtle oak, in a style that is less pungent and more restrained than many of its rivals.

A medium Müller-Thurgau – descended from the once-popular Mt Erin Müller-Thurgau – and a dryish, satisfying White Burgundy round out the white-wine range.

Vidal reds are gutsy and flavoursome, although both the Cabernet/Merlot and Cabernet Sauvignon have traditionally placed more emphasis on ripe, blackcurrant fruit character than on oak complexity. Top years have enough power to unfold well over several years.

Almost alone among the Hawke's Bay wineries, Vidal also has a solid reputation for Pinot Noir. Some vintages have produced wines that are tight and closed in their youth, the light fruit overpowered by assertive tannin; other vintages are fuller and rounder with a strawberryish palate, fruity and supple.

The St Aubyn's Claret is designed for early consumption. A blend of Cabernet Sauvignon's strength and the gentler Pinot Noir, it is typically fruity and full-flavoured with soft tannins.

Vidal a few years ago released a bottle-fermented sparkling wine from 1981, labelled succinctly as Vidal Brut. With its dry, sustained flavour and lifted bouquet, and the added benefits of bottle maturity, this ranked among the best New Zealand sparkling wines. Later vintages – based predominantly on Pinot Noir with one-third Chardonnay – and also a Methode Champenoise Rosé look equally promising.

WAIRARAPA

Judging from the five vintages of Martinborough wines currently in bottles, this Wairarapa hamlet is an outstanding new wine district on the rise.

One of the most silky, deep-scented Pinot Noirs ever made in this country – Martinborough Vineyards 1986 – and by far its most distinguished Pinot Gris – Dry River – have recently flowed from vineyards planted only a stone's throw apart. Five wineries have been established in Martinborough with more on the horizon.

The southern part of the North Island has inherited its own winemaking legacy. In 1883 a wealthy Wairarapa landowner, William Beetham, planted the first vines at his tiny Masterton vineyard. Romeo Bragato – who was later appointed New Zealand's first Government Viticulturist – visited Beetham during his 1895 national vineyard tour, and reported tasting a Hermitage wine of 'prime quality'. Following the prohibitionists' no-licence victory in Masterton in 1905, Beetham's vineyard was uprooted.

The first Martinborough vineyard was established by the then prominent publisher – and wine lover – Alister Taylor, on flats near the Huangarua River in 1978. The major impetus for the recent surge of interest in Martinborough winemaking, however, came from Dr Derek Milne's 1979 report, pinpointing similarities between Martinborough's climate and soils and those of premium French wine regions. Milne, a scientist with the DSIR's Soil Bureau, soon put his money where his mouth was, as a founding partner in Martinborough Vineyards.

Martinborough's winemakers share a conviction that their district is a sort of 'southern Burgundy'. According to the Martinborough Winemakers Association's promotional brochure, their study of relevant climatological and soil data indicated that 'conditions were similar to those in Burgundy'.

The figures back them up. Martinborough and Burgundy have roughly similar total rainfall figures (Burgundy 650–700mm per annum, Martinborough 750mm). The two districts also accumulate comparable heat readings (1150 degree days Celsius) during the vines' growing season. Thus, the Martinborough grapegrowers have planted predominantly Burgundy and Alsace grape varieties such as Chardonnay, Pinot Noir, Gewürztraminer, Riesling, Sauvignon Blanc and Pinot Gris.

Despite its location in the North Island, Martinborough's viticultural climate in fact resembles Marlborough's more closely than Hawke's Bay's. Martinborough's spring bud burst, for example, is typically two weeks behind Hawke's Bay's.

In March and April, the vital months leading into the harvest, Martinborough's average daily temperature of 14.7 degrees Celsius is more

BLUE SKIES AND DRY GRASS ON THE HILLS
ARE CHARACTERISTIC OF MARTINBOROUGH
IN AUTUMN. TOM DRAPER (LEFT) AND HIS
ASSISTANT WINEMAKER FOR THE 1988 VINTAGE,
HEIKO TUTT, IN THE TE KAIRANGA VINEYARD.

akin to Marlborough's 14.3 degrees than Hawke's Bay's 15.8 degrees Celsius. The autumn rainfall figures reveal the same story: both Martinborough and Marlborough are, on average, markedly drier than Hawke's Bay.

Droughts are a definite threat in summer, leading two of the wineries to install fixed irrigation systems in their vineyards. This relative dryness, however, also encourages the winemakers to hang their grapes late on the vines to achieve full fruit ripeness, without facing any undue risk of disease.

The chief weather drawback here is the wind. Martinborough is not only pummelled by strong southerlies from Cook Strait, but is also exposed to regular northwesterly gales; shelter belts are thus a necessity.

Soils are excellent. Although areas of heavy clay not ideally suited to vines exist, there are also highly sought-after pockets of gravelly silt loams overlying free-draining gravels. An area of high-quality, free-draining soils has already been delineated by the Winemakers Association, laying an early foundation for an appellation system which is designed to protect and promote Martinborough's vinous reputation.

Since 1986 the wines produced from grapes grown within the confines of this premium area, and also processed there, have been eligible to carry a handsome black and gold seal, guaranteeing their regional authenticity.

Few other vineyards are found in the southern part of the North Island. Pierre is a tiny winery at Waikanae, sixty kilometres north of Wellington on the west coast. Owner Peter Heginbotham, a Wellington optometrist, planted his three-hectare vineyard of Pinot Noir, Cabernet Sauvignon, Merlot, Müller-Thurgau, Chenin Blanc and Chardonnay in gravelly river silts in 1960. His debut commercial vintage was 1966. The wines I have tasted have been light and undistinguished.

Further north the Holly Lodge winery and tourist centre at Wanganui has for many years fashioned a range of basic table and fortified wines from bought-in fruit and grapes grown in the estate vineyard in Papaiti Road, on the banks of the Wanganui River.

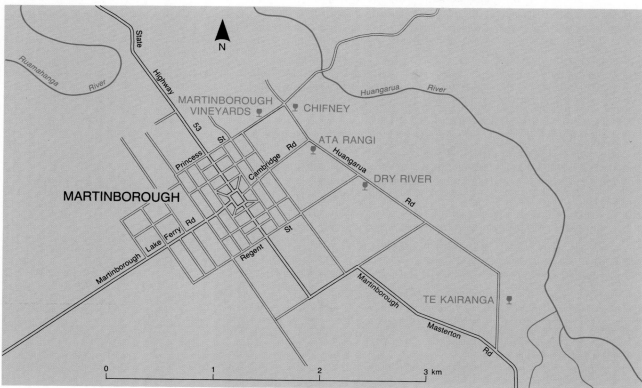

Clive Paton (39) has set up his Ata Rangi ('new beginning') winery to specialise in red wines.

After taking a diploma in dairying from Massey University, Paton went sharemilking before buying his Puruatanga Road property in Martinborough in 1980. He worked the 1981 vintage with Malcolm Abel and the 1982 vintage at Delegat's before erecting his own 600 square feet timber winery in 1987. Phyllis Pattie, formerly manager of Montana's Marlborough winery, then moved north to join him.

Paton's four-hectare vineyard of Cabernet Sauvignon, Merlot, Cabernet Franc, Pinot Noir, Gewürztraminer and Chardonnay is planted in free-draining gravelly soils beneath a shallow layer of top soil. Wind is a major problem, he says, and the vines also need to be irrigated during their early years.

Paton, who sees Pinot Noir as his 'biggest challenge', first sprang to prominence when his 1986 Pinot Noir collected a gold medal. Ata Rangi Pinot Noir is cherry-red to the eye, with a pleasant raspberryish fruit character and mouth-filling high alcohol.

Another winery specialty is Célèbre, a Cabernet Sauvignon/Shiraz/Merlot blend. With its brilliant, deep red hue, intensely smoky and slightly herbaceous bouquet, and bold, peppery flavour, this is a distinctive, rather Rhône-like red.

Although devoting most of his energy to reds, Paton is also eager to make a fat, Meursault-style Chardonnay, and barrel-fermented his first wine in 1988.

Ata Rangi's current annual production of only 1000 cases is planned to eventually rise to 3000 cases. Paton sells his wine by mail order or at the vineyard shop in early summer. 'The rest of the year, you see people turning into the gate and turning out again,' he says.

Ata Rangi

CLIVE PATON OF ATA RANGI – HIGH ALCOHOL REDS OF DISTINCTIVE BOLDNESS AND DEPTH.

Chifney

STAN CHIFNEY, WHO STARTED WINEMAKING AS A 'RETIREMENT HOBBY' AND ENDED UP NOT ONLY ASSISTING OTHER WINEMAKERS IN THE DISTRICT BUT ALSO COLLECTING A GOLD MEDAL FOR HIS OWN 1986 CHIFNEY CABERNET SAUVIGNON.

Stan Chifney, the snowy-bearded, sixty-eight-year-old owner of Chifney Wines in Huangarua Road, is one of the Martinborough 'originals' who planted his first vines in the winter of 1980. Bach and Mahler fill the air in his tiny winery, which produces only about 5000 bottles each year.

London-born Chifney arrived in this country sixteen years ago, after a career spent in vaccine manufacture in the Middle East and Nigeria. He and his wife Rosemary, having made their own fruit wines, thought winemaking would be an ideal retirement hobby.

In 1983 they erected their concrete-based winery with its partly subterranean cellar. Their two-hectare vineyard of Cabernet Sauvignon, Chardonnay, Chenin Blanc and Gewürztraminer, planted in loamy surface soils overlying stony subsoils, yielded its first commercial crop in 1984.

Chifney harbours reservations about the long-term viability of Chenin Blanc and Gewürztraminer in his vineyard; the Chenin Blanc ripens inadequately – and is thus made sweet to balance its tense acidity – and the Gewürztraminer, he says, has only made 'ordinary' wine.

About his ripe, gutsy Cabernets, however, Chifney has few doubts: 'This variety may prove to be our best wine.' The Easter Show gold medal awarded in 1988 to Chifney 1986 Cabernet Sauvignon – a deep garnet, berryish and firm-structured wine – was a real shot in the arm for the winery's reputation.

Dry River

Dry River, a Martinborough winery emerging with a high reputation, is owned by research chemist Neil McCallum – a genial forty-five-year-old who holds an Oxford doctorate in chemistry – and his wife Dawn. McCallum points out the double meaning of the name Dry River: not only is this a local geographic feature, but most of the wine styles under this label will also be dry.

The first vines were planted in 1979 on flat terrain, in river gravels underlying a few centimetres of light top soil. The vineyard, now covering three and one-half hectares, is close-planted in Gewürztraminer, Pinot Gris, Sauvignon Blanc, Chardonnay and Pinot Noir vines, trained on the Scott-

Henry system and not irrigated. The dry local climate and low soil fertility stress the vines, producing, says McCallum, small crops of intensely flavoured berries.

His corrugated-iron winery in Puruatanga Road is a traditional Wairarapa barn and McCallum describes his approach to winemaking as 'low-tech, involving minimum processing and placing an emphasis on cellaring qualities rather than short-term attractiveness for early drinking'. He avoids cold stabilising, gives his wines only one pre-bottling filtration, dislikes fining – it imparts softness but strips out desirable qualities, he says – and avoids giving his Gewürztraminer and Riesling skin contact, on the grounds that this causes premature aging.

McCallum is chiefly interested in producing white wines. His annual output is very low at 1000 cases, climbing eventually to 1500 cases.

Dry River wines are stylish, with plenty of extract, and are usually – although not always – bone dry. The Gewürztraminer has precise peppery/spicy varietal characteristics, without the pungent seasoning of the more ebullient Gisborne-grown examples of this variety. This is a 'fine-grained' (to borrow McCallum's adjective) dry wine of excellent weight and unusual flavour depth.

Dry River Pinot Gris is a revelation. McCallum tells the story of how his Pinot Gris vines, which he sourced from Mission Vineyards, are probably an old Alsace clone called Tokay à petit grain (small berry Pinot Gris) known for its low yields: only 4.5 tonnes per hectare in 1987. His wines are green-gold and savoury with a concentrated peachy/earthy varietal flavour and pungent bouquet. Here is a much-needed Chardonnay alternative.

The Dry River range also features a slowly evolving, estate-grown Fumé Blanc and a trio of wines based on Marlborough fruit: a Pinot Noir, a strapping, barrique-fermented Chardonnay, and a botrytised Riesling of delicate and fragile beauty.

NEIL McCALLUM AND HIS DAUGHTER – McCALLUM IS THE WINEMAKER WHO PROVED WHAT RICH FLAVOURS CAN BE COAXED FROM PINOT GRIS IN THE COOL, DRY CLIMATE OF MARTINBOROUGH.

Martinborough Vineyards

The highest-profile winery in the Wairarapa is unquestionably Martinborough Vineyards. Its prominence rests partly on its outstanding 1987 feat of scoring three gold medals – for its 1986 Pinot Noir, Fumé Blanc and Chardonnay – partly on its more commercial production scale (2000 cases, eventually rising to 5000); and partly on its release of part of this output through the merchant and retail trade, thereby making its wines more accessible to casual buyers.

This venture is a partnership involving scientist Derek Milne, his agriculturalist brother Duncan and his wife Claire Campbell, and chemist Russell Schultz and his wife Sue. The first vines were planted in 1980, in soils ranging from silt to stony areas over gravelly well-drained subsoils. Today in the ten-hectare vineyard there are three main blocks of Chardonnay, Sauvignon Blanc and Gewürztraminer, plus smaller plots of Pinot Noir and Riesling. Fruit is also bought in.

The first, 1984, vintage based on a mere two tonnes of grapes, yielded two outstanding wines: both the Pinot Noir – only 150 bottles were made – and Sauvignon Blanc unleashed enormous body and flavour length. The next challenge was to reproduce these standards in commercially available wines.

Twenty-seven tonnes were crushed in 1985, with the new coolstore winery's roof being erected only days before the harvest. In early 1986 Larry McKenna moved south from Delegat's to become the first qualified winemaker in the district. McKenna (37) is a talented, stocky Australian who, after gaining a Roseworthy diploma in agriculture, went to Delegat's in 1980 and headed Delegat's winemaking team from 1983 to 1986, before

LARRY McKENNA. HIS 1986 PINOT NOIR UNDER THE MARTINBOROUGH VINEYARDS LABEL HAS FAIR CLAIM TO THE TITLE OF THE BEST PINOT NOIR YET SEEN IN THE COUNTRY.

joining Martinborough Vineyards with immediate success.

The jewel in the Martinborough Vineyards range so far is its stunning 1986 Pinot Noir. This wine was hot-fermented – at temperatures peaking at over thirty degrees Celsius – with some whole berries and stalks being included in the ferment, and the skins being plunged by hand. Then it was matured in French oak barriques for twelve months.

Its appeal is immediate. It has a lovely fragrance and soft, generous, unmistakably Pinot flavour spread. Its achievement is that it has transcended the light berryish character of most New Zealand Pinot Noirs to reach the richer, earthy, mushroom-like standard of classic Pinot Noir.

Both the Chardonnay and Fumé Blanc are outstanding. With his barrel-fermented Chardonnay, McKenna is looking for a full, complex Meursault style; with his tank-fermented, but wood-aged, Fumé Blanc he wants the accent placed on gooseberry fruit ripeness. They are both robust and deep flavoured.

Martinborough Vineyards Gewürztraminer is also long and ripe on the palate, dry and firm: very Alsace in style. The Riesling, too, displays a delicious concentration of pure, apple and pineapple fruit flavours.

Few vineyards in the country can boast of a lineup of wines as intriguing and uniformly excellent as these.

Te Kairanga

TOM DRAPER, AMIDST PINOT NOIR VINES IN THE TE KAIRANGA VINEYARD, WITH JOHN MARTIN'S COTTAGE, BUILT IN THE 1860S, AT LEFT REAR.

Te Kairanga ('The place where the soil is rich and the food plentiful') winery in Martins Road is the latest arrival on the mushrooming Martinborough wine scene.

Tom Draper – a former building contractor and co-founder of one of Wellington's winetasting groups, the Magnum Society – and his wife Robin in 1983 bought Alister Taylor's vineyard, then in a run-down condition. After they brought in partners, the vineyards spread out over twenty-two hectares of free-draining stony terraces close to the Huangarua River. Cabernet Sauvignon and Merlot vines fill one-half of the vineyards, together with smaller plantings of Chardonnay, Gewürztraminer, Pinot Noir and Sauvignon Blanc. An irrigation system has been installed: 'I know how dry it can get here,' says Draper.

Draper quietly released his first wine, Te Kairanga Chardonnay 1986, in 1987. Stan Chifney made the 1986–1988 vintages of Te Kairanga wines, but in 1987 a concrete-walled, iron-roofed winery was erected and a full-time winemaker will be employed from 1989. Once production reaches around 5000 cases by 1990 – and it will eventually climb higher – Te Kairanga should emerge as one of the district's most widely seen labels.

A 120-year-old, pit-sawn timber cottage was recently removed from Martinborough township to the vineyard site. Originally built by the founder of Martinborough, John Martin, for a farm worker and his family, it now enjoys a new lease of life as Te Kairanga's sales and tasting facility.

NELSON

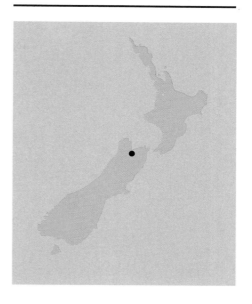

Whether Neudorf's Tim Finn or Hermann Seifried makes the finest Nelson wine is a question no doubt much discussed in that city's wine circles. No matter. What really counts is that both men are currently fashioning white and red wines as brimful of appeal as the achingly beautiful Upper Moutere hills they inhabit.

As a group, Nelson's wineries do not enjoy the high profile of those in the four principal growing regions: Gisborne, Hawke's Bay, Marlborough and West Auckland. When vinous talk turns to new and exciting areas, Canterbury and Martinborough invariably come up. The Waikato is often overlooked and so too is Nelson.

The reasons are not hard to find. Early German winemakers who landed at Nelson in 1843 and 1844 looked askance at the steep, bush-clothed hills and departed for South Australia. Other problems have included a shortage of large holdings suitable for viticulture and the region's distance from principal transport routes.

The undoubted climatic advantages for viticulture – warm summers and promisingly high sunshine hours – are reduced by the strong risk of damaging autumn rains as harvest approaches. In this respect Nelson parallels most North Island wine districts more closely than other South Island regions. Nelson winemakers thus sometimes struggle to match the sugar levels achieved over the hills in the relatively dry Marlborough climate.

Overshadowed by fruit, tobacco and hop growing, viticulture has always had only a modest foothold in Nelson province. Only about thirty hectares are under vines, less than one percent of the national vineyard area; the region is equally recognised for its cider and fruit wines.

Austrian-born Seifried, who established his vineyard in the hills at Upper Moutere in 1974, has so far produced the most wines. But others preceded him. In the 1890s, F.H.M. Ellis and Sons were 'substantial' winemakers at Motupipi, near Takaka, according to historian Dick Scott. Established in 1868, making wine from cherries and wild blackberries as well as grapes,

FROM THE LOVELY CLAY SLOPES OF THE UPPER MOUTERE FLOW CRISP CHARDONNAYS, RIESLINGS AND SAUVIGNON BLANCS, AND SUPPLE, LIGHT REDS.

the Ellis winery stayed in production for over seventy years, until it was converted into a woolshed in 1939.

Later, Viggo du Fresne, of French Huguenot descent, from 1967 to 1976 made dry red wine at a tiny, half-hectare vineyard planted in deep gravel on the coast at Ruby Bay. The vineyard, dating back to 1918, was originally established with Black Hamburgh table grapes; du Fresne took over in 1948 and waged a long, unsuccessful struggle to establish classical vines. After his Chardonnay, Sémillon and Meunier vines all failed – probably due to viruses – he produced dark and gutsy reds from the hybrid Seibel 5437 and 5455 varieties.

Victory Grape Wines is a pocket-size vineyard on the main road south at Stoke, near Nelson city. Irish-born Rod Neill, who named his winery in remembrance of Lord Nelson's ship, made his first trial plantings over two decades ago and began hobbyist winemaking in 1972. His loam clay soils are planted in Chasselas, Müller-Thurgau, Seibel 5455 and 'Gamay Beaujolais' vines.

Victory rose fleetingly to prominence at the 1980 National Wine Competition by scoring a silver medal for its 1978 Gamay Beaujolais – a light, pale and fruity red. Another silver at the 1987 Air New Zealand Wine Awards for its Seibel red proves ongoing success but, with production amounting to only a few hundred cases per year, Victory wines are rarely seen beyond Nelson.

In the past decade, however, the efforts of a small knot of enthusiasts – most prominently Hermann Seifried and Tim Finn – have put Nelson firmly on the New Zealand wine map. Tourists responding with ever-increasing enthusiasm to promotion of the Nelson wine trail are able to explore wines varying in quality from plain to world class in the most stunning vineyard settings in the country.

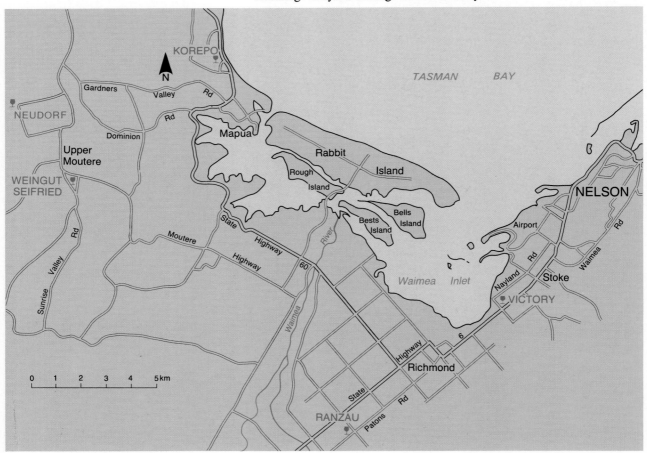

Korepo

T he winemaking tradition at Ruby Bay remains alive – in the same year that pioneering Viggo du Fresne completed his last vintage, Craig Gass planted the first vines at Korepo Wines. Korepo, says Gass, is Maori for 'no night', a reference to how the full moon on the sea illuminates Ruby Bay.

Nelson-born Gass is a highly extroverted forty-year-old. He gained a Massey University degree in food technology and then worked the 1972 and 1973 vintages at Villa Maria before establishing his own vineyard in 1976 on a north-facing, clay and gravel slope overlooking Ruby Bay. Today the four-hectare vineyard is planted in a diverse collection of grapes: Sémillon, Chardonnay, Sauvignon Blanc, Riesling, Gewürztraminer, Pinot Noir, Cabernet Sauvignon and Meunier.

Korepo only produces about 2000 cases of wine per year. Until recently, Gass and his schoolteacher wife Jane ran the vineyard and winery entirely by themselves. Then in 1987 the Gasses brought over a German winemaker, Franz Herbster from Baden, to work the vintage. Excited by Herbster's impact, they plan to regularly employ overseas winemakers in order to keep abreast of technological advances.

The Korepo range includes a dry Sauvignon Blanc, a German oak-aged Chardonnay, a Pinot Noir made from late-harvested, slightly raisined grapes, and a Gamay Beaujolais (once served to Queen Elizabeth at Nelson). I have tasted a solid Gewürztraminer and also 'Olly's Folly', a locally popular, pink sparkling, blended from Pinot Noir, Meunier and Chardonnay, showing a persistent bead and robust dry flavour. The gold medal awarded at the 1988 Easter Show to Korepo's botrytised Trockenbeerenauslese 1987 will give the winery's profile a valuable shot in the arm.

On peak summer days over 200 visitors pour into the Korepo vineyard restaurant, devouring rump steaks, lamb kebabs with satay sauce and king salmon steaks (all barbecued), or cold smoked salmon.

KOREPO'S VINEYARD SITE ON THE COAST AT RUBY BAY IS ONE OF THE MOST STUNNING IN THE COUNTRY. THE WINES, HOWEVER, ARE RARELY SEEN OUTSIDE NELSON.

Neudorf

IN THEIR IDYLLIC BACK-COUNTRY SETTING, TIM AND JUDY FINN MAKE CRISP, FLAVOURSOME SAUVIGNON BLANCS AND CHARDONNAYS, PLUS FRAGRANT, FRESH REDS.

Tim and Judy Finn of Neudorf Vineyards have a sophisticated approach to their livelihood – and a sophisticated lifestyle – that clearly reflects their academic, urban backgrounds. Neudorf, which derives its name from the surrounding district settled by Germans last century, lies not far from Weingut Seifried just off the Nelson-Motueka inland highway.

Tim Finn (42) was born in India and brought up in Wellington; he is an M.Sc. graduate and a former dairying advisory officer with the Ministry of Agriculture and Fisheries. His wife Judy, a former rural reporter for radio, is deeply involved in bottling, labelling, administration and sales.

For their first vintage in 1981, the Finns used an eighty-year-old stables on the property as a temporary winery. For 1982, Tim Finn built a proper macrocarpa winery, pitching its roof high to accommodate his fermentation and storage tanks inside.

The five-hectare vineyard is planted on clay soils, threaded with layers of gravel. Having experimented with numerous varieties, the Finns are now concentrating on Chardonnay, Sauvignon Blanc (both of which they have judged show a special affinity with the area) and Cabernet Sauvignon, plus small pockets of Sémillon and 'Gamay Beaujolais'.

Neudorf is famous for its Young Nick's Red, a floral and fragrant luncheon-style red made from 'Gamay Beaujolais' grapes. The success of 'Gamay Beaujolais' in Nelson (this is a misnomer – all 'Gamay Beaujolais' vines in New Zealand are actually a clone of Pinot Noir) encourages Tim Finn to attempt a 'serious' Pinot Noir style. He also hopes to produce a top Cabernet Sauvignon and is working in the vineyard to reduce its characteristic slightly green herbaceousness. In the years the Cabernet Sauvignon is considered not up to standard for varietal labelling, it is blended with Pinot Noir into a charming, plummy Blackbird Valley Claret.

Tim Finn feels strongly that Nelson is thus far underrated as a wine region, partly because of the lack of a large pool of trained, skilled winemakers. His wines back his enthusiasm up. Neudorf 1986 Chardonnay is savoury and penetrating, crisply acid, with a slight yeastiness reflecting its part fermentation in small French Nevers oak casks. This looks set for several years' graceful evolution in the bottle. The equally impressive 1986 Fumé Blanc (eighty-two percent Sauvignon Blanc and eighteen percent Sémillon) is a delightful harmony of the softer, gooseberryish Sauvignon Blanc and the crisp, grassy undercurrent of Sémillon.

In company with an equally promising 1987 Chardonnay, a biting 1986 Sémillon and a plum-coloured, light but attractively ripe 1987 Cabernet Sauvignon, Neudorf now has a lineup of labels that any winery would be proud of.

Ranzau

Ranzau is a rare label. Trevor Lewis, an amiable, forty-eight-year-old medical technologist, runs his small winery in spare hours after work and at weekends. On silty, stony soils at Hope, south of Richmond, his two-hectare vineyard planted in 1980 includes Riesling, Müller-Thurgau, Gewürztraminer, 'Gamay Beaujolais' and Cabernet Sauvignon.

This vineyard is a battleground, scene of an annual war between the beleaguered Lewis and the feathered vandals – blackbirds and thrushes – which usually plunder half his crop. Wire netting may prove to be the only safeguard.

In a tiny, concrete-block winery, Lewis each year since 1983 has produced about 300–400 cases of wine. His Gamay Beaujolais, perhaps not as fresh and fragrant as the best, nevertheless has respectable body and an overall red wine structure that eludes some of the more fancied labels, which too often veer towards rosé styles. I also enjoyed a gently spicy Gewürztraminer, which reflected advanced fruit ripeness in its mouth-filling alcohol and low acidity. Resting in a solitary Limousin oak puncheon was the promising 1987 Cabernet Sauvignon.

Lewis confesses that he loves tending his vines and wines but dons his marketing hat more reluctantly. Ranzau wines are sold at the vineyard during summer and also by mail order. Prices are as good as you could ask for.

TREVOR LEWIS – PRODUCING UNDER THE RANZAU LABEL A RIVULET OF SOUND NELSON WINES AT NOTABLY MODEST PRICES.

Weingut Seifried

Weingut Seifried, by far the largest Nelson winery, lies in undulating country near the village of Upper Moutere, several kilometres inland from Korepo. The Seifried label, proudly adorned with the Austrian eagle, early won respect when, from the first vintage, the Sylvaner 1976 won a silver medal.

Hermann Seifried (41) graduated in wine technology in Germany, and made wine in Europe and South Africa before arriving in New Zealand in 1971, as winemaker for the ill-fated venture by the Apple and Pear Board into apple-wine production. In spring 1974 Seifried planted his own vineyard in the clay soils of the Upper Moutere. A year later his wife Agnes, a Southlander, resigned her teaching job to join him in the winery. Today, she handles administration while Hermann – who is renowned in the wine industry for his voracious appetite for work – oversees production.

STARTING FROM SCRATCH FOURTEEN YEARS AGO, HERMANN AND AGNES SEIFRIED HAVE SINCE BUILT WEINGUT SEIFRIED INTO ONE OF THE LARGEST WINERIES IN THE SOUTH ISLAND.

The Seifrieds own three vineyards: the thirteen-hectare Sunrise Valley vineyard surrounding their ever-expanding winery; a twelve-hectare block in the Redwood Valley; and a newer vineyard planted at Rabbit Island. Output is higher than most wine drinkers realise at around 20,000 cases per year.

Riesling and Gewürztraminer are the two most featured varieties in the Weingut Seifried range. In some years, up to four different Rhine Riesling styles are produced: a Reserve Dry (two to three grams per litre of residual sugar); a Rhine Riesling (twelve grams per litre); a Late Harvest (freeze-concentrated bunches at thirty grams per litre); and a Beerenauslese (freeze-concentrated berries at 50–60 grams per litre). The Reserve Dry Rhine Riesling is a tangy, slightly austere wine with a pronounced flavour of tropical (pineapple) and citric (lemon) fruits. The Beerenauslese is clearly more elegant, much sweeter and again displays penetrating Riesling varietal character.

Four styles of Gewürztraminer, a Sauvignon Blanc, a Pinot Noir, a Gamay Beaujolais, a lightly sweet red, Refosca, aimed at non-red drinkers, and some excellent, currently much underrated Chardonnays are all part (and only part) of the broad Weingut Seifried range. The four silver medals and ten bronzes achieved at the 1987 Air New Zealand Wine Awards tell their own story regarding wine quality.

MARLBOROUGH

The emergence of Marlborough as the country's third most heavily planted wine region rates among the most crucial developments of the last fifteen years. From its endless rows of vines marching across the pebbly, pancake-flat Wairau Plains have flowed the deep-flavoured, scented white wines which – more than any rival region's – have awakened the world to the beauty of New Zealand wines.

Marlborough, the northeastern edge of the South Island, contains the inland Kaikoura Ranges, which reach an elevation approaching 3000 metres. The Wairau River, draining the ranges of silt and gravel, descends from the back country to the Wairau Plains; it is on the plains, formed by massive alluvial deposits from the river, that Montana, Corbans and others have planted their vines.

Sheep inhabited the Wairau Plains as early as the 1840s. Later, small and medium-scale mixed farming established a stronghold and recent decades have witnessed developing interest in peas, grass seed, lucerne, garlic and cherries. Not until 1973, however, did viticulture stake a claim.

Marlborough is one of the few South Island regions that is sufficiently warm for viticulture on a commercial scale. The heat summation figure, 1150–1250 degree days Celsius, is higher than at Geisenheim on the Rhine, in Germany, which has 1050–1250 degree days Celsius. Blenheim frequently records the highest total sunshine hours in the country, and this plentiful, although not intense sunshine affords the grapes a long, slow period of ripening. According to Montana, Marlborough's heat and sunshine are usually sufficient for 'good sugar levels to be attained in white grapes and adequate to good levels in red grapes'.

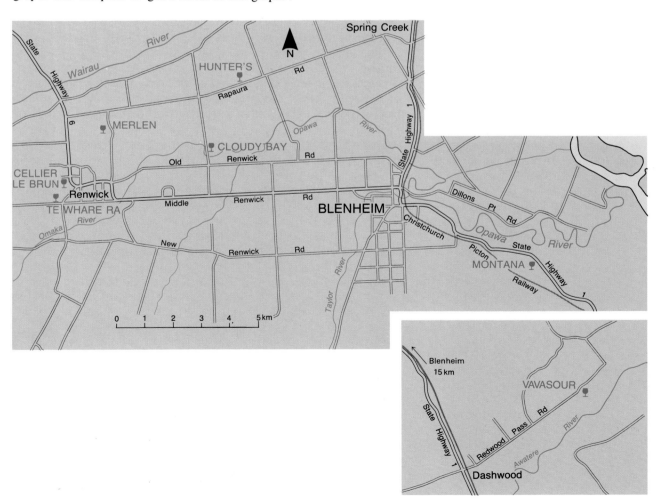

MERLEN, ONE OF THE LATEST ARRIVALS ON THE BURGEONING MARLBOROUGH WINE SCENE, AFFORDS A VEHICLE FOR THE TALENTS OF GERMAN-TRAINED ALMUTH LORENZ, WHO FASHIONED THE EARLY VINTAGES OF HUNTER'S WINES.

MONTANA'S PRESENCE IN MARLBOROUGH WAS ON A MAJOR COMMERCIAL FOOTING RIGHT FROM THE START. THE SHEER VOLUME OF WINE THAT RESULTED HAS HELPED MAKE MARLBOROUGH BY FAR THE MOST FAMOUS NEW ZEALAND WINE REGION OVERSEAS.

The risk posed by heavy autumn rains is lower than across the hills in Nelson. March is usually the driest month of the year; April rainfall, averaging sixty-one millimetres, compares favourably with the average seventy-two millimetres in Bordeaux during the harvest month.

Drought, caused by the warm, dry northwesterly winds that sweep across the plains, can pose problems, dehydrating the vines and severely reducing crop sizes. Most vineyards have installed a trickle-irrigation system, feeding water to the vines and greatly enhancing grape yields. Irrigation is most important during the vines' early years, before they have had the opportunity to develop an extensive root system. Late frosts also pose a risk − most are insufficiently intense to cause real damage but October, when three ground frosts strike on average, is a danger period; should temperatures drop below around minus 0.6 degrees Celsius, the vine shoots and flowers can die.

Owing to the relatively dry summers and low humidity in Marlborough, during the ripening season the vines are sprayed less frequently than in northern regions. Such dry weather diseases as powdery mildew pose more of a threat than botrytis and downy mildew, associated with wet climates. During the harvest month of April the average temperature is quite low, which by slowing the spread of disease allows the grapes to be left late on the vines to ripen fully.

Not all the various soil types found on the plains adapt well to viticulture. The preferred sites are moderately fertile, with friable top-soils overlying deep layers of free-draining shingle. These shallow, stony soils promote a moderately vigorous growth of the vine.

One problem facing viticulturists here is that soil types often vary enormously even within individual vineyards. According to Montana, 'it is common to find vigorous vines with a dense canopy and heavy crop in the same row as can be found stressed weak vines with little or no canopy. With such variability, harvest decisions become a compromise'. Vines planted in Marlborough's more fertile areas thus share the problem of too-dense foliage canopies found further north. Improved canopy control promises to bring a further upgrading of the quality of the region's fruit.

IN THE PREVIOUSLY UNPLANTED AWATERE
VALLEY, PETER VAVASOUR (RIGHT) AND
RICHARD BOWLING ARE CONFIDENT THEY CAN
PRODUCE CLARET-STYLE REDS OF A STANDARD
THAT WILL RIVAL THOSE OF THE NORTH
ISLAND.

In terms of area planted in grapevines, in 1986 Marlborough at 934 hectares was the country's third most important region, trailing Gisborne and Hawke's Bay. Between 1975 and 1986, Marlborough's share of the national area in vines rose steeply from seven to nearly twenty-four percent. Müller-Thurgau has proliferated, accounting for over one-third of all vines in the 1986 survey, but numerous other varieties are well established, notably Chardonnay, Riesling, Cabernet Sauvignon and Sauvignon Blanc, plus lesser amounts of Pinot Noir, Gewürztraminer, Pinotage, Chenin Blanc and Sémillon.

From the start, Montana has established a commanding presence and its pioneering move into Marlborough and Marlborough regional wines are discussed under the Montana entry on pages 164–68. Still the sole major company owning a winery in the region, its huge complex at Riverlands celebrated its tenth vintage in April 1987.

Penfolds and Corbans were much later to establish vineyards here. Penfolds' first contract vineyards were planted in the winter of 1979 and subsequently the company arranged contracts amounting to about 400 hectares. Its plans for a Blenheim winery, to be operational by 1983, were ultimately shelved and, until Montana purchased Penfolds, Penfolds' Marlborough grapes were trucked to the North Island.

Corbans commenced its vineyard development in the region in 1980 and – unlike Penfolds – planted its own company vineyards, notably Stoneleigh.

Almuth Lorenz, a former Geisenheim Institute student who made the early vintages of Hunter's wines – and later marketed a few wines under her own Lorenz label – with the backing of a group of investors has recently founded Merlen Wines, west of Hunter's in Rapaura Road. Lorenz says the winery's name is 'derived from the ancient name for Marlborough in England. The area was originally called Merlborough from the legend that Merlin the magician practised his arts there'. A superb (one is tempted to say spellbinding) 1987 Chardonnay launched the new label, to be joined by a Riesling, Sauvignon Blanc, Müller-Thurgau and Gewürztraminer.

Vavasour is a new company founded to make red wines. It will do so in the as yet untried Awatere Valley (pronounced 'Awatree' by the locals), situated east and over the hills from the more sweeping Wairau Valley, where all Marlborough's viticulture has hitherto been concentrated.

Vavasour is a name worth noting for three reasons: its pioneering of winemaking in the Awatere Valley; its unprecedented commitment to producing premium reds in Marlborough; and finally its glorious site on terraces bordering the Awatere River.

Peter Vavasour (37) is a slightly built, entrepreneurial Awatere Valley farmer who owns 'The Favourite', part of the Ugbrooke estate purchased by the Vavasour family in the 1890s. Vineyard manager Richard Bowling is a thirty-three-year-old viticultural expert, who served a seven-year stint with Corbans at Taupaki, and as second-in-charge of their Marlborough vineyards, before branching out as an independent viticultural consultant.

Bowling argues that the reds so far produced in Marlborough are not remotely indicative of the region's potential. In Peter Vavasour, he found a natural partner, one equally convinced of Marlborough's future in red wines, but commanding the financial resources and skills to do something about it.

Cabernet Sauvignon, Cabernet Franc, Merlot and Pinot Noir are the red grapes selected, with all except the Pinot Noir to be finally blended into a single red wine. Each variety is trellised and pruned according to its individual needs; Pinot Noir, for instance, has been planted on devigorating soils and trellised on single stakes. The grapes are all hand-picked. For cash-flow reasons, several hectares of white varieties, Sauvignon Blanc, Chardonnay and Sémillon, have also been established. The winery building costing $750,000 was erected in 1988.

The Marlborough wine trail now features a septet of wineries – Cellier Le Brun, Cloudy Bay, Hunter's, Merlen, Montana, Te Whare Ra and Vavasour – who in mid-summer join forces with the region's salmon, eel, mussel, honey, cheese, cherry, garlic and other producers to stage the much-acclaimed Marlborough Wine and Food Festival.

Cellier Le Brun

Daniel Le Brun (43) is a Champenois, the scion of a family of French Champagne makers stretching back over twelve generations to 1648. In search of new horizons, Le Brun came to New Zealand and at Renwick, near Blenheim, he discovered the combination of soil and climate he wanted. His ambition: to fashion a bottle-fermented sparkling wine in the antipodes able to challenge the quality of Champagne itself.

Le Brun speaks with a thick French accent. He was born at Monthelon, only a few kilometres south of Épernay and recalls 'the only thing for me to do was to carry on the family tradition'. However, after graduating from the École de Viticulture et Oenologie at Avize, he grew more and more frustrated by the very tight restrictions placed on the size of individual landholdings in Champagne.

After visiting New Zealand in 1975, he emigrated here the same year, and three years later met his future wife, Adele, in Rotorua. By 1980 they had purchased land just outside Renwick and had begun establishing their vineyard.

Labelled 'the mad Frenchman' by the locals after they got wind of his unorthodox winery plans, Le Brun set out to duplicate the cool subterranean storage conditions of Champagne by burrowing twelve metres into his Renwick hillside, to form steel-lined caves under four metres of earth. In these cool caves, varying only a couple of degrees in temperature between summer and winter, the Le Brun bottle-fermented sparklings age after bottling.

The classic varieties of Champagne are naturally featured in the fourteen-hectare Le Brun vineyard planted on flat river gravels: six hectares of Chardonnay, five hectares of Pinot Noir and three hectares of Meunier. The vines are densely spaced as in Champagne. Few contract-grown grapes are used.

Le Brun is intent on 'carrying on the old techniques – everything is handled according to Champagne tradition'. To make his beloved Methode Champenoise sparkling, he blends the base wine from the three varieties and across vintages. After adding yeasts and sugar for the second fermentation, the wine is then bottled and rests on its lees for one year.

Rather than laboriously handturning the bottles, they are then loaded into heavy metal-framed riddling machines called gyropalettes. Here, where the bottles stay for five days, they are automatically shaken every four hours. Then each bottle is disgorged, topped up, corked and wired.

And the wine? The Daniel Le Brun Methode Champenoise released in early 1986 opened up full-flavoured, yeasty and dry, showing a good straw colour and persistent bead – a good debut. This non-vintage Methode Champenoise is a blend of seventy percent Pinot Noir and Meunier and thirty percent Chardonnay. Subsequent releases have not been entirely consistent in quality.

Described as their 'crème de la crème', the Le Brun's purely Chardonnay-based Blanc de Blancs Methode Champenoise is stunningly bold for a style usually cast in the 'light and fresh' mould. Le Brun himself views New Zealand's bottle-fermented sparklings as 'bigger and fruitier' than their Champagne counterparts, principally due to their more advanced fruit ripeness.

The Le Brun range also includes a Methode Champenoise Rosé and a still Chardonnay, matured in Argonne oak 'foudres' (5000-litre casks), which displays a pungent yeastiness of taste reminding one of the sparklings.

DANIEL AND ADELE LE BRUN – THE FORMATIVE YEARS HAVE BROUGHT PROBLEMS BUT THEIR METHODE CHAMPENOISE WINES DISPLAY GREAT INDIVIDUALITY AND DEPTH OF FLAVOUR.

Regal Salmon Limited, a Marlborough Sounds and Stewart Island salmon producer, gained a controlling sixty percent interest in Cellier Le Brun in 1987. Daniel Le Brun, who has stayed on as the winemaker and is a director of the new company, declared his winery had been under-capitalised in its formative years.

After Regal Salmon's $700,000 capital injection, the Le Bruns and other original investors have a twenty-five percent shareholding and DFC Ventures owns the rest. Because salmon and top-class sparkling wines appeal to similar consumer markets, Regal Salmon sees its dual investments as 'a tremendous fit'.

On a lighter note, Le Brun recommends opening his wines not with an almighty flourish but 'with a whisper' – so as not to waste a drop.

Cloudy Bay

In the conviction that the quality of New Zealand-grown Sauvignon Blancs cannot be equalled in Australia, David Hohnen, part-owner of Cape Mentelle, a prestige Western Australian winery, has crossed the Tasman to set up a second winery in Marlborough. Cape Mentelle's reputation is based on having captured the Jimmy Watson Trophy – awarded to the top one-year-old Australian red – in successive years, with its 1982 and 1983 Cabernet Sauvignons.

Cloudy Bay, the name given to the district by Captain Cook, was finally chosen as the name of the new venture, but not before the name of a prominent local cape had been entertained but swifty rejected – Farewell Spit.

KEVIN JUDD, A MAN OF FEW WORDS, SHARPENED SELAKS' WINE QUALITY BEFORE HIS DEBUT WITH CLOUDY BAY, THE 1985 SAUVIGNON BLANC, SENT A RIPPLE THROUGH THE INTERNATIONAL WINE WORLD.

Cloudy Bay's declared intention is to make quality Sauvignon Blancs and Chardonnays, primarily for the Australian market. Construction of the robust, concrete-slab winery in Jackson's Road, Rapaura, began in August 1985 under the direction of Australian-born Kevin Judd (29), a Roseworthy College graduate who elevated the standard of Selaks' wines between 1983 and 1985. Judd, who had never tasted a New Zealand wine when he accepted the Selaks job offer, now has responsibility for the day-to-day running of Cloudy Bay. David Hohnen crosses the Tasman two or three times each year to work the Marlborough vintage and for crucial blending decisions.

Agreement has also been reached with Corbans to crush their Marlborough crop here until Cloudy Bay's own production reaches full capacity.

On flat land with stony, well-drained soils adjacent to the winery, the twenty-hectare Cloudy Bay vineyard of Sauvignon Blanc, Chardonnay and Sémillon was planted in 1986. Future plantings will add Pinot Noir, Shiraz and Merlot, and other varieties are also being trialled. Corbans supplied all the fruit for the early vintages but, long term, a fifty-fifty balance between estate-grown and bought-in fruit is the company's goal.

The first Cloudy Bay release, carrying an elegant uncluttered label depicting the Richmond Range, which overlooks the north side of the Wairau Valley, was a 1985 Sauvignon Blanc. A superb dry wine with a pungent bouquet and rich ripe flavour, avoiding any hint of stalkiness, its robust style was bound to appeal to Australian palates.

Judd seeks to produce Sauvignon Blanc having 'a lively gooseberries and lychees – rather than green peas – fruity character and a touch of oak complexity'. His adroitly structured blend includes about fifteen percent wood-fermented wine, an equal proportion of lower-acid Sémillon and also a hint (five grams per litre) of sugar which is barely perceptible. The emerging style is bracing and firm, distinctive for its mouth-filling body.

The Cloudy Bay range also includes a powerful Chardonnay, barrique-matured, and a lightish Cabernet Sauvignon, both making their debut from the 1986 vintage.

The toil required to establish a winery from scratch appears not to have drained the Cloudy Bay staff's humour. The sign at the gate when I called read: 'Sold out of wine. Our sales staff have gone fishing and our winemaker is dangerous if disturbed.'

Hunter's

Ernie Hunter, his spectacular career tragically cut short at the age of only thirty-eight, at the time of his June 1987 death in a motor accident had started to savour worldwide applause for the Marlborough wines he toiled so tenaciously and with such charisma to promote.

An ebullient Ulsterman, Hunter in his youth was once 'marched out of the Bogside at gunpoint'. He decided to leave Ireland after, at the age of seventeen, he 'saw a couple of kids barely old enough to talk thumping the hell out of each other. I bought my ticket the next day'.

After joining the retail liquor trade in Christchurch, he started a hotel wine club, then bought twenty-five hectares of land at Blenheim to grow grapes for Penfolds. After meeting Almuth Lorenz – a young German winemaker here on a working holiday – at a New Year's Eve party in 1981, at her suggestion he elected to plunge into commercial winemaking.

With Lorenz as winemaker the first, 1982 vintage of Hunter's wines was made under primitive conditions using borrowed gear at an old Christchurch cider factory. Observers were soon startled when, after entering six wines in that year's National Wine Competition, the fledgling company emerged with six medals, including three silvers. The promise in that performance was not fulfilled, however, in the 1983 vintage wines.

Suffering severe financial problems in 1984, Hunter was forced to sell his twenty-five hectare vineyard – although he arranged a supply contract with the new owner – and to lease out his vineyard restaurant. In exchange for a large cash injection, the Development Finance Corporation took

WINEMAKER JOHN BELSHAM UNDER THE
HUNTER'S LABEL PRODUCES WHITE WINES
BRIMMING WITH THE CLEAR, DEEP FLAVOURS
OF MARLBOROUGH-GROWN FRUIT.

JANE HUNTER, A HIGHLY QUALIFIED
VITICULTURIST WHO IS ALSO STUDYING
BUSINESS MANAGEMENT, MUST NOW
ALONE STEER HUNTER'S FUTURE.

a forty percent share of the company's equity.

Hunter now turned his formidable energy to export – and successfully shipped many thousands of cases of wine to the United Kingdom, the United States and Australia. In his widow Jane's words: 'Ernie didn't just sell Hunter's wines. When he was in New Zealand he always talked about Marlborough wines and when he was overseas he talked about New Zealand wines.' His most publicised successes came at the 1986 and 1987 *Sunday Times* Wine Club Festivals in London when the public voted his 1985 Fumé Blanc and 1986 Chardonnay as the most popular wines of the shows. 'A rampant attack on the world' is the way Bryan Mogridge, Montana's chief executive, later summed up Hunter's campaigns overseas.

His marketing efforts in this country were equally imaginative. The successful Marlborough Wine and Food Festival and the organisation of the Marlborough wine trail owed much to his drive. Mail-order customers were often bombarded with exuberant newsletters – 'Bedlam!' ran the heading on the spring 1986 newsletter – which, uniquely, even chronicled progress at other wineries in Marlborough.

After Ernie Hunter's premature death, his wife Jane stepped in as managing director. Born in 1954 into a South Australian grapegrowing family, she graduated in agricultural science from Adelaide University, majoring in viticulture and plant pathology. After a two year stint running a restaurant at Waikanae – 'I came to New Zealand to get away from the wine industry,' she says – she came to Marlborough in 1983 to take up a new post as Montana's chief viticulturist.

Following her husband's death, Jane thought about leaving the region. 'But then I thought, what's the point? We worked so hard to build it up. It would have been a waste if I'd walked away.'

The winemaker is John Belsham who, after five years spent at Château St Saturnin, a Médoc cru bourgeois, worked at Nobilo and then Matua Valley before coming south. Dr Tony Jordan, an eminent Australian oenologist, has been a consultant since the 1986 vintage.

The Hunter's winery in Rapaura Road, erected from coolstore materials in 1983, has since 'grown like Topsy' to handle its current output of 20,000 cases. Fruit is drawn from the eight-hectare estate vineyard – Chardonnay, Sémillon, Gewürztraminer and Pinot Noir in silty loams overlying riverstones – and from thirty-five hectares of contract vineyards.

Hunter's wines have deserved their acclaim. Although the Chardonnay and Fumé Blanc are the two flagships, these are also supported by a fine Gewürztraminer and Rhine Riesling. Deep-scented, elegant white wines of sustained flavour are the Hunter's hallmark.

The Chardonnay is one-third barrel-fermented and matured in new and once-used Demptos and Seguin Moreau Nevers oak puncheons. It usually combines enormous scale (over thirteen percent alcohol) with softness and a compelling, rich ripe flavour. Although enjoyable in its youth it is also packed with aging potential.

The Fumé Blanc, only twenty percent oak-aged, abounds with pungent Sauvignon fruit, crisp and fresh, barely toned down by the background hints of wood. There is also an excellent, non-oaked Sauvignon Blanc with pure, ripe gooseberry flavour in the classic Marlborough mould.

Hunter's Gewürztraminer Dry is a satisfying dinner wine: not too pungently spicy but flavoursome and with excellent palate weight. The Rhine Riesling is crisp, fragrant and full of fresh citric flavours. The Müller-Thurgau Dry, too, is a cut above average.

Hunter's Spring Creek Claret − the winery's first red wine − is a fresh, ruby red, showing pleasant berryish flavours in a smooth, soft style. The unusual blend − Cabernet Sauvignon and Pinot Noir − and absence of oak complexity hint that Hunter's have been 'marking time' with this wine. Its excellent basic fruit suggests the likelihood of finer reds to come. Indeed, John Belsham openly aspires to making a 'very good' Marlborough-grown Pinot Noir.

Te Whare Ra

Describing himself as a 'self-made, bootstraps winemaker' who is 'suspicious of received book wisdom on winemaking techniques', Allen Hogan under his Te Whare Ra label has fashioned several of this country's most rampantly botrytised sweet white wines.

Bay of Plenty-born Hogan (45) gathered his initial winemaking experience at a small Perth winery, then spent a couple of vintages with Montana at Marlborough and another vintage at the Te Kauwhata research station. He and his wife Joyce planted their first vines in Angelsea Street, Renwick in 1979.

'It felt right' when he first saw the land over which his future vineyard would spread. Today he has four hectares of irrigated Gewürztraminer, Sémillon, Riesling, Chardonnay, Cabernet Sauvignon and Merlot vines planted in variable loam and gravel soils.

The Te Whare Ra (House In The Sun) winery, begun in 1982, has been built from earth bricks with a timbered exterior. A beautiful leadlight glass panel in the entrance to the tasting room features the sun, vine leaves, a bunch of ripe grapes and a glass of red wine, accompanied by the motto 'Na Te Ra Nga Mamahi' (By Sun And Hard Work).

Te Whare Ra's varietal white wines are marketed under the Duke of Marlborough label (in memory of the crushing defeat inflicted by John Churchill, Duke of Marlborough, on the French in 1704 at the battle of Blenheim). Hogan makes distinctively 'big, high-alcohol styles as is to be expected with the late-harvesting techniques currently employed'. Oxidation − caused by leaking corks − marred one or two of the early releases, but with a set of strapping dry wines from 1985, Te Whare Ra arrived as a respected table-wine producer.

The Chardonnay, stainless-steel-fermented and matured for three months in new oak barriques, is remarkably robust (and tipsy-making), a blockbuster style drunk by heroes. Succulent, fat and slightly fiery, its style is well caught by Hogan's own 'knock your socks off' description.

Investors who each put up $100 to fund the winery's initial purchase of three barrels in which to mature its Chardonnay have been handsomely repaid with one hundred dollars worth of wine in the first year plus fifty dollars worth of wine in each of the two following years.

Other dry to medium whites include a big, spicy Gewürztraminer, a bitingly grassy Sémillon, a Flora (recommended with Chinese cuisine), Rhine Riesling (carrying ten grams per litre residual sugar) and an excellent, penetrating Fumé Blanc.

Te Whare Ra's narrow range of reds includes a QDR Pinot Noir for everyday thirst-quenching and a pair of Cabernet Sauvignons; the oak-aged version, labelled Sarah Jennings (after the Duke of Marlborough's wife) is a stocky and flavoursome wine, standing out as markedly riper and more robust than most Marlborough Cabernets have been.

The pearls in the Te Whare Ra lineup, however, are the stunning sweet whites. In 1979 Hogan noticed others ignoring the nobly rotten grapes in their Marlborough vineyards and determined to remedy this. Working with Rainer Eschenbruch at the Te Kauwhata research station later enhanced his knowledge of how to handle botrytised fruit.

Marlborough's cold autumn nights, followed by a heavy dew and high humidity in the morning, drying out later in the day, are tailor-made for the spread of favourable *Botrytis cinerea*, says Hogan. He uses both estate-grown grapes and fruit purchased from a larger wine company (a supply line which has its hazards – a 1987 Hogan newsletter revealed that 'politically it was extremely difficult to actually get hold of the material'). The wines are stop-fermented, leaving them with relatively low alcohol and soaring sugar levels.

The Botrytis Bunch Selection is a poised, honeyish, delectably botrytised wine, brimming with 110 grams per litre residual sugar, yet displaying a perfect alcohol/sweetness/acid balance. Even more stunning is the Botrytis Berry Selection, which is made from heavily raisined grapes from which Hogan only recovers under thirty percent of the normal amount of juice. Carrying 250 grams per litre of residual sugar, intensely botrytised and nectareous, this wine stands with the Rongopai Riesling Auslese at the forefront of this country's sweet white wines.

More than other winemakers, Hogan has put his relationship with mail-order customers on a personal footing by twice each year hosting Te Whare Ra tastings in cities from Auckland to Invercargill.

ALLEN HOGAN – HIS NECTAREOUS BOTRYTISED RIESLINGS AND MÜLLER-THURGAUS MUST BE RANKED AMONG THE MOST DELECTABLE WHITE WINES IN THE LAND.

CANTERBURY

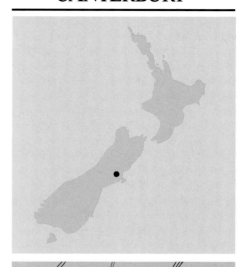

Ten years after the planting of the province's first commercial vineyard, Canterbury has emerged as a fully fledged wine region with half-a-dozen wineries up and running and a cluster of auspicious Pinot Noirs and Rieslings safely ensconced in bottles.

The climatic hazards for viticulture in Canterbury are more severe than for districts further north. Canterbury, although nearer the equator than many European wine regions, in cooler years can fail to accumulate the heat readings necessary to fully ripen grapes. In this respect it parallels parts of Germany. October spring frosts are a risk and April frosts can retard ripening.

Canterbury, however, like Marlborough, enjoys one vital advantage over most North Island winegrowing regions – low rainfall. During Canterbury's long dry autumns, the warm days and cool nights enable the fruit to ripen slowly, with high levels of acidity and extract. Müller-Thurgau is usually harvested in mid-April – a month or more later than in the North Island – and Riesling and Pinot Noir hang on the vines until May.

Most of the vineyards are located in two areas: south of Christchurch and at Waipara in North Canterbury. The soils in both districts are typically silty loams – shallower in the south – overlying river gravels, free-draining and in most seasons needing to be irrigated.

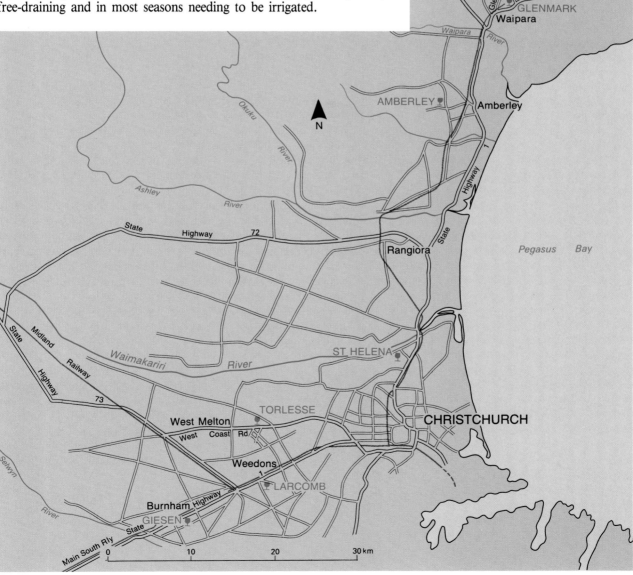

The fortunate viticultural combination of low rainfall and low to moderate soil fertility means that excessive vine foliage growth is not a problem here. Open vine canopies and dry weather also reduce disease problems and can encourage the development of 'noble rot'.

French peasants who landed in 1840 at Akaroa on Banks Peninsula carried vine cuttings, from which wine soon flowed for their domestic consumption. A century after their arrival, W.H. Meyers built a small winery, Villa Nova, in the Heathcote Valley. By 1945 he had a tiny vineyard of about 0.8 hectares planted in Verdelho – a Portuguese variety – Pinot Gris, Muscat and other grapes. Although wine was made, Meyers' vines were uprooted around 1949 after they failed to flourish.

The current resurgence of interest in Canterbury wine stems from research conducted at Lincoln College under the direction of Dr David Jackson. When the first grape trials commenced in 1973, research focussed on identifying the most suitable varieties for Canterbury's cool climate. After losing seventy percent of his vines in the first year to a late frost, Jackson began 'wondering if I really was making a mistake'.

Trial plantings of over sixty varieties have since demonstrated, according to the College, that Canterbury produces grapes of high acidity and high sugar levels. Jackson sees Canterbury as 'borderline' for such mid-to-late season ripeners as Sauvignon Blanc and such late-season ripeners as Cabernet Sauvignon, but Pinot Noir and Chardonnay are 'particularly promising'. The highest hopes are held for Riesling; this enthusiasm is reflected in the 1986 vineyard survey, which listed the five most popular varieties planted in Canterbury as (in order): Riesling, Müller-Thurgau, Chardonnay, Pinot Gris and Pinot Noir. Lincoln College is now winding down its programme of variety research and concentrating more on clonal evaluation, pruning and vine-management trials.

Torlesse is the newest label in Canterbury. Twenty-one shareholders, about one-half of them grapegrowers, with Development Finance Corporation assistance, have founded Torlesse Wines in West Melton about twenty kilometres from Christchurch, near the highway leading to the West Coast.

Danny Schuster, Torlesse's winemaker, is one of Canterbury wine's most passionate advocates. Born in Germany, Schuster gained a diploma in viticulture, oenology and wine evaluation, then worked in European vineyards and at research institutions in South Africa and Australia, before arriving in this country in the late 1970s. After establishing the winemaking trials at Lincoln College with David Jackson, Schuster guided St Helena's early vintages before joining Torlesse.

From the 1987 vintage has flowed a dry Gewürztraminer, two styles of Riesling, a Pinot Noir 'Beaujolais-style' and a blended, 'Chablis-style' Estate Dry White.

CANTERBURY'S LOW TO MODERATE SOIL FERTILITY AND LIGHT AUTUMN RAINFALL ARE WELL SUITED TO VITICULTURE – THE AMBERLEY VINEYARD IN NORTH CANTERBURY.

Amberley

mberley is a small North Canterbury winery, fifty kilometres north of Christchurch and two kilometres inland from Amberley township. Here, on a twenty-hectare property also devoted to sheep farming and mixed cropping, in 1979 Jeremy and Lee Prater began planting grapevines. Today, their gently undulating vineyard on north-facing Waipara loam-clay slopes includes five hectares of Riesling, Müller-Thurgau, Gewürztraminer, Sauvignon Blanc and Pinot Noir.

Prater (39), who was born in England, arrived in New Zealand in 1970 and later graduated with a B.A. from Canterbury University. He then spent four years in Switzerland – gaining a diploma in viticulture and winemaking from the Swiss Federal College, near Geneva – Germany and France, learning the ropes of cool-climate winemaking, and more than a year with Montana at Marlborough, before processing his first Amberley vintage in 1984.

In his insulated timber winery, Prater makes only about 1000 cases of wine per year, which will gradually climb to a maximum of 2000 cases. His first oak barrel arrived in September 1987.

To judge from the wines I have tasted – the 1987, 1986 and 1985 Brackenfield Rhine Rieslings, the 1985 Teviotdale Gewürztraminer and the 1987 and 1986 Glens of Tekoa Chardonnays – Prater is gradually coming to grips with the intricacies of cool-climate white winemaking. The Amberley range also features a medium Müller-Thurgau, a dry Riesling-Sylvaner and – coming up in the next couple of years – a Sauvignon Blanc and Pinot Noir.

JEREMY AND LEE PRATER – A QUIET START BUT THEIR VINEYARD AT AMBERLEY LOOKS LIKELY TO BE A SOURCE OF INTERESTING RIESLING AND PINOT NOIR.

Giesen

rom Hermann Seifried in the Upper Moutere hills to Danny Schuster – formerly at Lincoln College and St Helena, now at Torlesse – and Almuth Lorenz – previously at Hunter's, now at Merlen Wines – the impact of Austrian and German-born winemakers on the South Island has been sweeping. The German influence has been even more keenly felt of late since members of the Giesen family, hailing from Neustadt in the Rhine Valley, have founded the largest vineyard in Canterbury.

The Giesen property at Burnham, twenty-five kilometres south of Christchurch, is run by brothers Theodor (29), Alexander (28) and Marcel Giesen (23). The family, involved in granite construction in Germany, wanted to escape Europe's overcrowding and environmental problems.

Fumé Blanc
1987

RIESLING DRY
1987

Pinot Noir
1986

Cabernet Sauvignon/ Cabernet Franc/Shiraz
1986

(LEFT TO RIGHT) MARCEL, ALEXANDER AND THEO GIESEN. HAVING STUNNED MOST OBSERVERS BY SITING THEIR VINEYARD SOUTH OF CHRISTCHURCH, THEY NOW PRODUCE ONE OF THE MOST COMPELLING, FLAVOUR-PACKED DRY RIESLINGS IN THE COUNTRY.

Theo, after visiting New Zealand in the late seventies, returned to his home armed with several bottles of Weingut Seifried – and the conviction that the South Canterbury region is a southern Rhine. (The Giesens have even been known to ponder whether they ought to have established their venture still further south.)

After the family emigrated to New Zealand in 1979 – not necessarily intending to make wine, although they had owned vineyards in Neustadt – they were struck by the absence of local wineries servicing the Christchurch market. Planting commenced in 1981 and the vineyards now cover twenty-five hectares of Riesling – the flagship variety – Müller-Thurgau, Gewürztraminer, Chardonnay, Sauvignon Blanc, Cabernet Sauvignon, Merlot, Cabernet Franc, Pinot Noir and Shiraz. Many of the early vines perished in the stone-strewn soils – now irrigated – from the effects of drought and hasty planting. Other fruit is purchased from Canterbury and Marlborough grapegrowers.

The utilitarian, corrugated-iron and timber winery, dominated by a mammoth wine press, sits squarely in the centre of the vineyard. There is no refrigeration: since the grapes are harvested late in the season when the weather is turning cool, the Giesens simply run cold bore water down the outside of their tanks. The cellars are stocked with wine bearing a multitude of labels: the Giesens will individually label their wines for anyone purchasing a few cases. They are innovative, tireless marketers, conducting countless tastings.

Although 1984, the first vintage, produced some unhappy wines, young winemaker Marcel Giesen – who in 1986 graduated from Weinsberg College in Baden with a Kellermeister diploma – has swiftly lifted his performance. Giesen Pinot Noir is a fresh and soft red, giving ripe enjoyable drinking. There is also a successful Cabernet Sauvignon/ Cabernet Franc/Shiraz blend showing attractive peppery flavour and solid extract.

The range of whites includes a very fine dry Riesling, full and steely; a vibrant, lightly oaked Fumé Blanc featuring an eye-catching Evelyn Page painting, 'Still Life With Apricots'; and a robust Chardonnay matured in German and American oak barrels. Both the Müller-Thurgau and Gewürztraminer are pleasant commercial styles.

Giesen Blanc de Blancs Methode Champenoise was launched in a typically spirited fashion in 1987. According to the winery's press release: 'The French have threatened to take legal action against the Giesens for once labelling a sparkling wine as Canterbury Champagne . . . Mr Theo Giesen has lashed back at the French for what he considers to be a total insult to international industry . . . The Giesen wine estate now refuses to label any of its sparkling wines as Champagne even though the newly released Blanc de Blancs is a true methode champenoise wine. Says Theo: "We just could not insult such a fine wine".'

I n a converted haybarn on the main highway at Waipara on the Weka Plains, John McCaskey has founded Canterbury's northernmost winery.

McCaskey (50) has spent his lifetime farming his family's 392-hectare property, which originally formed part of George Henry Moore's 60,000-hectare Glenmark sheep station. The famous Glenmark homestead, destroyed by fire in 1891, is today the focal point of the winery's labels.

McCaskey's interest in winemaking was first fired over twenty years ago but, he says, it was not until the Glenmark irrigation scheme was under way that diversification could start. His first vines were planted in 1981.

Today McCaskey's two vineyards at Waipara, covering 4.5 hectares of light silt loams over a base of clay and gravels, feature Riesling as the principal variety with smaller plantings of Gewürztraminer, Chardonnay, Müller-Thurgau, Pinot Noir and Cabernet Sauvignon.

Winemaker Steve Harber, an American in his mid thirties, has come to Glenmark with over a decade's winemaking experience in California and a spell with Montana in Gisborne under his belt. Following the first vintage in 1986 of only a few hundred cases, production will swiftly rise to the desired annual output of around two thousand cases.

Two styles of Riesling have been marketed, the dry Weka Plains Rhine Riesling − the 1986 green-gold, with spine-tingling acidity and plenty of depth − and the medium Torokina Rhine Riesling. The reds, including the Hut Creek Pinot Noir, are produced 'basically for early consumption, with brief barrel contact', says McCaskey.

Glenmark

JOHN McCASKEY − PRODUCING REDS FOR EARLY DRINKING AND RIESLINGS LIKELY TO EVOLVE GRACEFULLY OVER SEVERAL YEARS IN THE BOTTLE.

Larcomb

Larcomb is a fledgling Canterbury winery – its label depicts the first four Canterbury ships – lying in Larcomb's Road, near Rolleston, south of Christchurch.

John Thom (41), a veterinarian-turning-viticulturist, and his wife Julie began planting grapevines in 1980 and four years later had their debut, a hundred cases of 1984 Breidecker. Tall, bearded and very enthusiastic about his fresh career ('most vets are frustrated farmers,' he says), Thom believes a veterinarian's training, with its emphasis upon hygiene and chemistry, affords a valuable background for winemaking.

The Larcomb vineyard currently encompasses four hectares of Pinot Noir, Riesling, Breidecker, Pinot Gris and Gewürztraminer varieties, planted in light sandy loams over river gravels. The corrugated-iron, polystyrene and plastic-lined winery erected in 1983 currently has an annual output of only 1000 cases, planned to eventually double.

Much of the wine is sold at Larcomb's delightful vineyard bar, which serves light lunches and wine by the glass (during summer only).

John Thom has slipped into the winemaker's role with apparent ease – his output shows signs of careful winemaking. The Breidecker variety, which grows readily and crops well in the Larcomb vineyard, forms the basis of his enjoyable vin ordinaire. Breidecker Dry (which is partnered by a Breidecker Medium) is a straightforward, clean and fresh wine, as this variety typically produces, showing very reasonable body. The Gewürztraminer is a light style of very delicate spiciness.

Larcomb Riesling is brimful of promise. The 1987 vintage, a pale green-tinged wine in its youth, is crisp and tight with excellent length of flavour – probably the best yet. The 1986 was lighter and more austere. The silver medal 1985 vintage is now light gold, with a wealth of classic Riesling characteristics.

The Pinot Noir is equally intriguing. A buoyant Canterbury red, cherryish to the eye, fragrant and supple, it is a non-wooded style, beautiful at a young age. Pinot Noir as ripe and savoury as the 1987 vintage should do wonders for this small vineyard's reputation.

JOHN THOM AND HIS WIFE JULIE – A PINOT NOIR THAT CONSOLIDATES THE REGIONAL REPUTATION PIONEERED BY ST HELENA, AND A PIERCING, PURE RIESLING.

St Helena

More than any other winery, St Helena put Canterbury firmly on the New Zealand wine map. It has the dual distinction of being the province's oldest commercial vineyard and the source of its most celebrated label – St Helena Pinot Noir.

Robin (42) and Norman Mundy (40) are down-to-earth, energetic men, combining an 'air of the soil' with undoubted business acumen. After nematodes rendered their potato farm unprofitable, they early took heed of the results of Lincoln College's pioneering viticultural research. By 1978 St Helena's first vines were planted at Coutts Island, near Belfast, twenty minutes' drive north of Christchurch.

Bounded by branches of the Waimakariri River, the vineyard needs no irrigation since the water table rises during drought conditions. Because the river flow encourages air movement, the vines also face a relatively low frost risk.

By the mid-eighties a twenty-nine hectare vineyard had been established principally in Riesling, Gewürztraminer, Müller-Thurgau and Pinot Gris, supplemented by smaller plots of Pinot Noir, Chardonnay, Pinot Blanc, Cabernet Sauvignon and Merlot. In 1987, following a successful export trip to the United States, Robin Mundy announced a major decision: to top-graft the entire vineyard – apart from a few hectares of Riesling – over to Pinot Noir and Chardonnay.

With winemaker Danny Schuster at the helm from the first vintage, 1981 until 1985, St Helena achieved gold medal status with its 1982, 1984 and 1985 Pinot Noirs. His white wines, as a rule, showed excellent body but sometimes were lacking in elegance. Interest now centres on the impact of Christchurch-born Mark Rattray (39), who has studied at the Geisenheim Institute and earned the industry's respect during his preceding terms at Montana and Penfolds.

A diverse array of wines has flowed from the brick-fronted, insulated aluminium winery erected in 1981. The majority of the Rieslings seen have been dry and full with lowish acidity – with the notable exception of the 1983 Late Harvest Rhine Riesling, which displayed a lovely, botrytised

NORMAN (LEFT) AND ROBIN MUNDY – THEY SWITCHED FROM POTATOES TO A PINOT NOIR THAT ELECTRIFIED THE CANTERBURY WINE COMMUNITY.

MARK RATTRAY – A PROVEN PERFORMER
AT PENFOLDS, HE NOW COMMANDS THE
WINEMAKING REINS AT ST HELENA, SINCE THE
DEPARTURE OF THE PINOT NOIR SPECIALIST –
AND AUTHOR OF A BOOK ON PINOT NOIR –
DANNY SCHUSTER.

bouquet but lacked acid steeliness to balance its sweetness. Müller-Thurgau has yielded pleasant, average wine, medium-sweet in style.

St Helena Ruländer (a synonym for Pinot Gris and Tokay d'Alsace) 1986 was fruity, sweetish and mild. Willow Creek Spaetlese 1987, a late-harvested and stop-fermented version of the same variety is more memorable, showing a touch of varietal peachiness. The 1987 Ruländer Auslese, made from shrivelled berries harvested in the last week of May, three weeks after the Spaetlese, is a gently peachy sweet wine with a mellow finish.

Chardonnay holds promise. After launching the first Canterbury-grown Chardonnay with its 1985 vintage, St Helena followed with the Nevers oak-fermented 1986, a robust, creamy wine, broad and soft.

Probably the most successful white overall has been the Pinot Blanc, typically a mouth-filling, white-burgundy style. The Pinot Blanc variety is heavier-cropping than Chardonnay but possesses less clearcut varietal character. It is grown in Alsace and also in Burgundy where, because it has good mouthfeel but less complexity, it is usually blended with Chardonnay. At St Helena, where it is usually matured in wood, its wine has been earthy, ripe-tasting, robust and dry – a tailor-made Chardonnay substitute.

But the much discussed Pinot Noir is the real success story so far. In a breakthrough for Canterbury wine the 1982 vintage scored a gold medal at the following year's National Wine Competition. Produced from ultra-ripe bunches aged in new French oak puncheons, this wine stood out for its dense colour and soft, mouth-filling palate.

The 1983 vintage, in which carbonic maceration played a greater role, was much lighter, but the 1984 brought a return to the full and savoury style of the 1982. Both the 1985 and 1986 vintages have also unleashed notable body, colour intensity and suppleness.

The fruit is harvested in mid-late May – in 1986 the vines had already dropped their leaves – at very high sugar levels. Up to and including the 1985 vintage, the slightly shrivelled grapes were hand-picked and twenty-five percent of the stalks were included in the fermentation. Since 1986 the fruit has been mechanically harvested and the practice of incorporating stalks abandoned.

During the ferment, which lasts sixteen to eighteen days, the cap of skins is plunged or pumped-over every eight hours. The wine is then transferred into Nevers oak puncheons for a year where it undergoes a malolactic fermentation.

Although lively debate in wine circles swirls around the issue of the extent to which this label captures the elusive character of Pinot Noir – the antagonists are evenly balanced and the issue is subjective – it remains a dark-hued, mouth-filling red of extraordinary concentration.

CENTRAL OTAGO

RIPPON VINEYARDS' ROLFE AND LOIS MILLS AND FAMILY WITH YOUNG HAWKE'S BAY WINEMAKER TONY BISH. IN LAKE WANAKA'S COLD AIR THEY POSE THE QUESTION: WHO NEEDS REFRIGERATION?

Central Otago
Rhine Riesling
1987
Late Harvest

VINTED AND BOTTLED BY
CENTRAL OTAGO WINE MAKERS
NEW ZEALAND

When claims first surfaced that parts of the cooler, and frequently drier, South Island enjoyed suitable climates for viticulture, they met in the north with a frosty reception. Tom McDonald once discounted the possibility of large-scale winemaking south of Cook Strait.

Montana researched and pioneered commercial wine production in the South Island at Blenheim fifteen years ago and then abruptly silenced its critics by releasing a stream of gold medal-winning Marlborough Rhine Rieslings and Sauvignon Blancs. Northern negativism regrouped when 'boutique' wineries later emerged in Canterbury – until St Helena electrified South Island winemakers by scoring a gold award with its 1982 Pinot Noir. Now, a small knot of enthusiasts are pioneering winemaking at the southern frontier – Central Otago.

Otago's inland basins and valleys yielded some of the earliest New Zealand wines. Jean Desiré Feraud was cultivating 1200 vines at his Monte Cristo farm near Clyde by 1870 and his wines, bitters and liqueurs commanded high prices on the goldfields. Known as 'Old Fraud' – as Mayor of Clyde he discovered the town's water right was not legally secured, so he resigned his office, and having taken legal action to have it transferred to himself, promptly embarked on an irrigation scheme – his Constantia wine captured a First Class of Merit award at the Dunedin Industrial Exhibition, and his Burgundy a Third Class of Merit at Sydney in 1881.

Then in 1895 Romeo Bragato, on loan from the Victorian government, toured the country to advise the government on the possibilities for winemaking in the colony. At Arrowtown, he tasted his first glass of New Zealand wine – made by a Mrs Hutcheson – and 'although made after the most primitive fashion, it reflected great credit on the producer . . .'

Bragato also found grapevines, tended by miners working the Clutha, flourishing outdoors at Cromwell and Clyde, and grapes fully ripened by February, 'a convincing fact to me that the summer climatic conditions here are conducive to the early ripening of the fruit'. Central Otago, he affirmed, was 'pre-eminently suitable' for winemaking.

At a public meeting later held in Dunedin, Bragato stirred up such enthusiasm that a Central Otago Vine and Fruitgrowers' Association was born. The word Vine however, was later dropped from the title, and the eagerly anticipated new wine industry never burgeoned in the interior.

The present resurgence of activity dates from the late 1950s with Robert Duncan, of Gilligan's Gully, who planted thousands of vine cuttings near Alexandra, but failed to protect his plants from birds and frost. Trials later conducted on the Earnsclaugh orchard of R.V. Kinnaird, across the Clutha from Alexandra, soon proved that fully ripe grapes could be harvested by the end of April, notably Müller-Thurgau and Chasselas.

Another trial block established in the 1970s by the DSIR under frost protection sprinklers at the research orchard at Earnsclaugh, successfully ripened the prized Pinot Noir and Gewürztraminer varieties.

The crunch question is whether this region is sufficiently warm to support commercial wineries. To properly ripen, grapes must receive a certain amount of heat during the growing season. Meteorological readings confirm that the district's climate is extremely marginal for viticulture, cooler even than Germany, the most hazardous of European wine countries (and the source of its most elegant white wines). It is clear that only the most painstakingly selected sites with sheltered, sunny meso-climates – heat-traps – will enable winemakers to succeed here.

Frosts pose another real danger, threatening tender spring growth as well as the ripening bunches in autumn: it will be crucial here to choose elevated vineyard sites with good cold-air drainage.

Dry autumn weather, however, is this region's vital viticultural asset, encouraging the winemakers to leave their grapes late on the vines, ripening undamaged by autumn rains.

Ann Pinckney, one of the rare breed – even endangered species, history would suggest – of Central Otago winemakers, lives on a stunning site above her one-hectare vineyard at Speargrass Flat, near the poplar-lined Queenstown-Arrowtown highway. This looks and feels like classic wine country.

Here, the thirty-five-year-old Lincoln College graduate has planted Gewürztraminer and Müller-Thurgau vines and erected a ten by seven-metre winery where, until her equipment was recently upgraded, she and her friends donned gumboots during the harvest and crushed the fruit by foot in buckets.

A Southlander, Pinckney is 'sick and tired of hearing bad things about the local climate' and is out to prove her point that 'the climate is there' to produce premium quality wines. From the 1988 vintage she produced about 170 cases under the Taramea label.

Over in the Gibbston Valley, television producer and reporter Alan Brady is also unravelling Central Otago's wine character. The Irish-born Brady, who purchased his briar-covered, hill-surrounded property twelve years ago, concluded 'it was an interesting piece of dirt'. He elected to do something a bit different with it and planted 350 vines in 1981 and 1982, to 'prove they would grow', and has lately planted more.

Each year until recently the bulk of his crop headed north to the Government research station at Te Kauwhata, where he says they were delighted with the fruit quality. In 1988 Brady's production amounted to about 200 cases, made at Ann Pinckney's winery.

The largest venture is Rolfe and Lois Mills' breathtakingly beautiful Rippon Vineyard, planted on a schist slope running down to the shores of Lake Wanaka. Mills (64), who planted his first vines in 1976 and then capped nine years of viticultural experiments with his first wine in 1985, now has four hectares established in Pinot Noir, Riesling, Gewürztraminer, Sauvignon Blanc, Müller-Thurgau, Breidecker and Chardonnay.

The Mills have recently appointed a trained winemaker, Tony Bish (27), who in the past worked at Corbans, Vidal, and Brown Brothers in Australia. Made in a temporary winery, the Rippon range includes a pair of Rieslings and Sauvignon Blancs in dry and late-harvest styles, a pair of Pinot Noirs in 'blush' and 'Burgundy' styles, a Müller-Thurgau and a Gewürztraminer. Rippon Sauvignon Blanc Late Harvest 1987 is clean and sweet, bold in alcohol but restrained in varietal character.

There are currently about eight hectares of vines scattered around Central Otago, in the Queenstown, Arrowtown, Wanaka, Cromwell and Alexandra areas. Not surprisingly for a region which boasts the most southerly vineyard in the world (at Alexandra 44° 36' south), Riesling is the variety most feel should excel here. Participants in the 1988 Second International Symposium for Cool Climate Viticulture and Oenology in Auckland described a couple of dry and late-harvest Rieslings from Central Otago as 'clean, with lots of flavour, showing great promise'.

Rob Hay, a young winemaker trained in Germany and at Babich and Korepo, has planted his vineyard at Chard Farm, high above the Kawarau River near Arrowtown, and will process his first vintage in 1989. This recent influx of experienced winemakers, sharing commitment and expertise, should capitalise more fully on Central Otago's promise – and coax a rivulet of elegant, deep-flavoured white wines from its majestic valleys.

CHAPTER FIVE

Buying, Cellaring and Drinking Wine

BUYING NEW ZEALAND WINE

*T*o sell wine in New Zealand is a privilege restricted to approved licence-holders – notably restaurants, hotels, wine resellers, 'wholesale' wine and spirit merchants and, of course, vineyards. For the wine buyer, each point of sale has its advantages and disadvantages.

A CORNER OF THE STYLISH WINERY SHOP AT MORTON ESTATE. VINEYARD VISITS OFFER AN UNPARALLELED OPPORTUNITY TO TRACK DOWN RARE LABELS, TASTE BEFORE YOU BUY, SAVE MONEY AND, IF YOU ARE LUCKY, MEET THE WINEMAKER.

VINEYARDS

Wine, they say, always tastes best at the vineyard. Why not explore one of the wine trails in West Auckland, Gisborne, Hawke's Bay, Martinborough, Nelson, Marlborough or Canterbury?

There are at least four compelling reasons for buying wine at the vineyard gate. The opportunity to try before you buy is a big advantage; scarce, private bin wines can often only be found here; prices are usually – although not universally – below the level at the wholesalers; and at small vineyards, the owner or winemaker is often behind the counter dispensing samples and insights into the wine world.

Add the relaxed pleasure of a day spent in the countryside and the sheer physical beauty of most of our vineyards, and you have the recipe for a memorable vinous outing.

Oddly, touring the vineyards to buy wine has yet to achieve the popularity here it deserves. The Giesen brothers were amazed upon their arrival in New Zealand in 1979 to find no wineries at all sited on the outskirts of Christchurch.

In Germany, the dozens of vineyards clustered around important towns are deluged each weekend with visitors buying several cases at a time – like the New Zealanders who buy case-loads of fruit from their local orchards. The Napa Valley, near San Francisco, is crammed on summer weekends with bumper-to-bumper winery traffic. By contrast, the several wine trails of New Zealand are relatively undiscovered.

An annual pilgrimage around the vineyards can uncover a hoard of treasures. The rules of the Air New Zealand Wine Awards prescribe that wines eligible for trophies must be on sale once the judging is finished – thus early November is the best period for pursuing special releases.

Be careful not to abuse the hospitality so freely bestowed at the wineries. Remember, in the winemakers' eyes you are there primarily to buy wine. Sampling is a privilege extended to help you make your selection. To try before you buy means precisely that.

Only about five percent of New Zealand wine is sold direct to the public over the vineyard counter. But some small wineries rely heavily on vineyard sales and for the wine enthusiast eager to explore the full array of local wines, vineyard visits are essential.

Mail-order is another, increasingly common, way to buy wine for those who lack the time to scour the countryside or live far from a favourite winery. The majority of small and medium-sized vineyards now operate a mail-order system, sending out newsletters – ranging in tone from businesslike to intimate – and new-purchase offers two or three times each year. Freight costs tend to be high for a solitary carton of wine, but you retain a direct link with the producer.

WHOLESALERS

Large volumes of wine are sold by so-called 'wholesalers', in reality wine and spirit merchants who also sell direct to the public. Most wine companies sell in large volumes to merchants, who warehouse the wine and then distribute to retailers (hotels, wine reseller shops and restaurants), who in turn sell directly to the public. But these merchant 'wholesalers' also operate their own sales outlets.

Through a very complex, rather incestuous set of company associations, many wholesalers are now in the hands of the two major brewery groups, who themselves are, or have been, shareholders in some leading wine companies. As a result, the consumer's freedom of choice may suffer – some merchants tend to heavily promote the products of their affiliated wine companies, making it more difficult for the smaller, independent wineries to achieve adequate exposure.

Wine merchants are only occasionally competent to give professional buying advice, although much needed effort is now starting to be channelled into specialist education. Also, the merchant's traditional role of selecting, holding and aging wine has been conspicuously ignored. However, although the law insists that at a wholesaler you must buy a minimum of eight litres, prices are normally cheaper here than anywhere other than the vineyards, and often a wide range is stocked.

HOTELS

Corner hotel bottle-stores typically offer only a very narrow selection of wines, so that being able to buy a single bottle is the only real advantage they offer. So lacking has been the management's understanding of wine on occasion that real finds have been made. Francis Colchester-Wemyss, in his *Souvenirs Gastronomiques*, recalls discovering thirty-five bottles of the great Bordeaux Château Latour 1899 in 'a New Zealand hotel'; the publican was happy to be rid of his old 'French Burgundy' at a price lower than his cheapest Australian imports.

Often hotels operate their own 'wholesale' departments which, in reality, are bottle-stores operating off reduced margins.

WINE RESELLERS

The local wine-reseller shops usually carry a wide selection and offer the convenience of single bottle purchases. But the wineshops, set up in 1948 to provide the New Zealand wine industry with an independent channel of distribution to the public, more often than not are unable to match the prices offered by the merchant 'wholesalers'.

Although discounting has spread recently, the average shelf price still does not encourage a bulk purchase. However, these shops are convenient and well-stocked outlets.

It must be said that the level of wine expertise still encountered in the majority of these shops is low. For specialised outlets, a more professional approach to staff education is sorely needed.

IN THIS AUCKLAND RETAIL OUTLET – THE VINTAGE WINE AND LIQUOR COMPANY IN PONSONBY ROAD – THE ACCENT IS ON NEW ZEALAND AND OVERSEAS WINES IN THE MIDDLE-TO-UPPER PRICE BRACKETS. YOU HAVE TO LOOK HARD TO FIND A WINE CASK.

RESTAURANTS

One of the dearest places to buy wine is in a licensed restaurant. Hotel dining-rooms which once opened fleetingly from 6 to 7 p.m. gave no encouragement to linger over a bottle of wine. But since 1961, when the Gourmet in Auckland became the first restaurant legally allowed to serve wine, hundreds of licensed restaurants around the country have aroused interest in New Zealand wine.

Mark-ups are commonly in the order of 100–200 percent – to cover the costs of tying up capital, storage, glasses, stewards' wages and so on.

Unless something outstanding is featured on the wine-list, order the meal first and then select the wines to suit. As an aperitif while pondering the menu, a bone-dry sherry or a dry white stimulates the appetite wonderfully. Should you want only a single bottle to be consumed throughout the meal, choose it to match the main course. A pleasant and common procedure is to consume a dry white wine with the initial courses, followed by a red wine or another white wine to accompany the main dish.

Care should be taken to ensure that the food and wines chosen complement each other, avoiding the danger that the flavour of one may swamp that of the other. Light wines should therefore be chosen to partner the more delicate dishes, and robust, full-bodied wines to partner strongly flavoured foods.

Delicate seafood dishes combine well with milder white wines such as Müller-Thurgau and Riesling. For heavier, flavoursome seafoods such as oysters, try the more assertive grape varieties – Chardonnay, Sauvignon Blanc or Gewürztraminer.

With steak and beef dishes, robust reds like Cabernet Sauvignon come into their own, the strong flavours of both the food and the wine affording an ideal match. Chicken, lamb and pork suit flavoursome white wines, such as Chardonnay and Gewürztraminer, or medium-bodied reds such as Pinot Noir and Pinotage.

If ordering a wine especially to accompany dessert, choose something unabashedly sweet – anything drier simply will not match the sweet food. At the very end of the meal, port, sweet sherry and red wine all combine admirably with cheeses.

Order the house wine if you want only a glass or two. Only recently, unfortunately, have some licensed restaurants realised that the house wine should not be the cheapest vin ordinaire they can lay hands on.

Be careful to order the precise style of wine you want. After the wine steward has opened the bottle is no time to decide that you would rather have a medium than a dry white. When the steward pours a little wine in your glass, you are merely checking that your chosen wine is in sound condition.

If you want to save money and enjoy your own wine, eat at a BYO restaurant. Bring-your-own restaurants have permits that authorise liquor consumption with a meal, and are entitled to charge for opening your bottle, providing glasses and so on. You pour your own wine.

AUCTIONS

The freakish sale by auction in 1987 of a rehoboam (five-litre bottle) of 1985 The Antipodean for $5100, has focussed the spotlight on the role of wine auctions here.

The 1986 Working Party on Liquor recommended a major freeing-up of the legal tape restricting wine auctions, but auctioneers are currently limited to acting on behalf of deceased estates or collectors who have no other proper method of disposal. According to auctioneers Peter Webb Galleries Limited, 'the benefits to be derived from bidding at a wine auction are numerous . . . here lies the opportunity to acquire fabulous and prestigious bottles that have long been out of circulation, and by the same token the chance to purchase young wines for extended cellaring or as an investment'.

It is essential to thoroughly research your prospective acquisition before the bidding starts. Do not treat the auctioneer's catalogue as divine law – Webb's 8 December 1987 catalogue lavished praise on Penfold's Grange Hermitage as 'Australia's consistently finest Cabernet'!

Some buyers have paid high prices for wines readily available from merchants at lower prices. Conversely, classic French wines have been snapped up by knowledgeable enthusiasts at, by world standards, bargain prices.

LABELLING

New Zealand up to 1980 had very incomplete labelling laws. Only the name of the wine producer, the volume of wine, and its percentage by volume of alcohol were mandatory. Such labelling laws − or the lack of them − allowed open season on the use of varietal names: a Cabernet Sauvignon, for example, was not required by law to contain any Cabernet Sauvignon juice at all.

Even today some bottles carry labels and names of doubtful validity. Are we entitled to assume that a New Zealand 'burgundy', for instance, in some respect resembles the original French Burgundies? (The proprietor of the now defunct Bordeaux Wines, in Henderson, when questioned once about the difference between his 'Bordeaux Claret' and 'Bordeaux Burgundy', replied: 'The Claret is fortified, the Burgundy is not'.) New Zealand, along with other New World wine nations, still arbitrarily apes the most famous European wine names, for obvious marketing reasons.

GIESEN'S LABELS PERPETUATE THE LINK BETWEEN FINE ART AND WINE LABELLING FIRST FORGED IN NEW ZEALAND BY COLLARD.

The position of wines labelled with the name of a particular grape variety is more clear-cut. Amendments to the wine-labelling regulations introduced in 1980 provided an important element of consumer protection. In essence, any wine named after any grape variety must contain at least seventy-five percent of the stated variety. A Pinot Noir, for example, should have no less than seventy-five percent Pinot Noir content. Australian regulations on varietal labelling are slightly tougher, demanding a minimum content of eighty percent of the stated variety.

Hybrid and *Vitis labrusca* wines cannot be labelled as varietals. Blends of two or more varieties must be named in order of the proportions used, with the predominant grape first; once again the named varieties must constitute no less than seventy-five percent of the overall blend.

In Europe, most consumers pay little heed to individual grape varieties and relatively few wines are labelled by grape variety. The practice in New Zealand, however, is for the great majority of the best wines to be sent into the world under the name of the principal grape used. A prestige Chardonnay will normally be sold as such; a 'Chablis', by contrast, probably has more humble grape origins.

The recent discovery that all 'Gamay Beaujolais' vines in New Zealand are a clone of Pinot Noir poses a legal – and marketing – problem for Gamay Beaujolais producers, because the law demands that varietal labels must be accurate.

Another danger area is the total absence in New Zealand of any regulations on regional labelling. A Cabernet Sauvignon grown in Gisborne, for instance, could be labelled Hawke's Bay without breaking any rules. Australia, by contrast, demands that any wine labelled with the name of a region must contain at least eighty percent wine from that region. This needs tightening up – where individual regions build a high reputation for quality, this can be eroded by a producer who gives in to marketing temptations and labels his wine with a misleading region of origin.

Equally, New Zealand still lacks any regulations on vintage labelling. Once again the Australians are much tighter on this, demanding that any wine bearing a vintage label must contain more than ninety-five percent wine made in the stated year.

Sparkling wines have their own nomenclature. The 1980 regulations avoid any reference to the term Champagne, neither approving nor ruling out its use on labels. Any sparklings labelled as 'bottle-fermented' may only contain CO_2 gas generated by their own natural fermentation. That last requirement also applies to 'Charmat process' or 'naturally fermented' wine, but the crucial difference is that any wine labelled 'bottle-fermented' must have had its secondary fermentation in a container of a capacity of five litres or less. (An exceedingly fine labelling distinction you should note is between the phrase 'fermented in *this* bottle', meaning the wine was produced by the traditional 'methode champenoise' technique, and the phrase 'fermented in *the* bottle', indicating the wine was made by the 'transfer' method.) The others may be produced in tanks of any size.

A carbonated 'bubbly' is entitled to no other term than 'sparkling wine'.

READING A NEW ZEALAND WINE LABEL

Wine labels vary around the world from the sterling prose efforts of many Australian wineries to the sparse, uncluttered labels of the top châteaux of Bordeaux. New Zealand labels, which by law are required to carry the producer's name and address, the country of origin, contents by volume and the alcohol content, fall into three broad categories according to the name of the wine: varietal, branded and generic.

Varietal wines, which tend to be the best and most highly priced, are labelled after the grape variety which constitutes at least seventy-five percent by volume of the wine – for example St Helena Pinot Noir – or the blend of varieties which also conforms to the same rule, for example Villa Maria Cabernet Sauvignon/Pinotage. That percentage, of course, may well be 100 percent. Branded wines may or may not specify the grapes used, but seek to achieve a consistent style, for example Cooks Chasseur, Babich Fumé Vert, Penfolds Chardon. Generic wines, such as Matua Valley Chablis or Collard White Burgundy, aim to conform to an internationally recognised wine style.

One or two vineyards, notably St Nesbit, are eschewing these more common approaches to labelling and – in the tradition of most French estate-bottled wines – marketing their wine solely under the name of the individual property.

**THE GENERIC
LABEL**

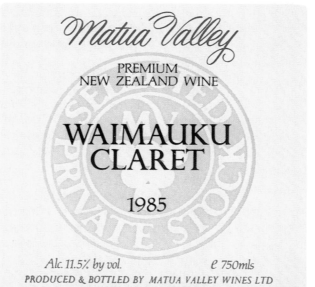

Producer

Country of Origin

Region of Origin
Generic Wine Name

Vintage

Alcohol Percentage by Volume

Contents by Volume
Name and Address of Producer

**THE BRANDED
LABEL**

Wine Colour and Style
Method of Production

Method of Production

Brand

Producer
Winery Name and Address
Country of Origin
Alcohol and Contents by Volume

**THE VARIETAL
LABEL**

Producer

Grape Variety

Vintage

Winemaker's name

Region of Origin

Contents by Volume

Alcohol Percentage by Volume
Winery Name and Address and
Country of Origin

VINTAGES

Does New Zealand experience good and bad vintages as do the European wine districts? Are vintage dates on wine labels of importance to the consumer?

The answer is yes. In Europe, the traditional emphasis placed on vintages as a guide to wine quality stems from the weather which can acutely affect ripening patterns in such northerly areas as Germany and Champagne.

New Zealand growing seasons also vary, from fine dry autumns such as 1986 and 1985 to near-disasters such as 1988. Flavour development in the berries and their sugar/acid ratios are closely related to the caprices of the weather. In fact, our climate is so variable that the concept of good and bad years for wine is rather clumsy: poor conditions for early ripening varieties like Müller-Thurgau and Chasselas, for instance, may be followed by an Indian summer that brings late grapes like Cabernet Sauvignon into the winery in peak condition. The 1985 vintage was a classic case of this.

Geographer H. de Blij, author of *Wine Regions of the Southern Hemisphere*, has succinctly summed up the broader factors underlying this vintage variability: 'New Zealand lies one thousand miles from the nearest landmass, so that it is totally exposed to maritime influences. To the north, a stable and persistent oceanic high pressure system prevails. The westerlies lie to the south. During the summer, the high pressure system tends to dominate, while the westerlies have stronger influence during the winter.

'But New Zealand's exposure permits subtropical and subpolar air to make contact along a front that often affects regional weather. Thus the country's weather is highly variable, and a warm, comparatively dry summer good for grape ripening may be followed a year later by a cloudy, grey and wet one.'

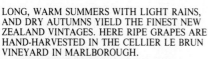

LONG, WARM SUMMERS WITH LIGHT RAINS, AND DRY AUTUMNS YIELD THE FINEST NEW ZEALAND VINTAGES. HERE RIPE GRAPES ARE HAND-HARVESTED IN THE CELLIER LE BRUN VINEYARD IN MARLBOROUGH.

RECENT VINTAGES

1976

Described by Nick Nobilo as 'the year of the decade' for the 1970s. Following very unpredictable weather in early summer, with heavy rain in December and January, later the weather improved. In Hawke's Bay the vintage was two to three weeks late and the fruit was high in sugar. Auckland enjoyed warm, sunny weather through February and March and the season, one to two weeks late, produced grapes with excellent sugar/acid balances. A few reds have proved outstanding.

1977

After a poor spring in which wet weather affected the crop at flowering, by late December most vines were several weeks behind. Following more settled weather in February and March, picking began towards the end of March, a month later than usual.

Hawke's Bay and Gisborne escaped the worst of the heavy rains which then descended on Auckland at the height of the vintage. But the sun was absent everywhere. Despite the late vintage, the grapes stayed high in acid, and sugar levels were below those of 1976. Overall 1977 was a year that produced ordinary wines.

1978

A wet spell before Christmas made this the third late vintage in a row. However, fine sunny conditions late summer and early autumn yielded a heavy crop, clean and ripe. Some memorable Chardonnays and Cabernet Sauvignons emerged.

1979

After a dry, settled spring and warm summer, by February this promised to be the best vintage for several years, but unusually heavy March rains ruined it: Hawke's Bay suffered its wettest March since 1923, and botrytis in Gisborne, and low sugars, meant this region was the worst hit of all. Only Marlborough produced grapes in reasonable condition – elsewhere the grapes came in rain-damaged, low in sugars and in the worst overall condition for many years.

The wines emerged with little depth and many proved short-lived.

As a rule the reds lacked body.

1980

A mediocre year. After another favourable spring the summer proved wetter and more cloudy than usual. Again it rained during the vintage period, although not so badly as in 1979. Gisborne encountered a spell of warm wet weather which led to a swift gathering of the grapes to minimise losses. Unseasonal winds gave the Marlborough vineyards one of their wettest years. Overall crops were heavy, clean, but not entirely ripe. Some good white wines emerged but the reds again proved disappointing.

1981

A low-volume, sound white and good red wine vintage. A difficult period at flowering in November produced small crops of white grapes throughout the country. The season was the best for whites since 1976, with clean grapes showing higher sugar levels than 1980. Yet, with February unseasonably cloudy, the vintage was not absolutely ideal, needing more sunshine to ensure maximum flavour development in the grapes.

The later-flowering reds escaped most of the adverse early weather and the fruit responded well to a sunny April. The 1981 reds showed good colour and flavour development, a needed lift after 1979 and 1980.

1982

A good yet not perfect vintage. Fine summer weather in January and early February was later marred by heavy rains late in February. Gisborne and Auckland were the regions most affected, while Hawke's Bay and Marlborough suffered to a lesser degree.

Yet 1982 overall produced grapes with higher sugars than usual. The wines emerged with reasonable character but subsequently were overshadowed by those of 1983. The reds maintained the improvement in quality noticeable from 1981.

1983

A much vaunted vintage that set new records both for quantity and quality levels.

The season was exceptionally dry, especially on the East Coast where the lack of rain led to drought. In Gisborne and Hawke's Bay the fruit quality was excellent, with sugar levels for most varieties being the highest ever recorded.

The grapes came in free from disease and with good acid levels. Although Marlborough growers were troubled by wind problems, overall, the 1983 vintage yielded the best fruit in memory.

The well-ripened grapes produced wines of higher alcohol than usual, showing plenty of body and aging potential. The higher sugars allowed winemakers to ferment such varieties as Sauvignon Blanc and Sémillon to dryness, rather than Germanising them with a touch of sweetness. From the beginning, the reds displayed deep colour and real intensity of flavour.

1984

After the intensely favourable publicity that surrounded the vintage of 1983, inevitably the 1984 harvest suffered a little by comparison.

The grape crop, down by one-third on the record 1983 level, was reduced by adverse weather at flowering, which affected the berry 'set'. In West Auckland a freak hail storm devastated several vineyards. Rain and humidity in February and March brought the fruit into the wineries at average sugar levels, and the 1984 wines, correspondingly, are lighter in body than those of 1983.

Yet in 1984 some white wines showed an abundance of flavour that often is associated with low-yield vintages. Most reds peaked early. Overall, an average year in terms of quality.

1985

After an ideal growing season in all districts – with particularly dry conditions in the North Island – heavy rains descended just as the harvest got underway.

The February rainfall brought greatest problems to the heavy crops in Gisborne, causing outbreaks of botrytis rot. In Hawke's Bay, with only half the Müller-Thurgau harvested, a heavy deluge fell in March, closing the Napier road. Later varieties, especially Chardonnay, Cabernet Sauvignon and Merlot, were picked in excellent shape and the 1985 Hawke's Bay Cabernet Sauvignons and Cabernet/Merlots are remarkably high in extract and firm-structured.

Auckland, favoured by a late spell of fine weather, had a memorable vintage, harvesting clean, very ripe grapes. The 1985 Auckland reds are very solid.

The Marlborough region experienced a wetter growing season than usual, but settled weather at harvest produced ripe, intensely flavoured fruit picked in very clean condition. The outcome has been some remarkably fragrant and penetrating white wines.

Overall a bumper vintage, yielding 78,000 tonnes.

1986

A variable vintage, with a clear contrast between some mediocre early ripening fruit and late-season varieties harvested in outstanding condition.

Following indifferent weather during the November flowering period, January and February proved unusually wet and humid. The Müller-Thurgau, Chenin Blanc and Chasselas crops suffered heavy outbreaks of rot; as a result most 1986 Müller-Thurgaus lack depth and staying power. A consistently dry and sunny autumn, however, enabled the late-season grapes to ripen fully on the vines. The Chardonnay, Sauvignon Blanc, Cabernet Sauvignon and Pinot Noir have all lived up to their early promise, the Chardonnays in particular showing unprecedentedly high alcohols and marvellously ripe fruit flavours. The Cabernet Sauvignons have less extract than the darker, more intense 1985s, but are fragrant and more supple.

In the wake of the vine-removal scheme, this vintage yielded a reduced crop of 63,000 tonnes.

1987

Inclement weather during flowering set the scene for a wet and difficult, low-yielding vintage. The Chenin Blanc crop fell by over thirty-three percent on 1986 and Gewürztraminer plummeted by over forty percent.

On the heels of a long dry spell in December and January the rains descended in early autumn. Early ripening varieties, particularly Müller-Thurgau, were hard hit by rot.

In Gisborne Denis Irwin reported 'a most frustrating vintage' and Hawke's Bay similarly suffered from the heavy downpours and rot. In Marlborough the early vintage was wet and cold.

Fortunately, drier and sunny weather in mid-late autumn lifted the standard of the late-ripening varieties. In their youth, the 1987 Chardonnays are crisper and more slender than the opulent 1986s. Reds vary from light to highly promising.

Overall a difficult year.

1988

One of the most difficult white-wine vintages in memory for winemakers relying upon North Island fruit.

1988, due to adverse weather at flowering and fruit set, and unprecedentedly heavy fruit losses to birds, shaped up early as a low-cropping year. A wet, humid February in most North Island districts triggered outbreaks of bunch rot in early season varieties, including Müller-Thurgau.

In early March cyclone Bola then dumped torrential rains on West Auckland, Gisborne and Hawke's Bay. For most winemakers the vintage immediately deteriorated into a 'salvage' operation.

Rot problems in Auckland forced the early to mid-season white varieties to be harvested with low sugar levels. In Hawke's Bay both yields and grape quality of the white varieties were generally down, although some pockets of superior fruit were harvested. In Gisborne – by far the hardest-hit region – many vineyards were wiped out by the unprecedentedly heavy flooding, their vines buried in up to sixty centimetres of silt and their crops submerged. Müller-Thurgau, Chardonnay and Gewürztraminer were the varieties worst hit. Overall yields in the Gisborne region dropped thirty percent.

Marlborough emerged largely unscathed, despite higher than average March rainfall. Canterbury and Martinborough, in stark contrast to other districts, experienced ripening seasons drier than normal.

A dry April in most districts later allowed the red fruit to be harvested in solid condition. In their infancy, the 1988 reds looked promising.

For consumers the outcome was a shortage of premium wines and, overall, a drop in wine quality.

WINE COMPETITIONS

Too many of us rely on the opinions of too few on which are the country's top wines. Medals and trophies awarded at the American Express-sponsored Easter Show Wine Competition, staged in February, and the Air New Zealand Wine Awards, held in late October, are always publicised with much fanfare, arousing intense interest among wine enthusiasts and accelerating public demand for those wines scoring the higher awards. The time is right, therefore, for a look at the strengths and weaknesses of wine competitions here.

Two strong arguments are often advanced in support of the need for competitive judgings. Winemakers learn from the rejection of their mediocre and faulty wines, and from the approval given to quality entries, whether they are heading in the right direction. And the public are given guidance through the maze of competing labels in the marketplace to the most successful individual wines, wine styles and vineyards.

The basic judging procedure is straightforward. According to the Wine Institute, organiser of the more prestigious Air New Zealand Wine Awards, each entry is evaluated 'on the basis of twenty points, with a maximum of three for colour and clarity, seven for aroma and bouquet, and ten for taste and general characteristics. The marks of the judges are totalled and averaged. Any wine averaging eighteen points or more receives a gold award, 16.5 to 17.9 points a silver, 15 to 16.4 points a bronze'.

The judging panels are a blend of winemakers, and others who are not professionally engaged in the industry on a full-time basis. John Comerford, a Lower Hutt lawyer, presided as chairman of judges over the 1986 National Wine Competition, with winemaker judges Joe Babich, Bruce Collard, Michael Brajkovich and Ian McKenzie (of Seppelt in Australia). Bob Campbell, then Corbans' public relations manager; Geoff Kelly, a Lower Hutt soil scientist; Christchurch medical professor Don Beaven; and Sarah Morphew, an English Master of Wine, completed the panels.

Facing an array of 592 entries, these skilled tasters awarded thirty-seven gold, 130 silver and 164 bronze medals. Only fifty-six percent of the wines gained an award, a dramatic decline from the eighty-three percent award rate of only two years before – confirming not that the local wine standards are plummeting, but that, as John Comerford put it: 'An award was only given if the wine was meritorious . . . The days of awarding medals to sound but undistinguished wines have now passed'.

So far, so good. Competitions are the most accurate and objective way of evaluating wines that we fallible humans have. The danger, however, is that too many wine enthusiasts are treating medals as a sole definitive assessment of wine quality, attributing to medals something of the status of divine law.

These contests are far from flawless. Judges are human and can easily be wrong. The wine scandals in Bordeaux and Italy in the 1970s occurred partly because professional tasters were unable to distinguish the adulterated wines from genuine wines by taste.

American judge Leon Adams recalled 'one sincere fellow who, although he served on wine juries for many years, couldn't tell a Cabernet from a sweet vino'. Dan Murphy, an Australian judge, even encountered a colleague who 'quite frankly, was mad. He could get away with his mental imbalance most of the time, but on the whole his judgements were poor'.

Awards made in New Zealand today are a far more realistic guide to quality than those made a decade ago. Des Lagan, who judged at the 1971 National Wine Competition, later recalled how one richly deserving wine was overlooked for a medal: 'a fact for which some of my brother judges must accept responsibility. It was a classic wine from a classic grape

WINE AWARDS 1987–1988

1988 American Express Easter Show Competition

GOLD MEDALS

CHARDONNAY
Collard Rothesay 87
Collard Rothesay 86
Hunter's 87
Martinborough Vineyards 87
Morton Estate Winery Reserve 86
Villa Maria Barrique Fermented 87
Villa Maria Reserve 86

GEWÜRZTRAMINER
Vidal Reserve 86
Villa Maria Reserve 87
Villa Maria Reserve 86
Villa Maria Reserve 85

SAUVIGNON BLANC
Hunter's Fumé Blanc 87
Villa Maria Reserve 86
Weingut Seifried 85

RHINE RIESLING
Corbans Marlborough 83
Robard and Butler Amberley 86

SWEET WHITES
Collard Botrytised Rhine Riesling 86
Cooks Late Pick Müller-Thurgau 83
Corbans P.B. Auslese 80
Delegat's Proprietor's Reserve Auslese 86
Korepo Trockenbeerenauslese Botrytised 87

CABERNET SAUVIGNON
Chifney 86
Cooks P.B. Fernhill 85
Delegat's Proprietor's Reserve 86
Villa Maria Reserve 86

BLENDED REDS
Cooks Hawke's Bay Cabernet/Merlot 86
Corbans P.B. Cabernet/Merlot 86
Villa Maria Reserve Cabernet/Merlot 86

PORT
Cooks P.B. Vintage 82
Pleasant Valley Founders

1987
Air New Zealand Wine Awards

GOLD MEDALS
CHARDONNAY
Babich Irongate 87
Collard Hawke's Bay 87
Cooks Private Bin 84
de Redcliffe 87
Morton Estate Winery Reserve 86
Robard and Butler 86
Vidal Reserve 86
Villa Maria Reserve 86
Villa Maria Barrique Fermented 86
GEWÜRZTRAMINER
Pacific Willowbrook 86
Villa Maria Reserve 85
Villa Maria Reserve 86
RHINE RIESLING
Collard 87
Coopers Creek 87
Millton Medium 87
Montana Marlborough 87
SAUVIGNON BLANC
Delegat's Selected Vintage 86
Villa Maria Reserve 85
Villa Maria Reserve 86
SÉMILLON
Villa Maria Reserve 85
MEDIUM SWEET WHITES
Collard Botrytised Rhine Riesling 86
SWEET WHITES
Corbans Noble Rhine Riesling 86
Delegat's Proprietor's Reserve Auslese 85
Delegat's Proprietor's Reserve Auslese 86
Montana Auslese 85
CABERNET SAUVIGNON
Babich Hawke's Bay 85
Cooks Fernhill 84
Cooks Fernhill 86
Matua Valley 85
Villa Maria Reserve 86
CABERNET SAUVIGNON/MERLOT
Esk Valley Private Bin 86
Villa Maria Reserve 86
PINOT NOIR
Martinborough Vineyards 86
SPARKLING
Montana Bernadino Spumante
Morton Estate Methode Champenoise 85

and it was this that probably had some judges puzzled'.

Our judges today are technically highly trained, enjoy the confidence of the wine industry itself – and only unsuccessful exhibitors would dare challenge their sanity.

But if you use medal lists as your principal buying guide, be prepared for a share of disappointments. Judges do not allocate medals to a wine because they find it appealing; they measure wines against a set of such specifications as colour, acidity, tannin, varietal character and freedom from faults. A gold medal is no guarantee that you, personally, are going to enjoy a wine.

Nor is there any absolute guarantee that the wine sample allotted a high medal is identical to the wine retailing under the same label in your corner store. Entries in the small production categories at the shows are delivered to organisers by the wine companies themselves, with rumours occasionally surfacing of special batches of wine being set up specifically to capture awards.

A host of wineries do not even enter the competitions. Notable absentees from the 1987 Air New Zealand Wine Awards included The Antipodean, Ata Rangi, Bellamour, Brookfields, Cloudy Bay, Dry River, Eskdale, Giesen, Goldwater, Cellier Le Brun, Matawhero, Ngatarawa, C.J. Pask, Rongopai, St George, St Nesbit, Kumeu River, Soljans, Stonyridge, Te Mata and Te Whare Ra.

Some simply feel no need to enter; others have withdrawn following disappointment with their results; others believe anything less than a gold medal could harm their prestige and consequently prices; others criticise the timing of the events; others are unhappy about the repeated success of small batches of reserve wines which the public cannot buy.

Recently a cluster of inconsistent awards to individual wines has further highlighted the danger of giving too much weight to medals. Nobilo's excellent 1985 Dixon Chardonnay walked off with a London gold medal, plus the Decanter Trophy for the New Zealand wine showing the strongest export potential, then failed to score any award at all at the 1986 National Wine Competition. That fate it shared with Babich 1985 Irongate Chardonnay, which previously took a gold medal at the 1985 National Wine Competition and the Vintners Trophy as the best current vintage dry white table wine.

These marked inconsistencies have also shown up between New Zealand and Australian competitions. Corbans Private Bin Chardonnay 1984, a bronze medal winner at home in October 1986, one month later collected a gold medal in Canberra at the Australian National Wine Show, topping its class. In a reversal of this outcome, Vidal Reserve Chardonnay 1985, the champion table wine at our 1986 National Wine Competition, crashed to a 'no award' in Canberra. Bob Campbell believes these confusing discrepancies point to 'a different Australian perception of the definition of top Chardonnay'.

The heart of the problem is style bias. Such complex wines as Chardonnay – owing to the nuances of barrel fermentations, wood-aging, malolactic fermentations etc. – are much harder to judge than more obvious wines such as, for instance, Sauvignon Blanc. Varying definitions of desirable styles bring in their wake varying and inadequate medal results.

The problem has surfaced before with red wines, less with Cabernet Sauvignon than with Pinot Noir and Pinotage. Nobilo's 1983 Te Karaka Pinotage dropped from a 1985 Easter Show gold award to nothing at the 1985 National Wine Competition, prompting a refusal from Nick Nobilo to accept that his gold medal red was no longer worthy of at least a silver.

Another hot topic after the 1986 National Wine Competition was the number of prestigious labels rigorously excluded from the medals list for showing slight faults. Judges – particularly winemaker judges – are acute at detecting defects – oxidation, hydrogen-sulphide, volatility, mustiness and so on – which in small degrees are not discernible by the vast majority of wine consumers.

Arped Haraszthy noted in 1889, in his *Wines and Vines of California*, that 'the difference in a trial of wine by the consumer and the expert, is that the former seeks for something agreeable, something to praise; whilst the latter seeks for a fault, a blemish, or something to condemn'. It seems foolish to condemn a wine to the status of no award because of a minor technical blemish when in all important respects it is outstanding.

One final problem: blind tastings favour assertive, 'sledgehammer' wines over those with more subtle qualities. This is the reason high impact Californian wines often outpoint fine French wines in comparative sessions. That rounded, subtle wine you would enjoy drinking several glasses of can be easily overshadowed by blockbusters full of oak, acid and tannin. Some of the most drinkable wines ever made in New Zealand have not shone in competition.

It is also clear, however, that many of the country's top wines do achieve brilliant success under the judges' scrutiny. The trio of gold medals awarded at the 1986 National Wine Competition to Montana Marlborough Sauvignon Blanc from the 1984, 1985 and 1986 vintages, and an equally emphatic trio awarded to Cooks Fernhill Cabernet Sauvignons from 1983, 1984 and 1985, spoke not only of the lofty standard of these wines, but of consistency of judging too.

So treat these medals with the respect they deserve – as a valuable and independent quality analysis – but refrain from worship.

CELLARING

What happens to wine as it ages is still largely a mystery. To some extent a maturing wine undergoes a slow, controlled oxidation, not so much from the tiny amount of air that enters the bottle through the cork, but rather from the presence of air in the wine when it was bottled. With age the acidity declines and the alcohol, acids and other components are transformed into complex compounds such as esters and aldehydes. The bouquet and flavour develop complexity, one of the hallmarks of a mature wine

The old belief that New Zealand whites do not keep well is incorrect. Even Müller-Thurgau, the most common variety, has the ability to age well over many years. Most of this wine is consumed long before it has even approached its potential. I recently found Corbans 1965 Riverlea Riesling was still alive and healthy entering its third decade.

Such varieties as Riesling, Chardonnay, Sauvignon Blanc, Gewürztraminer, Sémillon and Chenin Blanc all need two to five years to mature. It is difficult to be precise about the long-term aging prospects of these varieties, as only recently have they been widely established in New Zealand. Barely a handful of the post-1980 local white wines in my personal cellar, however, could be classed as 'over the hill'.

Our best reds are able to develop gracefully over a decade and beyond. The early McWilliam's Cabernet Sauvignons from the mid and late 1960s are mostly still intact although fading. One reason for the supremacy of Cabernet Sauvignon among red grapes is that its high levels of alcohol, acid and tannin allow it to develop over a long period. J.R. Roger's book

1987
International Wine and
Spirit Competition
London

GOLD MEDALS
CHARDONNAY
Babich Irongate 86
Corbans P.B. Chardonnay 84
Morton Estate Winery Reserve 85
Villa Maria Reserve 86
GEWÜRZTRAMINER
Pacific Willowbrook 86
Villa Maria Reserve 86
SAUVIGNON BLANC
Hunter's 85
SWEET WHITES
Montana Auslese 82
VINTAGE PORT
Cooks 82

1987
Australia National Wine Show
Canberra

GOLD MEDALS
RHINE RIESLING
Collard Marlborough 86
SAUVIGNON BLANC
Collard Rothesay 87
Selaks 87

on Bordeaux has a memorable and amusing description of the 1945 vintage: 'exceptionally great . . . full and round . . . wines to lay down with'.

Choose reds with plenty of body, acidity and tannin. Only Pinot Noir, Pinotage, Merlot and Cabernet Sauvignon in New Zealand have proved themselves to respond well to medium-term aging. At three to five years old, most Pinotages and Pinot Noirs are nearing their best – soft and fruity – and thereafter sometimes lack staying power. Among fortified wines, the flush-corked vintage ports are the only ones that improve markedly after bottling.

IN THIS TYPICALLY IMPROVISED PRIVATE WINE CELLAR, HUMBLE BEER CRATES AND CARTONS STORE THEIR TREASURES PERFECTLY SATISFACTORILY.

Rather than entering a couple of bottles of a myriad different labels in your cellar, be more selective and buy in case or half-case lots. By opening a favourite wine say, once a year for a decade, you can trace its ascendancy from brash youthfulness through maturity to mellow old age. By the time you reach bin's end it will taste like an old friend – broaching that final bottle can be a melancholy affair.

As wine is a natural, living substance it is vulnerable to external influences. Be sure to position your cellar in a cool area with even temperatures. Cool conditions foster a long, slow development in wine; higher temperatures hasten the maturing process but prevent wines from reaching their full potential. Rapid fluctuations in temperature must also be avoided; so must vibrations and direct sunlight.

For storage materials, the commercial wine racks are useful for a small cellar. Beyond that, beer crates stacked on their sides are hard to beat – cheap but functional. Place your bottles in a horizontal position to ensure contact between the wine and corks, and as far as possible avoid repeated handling.

TASTING AND DRINKING WINE

Serving and tasting wine need not be an elaborate process: you can simply pull the cork, fetch a glass and drink the wine. All over the world wine is most often consumed casually, as a thirst quencher, with no ceremony at all. The following suggestions are for those other occasions, when you are in the mood to treat wine appreciation seriously.

The opening of the bottle is simple enough. Cut the capsule off sufficiently below its top to prevent contact with the poured wine. If necessary, wipe the lip of the bottle clean. To extract the cork, use a wine-waiter's knife or any of the several other devices available – the advantage of the knife is that it houses both a blade and a corkscrew. When opening sparkling wine, hold your thumb firmly over the cork, then twist the bottle sideways and downwards.

Pour your wine into glass rather than pottery or silver, if you want to study its appearance. Select a glass with a large bowl and a stem that allows the glass to be handled without touching the bowl. Half fill the glass, leaving room for the wine to be swirled around. As you finish pouring, give the bottle a quick sideways twist to prevent any drips falling.

White wines should be tasted cool, not cold: an overly chilled wine loses its bouquet and nuances of flavour. In winter whites can be served at room temperature; summer calls for an hour in the refrigerator or a short plunge in an ice-bucket. Light, dry styles are at their best when served less chilled than sweet wines and sparklings.

Red wines taste best at spring or autumn room temperature. In the cooler seasons, avoid warming a red hurriedly in front of a fire or heater – instead, leave it in the hot-water cupboard, well away from the pipes, for a half-day or so. If you are forced to open a too cool bottle of red, try warming the wine by nursing the bowl of the glass in your hands.

Breathing red wine by pulling the cork achieves almost nothing, since only the wine in the neck of the bottle has any contact with the air. Rather, pour the wine back and forth between the bottle and a decanter several times, or allow it to breathe in a decanter for a couple of hours. An old wine that has thrown a sediment will need decanting too. Stand the bottle upright, preferably for a couple of days, then carefully pour out the wine into the decanter, stopping when the sediment reaches the shoulder of the bottle.

Now on to the tasting. Hold the glass before a sheet of white paper – to eliminate background colours – and then tilt the glass and look closely at the wine near the lip. Grape varieties, wine styles, and wines of different ages can often be identified by their characteristic shades of colour.

A white wine should be distinguishable by its appearance from a glass of water; pale green or straw are the usual colours for a youthful wine. The colour deepens as the wine matures, turning gold in maturity and yellow-brown in old age. Advanced browning is a sign that the wine has oxidised.

Youthful reds have a purplish hue that turns red with age and eventually starts to brown when full maturity is reached. Deep colour in a red also indicates the probable presence of plenty of tannin, acid and extracts.

Apart from the precise colour, wine clarity is also important. Is the wine clear and free of suspended material? Any cloudiness or haze is undesirable.

Now, gently swirl the wine before raising the glass to your nose. The bouquet should be appealing, free of unpleasant odours, and should communicate something about the grapes from which the wine was made, its vinification, perhaps its age and country of origin. A young Müller-Thurgau, for example, has an immediately recognisable, fruity and fresh smell.

– N.Z. HERALD, 15·10·77

WINE GLASSES

Wine glasses are sold in a confusing array of sizes and shapes. One glass, however, will suffice for all occasions and all wine styles, provided it is clear, stemmed, and has a generously proportioned bowl that narrows at the top.

Clear glass, or crystal, is necessary to allow a clear view of the wine; the stem prevents unnecessary touching of the bowl, which can warm a chilled white wine; a bowl of decent proportions allows the drinker to swirl the wine to savour its bouquet; and the taper at the top of the bowl concentrates the bouquet.

This common glass is too small to allow a decent serving to be comfortably swirled.

An ideal all-purpose wine glass.

A standard sherry glass, also useful for port.

The sense of smell can be extraordinarily accurate in pinpointing the nature of an individual wine. Pay heed especially to your initial impression – the sense of smell is rapidly fatigued – and often this first impression will be confirmed on the palate.

Now, tasting the wine: hold it in your mouth while drawing air in over the tongue; you will notice that the flavour is accentuated. This technique helps to bring out some of the myriad taste elements that are the very essence of pleasure in wine.

Sweetness is measured on the front of the tongue, acidity on the sides and bitterness or astringency at the back. Are there any foreign or unpleasant flavours present? 'Body' is the relative fullness of the wine in the mouth; a Gamay Beaujolais will feel relatively light-bodied and this is part of that grape's appeal; a Cabernet Sauvignon should be more weighty. Look for overall balance. A mature red should taste of fruit foremost, with the oak and tannin flavours secondary. A fine balance between sweetness and acidity is very important for a medium white wine. In a well-made wine the component flavours will all be in harmony.

After the wine has been swallowed comes the 'finish'. Ordinary wines slip down with little remaining trace, but a long, trailing finish is one of the identifying marks of a wine of true quality. The taste of a superb red wine can stay with you long after the wine itself leaves your mouth.

Tasting wine 'blind' is great fun and equally instructive. Merely by masking the label, the powerful preconceptions we all bring to wine, based primarily on reputation and price, can be set aside, allowing the wine in the glass to speak boldly and unambiguously for itself.

A VOCABULARY OF WINE TASTING

A knowledge of the following terms is useful when reading other people's descriptions of wine, or trying to formulate one's own tasting notes.

Acetic	wine soured by contact with air, vinegary.
Acidity	tart, sharp taste in wine, normally from natural grape acids.
Aftertaste	the last impression lingering in the mouth after swallowing.
Aroma	that part of the 'nose' derived from the grape itself. See Nose.
Astringent	having a mouth-puckering character, caused by tannin from grape skins, seeds and wood storage.
Balance	the harmony of flavour constituents.
Blackcurrants	the smell and taste of some red wines is likened to this fruit, particularly Cabernet Sauvignon.
Body	fullness or weight of wine in the mouth, largely related to alcohol level.
Bouquet	that part of the 'nose', or smell, which develops as a wine matures in casks and bottles. See Nose.
Bright	clear, with no suspended matter.
Clean	free from obvious defects.
Coarse	rough, of poor-quality material or poorly made.
Cloudy	with suspended matter present in the wine.
Complex	showing subtle integration of various taste and smell factors.
Condition	clarity and soundness.
Corked	tainted by a mouldy cork.
Dry	where all or nearly all sugar has been fermented into alcohol – where sweetness is absent.

Earthy	having the smell and taste of the soil.
Elegant	showing finesse.
Firm	showing tannic/acid backbone, not flabby or soft.
Finish	same meaning as Aftertaste.
Flowery	appealingly aromatic; commonly used in describing Riesling and Müller-Thurgau.
Fruity	with pronounced flavour and fragrance of the grape, the term being commonly used of slightly sweet wines.
Hard	having the hardness of flavour which tannin imparts to young red wines.
Honey	this is sometimes referred to in describing the bouquet of good sweet white wines.
Medium	level of residual sugar between dry and sweet.
Mellow	having a softness derived from maturity.
Nose	Aroma and Bouquet combined.
Oak	character imparted to wine by wood maturation.
Oxidised	having a browning of colour and taste deterioration caused by exposure to air or excessive aging.
Ripe	tasting of well-ripened fruit – not green or sour.
Rough	low grade, poorly made wine.
Round	smooth and well-balanced.
Ruby	full red colour of young wine, especially port.
Soft	gentle finish.
Spicy	having a taste as though some spice were present, a character most pronounced in Gewürztraminer.
Sulphury	having an unpleasant excess of the preservative sulphur-dioxide.
Supple	not hard, having an agreeable soft character.
Sweet	with residual sugar; in New Zealand this usually means sweeter than medium.
Tannic	a wine showing strongly the presence of tannin from the grape skins, pips and oak storage. Especially in young reds.
Tawny	faded amber of old wine, especially port.
Thin	deficient in body, almost watery.
Volatile	bacterial spoilage causes an excess of volatile acids (acetic acid or ethyl acetate).

WINE GLASSES

Two champagne glasses – the thin tulip style concentrates the bouquet, and disperses the bubbles less rapidly than the once popular saucer-shaped style.

This tulip-shaped glass has a long stem suitable for serving lightly chilled white wines.

A classic design for serving red wines.

A SELECT BIBLIOGRAPHY

This bibliography is based on the most valuable published material used by the author during research for successive editions of this book.

All listings have been organised into one of several categories: Books, University Theses, Government Publications, Wine Magazines and Newsletters, and Miscellaneous Items. The multitude of wine columns also appearing in magazines and newspapers throughout the country constitutes another rich mine of wine material. (Any reader dedicated enough to subscribe to a press clipping service will rapidly be inundated with more words on wine than anyone can comfortably digest.)

Alternative starting-points are S.M. Bradbury's *Wines and Winemaking in New Zealand: A Bibliography*, Wellington Library School, 1970, and my own *A Bibliography of New Zealand Wine to 1981*, Auckland Public Library, 1983.

Books

Beaven, D., *Wines for Dining*, 1977.

Beaven, D., Donaldson, I. and Watson, G., *Wine – A New Zealand Perspective*, (undated).

Beaven, D. and Schuster, D., *Wine: Care and Service*, 1985.

Bollinger, C., *Grog's Own Country* (2nd ed.), 1967.

Buck, J., *Take a Little Wine*, 1969.

De Blij, H., *Wine Regions of the Southern Hemisphere* (USA), 1985.

Eldred-Grigg, S., *Pleasures of the Flesh: Sex and Drugs in Colonial New Zealand 1840-1915*, 1984.

Evans, L. (ed.), *Australia and New Zealand Complete Book of Wine*, 1973.

Graham, J.C., *New Zealand Wine Guide*, 1971.

Graham, J.C., *Know Your New Zealand Wines*, 1980.

Graham, J.C., *Jock Graham's Wine Book*, 1983.

Jackson, D. and Schuster, D., *Grape Growing and Wine Making: A Handbook For Cool Climates*, 1981.

Jackson, D. and Schuster, D., *The Production of Grapes and Wines in Cool Climates*, 1987.

Johnson, H., *Hugh Johnson's Wine Companion* (London), 1983.

New Zealand Wine and Food Annual (4th ed.), 1985.

Reid, J.G.S., *The Cool Seller*, 1969.

Robinson, J., *Vines, Grapes and Wines* (London), 1986.

Saunders, P., *A Guide to New Zealand Wine*. Published yearly since 1976.

Scott, D., *Winemakers of New Zealand*, 1964.

Scott, D., *A Stake in the Country: A.A. Corban and Family 1892-1977*, 1977.

Scott, D., *Seven Lives on Salt River*, 1987, (see Chapter 4, 'He Made the Vine Flourish', pp. 57–73).

Southern, E., *New Zealand Wine and Cheese Guide*, 1969.

Stewart, K., *The Wine Handbook*, 1988.

Thorpy, F., *New Zealand Wine Guide*, 1976.

Thorpy, F., *Wine in New Zealand*, 1971. (Revised ed.), 1983.

Trlin, A.D., *Now Respected, Once Despised: Yugoslavs in New Zealand*, 1979, (see Chapter 4, 'The Winemakers', pp. 81–98).

Young, A., *Australian New Zealand Wine Year Book* (Melbourne), 1986.

University Theses

Bradding, R., 'Future Directions for MAF Viticultural Research in New Zealand', University of Waikato Bachelor of Management Studies Report, 1987.

Cooper, M.G., 'The Wine Lobby: Pressure Group Politics and the New Zealand Wine Industry', University of Auckland M.A. Thesis, 1977.

Corban, A., 'The History, Growth and Present Disposition of the New Zealand Wine Industry', Dissertation for a Diploma in Biotechnology, Massey University, 1974.

Corban, A.C., 'An Investigation of the Grape Growing and Winemaking Industries of New Zealand', University of New Zealand M.D. Thesis, 1925.

Forder, P.G., 'The Te Kauwhata Viticultural Research Station', University of Auckland M.A. Research Essay, 1977.

Marshall, B.W., 'Kauri-Gum Digging 1885–1920', University of Auckland M.A. Thesis, 1968.

Moran, W., 'Viticulture and Winemaking in New Zealand', University of Auckland M.A. Thesis, 1958.

Townsend, P., 'Location of Viticulture in New Zealand', University of Auckland M.A. Thesis, 1976.

Trlin, A.D., 'From Dalmatia to New Zealand', Victoria University M.A. Thesis, 1967.

Zuur, D., 'Ampelographic Studies of New Zealand Grape Varieties', University of Waikato M.Phil. Thesis, 1987.

Government Publications

Berrysmith, F., 'Viticulture' (rev. ed.), 1973.

Bragato, R., 'Report on the Prospects of Viticulture in New Zealand', 1895.

Bragato, R., 'Viticulture in New Zealand with Special Reference to American Vines', 1906.

Brocx, B. Monique, 'New Zealand Grape Variety Survey, 1983'. Ministry of Agriculture and Fisheries Research Paper 2/84, 1984.

Buchanan, G.A., 'Grape Phylloxera in New Zealand'. Department of Agriculture, Victoria, Australia, Study Tour Report, Series No. 78, 1982.

'The Chemical Composition of some Experimental New Zealand Table Wines', DSIR Report No. CD 2290, Sept. 1979.

'The Chemical Composition of some Musts and White Wines from the Henderson Valley and Kumeu Areas', DSIR Chemistry Division Report No. CD 2222, June 1976.

'The Chemical Composition of some New Zealand Red and Rosé Wines', DSIR Chemistry Division Report No. CD 2247, Dec. 1976.

Conference of New Zealand Fruitgrowers and Horticulturists, Dunedin, June 1901, NZ Department of Agriculture.

'Control of Vine Diseases and Pests Occurring in New Zealand', NZ Department of Agriculture, Bulletin No. 134.

The Customs Tariff (Wine) Amendment Order, 1975.

Garrett, R. and Smith S., 'Wine Industry Assistance Package', Ministry of Agriculture and Fisheries, Economics Division, 1986.

'Grape Varieties for New Zealand', Department of Horticulture, Lincoln College, Bulletin No. 21, 1977.

'The Grape Experiments at Lincoln College', Department of Horticulture, Lincoln College, Bulletin No. 36 (2nd ed.), June 1984.

Interdepartmental Overview Committee, Mid Term Review of the Wine Industry Development Plan to 1986, 1985.

New Zealand Department of Agriculture and Fisheries, Annual Reports.

New Zealand Department of Trade and Industry, Public Tariff Inquiry, Report No. 199 to the Tariff and Development Board, August 1973.

Oenological and Viticultural Bulletins, Ruakura Agricultural Research Centre.

Papers in Viticulture, Lincoln College, Bulletin No. 22A, 1978.

Papers in Winemaking and Wine Evaluation, Lincoln College, Bulletin 22B, 1978.

'Phylloxera-resistant Vines', NZ Department of Agriculture, Bulletin No. 276, 1947.

Proceedings of Vintage '85 Seminar, Te Kauwhata Research Station Oenological and Viticultural Bulletin No. 46, 1985.

Proceedings of Vintage '86 Seminar, Te Kauwhata Research Station Oenological and Viticultural Bulletin No. 47, 1986.

Proceedings of Vintage '87 Seminar, Te Kauwhata Research Station Oenological and Viticultural Bulletin No. 51, 1987.

Proceedings of the Winter Pruning Field Day, Te Kauwhata Research Station Oenological and Viticultural Bulletin No. 48, 1986.

Report and Evidence of the Royal Commission on the Kauri Gum Industry in New Zealand, AJHR, A-12, 1898.

Report No. 76C to the Tariff and Development Board, Certain Wines and Spirits, NZ Department of Industries and Commerce, 9 June 1970.

Report of the Colonial Industries Commission, AJHR, H-22, 1880.

Report of the Flax and Other Industries Committee on the Wine and Fruit Industry, AJHR, I-6B, 1890.

Report of the Industries Commission, AJHR, I-12, 1919.

Report of the Industries Development Commission: The Wine Industry Development Plan to 1986, 1980.

Report of the Licensing Committee, AJHR, I-17, 1960.

Report of the Licensing Control Commission 31 March 1955, AJHR, A-3.

Report of the New Zealand Commission to Inspect and Classify the Kauri Gum Reserves in the Auckland Land District, AJHR, C-12, 1914.

Report of the Review Committee on New Zealand Wine Statistics, Department of Statistics, 1983.

Report of the Royal Commission on Licensing, 1946.

Report of the Royal Commission on the Sale of Liquor in New Zealand, 1974.

Report of the Winemaking Industry Committee, AJHR, I-18, 1957.

Report on the Review of Excise Duties on Alcoholic Beverages and Tobacco Products, Excise Review Committee, June 1988.

Report to the Prime Minister on Investigation of Grape Surplus by Officials Committee, 1983.

The Wine Duty (South Africa) Order 1938, Statutory Regulations, 1938.

Wine in New Zealand, published annually in the 1960s by the NZ Department of Industries and Commerce.

Wines and Certain Other Fermented and Spiritous Beverages, Tariff and Development Board, Public Hearing, 6-8 August 1973, Transcript of Proceedings.

Wine Magazines and Newsletters

Cuisine, first issue Jan-Feb. 1987 (six issues yearly).

Kelly, G.C., New Zealand Wine Supplement (in Cuisine), Jan-Feb. 1987.

Saunders on Wine (a fortnightly newsletter).

The New Zealand Wineglass (latterly Pacific Wineglass) appeared monthly from 1980 to 1986.

The Wine Report (a monthly newsletter).

Wine Review was published from 1964 to 1978 (quarterly).

Ayto, J., 'A Review of the Policy and Economics of Selective Taxation on Wine', New Zealand Institute of Economic Research, July 1986.

'Grape Quality – Grape Pricing', Proceedings of Inaugural Seminar, New Zealand Society for Viticulture and Oenology, October 1985.

A Hawke's Bay Regional Wine and Grape Industry Study, Hawke's Bay Vintners, July 1985.

'Improving Wine Quality in the Vineyard', Proceedings of the Second Seminar, NZ Society for Viticulture and Oenology, 1986.

Industry Study and Development Plan 1978, Wine Institute of New Zealand, 1979.

Kliewer, M., 'Review of Viticulture Research and Extension Programme in New Zealand' (for NZ Grape Growers' Council), 1987.

'Quality Winegrowing – An Industry Perspective', Proceedings of Seminar, New Zealand Society for Viticulture and Oenology, October 1987.

Southern Horticulture Grapegrower and Winemaker, No. 3, 1985–1986.

Wine Institute of New Zealand, Annual Reports.

Miscellaneous

INDEX

Entries in bold type indicate vineyards. Entries in italics indicate grape varieties. Page numbers in bold refer to main entries while page numbers in italics refer to pictures.